Gender on the Edge

Gender on the Edge
Transgender, Gay, and Other Pacific Islanders

Edited by Niko Besnier and Kalissa Alexeyeff

University of Hawai'i Press
Honolulu

19 18 17 16 15 14   6 5 4 3 2 1

Library of Congress Cataloging-in-Publication Data
Gender on the edge : transgender, gay, and other Pacific islanders / edited
by Niko Besnier and Kalissa Alexeyeff.
    pages   cm
  Includes bibliographical references and index.
  ISBN 978-0-8248-3882-9 (cloth : alk. paper)
  ISBN 978-0-8248-3883-6 (pbk. : alk. paper)
  1. Transgender people—Oceania. 2. Gays—Oceania. 3. Sex role—
Oceania. I. Besnier, Niko, editor of compilation. II. Alexeyeff, Kalissa,
editor of compilation.
  HQ77.95.O3G46 2014
  306.76'8—dc23
                                                        2013040578

Published with financial support from the Amsterdam Institute
of Social Science Research

Designed by Janette Thompson (Jansom)

Printed by Sheridan Books, Inc.

Contents

CHAPTER 1

Gender on the Edge

Identities, Politics, Transformations

Kalissa Alexeyeff and Niko Besnier

Gender is on the edge. Being on the edge is both a position of power and one of marginality, and it is this paradox that we address in this book. We first situate gender on the cutting edge in terms of the position it has come to occupy, in the course of the last half-century, in intellectual debates. These debates have catapulted gender to the center of the important social, political, and cultural questions that anthropologists and other social scientists address—such as kinship, the division of labor, political institutions, religion, law, and the economy. Yet gender is also on the edge, in the different sense of often being marginalized in, for example, current theoretical concerns with globalization, colonialism, history, and other large-scale dynamics, so that feminist scholars constantly have to remind us of the fundamental role that gender plays in global and historical contexts. Gender, as well as the category to which it is yoked, sexuality, is in fact central to the way in which the intimate relates to the global and everything in between, and this role continues to call for a radical rethinking of empirical and theoretical approaches to classic social scientific topics.

In this book, gender is also on the edge in a different way. Here we are concerned with forms of gender and sexuality that question and transcend what is generally seen as a normative order that requires no explanation (though in fact it does). The practices and categories that we seek to understand have been variously referred to as "betwixt-and-between," "liminal," or "transgender"—here we refer to them collectively as "non-heteronormative." Since the aim of this collection of essays is to explore the relationship between these different configurations, the term is particularly apt for our purposes (despite the negative prefix running the danger of emphasizing marginality over embeddedness). "Heteronormative" has gained currency to refer to structures, relationships, and identities that conform to and affirm hegemonic gendering and sexuality (Warner 1991). The concept builds on Rubin's (1975) oft-cited "sex/gender system" and Rich's (1980) equally influential "compulsory heterosexuality." It is vaguer than concepts like "mainstream" and "heterosexual," which is precisely what makes it useful, particularly in cross-cultural comparison and in the negative. In contrast to other alternatives, "non-heteronormativity" leaves open the possibility that the dynamics at play may be a matter of gender, sex, sexuality, or yet other categories. The concept is particularly apt for our purposes because it exposes these power dynamics.

Non-heteronormative gender and sexual categories may be on the edge, yet we cannot understand the normative without an exploration of what falls outside it, what gives it definitional power. Around the world, these categories have long been reduced to the exceptional status of pathological and marginal subjects, but are now viewed as pivotal to important questions about the constitution of gender and sexuality, as well as to much larger issues concerning structure and agency, power and inequality, local–global tensions, and the relationship of the past to the present.

The gendered subjects whose lives we explore in this book are on the cutting edge of their own societies, and their position constitutes a third way in which we conceptualize the edginess of gender. Non-heteronormative Pacific Islanders are at once part and parcel of their societies and subversive of the social order. They are deeply enmeshed with what many think of as "tradition," but they are also the heralds of the new, the experimental, and the exogenous. Suspended between the visible and the invisible, the local and the global, the past and the future, and what is acceptable and what is not, they call for a rethinking of morality, what "acceptance" (or "tolerance") means, and the very relationship between agents and structures. They bring new ways of being in and thinking about the world, to the delight of some and the indignation of others. Their very existence embodies the contradictions of the contemporary social order.

We also explore gender on the edge in a fourth way, as it manifests itself in what is considered to be one of the more marginal areas of the world, the Pacific Islands. While the region has in the course of history preoccupied the imaginations of those who thought they controlled the world (as it did in late eighteenth-century Britain and France), the Pacific Islands were at other times in history what travelers merely passed through on their way to larger, richer, and more populated regions of the world. They were an afterthought of the global Western empire-building enterprise, even though they loomed large in the colonial imagination, particularly around questions of gender and sexuality. For those who inhabited them, the Pacific Islands had a different configuration that placed relationships, connections, and movements between them across vast distances at the center of their definition: they were a "sea of islands," rather than islands lost in a vast ocean (Hau'ofa 1994). These different positions underscore the uncanny way in which what is on the edge from one perspective is at the center from another perspective. We situate gender in the tension between these perspectives.

The chapters in this collection focus on the transgender and cognate categories in a broad range of Pacific Island societies, seeking to tease out similarities, differences, and generalizations. The contributors are trained in a variety of disciplines (anthropology, sociology, political science, cultural studies, social work, gender studies, media studies, legal studies, and of course Pacific Island studies) and national intellectual traditions (those of North America, Australia, New Zealand, Western Europe, Japan), but are committed to cross-disciplinary and cross-national dialogues. They have based their analyses on an intimate engagement with the materials they analyze, an intimacy based on involvements that range from being indigenous to the societies in question, to life-historical grounding in them, to long-term ethnographic work conducted in their midsts. All contributions centralize the importance of combining robust theory with empirical material. Individually and collectively, the chapters address questions central to our social scientific understanding of gender, structure and agency, power and inequality, local–global dynamics, and the relationship of the past to the present. This book is appearing at a particularly pertinent juncture in history, as gender and sexuality are undergoing fundamental transformations in the societies of the Pacific region—transformations that are brought about by a broad variety of factors, from the resource extraction industries to the diasporic dispersal of populations, from the turn to neoliberalism to the emergence of new religious moralities, from the commodification of bodies in the tourism and sport industries to the militarization of societies. Even though these changes are not universally welcome to everyone in Pacific Island societies, their gendering and sexualization demand analytic attention.

From Identities to Practices

The 1997 national conference of the Methodist Church of New Zealand was the stage of a bitter dispute over the ordination of lesbian and gay clergy. The dispute ended with the breakaway from the church of congregations "who could not live with the increasingly radical liberal theology of the Methodist Church of New Zealand and acceptance of Ministers living in sexual sin" (Wesleyan Methodist Church of New Zealand 2009). The breakaway groups, made up principally of Tongan, Samoan, and Fijian members, in addition to Pākehā (White New Zealander) evangelicals, were ministered by a Tongan pastor-at-large and former president of the church, Tavake Tupou. They eventually formed, in 2000, the Wesleyan Methodist Church of New Zealand. Similar fault lines emerged in the Australian Uniting Church Assembly, pitching Pacific Island members against mainstream congregants, although there, congregation fission did not occur (ABC Radio Australia, *Pacific Beat,* 2011).

How do we reconcile these situations, in which Pacific Islanders express deep hostility toward non-mainstream sexualities, with the conspicuous visibility in everyday life of non-heteronormative people in many Pacific Island societies? How can rejection and acceptance rub shoulders in such a spectacularly contradictory fashion? These seemingly incommensurable positions cannot simply be explained away as the result of Christian dogmatism interloping upon a "traditional" laissez-faire, since in many parts of the Pacific Christianity is so intricately intertwined with the sociocultural order that it is *defined* as tradition. In addressing these problems, the contributors to this book all take as a given that categories, identities, social practices, and moralities are by definition complex and replete with apparent contradictions.

In the West, non-heteronormative gender and sexuality exist in a number of forms. Lesbian, gay, and bisexual persons are defined by an (at least partial) affective affinity with and sexual attraction to people of the same gender. "Transgender" (an umbrella term for a diverse group of people formerly referred to by such terms as "transsexuals," "transvestites," "gender inverts") refers to persons whose experiential gender is at odds with their ascribed gender. The term "transgender" has had both an enabling and a restricting effect on people's self-understanding: "On the one hand, it validates those people who adopt transgender as a meaningful category of self-identity; but it also draws attention to how people are identified by others as being transgender even though they may not necessarily use this term in talking about themselves" (Valentine 2007, 26).[1] Also conflated with these categories of sex and gender are the intersex, into which fall persons whose chromosomal structure, physiology, or hormonal function generate, for a wide diversity of reasons, ambiguities about their sex at birth and beyond. While they differ in their constitution, visibility, and politics, these various categories also exhibit similarities that are reflected in the use of various acronyms, from LGB to LGBT and LGBTQI, which have gained widespread currency over the last four decades, with both useful and problematic consequences.

In non-Western contexts, non-heteronormative gender and sexuality take the form of locally specific categories, such as South Asian *hijra* and *koti*, Thai *kathoey*, Indonesian *waria* or *banci*, or what is commonly referred to as "two spirit people" in Native North America. In the Pacific Islands, a variety of terms are used to refer to individuals who embody non-heteronormative identities, such as *leitī* in Tonga, *fa'afafine* in Samoa (plural form, *fa'afāfine*), *'akava'ine* or *laelae* in the Cook Islands, *māhū* and *raerae* in Tahiti. This book is an exploration of the ways in which non-normative gendering and sexuality in the Pacific Islands are metonymic of a wide range of sociocultural dynamics—dynamics that are at once local and global, historical and contemporary.

In contemporary Western ideologies, sexual identity (as well as identity *tout court*) is understood as being a property of persons. Sexuality is an issue of "being" and only incidentally an issue of relatedness to others. One *is* male or female, and consequently one *is* a man or a woman and performs these identities socially. Gender performance is thus merely an index of one's essence. Yet, as anthropologists have amply demonstrated, this theory of sexuality is far from universal and in fact probably operates at the level of ideology even in Western contexts. In many other societies, sex and gender are much more squarely matters of interpersonal relationships, of dispositions that enable and restrict social action. Thus it is not surprising that many chapters in this book (among others, those of Dolgoy, Ikeda, and Kuwahara) foreground the importance of family relations (including fictive families), friendships, and other forms of relatedness to understanding non-heteronormative identifications in Pacific Island societies. In such contexts, persons whose subjectivity is at odds with their sexual status emerge as a sociological puzzle rather than a psychological problem, and the mismatch tends to be managed by reassigning the person to a different social category.

Needless to say, this contrast is a gross oversimplification, particularly in a world in which all boundaries are porous, and thus all fashions of being and doing are constantly informed by other ways of being and doing. Yet it does lead us to relativize the privileging of identities in social scientific research on transgender and related categories in the Pacific Islands (as well as elsewhere), which continues to be dominated by the question, "Who are these people?" Rather than focusing on categories as objects of analysis, we argue that a focus on relationships or, more broadly, social practices may provide a much more fruitful handle on the world around us.

This shift enables us to rethink in a productive manner an issue that has monopolized attention—namely, terms for categories of non-heteronormativity. Do we refer to Tongan *leitī*, Cook Islands *'akava'ine*, or Fijian *qauri* as "transgender," "queens," or simply "homosexuals"? What do we gain or lose by applying these labels, and who decides? What do we do about derogatory and stigmatizing terms like "*poofta*" (as it is often rendered in the Pacific Islands) and "fairy," which are nevertheless widely used? Frequently, terminological discussions conflate description and enactments, words and meanings, and fail to account for the instability of categories across time, context, and place. For example, we have all witnessed people in the Pacific Islands performing one kind of identity while living in the islands and taking on a very different persona when they migrate (Farran, Tcherkézoff, this volume). Similarly, people themselves enact gender and are gendered by others in different ways, for example, according to whether they find themselves in formal situations (where rank, kinship, and propriety are foregrounded) or in casual company; but contexts can be subject to different definitions, which may lead to conflict as easily as it can lead to experimentation (Good, Presterudstuen, Stewart, this volume).

Terms are not just descriptive but performative, and with the performative comes the political. For example, in the ethnically tense context of Aotearoa New Zealand, gay and transgender Maori people in the 1980s began calling themselves *takatāpui*, utilizing a term that appears in nineteenth-century Maori–English dictionaries, where it is defined as "Going about in company, familiar, intimate" (Williams 1957, 369), although whether or not it implied anything about gender and sexuality at the time is entirely unknown.[2] Since then, this term has gained traction, particularly among those who seek to claim the legitimacy of being at once indigenous and nonheterosexual on the one hand and, on the other, are keen to distance themselves from Pākehā gay and lesbian identities and remain true to Māoritanga.

Often, debates around terms are really about something quite different, namely, the specificities of local contexts and who has the power to define localness. Debates about local legitimacy are invariably based on a binary oppositional contrast: Tongans define themselves in opposition to (a highly reified version of) the culture of the Pālangi (New Zealanders, Australians, Americans, etc.); Cook Islanders in opposition to Papaʻā; and Maori people in opposition to Pākehā. The oppositional group may differ according to the purpose of the comparison, but the binary nature of the comparison is oddly resilient. There may be a great deal of similarity in the behaviors, self-understandings, and beings-in-the-world between groups, but all comparisons between self and other emphasize differences and obscure similarities, as Fredrik Barth's (1969) foundational work on ethnicity as the creation of boundaries demonstrated long ago. So when Hawaiian non-heteronormative people assert themselves as *māhū*, thereby claiming the legitimacy of a traditional grounding based on historical continuity, they are distancing themselves from mainstream gays and lesbians of other ethnicities in Hawaiʻi and the postcolonial hegemony in which they are implicated (Ikeda, this volume).[3]

While we are sympathetic with efforts by non-heteronormative groups to distance themselves from terms that are "imposed" on them "from the outside," particularly in settler societies of the Pacific region (Hawaiʻi and Aotearoa New Zealand), we also stress that, ultimately, words are just words. There is nothing inherently problematic with using the term "transgender" or "gender liminal," for example, to refer to certain forms of Pacific Island non-heteronormativity, as long as one understands the cultural and political specificities of the context to which it is applied.[4]

Here we insist on two points. One is that comparisons are most useful when they involve more than two contrasting categories. Gender and sexual configurations in Tahiti should be understood against the background of cognate configurations in Samoa, Tonga, the Cook Islands, and Fiji. The other point is that all categories are constructs, generated in the very process of comparison, rather than essentialized entities that antedate the act of the comparison. Thus the fact that *māhū*, *ʻakavaʻine*, and *faʻafāfine* are often asserted to be completely different from transgender or gay categories in the West results from the way in which Western transgender is constructed in the very act of difference making. The categories are indeed different, but there are also important overlaps, in that Pacific Island non-normative genders and sexualities share commonalities (in their self-definition, political struggles, anxieties for the future, etc.) with those of postindustrial urban societies. In addition, people have a notable capacity to redefine who they are over the course of their lives, shifting from one category to another, sometimes at very short notice (Valentine 2007).

The terminology used to describe non-heteronormativity by both scholars and those who identify with this identity is temporally and contextually unstable. For example, in the Cook Islands in the late 1990s, the term *laelae,* a borrowing from Tahitian *raerae* (see Elliston's and Kuwahara's chapters), was the most commonly used term to describe both "traditional" transgender categories and individuals considered to be "gay." The term's connotations ranged from neutral to negative depending on who was using it and for what purpose. In the mid-2000s, transgender Cook Islanders no longer found this term acceptable, preferring instead to call themselves *'akava'ine,* calqued on the Samoan term *fa'afafine,* to which they had been exposed through diasporic networks. At the same time, the new term constitutes a local reclamation: before this time, *'akava'ine* had referred negatively to young women who were "above themselves," "did not know their place," and displayed overtly individualistic and immodest behaviors (Alexeyeff 2009a, 88), similarly to Tongan *fokisi* (Good, this volume). Transgender Cook Islanders appropriated the term to indicate that they are indeed "in the spotlight" through their glamour and sophistication. In contrast, non-heteronormative males in Samoa, at least until recently, rejected the term by which they are known to the rest of society (and, further afield, to New Zealanders and Australians)—namely, *fa'afafine*—because it foregrounds a sexual persona from which they wish to distance themselves (Tcherkézoff, this volume). Terms may thus be unstable over time, just as they are at any given moment the focus of contestation.

At the other end of the spectrum, one encounters efforts from other quarters that strive to go in the opposite direction by erasing difference and local specificity. Perhaps the most egregious example is to be found in the work of a team of Canadian evolutionary psychologists who visited Samoa repeatedly in the first decade of the new millennium and published a series of papers about Samoan *fa'afāfine,* at least one of which was disseminated to the media with great fanfare (Vasey and VanderLaan 2010). Following recent trends in evolutionary models of human sexuality (Bailey 2003), the researchers shift away from working with categories like "heterosexual" and "homosexual," using instead the neologisms "androphilia" and "gynephilia" to refer to sexual attraction to men and women respectively regardless of the person's gender, terms that become definers of categories of people. This categorization enables Vasey and his colleagues to lump together *fa'afāfine* in Samoa with gay men in Western contexts and claim to (finally!) solve the problem that same-sex erotic attraction represents for evolutionary theory: it is an adaptation to the demands of child care, whereby the androphilic would "sacrifice" their own fertility in order to attend to their nephews and nieces. The problems with the astounding configuration of methods, assumptions, and conclusions presented in this body of work are too numerous to spell out (cf. Jordan-Young 2010, 159–167, Schoeffel, this volume).[5] Suffice it to say that defining *fa'afāfine* in Samoa solely in terms of the gender of the object of their sexual attraction, and then to conflate them with gay identity in the West, obliterates the enormously complex ways in which sex, gender, and sexuality are interwoven, in Samoa and elsewhere, complexities that every chapter of this book highlights.

Ultimately, ad nauseam debates about whether categories are similar or different, or assertions to the effect that a term is in and others are out, are unproductive. We argue instead that we need to shift our attention from "who people are" to "what people do," to what effect, with what intentions, and according to whom. This theoretical position is squarely embedded in the shift that anthropological and sociological theory has undergone since the 1980s with the turn to practice theory (Bourdieu 1977).

Practice is "anything people do," particularly acts that have "intentional and unintentional political implications" (Ortner 1984, 149). A focus on social practice allows us to understand categories as shifting and complex rather than bounded. It provides the tools to understand change but also comes to grips with the fact that who we are is the result of performativity and repetition across different structural fields, repetition that can be interrupted at any moment (Butler 1990; Stryker 2006, 10). It also necessarily politicizes categories and actions. To varying degrees, contributors to this collection address how identities and categories emerge out of practice rather than the reverse.

The authors of the contributions to this collection distance themselves from the straightjacket of identity definitions, realizing fully the futility of attempting to define identities of any kind, particularly when these attempts have the effect of isolating identities from other dynamics at play in society and culture and in the local, the state, and the global, as we discuss further in the following sections. They engage squarely with the fact that identities do things, that they are performed in daily life, that they are transformed through events and movements, that they generate history and are the product of history, that they are constrained or liberated by legal constructions, and that they are constantly negotiated alongside other forms of identity. The chapters take seriously, for example, the moving and blurred boundary between transgenderism and homosexuality, and shy away from simplistic explanations in terms of "tradition" versus "modernity," or "identity" versus "practice," or "rural" versus "urban." Through its engagement with the complexities of these questions over time and space, this collection provides a model for future endeavors that seek to embed gender and sexuality in a broad field of theoretical import.

From Practice to Politics

One central aim of this book is to understand non-heteronormative practices in terms of their social, cultural, political, and historical contexts. All too often, non-heteronormative practices and people have been isolated as a separate category to be studied independently from other dynamics in society and culture, in the same way that women in the early days of feminist scholarship were approached as a marginal category of analysis separate from forces such as politics, the economy, and religion—despite the fact that these are often deeply implicated in gender and sexuality (Brownell and Besnier 2013; di Leonardo 1991; Freeman 2001; McKinnon 2000). Here we seek an understanding of the way in which non-mainstream gendered practices and identities are produced by hegemonic sociocultural dynamics, and how they in turn produce the social order through compliance, resistance, or anything in between. The social order is of course deeply political, and is so in different ways. We find politics in representations, in actions, and in symbols. We find politics in the intimacy of the private home, and in the corridors of government buildings. And everywhere gender looms large.

This politics is historical, and the history of gender in the Pacific Islands is implicated in the history of contact between Westerners and Islanders. Historically, the Pacific Islands have occupied a privileged position in Western making of meaning about gender and sexuality, and thus the politics of gender was a global politics right from the beginning of modernity. This meaning making began in the Enlightenment and Romantic eras with European travelers' mythologizing of the region, often based on their misunderstandings of Islanders' actions (Cheek 2003; Manderson and Jolly

1997; Sahlins 1985; Tcherkézoff 2004, 2008). From initial contact between Europeans and Pacific Islanders, the former constructed the latter as sexualized beings—whether positively, as in Tahiti, or negatively, as in Melanesia. In turn, Islanders themselves sexualized Western colonial agents, albeit in a different way. At the same time, these dynamics operated very far from the Pacific, as in Romantic debates in Europe that utilized what Europeans thought they had seen in the Pacific Islands to reconsider their own sexuality. These observations and interpretations showcased heteronormativity; in the few instances in which non-heteronormative people and practices were even mentioned (in travelers' or missionaries' accounts, for example), it was to condemn them and reaffirm a very conservative morality.

A particularly puzzling fact is that the only clear accounts of such persons and practices at the time of contact with Europeans in the late eighteenth century refer to Tahiti (Oliver 1974, 369–374). Europeans who visited other Pacific Islands made no mention of non-heteronormativity, even though most were well versed in contemporary descriptions of Tahiti, and in one (albeit ambiguous) case, a commentator who spent four years in Tonga in the first decade of the nineteenth century appears to deny its existence (Martin 1817, 2: 178). Yet today, non-heteronormative persons are present in virtually all island societies of Polynesia and perhaps Micronesia, and increasingly visible in Melanesia (Stewart, this volume). While of course we cannot know whether practices or identities existed at the time they were not mentioned in historical records, we do have ample evidence that historical contact and the ensuing colonialism are complicit in transforming the gender and sexual configuration of both island cultures and the cultures of the colonizers (Clancy-Smith and Gouda 1998; Gouda 1996; Stoler 1995).

While much of the work that deals with these issues focuses exclusively on heteronormativity, we ask whether the historical emergence of transgender categories in the Pacific could be the product of similar dynamics of contact, power, and exchange, which are not reducible to a simple process of importation. In what Sahlins (1985) calls the "structure of the conjuncture," dynamics that were present but not visible in society may emerge at the moment of contact. The cross-cultural encounter, particularly when it involves widely different kinds of people, is after all a performative moment, in which theatricality, artifice, and improvisation all figure prominently (Balme 2007; Dening 1980; Herbert 1980; Wallace 2003). In a more recent historical context, Tahitian transgender categories were fundamentally transformed by the neocolonial presence of French military personnel in the 1960s (Elliston, this volume), which suggests that comparable transformations may have taken place in earlier times about which we have little solid information (a hypothesis that Mageo [1992, 1996] develops for Samoa, albeit in a speculative way). It is no coincidence, we surmise, that we find that performativity is so central to some of the non-heteronormative categories that we analyze in this book (see, e.g., Pearson, Presterudstuen, Tcherkézoff, and Ikeda, this volume).

From the early twentieth century, anthropologists jumped into the fray with psychosocial analyses of sexuality in Pacific Island societies that grappled with the theoretical debates of their times. Here we think of Margaret Mead (1928), Bronislaw Malinowski (1929), and Ralph Linton (1939), with Mead's famous depiction of "sexual freedom" among Samoan adolescents and Malinowski's equally famous account of equally liberal sexuality in the Trobriand Islands standing out as particularly salient for the times. Mead claimed that Samoans were permissive of same-sex play among adolescents. She relates encountering one "deviant," a twenty-year-old who made "continual sexual advances to other boys"; girls regarded him as "an amusing freak," but men looked upon him with "mingled annoyance and contempt" (1928, 148). Malinowski, in contrast, reported that Trobrianders considered same-sex relations contemptible and makes no mention of gender crossing. With the exception of a handful of popular accounts of "sexuality in the islands" (Beaglehole 1944; Marshall 1971; Suggs 1966), early anthropological works make either only passing mention or no mention of non-heteronormative persons and practices. Nevertheless, these works established youth as an important subject for anthropological investigation. Issues associated with this life stage such as sexual intrigue, sexual experimentation, and courtship, as well as the societal acceptance of these practices during this period, laid the ground for later generations of scholars working on young people in the Pacific (e.g., Lepani 2012; Lepowsky 1998; Elliston, this volume). The first sustained account of transgender Pacific Islanders is arguably a brief but consequential article (1971) by psychiatrist-turned-anthropologist Robert Levy, which he incorporated into his 1973 book, *Tahitians: Mind and Experience in the Society Islands*, a groundbreaking work in psychological anthropology at the time. Levy developed a functionalist argument to the effect that Tahitian society needed a transgender figure to resolve the potential anxieties surrounding the differentiation of genders. The *māhū* was supposed to demonstrate to Tahitian men how not to be a man. Levy supported this argument by claiming that every village in Tahiti had only one *māhū*, because that was all that was needed, and this myth has been repeated over and over again in popular accounts. Levy's understanding of the place of *māhū* in Tahitian society has been subjected to critical deconstruction (e.g., Besnier 1994; Elliston, Schoeffel, this volume) for, among many other things, robbing the category of any kind of agency.

Besnier's 1994 chapter, "Polynesian Gender Liminality through Time and Space," marked a distinct shift in the study of non-normative gender and sexuality in the Pacific Islands. While more programmatic than ethnographically grounded (since at the time few ethnographic accounts of non-heteronormativity were available), it engaged with broader theoretical and cross-cultural analysis of gender and sexual politics. Anticipating the critique of the binary nature of comparison we developed in the previous section, Besnier opened the framework of comparison by engaging with works on non-normative genders in societies beyond the Pacific, searching for analytic insights comparatively. At the time, the notion of "third gender" was in fashion in the social sciences and in the popular imagination. Thirdness is perhaps most useful if one interprets it as referring to "otherness" (as in "the Third World" or the Lacanian symbolic), as cultural theorist Marjorie Garber argues in her classic *Vested Interests* (991, 11–13); but the problem is the persistence of the term's numerical meaning, the illusion that transcending the strictures of binary gender is just a matter of adding one more category without thinking through the implications of such a move. Ultimately, thirdness fails to capture the complex interaction among gender, sexuality, and the social, economic, and political contexts in which they operate.

Ironically, while Besnier's chapter appeared in an edited book entitled *Third Sex, Third Gender,* he argues against giving the notion too much analytic weight. A more productive line of thinking engages with the way in which gender and sexuality are implicated in structures of inequality (be they of rank, social class, ethnicity, indigeneity, etc.) and of unequal access to material or symbolic resources. This approach then enables us to understand non-heteronormativity in all its complexity: as highly variable in its manifestations from one person to another, from one context to another, and from one society to another; as shifting over time, whether in the course of history or the course of a lifetime; and as porous and unstable, as people take on gender and sexual attributes according to their own needs and aspirations or those of other people around them. We thus find, for example, a recurrent association between non-heteronormative practices and identifications with the liminality of adolescence, either in the form of persons crossing gender lines during their youthful years (before marrying and "settling down") or in the form of adolescents' sexual relations with a transgender person (Elliston, this chapter). Focusing on these complexities amounts to engaging with the way in which subjectivities and structures are intertwined with one another.

Some of these complexities come to the fore in the works of a number of transgender and gay Pacific Islanders and Maori people in recent years (e.g., Hutchings and Aspin 2007; Pulotu-Endemann and Peteru 2001). Some of the most sophisticated works in this vein have utilized modes of communication beyond print media and have creatively transcended the boundary between seriousness and humor, between aesthetics and politics, and between the identity politics and other forms of political action. Samoan artist Dan Taulapapa McMullin's hilarious three-minute 2001 video (McMullin 2007) draws on traditional Samoan forms of comedy or *fale aitu* (see Pearson, Schoeffel, and Tcherkézoff, this volume) to draw a trenchant critique of both neocolonialism and the complex configurations of the local through the eyes of a *fa'afafine* named Sinalela (Samoan for "Cinderella").

Questions of morality constitute a key puzzle for contributors to this book, although they do not necessarily couch the problems in these terms. People in all societies have a propensity to live by often seemingly contradictory moral standards. For example, in the Cook Islands, "straight" women and men can be heard vilifying *'akava'ine*'s alleged sexual immorality while at the same time relishing the company of their *'akava'ine* friends, engaging in very overt sexual banter with them if they are men and laughing with abandon at their lewd stories if they are women. Similarly, in Tonga, *leiti* are valued congregation members in most established churches because of their dedication to the activities of the church; yet bringing up the presence of *leiti* with church officials invariably elicits serious condemnation, complete with biblical quotations. These apparent contradictions cannot simply be explained away as matters of "context appropriateness" or "hypocrisy," even though there is a polarization of moral stances according to the degree of visibility of practices. Tcherkézoff (this volume) analyzes sexual relations as always confined to an "invisible" world outside the realm of society and culture, and since Samoans consider non-heteronormative relations as always sexual, they cannot be part of society.

Still, we contend that morality is by definition based on multiple frames of reference, which allow for the coexistence of seemingly contradictory moral stances. These do not necessarily map onto differences in context in any straightforward manner. In fact, arguing that different contexts elicit different moral judgments of the same action or person simply shifts the burden of analysis to the task of explaining how contexts can coexist while being defined by incompatible moralities. The situation is even more complex in many of the societies that we focus on in this book, many of which are diasporic or multicultural, and all of which have undergone tremendous moral transformations in the relatively recent past through missionization, colonialism, postcolonialism, and globalization. For example, debates about the religious ordination of lesbians and gay men in industrial countries of the Pacific Basin, as illustrated above, or the move to extend the right to marry to same-sex unions can have complex transformative effects on societies that are both island-based and diasporic (Farran, this volume). Through their strong connections to New Zealand and other countries, Tongans have become increasingly aware of the concept of "child molestation," casting an entirely new light on casual sexual encounters between *leitī* and adolescents. Moralities are thus potentially informed by multiple overlapping cultural frames. This is where attention to social practice becomes useful and important, in that it forces us to see action and context as mutually constitutive. This is also why terms like "acceptance" and "rejection" are not useful analytic tools to characterize the relationship among categories, actions, and moral judgments—they also imply that people have a pre-social identity that they present to the rest of society for moral evaluation.

Most popular accounts of non-heteronormativity in Pacific societies maintain that "traditional" forms of transgender were more "authentic" and thus morally "acceptable" to mainstream society because they were defined in terms of gender rather than sexuality. But then "foreign-influenced" modernity gradually sexualized the identity and rendered it "inauthentic," bringing about a withdrawal of societal acceptance and the emergence of moral condemnation (e.g., Croall 1999; Harker 1995; Xian and Anbe 2001). While this scenario accords with what many Pacific Islanders themselves maintain and is reproduced uncritically in some academic works (e.g., James 1994; Schmidt 2010), we find it deeply problematic for a number of reasons. First, it places the burden of morality on non-heteronormative individuals, as opposed to understanding them in the context of their relationships with other people, including those they have sex with, whether on the beaches of traditional villages or in the back alleys behind the urban nightclub. Second, this account erases sexuality from the "traditional" transgender, an erasure in which anthropologists and other commentators have been complicit, as Pearson argues (this volume; see also Wallace 2003). Third, it is predicated on an overarching contrast between "tradition" and "modernity," whereby the former is the historical antecedent to the latter, while we know well that both "tradition" and "modernity," and the different moral orders with which they are alleged to be associated, are the products of active construction. This is dramatically illustrated by the different moral evaluations of two transgender categories, *māhū* and *raerae*, on Tahiti and Bora Bora, even though the two islands are only separated by 160 miles and are part of the same cultural and political entity (Kuwahara, this volume). On Tahiti, while *māhū* are valued as custodians of "tradition," *raerae* are immoral and inauthentic because of their associations with the French colonial presence, especially the military, who are supposed to patronize *raerae* sex workers. On Bora Bora, in contrast, where there is no military presence, both *māhū* and *raerae* are equally valued for their labor in the luxury tourism industry and their roles in families. Here, the contrast between tradition and modernity, and the concomitant moralities, are the products of geopolitical dynamics whose effect can vary radically within the same territory.

More generally, both gender and sexuality are embroiled in the same set of sociocultural and political dynamics, and work in tandem with one another so as to produce moral hierarchies (Rubin 1975, 1984). The chapters in this book all build on these various insights, exploring the specificities of each ethnographic situation through the lens of comparison and of theoretical frameworks that extend beyond the Pacific. They investigate contradictory moralities—some religious, others secular, some local, others global—and the negotiations that these contradictions generate in people's lives. They are attentive to the consequences of poverty and marginality in shaping the gendering of subjects as well as their sexual lives. Lack of economic and social capital can engender alienation, but it can also be the basis for the creation of new social and political formations, such as fictive kinship ties, adoption, friendships, and networks that can reach beyond the confines of the local (Dolgoy, Ikeda, and Stewart, this volume).

Local, Regional, and Global

Non-heteronormative people of all kinds define themselves in both local and non-local terms. Both the local and the nonlocal, however, operate on different scales, encompassing different geographical, social, political, and cultural frames of reference that refract one another. For example, the nonlocal may be regional or global, and "region" and "global" may be defined differently for different purposes. Similarly, the local itself may be quite complex, as people in many societies (particularly in the postcolonial world) contest among one another what is local and who is entitled to define the local (in terms of culture, morality, authenticity, or relevance). The constant awareness of different frames of reference results in a bifocality of life (Besnier 2011, 12–17), as people live and act both in the "near-sightedness" of the here and now while constantly looking over each other's shoulders at a larger audience, which can consist of diasporic compatriots, foreigners, agents of new moralities, or providers of development aid. Some people are better versed in this bifocality than others, because they are more experienced at it or have more to gain from it, and some forms of non-heteronormativity have an uncanny tendency to place themselves right at the center of bifocal negotiations (Good, this volume).

A comparative approach such as the one we are encouraging here seeks to understand identity formations in contrast to one another, while also being attentive to the fact that they always inform one another, particularly in the context of the regional and global circulation of information, political action, legal concepts, and moral regimes. For example, transgender and gay Westerners often seek inspiration from "traditional" transgender categories, through which they develop a somewhat romantic critique of what they see as the restrictive sexual binary of Western modernity (Towle and Morgan 2002). Concurrently, some non-heteronormative people in other societies are increasingly accessing body modification procedures (e.g., sex-reassignment surgery or hormone therapy) made possible by advances in Western medical technologies, enabling the emergence of new identities. To complicate matters further, the international distribution of medical competencies in matters of sex transformations has now shifted to non-Western countries, as illustrated by Thailand having emerged as a world center of expertise and a major destination for transgender medical tourism (Aizura 2010). The global flow of people, information, technology, and other material and symbolic forms provides individuals with new forms of self-definition and self-understanding. While some Pacific Islanders undertake body-modification surgery (Kuwahara, this volume), most male-bodied non-heteronormative people in the Pacific have little desire to cover up their maleness completely so as to "pass" as women. Some view themselves as possessing the best physical attributes of both sexes, and there is a wide range of interpretations of feminine appearance depending on individual dispositions and context (Alexeyeff 2008).

One vector through which identities and practices are being transformed in the interface of the global and the local is the increased importance of nongovernmental organizations throughout the developing world (Jolly 2010; Lind 2009). NGOs operate within a neoliberal logic characterized by the withdrawal of the state from the economic and social structure of society, a space that is being filled by other agents—from large-scale United Nations agencies and international finance institutions, to churches, grassroots organizations, and private interests (Fisher 1997). The material resources that invariably back up these organizations help them gain a foothold in local contexts, where these resources provide them legitimacy.

Recent years have witnessed a proliferation of NGOs relating to gender and sexuality, relating in particular to HIV prevention efforts even in parts of the region where the predicted HIV pandemic has yet to materialize to any significant proportion, as well as to gender equality, violence, and human rights. These efforts have brought people from all corners of the Pacific region together in multiple associations, workshops, conferences and networks, through which they can identify common goals and agendas.

While the ideology of HIV prevention has been careful over the years to eschew the stigmatizing effect of identifying groups at risk, preferring instead to focus on risk practices and later risk situations, in practice on-the-ground efforts end up targeting specific groups of people. In the Pacific as elsewhere, these have invariably been the transgender, even though other social categories of people are equally, if not more, vulnerable to HIV infection. However enlightened NGO efforts may be, their translation into local contexts invariably runs the risk of highlighting certain aspects of local moralities and downplaying others. At the same time, NGOs invariably operate with the assumption that openness about sexual practices and other morally charged matters is healthy and desirable, and can bring about significant and perhaps useful transformations in what can or cannot be said, in what can be visible or not. These transformations, however, do not operate without contestation and conflict (Good and George, this volume).

What has been called the "NGO-ization" of the world has other possible consequences. One is the efflorescence, narrowing down, and modification of local identifications. For example, the neologic acronym MSM, "men who have sex with men," has emerged around the region, because it has immediate traction from which international aids money flows and national responses take place (Eves and Butt 2008; more generally, Boelstorff 2011; Reddy 2005). However, the local response may be mitigated: in Fiji, for example, the term elicits snickers among the mainstream (George, this volume). In contrast, non-heteronormative people in the region increasingly understand themselves in terms of categories like LGBT, particularly when this categorical shift is encouraged through the availability of trips to overseas conferences and the new networking possibilities they offer, and in the training workshops and festivities that accompany them. Through efforts like these, the pleasures of sex, traveling, and partying go hand in hand with global development discourse of sexual risk and danger (Jolly 2010).

While NGO activity takes up the issue of sexuality narrowly as an issue of HIV and STD prevention, local non-heteronormative individuals also frame these networks to address local agendas, some of which have little to do with sexuality. For instance, the Te Tiare Association, a Cook Islands NGO founded by local *'akava'ine*, frames its constitution in terms of a global human rights discourse (e.g., Objective 2.2: "raise public awareness of the human rights abuses suffered by aka vaine [*sic*] in the community"); but it is also active in relation to local priorities, for example, by organizing entertainment for fund-raising (particularly for schools) and mentoring "young queens" in their job-seeking endeavors. This group was formed after one *'akava'ine* attended a "Love Life Fono" organized in 2007 by the New Zealand AIDS Foundation. From there she decided the Cooks should have an organization similar to transgender organizations in Samoa and Tonga. As part of Te Tiare's launch in 2008, "sisters" representing other Pacific Nations transgender organizations were invited and attended, further underlying the pan-regional connections being forged through local, diasporic, and global networks.

Concurrently, the larger context that informs people's lives is itself shifting in both geography and scale. NGOs can also encourage identification with a "region," through the workings, for example, of such organizations as the Pacific Islands AIDS Foundation, with funding from New Zealand. Alternatively, the exact constitution of a "region" may be the result of expedient lumping together of numerous countries by large-scale agencies like the UN, for whom the Pacific Islands, being relatively insignificant in terms of population, are affixed to a much larger "Asia-Pacific" entity. This configuration has the advantage of potentially involving Pacific Islanders in circuits of information and resources of much greater scale. At the same time, it runs the risk of relegating the Pacific Islands to the status of an appendage, an afterthought of the global, and of obscuring the fact that being on the edge can be a position of great productivity (Jolly 2001; Teaiwa 2001). Intellectuals and the infrastructures in which they operate (e.g., institutions, funding agencies, publishers) can unwittingly contribute to this political marginalization by conflating very different dynamics and concerns and obliterating local specificities. While the notion of "region" is "a theoretically and politically necessary fiction" (Johnson, Jackson, and Herdt 2000, 361), it is always problematic.

At the same time, flows of ideas about sexuality and the mediating role it plays between the person and the social context transcend regional boundaries, proverbially harnessing all local specificities to the global. This is what Altman (2001) has termed "global sex," the hypothesis that the forces of globalization are enacting changes in local contexts that bring about both increased homogeneity and greater inequality in matters of sexuality around the world. In the context of these global transformations, identities themselves are changing, from a broad diversity of local configurations that may involve a constellation of identifications based on gender, sexual desire, kinship, religion, and labor, to a much narrower focus on sexuality as the primordial definer of who one is. For example, according to Altman, categories like *banci* and *waria* in Indonesia, *bakla* and *bantut* in the Philippines, and *kathoey* and *tomdee* in Thailand are increasingly morphing into a global gay identification produced through Western-inflected media images, consumer goods, and discourses of sexual rights, resulting inter alia in buff gay gym rats and lipstick lesbians waving rainbow flags in pride parades in all corners of the urban world. This explains why many mainstream Pacific Islanders (alongside people in many other parts of the world) often maintain categorically that "homosexuality" (a term that generally conflates categories of gender and sexuality) is a "Western scourge"—which is correct if one thinks of "homosexuality" as principal definer of who one is, as opposed to a practice that has no relevance as a marker of personal or group identity (Schoeffel, this volume).[6]

Altman is careful to acknowledge that these transformations are messy, with different modes of identification coexisting and overlapping. He is also critical of the dominance of the West, and in particular of the United States, in determining the direction of these changes, and of the central role that they accord to commodification and neoliberalism. In addition, while global sex appears to enact a liberatory politics everywhere, in fact it operates within an uneven playing field. Urban middle classes, for example, benefit from the cosmopolitan freedom promised by global sex, while those outside its reach do not. Similarly, global liberatory politics also go hand in hand with the global circulation of new forms of oppression, under the guide of religious fundamentalism for example (Morris 1997), and can generate new local forms of sexual repression (a point that Massad [2002] would later controversially elaborate; contrast Farran, this volume).

The global sex hypothesis speaks to a number of issues that we raise. Like all grand narratives, it has been subjected to critical scrutiny, particularly by anthropologists concerned with the complexities of the local politics, identifications, and transformations (Alexeyeff 2009a; Besnier 2002; Jackson 2009; Reddy 2005; Rofel 2007). For us, one of its major problems is that it is reminiscent of the problematic evolution from "morally acceptable" tradition to "morally problematic" modernity that we critiqued in the previous section. Yet it does bring to the fore the impact of capitalism, principally in its neoliberal forms, on the sexed and gendered person, demanding a political economy of sexuality. But this political economy must also remain cognizant of other politics (diasporic dispersal, nationalism, militarism, etc.) and of the fact that the global may affect the local but the global is also produced through the local. This volume seeks to understand non-heteronormative people in a local context of all social relationships, among not only other transgender affines but also non-transgender friends and relatives. Transgender individuals interact with, evaluate, and are evaluated by others around them whether of mainstream gender and sexuality or not. The local, in other words, is as complex and shifting as global and regional dynamics.

Where to Next?

The following chapters go to great lengths in exploring unchartered territory, but also leave a number of questions open, simply because they have not been subjected to empirical investigation. The first is a regional question: most contributions focus on the Polynesian region, reflecting the unexplored status of non-heteronormative sexuality throughout the Melanesian region and in many parts of Micronesia (Dvorak's and Stewart's chapters being the exceptions). The silence over contemporary forms of non-het-eronormativity in Papua New Guinea societies is puzzling in light of the well-trodden ground occupied in anthropological theory in the 1980s and 1990s by discussions of "ritualized homosexuality" (e.g., Elliston 1995; Herdt 1984; Knauft 1985) associated with male initiation rituals that were once practiced, in varying configurations, in societies dispersed across the Highlands and along the south coast of New Guinea until they were dis-placed by colonial and missionary sexual regimes (Knauft 2003). Similarly, rampant sexual violence, sex work, and HIV in many parts of contemporary New Guinea have preoccupied practitioners as well as scholars (Eves and Butt 2008; Hammar 2010; Lepani 2012; Wardlow 2006). Yet gender and sexual variance is seriously under-studied in that era of the region, reasons for which constitute a particularly puzzling question to which we do not have a clear answer.

One contrast that arises between the material on Papua New Guinea presented in Stewart's chapter and that in other chapters is the hypervis-ibility of transgender individuals in many parts of Polynesia. Polynesian transgender people are hypervisible, both in the sense of refusing to remain hidden or obscured, and in the fact that transgender individuals and repre-sentations turn up in expected and unexpected contexts and in the darned-est places, at times making for uncomfortable or surprising negotiations of meaning. The situation in Papua New Guinea is strikingly different, in that there non-heteronormative individuals report a strong sense of isola-tion from their families and from the public sphere, where they feel they can rarely be "out" for fear of violent retribution (similar issues also emerge in Ikeda's materials about Hawai'i). But then again, Papua New Guinea is not coterminous with "Melanesia." Vanuatu's first drag queen, named Masi, performed in Port Vila in 1999, apparently for the first time ever, in front of her home island community, Tanna, reputed to be the most aggressively hypermasculine island in the country, and the response from the large crowd was one of celebration, humor, and delight (John Taylor, personal com-munication, May 2012). Here, the alleged contrast between Polynesia and Melanesia evaporates, suggesting that many additional factors are at stake.

A second area of research that remains underexplored is female non-heteronormative practices and identifications, which Tcherkézoff alone addresses in this book (see also Elliston 1999 and, in more tangential fashion, Pearson, this volume). His analysis uncovers major disjunctures between the person of the Samoan *tomboy* and that of the *fa'afafine* (or *fa'ateine,* the term he prefers), disjunctures that explain the invisibility of the former in contrast to the conspicuousness of the latter in Samoa, elsewhere in the Pacific Islands, and in diasporic communities. How do the forces of the global unsettle the silence that surrounds female non-heteronormativity, and how do the resulting dynamics resemble or differ from those that reshape male non-heteronormativity? These and a host of other questions remain to be addressed seriously.

A third set of issues that demands attention is the subjectivity of men who do not identify as *fa'afafine, leitī,* or *'akava'ine,* but who engage in sexual relations with members of these social categories, occasionally in preference to heteronormative sexual relations. From the perspective of mainstream Pacific Island societies, these questions are deeply unsettling, as illustrated by Kalissa Alexeyeff's (2009b, 113) anecdote about naïvely assuming that one of her straight Rarotongan interlocutors would identify as gay because he had a *'akava'ine* partner, and nearly getting beaten up by him as a result. For mainstream society, these questions raise uncomfortable issues about the permeability of "cultural" boundaries (dislodging, for example, the assertion that "homosexuality" is not local) and about the fragility of masculinity beneath a veneer of gendered stability and power. Similarly, we know next to nothing about the emergence of gay identities among Pacific Island men, primarily in diasporic communities but not exclusively so, and their relationships to other manifestations of non-heteronormative identifications and to global forms of same-sex identification.

Finally, while (post)colonialism and its configuration through sexuality figures in many of the chapters of this book (e.g., Dvorak, Elliston, Farran, George, Ikeda, Kuwahara, Pearson, Stewart, and Teaiwa), the topic demands considerably more attention. Broadly speaking, the sexualization of colonialism has garnered much greater attention in its historical forms than in its contemporary manifestations, and this attention has been largely confined to heteronormative relations, with a few exceptions (e.g., Bleys 1996). Yet the mapping of contemporary (post)colonial relations onto sexual desire raises a host of theoretically important questions that remain to be addressed in the Pacific and elsewhere. For example, how are same-sex relations between Westerners and Islanders embedded in a historical and contemporary context of structural relations between island nations and metropolises? How do they in turn inform these relations by contributing, for example, to the racialization of postcolonial relations (cf. Constable 2003; Kelsky 2001)? Why are so many same-sex relations between Western men and Island men in diasporic communities so frequently informed by an age difference that always has the same configuration, reminiscent of the mutual attraction between older white "rice queens" and younger Asian "potato queens" in much of Asia (Ayres 1998; Jones 2000)? The complicated structuration of sexual desire, material desire, and parameters of social inequality (e.g., age, ethnicity, race) deserves considerably more analytic attention.

We have assembled this book with the aim of inspiring a new generation of researchers to engage with questions of gender and sexuality in the Pacific and beyond, so these questions progressively migrate from the edge to the center.

Acknowledgments

Over the years, Alexeyeff's research in the Cook Islands has received support from the Thomas and Ruth McArthur Fellowship Fund, the Australian National University, and the University of Melbourne. Besnier's research on Tongan *leitī* has garnered funding from the Wenner Gren Foundation for Anthropological Research, the Marsden Fund of the Royal Society of New Zealand, and the Netherlands Organisation for Scientific Research. We thank the University of Melbourne Faculty of Arts for granting Niko a Visiting Fellowship in 2012, which enabled us to complete this book. Mahmoud abd-el-Wahed, Deborah Elliston, Sue Farran, Mary Good, Linda Ikeda, Ian Lincoln, Rachel Morgain, Benedicta Rousseau, John Taylor, and Serge Tcherkézoff provided useful comments on earlier drafts of this introduction. Two scholars reviewed the entire book manuscript anonymously for the press and offered excellent advice; one, Maria Lepowsky, provided meticulous comments on every single chapter. Finally, we thank Masako Ikeda of University of Hawai'i Press for her enthusiastic support of this project and Barbara Folsom for her expert copyediting.

Notes

1   In a similar vein, Susan Styker finds that "the conflation of many types of gender variance into the single shorthand term 'transgender,' particularly when this collapse into a single gender of personhood crosses the boundaries that divide the West from the rest of the world, holds both peril and promise" (2006, 14).

2   We know from the work of such scholars as Smith-Rosenberg (1975) that Victorian-era friendships in the West were deeply intimate and physical, but did not necessarily involve sexual intimacy or define those involved as

nonheterosexual. This is the lens through which missionary linguists in the nineteenth century viewed Maori sociality.

3   At the same time, they have to contend with calls for the "re-masculinization" of indigeneity as part of the Hawaiian sovereignty movement, which seeks to redress the simultaneous feminization and commodification of Hawaiian identity (e.g., in hula dancing in tourist resorts), but at the same time has the effect of marginalizing *māhū* and condoning homophobia (Tengan 2008, 159–161).

4   In the report of a regional training workshop for AIDS education sponsored by the New Zealand AIDS Foundation, for example, one Samoan representative is quoted as saying, "Often psychologists and anthropologists label us with terms that we don't like" (Akersten 2008). One activity of the workshop consisted in sorting through terms in three categories: hated (e.g., "queer," "third gender," "*laelae*"), acceptable ("transgender," "gay," "*akava'ine*"), and loved ("*takatāpui*," "*fa'afafine*," "girl").

5   It is interesting that it never seemed to have occurred to the researchers to broach the issue of "straight" men's erotic attraction to *fa'afafine*, even though it is, in their terminology, "androphilic" behavior. Nor do they seem to be aware of the fact that, in Samoa and elsewhere in Western Polynesia, there is no category "uncle": as anthropologists have known at least since Radcliffe-Brown (1924), a crucial and deeply relevant distinction is made in societies of Western Polynesia between uterine and paternal uncles. The uterine uncle (straight or not) has a nurturing relationship with his sister's children, to whom he is inferior in rank. Father's brothers, in contrast, are not distinguished terminologically or behaviorally from fathers, and, like the latter, their relationship with their male sibling's children is distant and authoritarian (whether they are straight, gay, transgender, or anything else). One wonders what kinship relationship the researchers' subjects were thinking of when filling out the questionnaires on which this research was based.

6   In this respect, they are in good company: African politicians and intellectuals are quick to define homosexuality as "un-African" and the "White man's disease," thereby authorizing extraordinary forms of repression against gay- and lesbian-identified citizens (Epprecht 2008; Hoad 2007).

References

ABC Radio. 2011. *Pacific Beat: Pacific Churches in Australia Upset over Gay Ministers;* http://www.radioaustralia.net.au/international/radio/onairhighlights/pacific -churches-in-australia-upset-over-gay-ministers (accessed March 2012).

Aizura, Aren Z. 2010. Feminine Transformations: Gender Reassignment Surgical Tourism in Thailand. *Medical Anthropology* 29: 424–443.

Akersten, Mark. 2008. Supporting our Sisters in the Pacific; http://www.gaynz .com/articles/publish/21/article_6339.php (accessed May 2012).

Alexeyeff, Kalissa. 2008. Globalizing Drag in the Cook Islands: Friction, Repulsion, and Abjection. *The Contemporary Pacific* 20: 143–161.

———. 2009a. *Dancing from the Heart: Movement, Gender and Cook Islands Globalization.* Honolulu: University of Hawai'i Press.

———. 2009b. Dancing Sexuality in the Cook Islands. In *Transgressive Sex: Subversion and Control in Erotic Encounters,* ed. Hasting Donnan and Fiona McGowan, pp. 113–130. New York: Berghahn.

Altman, Dennis. 2001. *Global Sex.* Chicago: University of Chicago Press.

Ayres, Tony. 1998. *China Dolls.* Documentary (28 min.). Helen Bowden, producer.

Bailey, Michael. 2003. *The Man Who Would Be Queen: The Science of Gender-Bending and Transsexualism.* Washington, DC: Joseph Henry Press.

Balme, Christopher. 2007. *Pacific Performances: Theatricality and Cross-Cultural Encounter in the South Seas.* New York: Palgrave Macmillan.

Barth, Fredrik. 1969. *Ethnic Groups and Boundaries: The Social Organization of Culture Difference.* Oslo: Universitetsforlaget.

Beaglehole, Ernest. 1944. *Islands of Danger.* Wellington, NZ: Progressive Publishing Society.

Besnier, Niko. 1994. Polynesian Gender Liminality through Time and Space. In *Third Sex, Third Gender: Beyond Sexual Dimorphism in Culture and History,* ed. Gilbert Herdt, pp. 285–328. New York: Zone.

———. 2002. Transgenderism, Locality, and the Miss Galaxy Beauty Pageant in Tonga. *American Ethnologist* 29: 534–566.

———. 2011. *On the Edge of the Global: Modern Anxieties in a Pacific Island Nation.* Stanford, CA: Stanford University Press.

Bleys, Rudi. 1996. *The Geography of Perversion: Male-to-Male Sexual Behavior outside the West and the Ethnographic Imagination, 1750–1918.* New York: NYU Press.

Boellstorff, Tom. 2011. But Do Not Identify as Gay: A Proleptic Genealogy of the MSM Category. *Cultural Anthropology* 26: 287–312.

Bourdieu, Pierre. 1977. *Outline of Theory and Practice.* Cambridge: Cambridge University Press.

Brownell, Susan, and Niko Besnier. 2013. Gender and Sexuality. In *The Handbook of Sociocultural Anthropology,* ed. James G. Carrier and Deborah B. Gewertz, pp. 239–258. London: Bloomsbury.

Butler, Judith. 1990. *Gender Trouble: Feminism and the Subversion of Identity.* New York: Routledge.

Cheek, Pamela. 2003. *Sexual Antipodes: Enlightenment Globalization and the Placing of Sex.* Stanford, CA: Stanford University Press.

Clancy-Smith, Julia A., and Frances Gouda, eds. 1998. *Domesticating the Empire: Race, Gender and Family Life in French and Dutch Colonialism.* Charlottesville: University of Virginia Press.

Constable, Nicole. 2003. *Romance on a Global Stage: Pen Pals, Virtual Ethnography, and "Mail Order" Marriages.* Berkeley: University of California Press.

Croall, Heather. 1999. *Paradise Bent: Boys Will Be Girls in Samoa.* Documentary (52 min.). Heather Corall, producer.

Dening, Greg. 1980. *Islands and Beaches: Discourse on a Silent Land, Marquesas, 1774–1880.* Melbourne: Melbourne University Press.

di Leonardo, Micaela, ed. 1991. *Gender at the Crossroads of Knowledge: Feminist Anthropology in the Postmodern Era.* Berkeley: University of California Press.

Elliston, Deborah. 1995. Erotic Anthropology: "Ritualized Homosexuality" in Melanesia and Beyond. *American Ethnologist* 22: 848–867.

———. 1999. Negotiating Transnational Sexual Economies: Female Māhū and Same-Sex Sexuality in "Tahiti and Her Islands." In *Female Desires: Same-Sex Relations and Transgender Practices Across Cultures,* ed. Evelyn Blackwood and Saskia E. Wieringa, pp. 232–252. New York: Columbia University Press.

Epprecht, Mark. 2008. *Heterosexual Africa? The History of an Idea from the Age of Exploration to the Age of AIDS.* Columbus: Ohio University Press.

Eves, Richard, and Leslie Butt, eds. 2008. *Making Sense of AIDS: Culture, Sexuality, and Power in Melanesia.* Honolulu: University of Hawai'i Press.

Fisher, William F. 1997. Doing Good? The Politics and Antipolitics of NGO Practices. *Annual Review of Anthropology* 26: 439–464.

Freeman, Carla. 2001. Is Local : Global as Feminine : Masculine? *Signs* 26: 1007–1037.

Garber, Marjorie. 1991. *Vested Interests: Cross-dressing and Cultural Anxiety.* London: Routledge.

Gouda, Frances. 1996. *Dutch Culture Overseas: Colonial Practice in the Netherlands Indies, 1900–1942.* Amsterdam: Amsterdam University Press.

Hammar, Lawrence. 2010. *Sin, Sex and Stigma: A Pacific Response to HIV and AIDS.* Wantage, Oxfordshire: Sean Kingston.

Harker, Caroline. 1995. *Fa'afafine: Queens of Samoa.* Documentary. Susan Nemec, producer.

Hau'ofa, Epeli. 1994. Our Sea of Islands. *The Contemporary Pacific* 6: 148–161.

Herbert, T. Walter. 1980. *Marquesan Encounters: Melville and the Meaning of Civilization.* Cambridge, MA: Harvard University Press.

Herdt, Gilbert H., ed. 1984. *Ritualized Homosexuality in Melanesia.* Berkeley: University of California Press.

Hoad, Neville W. 2007. *African Intimacies: Race, Homosexuality, and Globalization.* Minneapolis: University of Minnesota Press.

Hutchings, Jessica, and Clive Aspin, eds. 2007. *Sexuality and the Stories of Indigenous People.* Wellington, NZ: Huia.

Jackson, Peter. 2009. Capitalism and Modern Queering: National Markets, Parallels among Sexual Cultures, and Multiple Queer Modernities. *GLQ* 15: 357–395.

James, Kerry E. 1994. Effeminate Males and Changes in the Construction of Gender in Tonga. *Pacific Studies* 7(2): 39–69.

Johnson, Mark, Peter Jackson, and Gilbert Herdt. 2000. Critical Regionalities and the Study of Gender and Sexual Diversity in South East and East Asia. *Culture, Health & Sexuality* 2: 361–375.

Jolly, Margaret. 2001. On the Edge? Deserts, Oceans, Islands. *The Contemporary Pacific* 13: 417–466.

Jolly, Susie. 2010. Why the Development Industry Should Get Over Its Obsession with Bad Sex and Start to Think about Pleasure. In *Development, Sexual Rights and Global Governance,* ed. Amy Lind, pp. 23–38. London: Routledge.

Jones, Rodney H. 2000. "Potato Seeking Rice": Language, Culture, and Identity in Gay Personal Ads in Hong Kong. *International Journal of the Sociology of Language* 143: 33–61.

Jordan-Young, Rebecca M. 2010. *Brain Storm: The Flaws in the Science of Sex Differences.* Cambridge, MA: Harvard University Press.

Kelsky, Karen. 2001. *Women on the Verge: Japanese Women, Western Dreams.* Durham, NC: Duke University Press.

Knauft, Bruce M. 1985. *Good Company and Violence: Sorcery and Social Action in Lowland New Guinea Society.* Berkeley: University of California Press.

———. 2003. What Ever Happened to Ritualized Homosexuality? Modern Sexual Subjects in Melanesia and Elsewhere. *Annual Review of Sex Research* 14: 137–159.

Lepani, Katherine. 2012. *Islands of Love, Islands of Risk: Culture and HIV in the Trobriands.* Nashville, TN: Vanderbilt University Press.

Lepowsky, Maria. 1998. Coming of Age on Vanatinai: Gender, Sexuality, and Power. In *Adolescence in Pacific Islands Societies,* ed. Gilbert Herdt and Stephen C. Leavitt, pp. 123–147. Pittsburgh, PA: University of Pittsburgh Press.

Levy, Robert I. 1971. The Community Functions of Tahitian Male Transvestites. *Anthropological Quarterly* 44: 12–21.

———. 1973. *Tahitians: Mind and Experience in the Society Islands.* Chicago: University of Chicago Press.

Lind, Amy. 2009. Governing Intimacy, Struggling for Sexual Rights: Challenging Heteronormativity in the Global Development Industry. *Development* 52: 34–42.

Linton, Ralph. 1939. Marquesan Culture. In *The Individual and His Society: The Psychodynamics of Primitive Social Organization,* ed. Abram Kardiner, pp. 197–250. New York: Columbia University Press.

Mageo, Jeannette. 1992. Male Transvestism and Cultural Change in Samoa. *American Ethnologist* 19: 443–459.

———. 1996. Samoa, on the Wilde Side: Male Transvestism, Oscar Wilde, and Liminality in Making Gender. *Ethos* 24: 588–627.

Malinowski, Bronislaw. 1929. *The Sexual Life of Savages in North-Western Melanesia.* New York: Beacon Press.

Manderson, Lenore, and Margaret Jolly, eds. 1997. *Sites of Desire/Economies of Pleasure: Sexualities in Asia and the Pacific.* Chicago: University of Chicago Press.

Marshall, Donald S. 1971. Sexual Behavior on Mangaia. In *Human Sexual Behavior,* ed. Donald S. Marshall and Robert C. Suggs, pp. 103–162. New York: Basic Books.

Martin, John. 1817. *An Account of the Natives of the Tonga Islands, in the South Pacific Ocean, with an Original Grammar and Vocabulary of Their Language, Compiled and Arranged from the Extensive Communications of Mr. William Mariner, Several Years Resident in Those Islands.* London: Printed for the author.

Massad, Joseph. 2002. Re-Orienting Desire: The Gay International and the Arab World. *Public Culture* 14: 361–386.

McKinnon, Susan. 2000. Domestic Exceptions: Evans-Pritchard and the Creation of Nuer Patrilineality and Equality. *Cultural Anthropology* 15: 35–83.

McMullin, Dan Taulapapa, dir. 2001. *Sinalela.* Video (3 min.); http://www.youtube .com/watch?v=6hvJQTyTSZg (accessed May 2012).

Mead, Margaret. 1928. *Coming of Age in Samoa: A Psychological Study of Primitive Youth for Western Civilisation.* New York: William Morrow & Co.

Morris, Rosalind C. 1997. Educating Desire: Thailand, Transnationalism, and Transgression. *Social Text* 15(52–53): 53–79.

Oliver, Douglas L. 1975. *Ancient Tahitian Society.* Honolulu: University of Hawai'i Press.

Ortner, Sherry B. 1984. Theory in Anthropology since the Sixties. *Comparative Studies in Society and History* 26: 126–166.

Pulotu-Endemann, F. Karl, and Carmel L. Peteru. 2001. Beyond the Paradise Myth: Sexuality and Identity. In *Tangata o Te Moana Nui: The Evolving Identities of Pacific Peoples in Aotearoa/New Zealand,* ed. Cluny Macpherson, Paul Spoonley, and Melani Anae, pp. 122–136. Palmerston North, NZ: Dunmore Press.

Radcliffe-Brown, Alfred R. 1952 [1924]. The Mother's Brother in South Africa. In Alfred R. Radcliffe-Brown, *Structure and Function in Primitive Society,* pp. 15–31. London: Routledge & Kegan Paul.

Reddy, Gayatri. 2005. *With Respect to Sex: Negotiating Hijra Identity in South India.* Chicago: University of Chicago Press.

Rich, Adrienne. 1980. Compulsory Heterosexuality and Lesbian Existence. *Signs* 5: 631–660.

Rofel, Lisa. 2007. *Desiring China: Experiments in Neoliberalism, Sexuality, and Public Culture.* Durham, NC: Duke University Press.

Rubin, Gayle. 1975. The Traffic in Women: Notes on the Political Economy of Sex. In *Toward an Anthropology of Women,* ed. Rayna Reiter, pp. 157–210. New York: Monthly Review Press.

———. 1984. Thinking Sex: Notes for a Radical Theory of the Politics of Sexuality. In *Pleasure and Danger: Exploring Female Sexuality,* ed. Carole Vance, pp. 267–319. Boston: Routledge.

Sahlins, Marshall. 1985. *Islands of History*. Chicago: University of Chicago Press.

Schmidt, Joanne. 2010. *Migrating Genders: Westernisation, Migration, and Samoan Fa'afafine*. Farnham, UK: Ashgate.

Smith-Rosenberg, Carroll. 1975. The Female World of Love and Ritual: Relations between Women in Nineteenth-Century America. *Signs* 1: 1–29.

Stoler, Ann L. 1995. *Race and the Education of Desire: Foucault's History of Sexuality and the Colonial Order of Things*. Durham, NC: Duke University Press.

Stryker, Susan. 2006. (De)Subjugated Knowledges: An Introduction to Transgender Studies. In *The Transgender Studies Reader*, ed. Susan Stryker and Stephen Whittle, pp. 1–17. New York: Routledge.

Suggs, Robert C. 1966. *Marquesan Sexual Behavior*. New York: Harcourt, Brace & World.

Tcherkézoff, Serge. 2004. *Tahiti 1768: Jeunes filles en pleurs: La face cachée des premiers contacts et la naissance du mythe occidental (1595–1928)*. Papeete: Éditions des Îles au Vent.

———. 2008. *"First Contacts" in Polynesia," The Samoan Case (1722–1848): Western Misunderstandings about Sexuality and Divinity*. Canberra: ANU E-Press.

Teaiwa, Teresia K. 2001. Lo(o)sing the Edge. *The Contemporary Pacific* 13: 343–365.

Tengan, Ty P. Kāwika. 2008. *Native Men Remade: Gender and Nation in Contemporary Hawai'i*. Durham, NC: Duke University Press.

Towle, Evan B., and Lynn M. Morgan. 2002. Romancing the Transgender Native: Rethinking the Use of the "Third Gender" Concept. *GLQ* 8(4): 469–497.

Valentine, David. 2007. *Imagining Transgender: An Ethnography of a Category*. Durham, NC: Duke University Press.

Vasey, Paul L., and VanderLaan. 2010. An Adaptive Cognitive Dissociation between Willingness to Help Kin and Nonkin in Samoan Fa'afafine. *Psychological Science* 21: 292–297.

Wallace, Lee M. 2003. *Sexual Encounters: Pacific Texts, Modern Sexualities*. Ithaca, NY: Cornell University Press.

Wardlow, Holly. 2006. *Wayward Women: Sexuality and Agency in a New Guinea Society*. Berkeley: University of California Press.

Warner, Michael. 1991. Introduction: Fear of a Queer Planet. *Social Text* 9(4): 3–17.

Wesleyan Methodist Church of New Zealand. 2009. Our History: Where We Came From; http://www.wesleyan.org.nz/about/ourhistory-our-history/our -history/ (accessed March 2012).

Williams, William H. 1957 [1862]. *A Dictionary of the Maori Language*. Wellington, NZ: Government Printer.

Xian, Kathryn, and Brent Anbe, dir. 2001. *Ke Kūlana He Māhū: Remembering a Sense of Place*. Documentary (67 min.), distributed by Zang Pictures.

PART I

Historical Transformations

CHAPTER 2

Queer History and Its Discontents at Tahiti

The Contested Politics of Modernity
and Sexual Subjectivity

Deborah Elliston

This chapter is motivated by questions about the uses of history in queer narratives of the present: how narratives of the past are (re)made through contemporary experiences of sexual desire and gendered belonging; how such narratives are employed in the service of projects of queer self-making—that is, the crafting of queer subjectivity, personhood, and identification; and, more reflexively, how we as anthropologists grapple with our own uses and sitings of history in ethnographies of sexuality.

I engage these questions by examining a contemporary contest to legitimize queer identities among people of the Society Islands of French Polynesia (referred to here as "Islanders" or "Polynesians"), an overseas territory of France in the Pacific commonly known as "Tahiti and its Islands" (referred to here as "the Islands").[1] The formulation of this contest in the Islands raises questions about intersections of the uses of history and the politics of modernity in relation to queer sexualities. Basing it on field-work in Papeete, Tahiti, as well as on the Society Islands of Huahine and Moorea, I examine how the queer gender subjects known locally as *raerae* are bidding for social acceptance in part by critiquing the social acceptance given to *māhū*. *Raerae* are male-bodied, femininity-performing, men-desiring subjects who entered the Polynesian scene of sexual/gender possibility within the past forty or so years. *Māhū*, in contrast, are represented as indigenous to the Islands and commonly referred to in discourses of Polynesian cultural tradition. Translated by Polynesians as meaning "half-man, half woman," *māhū* is primarily a gender category, yet it is one that also licenses *māhū* sexual desires to be directed toward either men or women, as I shall discuss later.[2] As a category, *māhū* thus allows for same-sex sexual desire and practice but does not necessarily entail or require it. Such ambiguity about *māhū* sexuality, in turn, enables the common practice among non-*māhū* Polynesians of ignoring *māhū* sexual practices altogether.

My more specific motivation for this analysis is the emergence among *raerae*, within the past decade, of a distinctly critical discourse about *māhū*, in which *raerae* castigate *māhū*—specifically male-bodied *māhū*—as "cowards" who "hide" in the ambiguities around their (homo)sexual desires.[3] This discourse represents *māhū* as deliberately manipulating the "half-man, half-woman" designation to position their sexuality ambiguously and thus to sidestep issues of their own queer desires. In contrast to their denouncements of *māhū* "cowardice," *raerae* characterize themselves as brave, courageous, and the more "authentic" and "legitimate" queer gender subjects—not because of the long cultural history, culturally "authentic" status, and social acceptance possessed by *māhū*, but rather because they are "honest" about who and what they are: namely, male-bodied, femininity-performing subjects who sexually desire men and do not "hide" their queer desires but instead make them abundantly clear to themselves and all who see them.

Two key uses of history animate this critical discourse by *raerae*, both of which take shape by contrasting the meanings of *raerae* and *māhū* as local categories and sites of identification. The first is the use of history in narratives of *māhū* and *raerae* origins and historicity. The second is the use of history in narratives of *raerae* subjectification—their life histories and stories of coming into their identifications as *raerae*—which are also developed in contrast to and distinct from those of *māhū*. Both of these uses of history, I argue, also hold lessons for specifically anthropological uses of history in the crafting of the narratives we tell, and particularly in our ethnographic representations of sexuality and desire.

Māhū: "Half-Man, Half-Woman"

The local translation of *māhū* as "half-man, half-woman" emphasizes that first and foremost *māhū* is a gender category, and one we may best think of as "bilateral." This gender category describes Polynesians who draw on a combination of masculine and feminine gender signs and practices but who are represented as behaving more generally "in the manner of" their sexed-body opposite: female-bodied *māhū*, for example, are commonly described as behaving "in the manner of men," while male-bodied *māhū*, the focus of this chapter (and thus referred to simply as "*māhū*" from this point forward), are commonly described as behaving "in the manner of women."

Among the gendered signs that *māhū* deploy, the most fundamental one is labor. Most *māhū* engage in forms of labor coded as feminine: sewing, craft making, hairdressing, service work at hotels and restaurants, pink-collar office work, and childcare, for example. *Māhū* narratives of their own coming into their identifications as *māhū* unanimously privilege labor practices as the initial and primary sign of their *māhū* identifications; an early preference for "women's work"—most often helping their mothers with housework—is commonly counterpointed in their narratives by an explicit and vehement rejection of the traditional labors associated with men ("men's work"), especially the hallmark men's labor practice of subsistence gardening (making *fa'a'apu*). Indeed, a childhood memory of helping their mothers in the home and refusing to help their fathers in *fa'a'apu* work is most commonly cited as the defining moment of a *māhū's* identification as *māhū*.

This primary emphasis on labor practice is consistent with anthropological findings on other transgender, "third gender," and "gender liminal" subjects across the culture region of Polynesia and beyond. In his overview of regional commonalities in what he formerly termed "gender liminality," for example, Besnier (1994, 296) emphasizes that "[g]ender-liminal persons are most fundamentally distinguished by the nature of their labor contribution" and, more specifically, that "the [male-bodied] gender-liminal person in Polynesia is commonly thought to excel in women's tasks." Similar descriptions are found in ethnographic studies of the Samoan *fa'afafine* (Mageo 1992), the Tongan *fakaleitī* or *fakafefine* (Besnier 1997), the Cook Island *laelae* (Alexeyeff 2000), and the Tuvaluan and Gilbertese *pinapinaaine* (Besnier 1994), among others.

In addition to labor practices, *māhū* use a variety of embodied performances to produce what Alexeyeff refers to as "gender as performed affective comportment" (2000, 299): gesture, stance, intonation patterns, voice pitch, and more are all used to signify femininity. *Māhū* may also incorporate styles of bodily adornment that either conjoin or alternate between masculine and feminine repertoires; long hair and a plucked beard are requisite, for example, while dress is more varied. Most *māhū* wear masculine-coded or gender-neutral clothing in public spaces (e.g., shorts and T-shirts), including at work (e.g., pants and shirt), whereas they wear feminine-coded clothing (e.g., *pāreu,* a sarong-type garment worn by women) around the house.

Throughout the Society Islands, evaluations of *māhū* are, on the whole, remarkably accepting. Polynesians commonly represent *māhū* as "natural," with their "naturalness" explained and authorized in a variety of ways that draw on and use "history." First, among both *māhū* and non-*māhū* Polynesians, it is often explained by invoking an individual *māhū*'s biographical history of "being that way." *Māhū* are thought to show signs of their *māhū* subjectivity at a very young age, with the central sign (again) being a preference for cross-gender labor. The facts that such preferences and behaviors appear while a child is still young, and that they have been consistently present over the individual's life course, are taken locally as evidence that *māhū* subjectivity is "natural" to the person.

Second, the "naturalness" of *māhū* is commonly authorized by reference to Polynesian cultural history and "tradition." Polynesians have explained to me, for example, that "we [Society Islanders] have always had *māhū,*" and "*māhū* are unique to Polynesia." With a clear sense of pride, one cultural activist told me, "*Māhū,* you only find that here, it's Polynesian tradition." Such representations draw on a specific use of history: namely, the ubiquitous references to *māhū* found in the earliest European voyager accounts of social life in the Islands, widely known among Polynesians. Voyager narratives from the eighteenth and nineteenth centuries, for example, make consistent—albeit oftentimes scandalized—references to *māhū,* describing them as present throughout Tahiti and the other Society Islands, and from the bottom of the social hierarchy up to the ranks of the most sacred Polynesian chiefly rulers. In his three-volume compendium, *Ancient Tahitian Society,* Douglas Oliver (1974, 369–374) drew together a wide variety of eighteenth- and nineteenth-century voyager and missionary sources detailing European accounts of and encounters with (male-bodied) *māhū.* Most include descriptions of *māhū* similar to the following by the missionary Wilson (1799, 156): "In various districts of the island there are men who dress as women; work with them at the cloth; are confined to the same provisions and rule of eating and dressing; may not eat with the men, or of their food, but have separate plantations for their peculiar use" (in Oliver 1974, 370).

Such European accounts often commonly make reference to "other practices too horrible to mention" (Wilson 1799, 198), "abominable" acts (Edwards and Hamilton 1915, 113; in Oliver 1974, 370), and "the abominable sin of sodomy" (John Jefferson, journal entry for August 22, 1800, in Oliver 1974, 371). The missionary John Jefferson, for example, described in one of his journal entries for February 12, 1801, walking in on "The chief of Haryana . . . committing an act of bestiality with another man . . . having in his mouth the other's _____" (John Jefferson, Journal of the Missionaries Proceedings on Otaheite, London Missionary Society Archives, SOAS, in Oliver 1974, 371). Such scandalized judgments of *māhū* sexual practices prompted Captain Bligh (1789 [1789], 2: 16–17, in Oliver 1974, 369) to examine one *māhū's* "privacies" in order to determine why, "in so prolific a country as this, Men should be led into such sensual and beastly acts of gratification."

A historicizing narrative of *māhū* as "traditional" and "culturally authentic" has been further authorized, in some interesting and problematic ways, by Robert Levy's (1971, 1973) ethnographic representations of the established place of *māhū* in Polynesian social life of the 1960s. Levy, a psychoanalytically trained anthropologist, described *māhū* as a "traditional" and ubiquitous part of rural Polynesian village life where, he asserted, they live at a density of "one *māhū* in each village" (1971, 12).[4] This spatial— and suspiciously even—distribution of *māhū* across the social geography of the Society Islands further solidified the historicizing narrative of *māhū* as an intrinsic part of "authentic" and "traditional" Polynesian "culture." Since first published in the 1970s, it has circulated widely in tourist publications, journalistic reporting, and popular-culture productions, from music videos to television documentaries, much of which has been oriented toward metropolitan French residents as well as foreign visitors and tourists. During my fieldwork, for example, tourists routinely asked me about "the" village *māhū,* and e-mail queries I periodically receive from filmmakers and journalists interested in *māhū* invariably presume that the "one *māhū* per village" claim is fact.

While Levy's representation of "one *māhū* in each village" has not been taken up by Polynesians locally, his cultural "tradition" signification has further solidified Polynesians' ideology of *māhū* "authenticity." This phenomenon thus offers anthropologists some valuable lessons, not least of which is its showcasing of the dangers of positivist approaches bent on quantification that seek to freeze complex social dynamics—in this case the privileged reception given to quantitative representations ("one per village") over more complex qualitative and historically nuanced approaches to cultural productions. It also offers a cautionary lesson about the recirculation of anthropological knowledge claims, and specifically the extent to which knowledge claims may be much more prone—and vulnerable—to recirculation when they concern sexuality.

The (De)Sexualization of *Māhū*

What is curiously absent from these varied uses of history in the authorizing and explanatory narratives around *māhū* is much mention of *māhū* sexual practice. This absence is particularly striking because the vast majority of *māhū* are sexually involved with men. Indeed, their sexual involvements with and desires for men are intricately and inextricably woven into the fabric of their lives, from the everyday—a *māhū* bank teller flirting with a customer—to their hopes and aspirations for a future blissful life in a couple with a particular man.

In addition to taking adult men as lovers, in *māhū* narratives I have collected that recall events as far back as the 1950s, *māhū* consistently describe themselves as sexually active with the teenage boys and younger unattached men (*taure'are'a*) of their neighborhoods in Papeete and its urban surroundings as well as in villages on the outer islands (see also Levy 1971, 1973). Young *taure'are'a* men "go visit the *māhū*" they know in order "to get off" (*tirer leur coup*) in sexual relationships that are consistently described as nonreciprocal, at least until quite recently: "I gave him pleasure; it stopped there," as one *māhū* characterized it.[5] The most common sexual practices of *māhū* exemplify this: oral sex (performed by the *māhū* on the man, never performed on the *māhū*) and interfemoral sex ("between the thighs" of the *māhū*, never those of his lover).[6]

A *māhū* in his early fifties tried to explain the structure and texture of these interactions during an interview we had in 2003:

> Here [in Papeete] one lives in a neighborhood [*quartier*], so in a given neighborhood there's a *māhū*. A *māhū*, that's me. And in the neighborhood one has some boys, true boys [*vrais garçons*]. And because we have all known each other from the time they were little, we are all acquainted with one another. Because of that these boys prefer to come to see me than to see another [*māhū*] who may come into the neighborhood. . . .[7]

> In terms of sexuality . . . you have a *māhū* in the neighborhood and all of the boys of the neighborhood have sex with him.

I'm talking only about sex: the sentiments, there are none [on the part of the boys]. There are none. It's only sex, until the day the boy meets up with a girl . . . and then he'll go with her. . . .

Up until then, the boy will have benefited very well from the *māhū*—for maybe ten years, yes?—and the *māhū*, he may be truly amorous [toward the boy]. But then, well, after the boy gets with a girl [that's that]. (Interview, June 21, 2003)[8]

Despite the ubiquity of sexual relationships between *māhū* and young men, the sexuality of *māhū* is consistently obscured, and it is the gender-coded meanings of *māhū* that are foregrounded by other Polynesians, and especially by Polynesian men. Indeed, Polynesian men I've interviewed about this have at times quite adamantly asserted that, while a very few *māhū* may have sex with *taure'are'a* or with men, the vast majority of them are either celibate or married to women. Polynesian women, in contrast, commonly assert that male-bodied *māhū* have sex with men, and particularly with young men. When I've asked women about the discrepancies between their accounts and men's accounts of *māhū* sexual practice, some have actually laughed at me for taking men's claims seriously. As one woman chided me, "But of course they lied to you. . . . all the men here have been with *māhū* but they don't talk about it."

With the "half-man, half-woman" designation that defines *māhū* gender positioning comes the possibility of *māhū* taking lovers who are same-sex-bodied but gender-opposite. The cultural logic of (male-bodied) *māhū* sexual desire for men is founded in the part of the *māhū* that is "half-woman." *Māhū* sexual desire takes shape through what I have called elsewhere, with appreciation to Judith Butler (1990), a Polynesian heterosexual matrix—that is, a widely shared understanding among Polynesians that all sexual desire is structured through, and only coherent in relation to, gender difference: sexual desire is always oriented to one's gender opposite. Women are held to desire men, and men to desire women, and thus a *māhū*'s sexual desire for men is founded in his feminine "half."[9]

Raerae: From Māhū Born

In contrast to the historically deep representations of *māhū*, accounts of the history of *raerae* that I've gathered from both *raerae* and *māhū* agree that both the term "*raerae*" and the persons it refers to did not emerge in the Islands until the 1960s (see also Montillier 1999, 201; Kuwahara, this volume). In the cosmopolitan city of Papeete on Tahiti island, the capital of the territory of French Polynesia, the queer gender category *raerae* has been positioned and developed today in dialogue with the three mainstays of Polynesians' sex/gender system, all of which bear the authority of having historical roots that predate the arrival of the first Europeans in the 1760s: *vahine* (woman), *tāne* (man), and, of course, *māhū*. To a lesser extent, the contemporary meanings of *raerae* are also negotiated in relation to an ever-increasing variety of queer (but not necessarily gendered) categories and identifications for male-bodied and female-bodied same-sex desiring subjects: *pédé, gay, petea, homo, lesbienne, tamāhine raerae,* and *gouine,* among others (see Elliston 1999). The dynamics of these negotiations, however, raise questions related to what I would critically term "the global gay thesis" (see Altman 1996) and lie beyond the scope of this chapter.

The period to which the emergence of *raerae* is dated, the 1960s, was a period of rapid and dramatic social change in the Society Islands. It was inaugurated by France's relocating its nuclear testing program from Algeria, which was then on the verge of independence, to its overseas territory of French Polynesia, of which the Society Islands archipelago is a part. Along with the new nuclear use France began to make of the territory came a significant change in the French state's investments in and approach to the Islands; in part "to encourage local acquiescence" to nuclear testing (Henningham 1992, 127), France began pouring money into the territory, quickly and effectively transitioning Islander society from a primarily subsistence-based economy to a cash economy. Today, the territory is substantially a consumption-driven, remittance- and market-based economic dependency of France.

Accompanying the 1960s cascade of money into the territory was a stampede of metropolitan French men. Upwards of 20,000 French military and civil personnel came to Tahiti in the early 1960s, and to the city of Papeete specifically, to work on the nuclear testing program and adjacent projects of infrastructural support for the testing program: building an international airport, for example, as well as developing road systems, sewer systems, electrical grids, hospitals, housing, and the like (Rallu 1991, 183). Among other effects, the sudden influx of 20,000 or more French men to an island with a total population, at the time, of about 45,000— in a territory where the entire population in 1962 totaled about 85,000 (Henningham 1992, 130)—promoted the development of a booming sex trade (Bauer 2002, 95).

The story of this historical development, from the perspectives of older *raerae* and *māhū* today, is that it was *māhū* who first began to provide sexual services to French men in exchange for money (see also Bauer 2002, 95–100), and primarily to French sailors around Papeete's port. That *māhū* stepped up to provide commercialized sexual services to French men in this initial period is not as anomalous as it might first appear. First, and as Bauer (2002, 95) rightly situates it, women's prostitution was a rarity in Papeete and in French Polynesia more broadly. While Polynesian women certainly have a long history of sexual relationships with foreign men, they have insistently and consistently framed such relationships on the model of boyfriend relationships, not sex-for-money exchanges. Thus does Bauer argue that, for sailors and other French men in the 1960s, *māhū* presented an alternative to the "demands" of having Polynesian girlfriends (Bauer 2002, 97).

Second, as discussed previously and as supported by life stories I've gathered from *māhū* over the years, *māhū* sexual practices have substantively included a form of sexual servicing in which young men and teenage boys known to a specific *māhū* go to "visit the *māhū*" for sex. The shift from the practice of sexually servicing young Polynesian men to sexual soliciting foreign French men, and ultimately to the direct marketing and selling of sexual services to a substantially foreign clientele, may best be seen as part of the broader commercialization and marketing projects that began in earnest in this French colony in the 1960s—projects that articulated France's "modernization" of the territory, economically as well as socially.

Yet from the perspective of the French men, sailors and otherwise, arriving at the Papeete ports in the 1960s, Polynesian *māhū* were not the obvious prospective sexual partners, nor were they obvious as sex workers. While local Polynesian understandings of *māhū* included their practices of same-sex sexuality and sexual servicing, the performance of *māhū* gender involved *both* masculine and feminine components (i.e., "half-man, half-woman"). According to contemporary *māhū* and *raerae* narratives, *māhū* of the 1960s who sought boyfriends and clients among the newly arriving French men flush with francs found that the more they "feminized" themselves, the more successful they were in attracting these foreigners. "Feminizing" their gender performances (through dress, makeup, and more) helped these *māhū* to compete with Polynesian girlfriends and produced increased earnings. Accordingly, in providing sexual services to French men in exchange for money, these *māhū* were seen to be offering them an alternative to the "demands" of Polynesian girlfriends—specifically, "demands" for gifts and relationships (Bauer 2002, 97).Within a few years, by the latter 1960s, the term *"raerae"* is said to have emerged to identify and distinguish these more "feminized" *māhū* from other, regular, *māhū*.

In striking contrast to the ease with which Islanders explain the term *"māhū,"* the term *"raerae"* cannot be etymologically and morphologically taken apart to shed light on—or play with—its meanings. A *reo Māʻohi* word like "Huahine," for example, the name of the outer island where I have lived during most of my fieldwork periods in the Islands, is etymologically comprised of the morphemes *"hua"* and *"vahine."* Following the Tahitian Academy's *Faʻatoro Parau* Tahitian–French Dictionary (Académie Tahitienne–*Fare Vānaʻa* 1999), *"hua"* is an adverb meaning "many, completely, truly, or exactly"; it also is a noun that refers to the Polynesian outrigger canoe, the testicles of animals or human men, and eggs. *"Vahine"* means "woman, wife, mistress, female lover." The island of Huahine in silhouette is said to resemble a reclining woman, and Islanders translate the island's name as referring to a beautiful woman provocatively reclined as she waits in anticipation for her lover, the god Hiro, to arrive.

Such folk etymological complexities—ubiquitous in Polynesian languages spoken throughout the culture area of Polynesia—are precisely the basis for the elaborate tradition of punning so widely reported in the scholarship. The word *"raerae,"* however, is remarkable in having no such etymological or morphological significances: it has no component parts and no known etymology or grammatical motivation to native speakers. When asked about the meaning of the word, Islanders, who usually respond to such requests by parsing the word and explaining its component morphemes, are unable to disassemble it; nor can they historicize it through myths. It is a creation of the 1960s.[10]

Consuming Desires

As the preceding account suggests, the genesis of the queer gender category *raerae* is locally sited squarely within the development of capitalist market relations in the Islands and the attendant intensification of the discourses and projects of modernity that were a part of the "modernization" of the Polynesian economy and people by the French colonial state (itself undertaken in the interest of securing France's nuclear testing program). This historical genesis has significant entailments for contemporary *raerae* struggles to legitimize their queer gender identifications, and all of these revolve in some way around the associations between *raerae* and the projects—and politics—of modernity.

First, part of the signification of *raerae* as a "recent" innovation is the shading of it as culturally inauthentic—in sharp contrast to the cultural authenticity attributed to *māhū* through the authority of historical depth. Also in contrast to the social acceptance extended to *māhū*, *raerae* are denied respectability in the evaluations of most Polynesians. Ubiquitous targets of verbal and physical harassment by young Polynesian men in particular, *raerae* are maligned, castigated, ridiculed, and even targeted for beatings. Many *raerae* I've known avoid going out of their homes during the day to avoid such harassment; others, if they do venture out, do so nervously, anxiously, and in drag (dressed like boys/men). Indeed, younger *raerae* migrate to the capital city of Papeete precisely to escape the kind of harassment and marginalization they report as commonplace in outer island villages.

Second, since their emergence in the 1960s, *raerae* have been indelibly associated with sex work. In the Society Islands today, by far the vast majority of sex workers are not women at all but rather turn out to be *raerae*, and often enough to the surprise of their predominantly French clients. It is thus not only in stereotypes and popular understandings that *raerae* are fundamentally associated with sex work: since I first began research in the Society Islands in 1993, all of the many *raerae* I have known have, for some period of their lives as *raerae*, engaged in sex work.

The phrase "for some period of their lives as *raerae*" is meant to indicate, first, that these Polynesians move in and out of their identifications as *raerae*: it is not an "identity" in a fixed or essential sense. Several *raerae* I knew in 1993, for example, were men married to women and raising children with their wives a decade later. One *raerae* I first came to know in 1994 had, by late 1995, twice decided he would no longer be a *raerae*, remaking himself each time as a young man in comportment, dress, and social habits (hanging out with other young men rather than with *raerae*); and by 2003 he had been living as a *tāne* (man) for the past five years. Second, it is during the periods of their lives when they identify as *raerae* that they, at some points during those periods of identification (and usually for most of those periods), engage in sex work. Another way of stating this would be that, although not all *raerae* are sex workers, all *raerae* have at some point engaged in periods of sex work (as *raerae*).

For many Polynesians, this association with sex work is problematic, although not because sex work itself is particularly so. The first set of challenges this association produces stems from the centrality that Polynesians assign to labor practice in defining and authorizing gender. As discussed above, *māhū* gender performances rely on labor practices for a key part of their authority: it is the logic that animates male-bodied *māhū* engaging in forms of labor associated with women. More broadly, throughout the Society Islands, forms of labor have long been complexly interwoven with gender and gender positionings, and by that I am not simply referring to a gendered division of labor. Rather, labor forms have been used both to "read" an individual's gender positioning and to "write" or authorize one's own gender positioning. Indeed, labor and gender have been so closely bound together in Polynesian society that a subject's labor practice may often be central to others' very recognition of that subject's gender, as well as to the person's own authentic claim to a particular gender identification. As part of these dynamics, subjects are understood as choosing gender-coded labor practices because those practices reflect, and in an important sense produce or constitute, their gender identifications. For most Polynesians, however, sex work is not a gender-coded labor practice: it is not women's work. Indeed, there have been and are very few women sex workers in the Islands. Rather, sex work is a labor practice associated with *raerae*.[11]

Second, the association between *raerae* and sex work is problematic because this labor practice in which they specialize is an exclusively market-based labor form: the sale of sexual services. It is thus a labor practice that, in the Society Islands, lacks any ties to "traditional" forms of gendered labor, which are embedded in systems of exchange and kinship. It is also a labor practice that is oriented almost exclusively to a foreign clientele, predominantly French men, in a French colonial context where the French are, to phrase it gently, not collectively liked. In combination with the importance of labor practice to defining and authorizing gender, these features of *raerae* sex work locate their labor form outside the frameworks within which labor practices locally achieve legitimacy and respectability.

Finally, the ways in which *raerae* fashion themselves as queer gendered subjects also generates challenges to their bids for legitimacy and respectability. *Raerae* gender performances are enacted through the consumption of particular modernist fantasies of gendered sexuality, modeled after what I have elsewhere termed "the Global Femme" (Elliston 2005). This is mass-mediated Euro-American fashion-model femininity, beautiful in cover model ways—thin, ever-youthful, scantily clad, made up in cosmetics, glamorous, and white (cf. Besnier 2002 on Tonga; Alexeyeff 2009 on the Cook

Islands). *Raerae* constitute themselves as queer gender subjects by working to embody this *ur*-model of cosmopolitan (white) femininity through
styles of dress that are both deliberately revealing and of cosmopolitan
fashion (skirts that barely cover their bottoms, thigh-high dresses of slinky
fabrics, stiletto heels, go-go boots); comportment that includes modes of
standing and walking that emulate supermodels (one foot placed precisely
in front of the other when walking); and effusively stylized manners of
gesturing and talking. The femininity that *raerae* perform thus participates
far more in modernist fantasies of (white) femininity than it does in local
gender iconography. As a result, the status of *raerae* as feminine subjects
ends up being read locally as something other than womanhood. *Raerae*
use of modernist commodities extends to their taking into their very bodies
idealizations of modernist feminine sexuality—for example, reconfiguring
their boy bodies through hormones, depilation, dieting, tanning, and other
bodily disciplines and modifications. While at one level this speaks to the
logic of gender/sexual production in the Islands, in which gender is taken
as the ground of sexual desire and desirability, it also speaks to the logic of
the market, in which commodities are (problematically) imbued with an
almost magical power to confer claims to identity. Such claims to (gender)
identity, however, are neither credentialed nor legitimated through regular
Polynesian channels.

Narratives of *Raerae* Subjectification

As the foregoing suggests, the critical discourse *raerae* have developed contesting *māhū* claims to legitimacy and respectability is best situated in relation to the politics and projects of modernity, as well as in relation to the
uses of history within these politics and projects. But a second set of historical representations shapes the *raerae* critique of *māhū*. While eighteenth-
century voyagers like Captain Cook and twentieth-century anthropologists
like Robert Levy are reference points in the Polynesian discourse on *māhū*,
less public but no less authoritative histories are also "written" daily in the
stories that *raerae* and *māhū* themselves tell. Here, the uses of history take
the form of life stories, biographies, and related narrative productions in
which *raerae* describe their queer gender subjectivities and chart how they
arrived at their queer gender positionings. Along the way, they position
māhū, at best, as underdeveloped in their self-understandings and, at worst,
as cowardly hypocrites.

Raerae with whom I've been working use a quite specific set of spatial metaphors to account for their sexual desires for men. In their life stories they describe the relationships among gender, desire, and the sexed body first in terms of having femininity—and only femininity—"inside" themselves (*dedans; à l'intérieur*). This femininity they then "push" (*pousser*) to the "outside" of themselves (*dehors; à l'extérieur*). Such "pushing" motivates their gender performances, that is, their feminine dress and stylized Global Femme comportment. In the accounts I've collected, *raerae* have narrated such "pushing" sometimes in the active voice and sometimes in the passive. In the somewhat more common impersonal construction, for example, a *raerae* will say, "*ça pousse*," which translates as, "it [femininity] pushes [itself]" from the inside to the outside. In the more active voice, as one *raerae* phrased it, "We [*raerae*] push it [femininity] to the exterior and take it further, much, much further [*plus loin*] than *māhū*."

It is this "interior" femininity that *raerae* (and others) see as founding and directing *raerae* sexual desires for men—specifically for "real" men, namely men who desire women. Similarly, it is their exteriorized performances of that interior femininity that account for why "real" men are sexually attracted to them. *Raerae* gender performances, then, serve to exteriorize their "interior" femininity to make evident their own desires to have sex with men and, as part of that, to attract men to sleep with them because men are understood as being exclusively attracted to femininity.

By way of comparison, *māhū* use exactly the same spatializing metaphor to describe their gender identifications and its entailments for their sexual desires. But, unlike *raerae,* they say they have *both* masculinity and femininity "inside." In keeping with their "half-man, half woman" characterization, *māhū* narrate themselves as having "two sides" "inside" themselves: a feminine side (*le côté féminin*) and a masculine side (*le côté masculin*). Consistent with that, *māhū* gender performances draw on signs of *both* masculinity and femininity. Thus, for (male-bodied) *māhū,* the exteriorizing of their feminine "side" is much more attenuated than is *raerae* exteriorizing. This, *māhū* explained to me, is why, for example, *māhū* do not cross-dress in public; it also accounts for why there is so much variability in *māhū* use of stereotyped feminine styles of comportment. The only consistent and necessary marker of *māhū* gender identification *as māhū* is labor practice: it is in and through the work they do, the labor forms they practice, that they consistently and clearly position themselves as gender "bilateral" subjects.

It is precisely on this account of *māhū* having both masculinity and femininity "inside" and their attendant and attenuated exteriorizing of their feminine sides that *raerae* base their critique. "They're cowards," *raerae* repeatedly told me, in a discursive move that, notably, contrastingly positions themselves as bravely and honestly revealing themselves for who they really are. *Māhū,* in contrast, they criticize as hypocrites and cowards for "hiding" (*cachant*) their feminine side, not showing it in public, and in not doing so, concealing from others the sexual desires for and relations with men that, *raerae* emphasize, the vast majority of *māhū* both feel and practice.[12]

Building on this spatial metaphor of interior gender that is pushed to the exterior, a metaphorical understanding of gender identification and performativity that is shared and used by both *māhū* and *raerae, raerae* have also developed a critical account of *māhū* as underdeveloped in their self-understandings. This account uses the authority of *raerae* biographies, and specifically their version of "coming out" stories, to build a critique that revolves around the comparative meanings of and relationships between *māhū* and *raerae* as (queer) gender identifications.

Raerae narratives describing their "realizations" that they were *raerae* are strikingly standardized, to such an extent that they constitute a kind of Polynesian analogue to American gay and lesbian "coming out" stories. In their narratives, *raerae* describe their process of realization as a pathway or road (*le chemin*) that leads to their current identification. In the standard narrative, a *raerae* begins on the pathway as a *garçon* (a [regular] boy) who, at a fairly young age (sometimes three or four, more often seven or eight years old) realizes that he is "different" from other boys. In their narratives, *raerae* most often exemplify this difference as finding themselves drawn to housework (women's work) and enjoying it and, conversely, as being repelled by men's work, especially subsistence gardening.[13] So far, this standard narrative aligns directly with *māhū* narratives I've collected about how *māhū* come to the realization that they are *māhū*. As a result, it is not surprising that, as the pathway continues, by the time the *raerae* reaches the age of ten or eleven, she has come to think of herself as *māhū*. The reason for this, *raerae* say, is that they are boys but they feel they have "some" femininity inside them: positioning or identifying themselves as *māhū* at this point allows them to account for and authorize their feminine "side." Subsequently, however, and usually by their mid- to late teenage years, a *raerae* realizes that she is not a *māhū* after all. Rather, because she has come to understand herself as having exclusively femininity "inside" her male body, she is actually a *raerae*.

Up to the final step of identifying "only" femininity inside themselves and thus realizing they are "really" *raerae, māhū* and *raerae* narratives of "the pathway" to (queer) gender subjectivity are virtually identical. They do not differ in their commitments to or in their use of the Polynesian hetero-sexual matrix to mediate their self-understandings of their same-sex desire. That, for both *raerae* and *māhū,* is founded in their "exclusive" (for *raerae*) or "half" (for *māhū*) identifications with femininity.

Instead, the differences lie, first, in a kind of quantification of their "interior" femininity, that is, whether it is exclusive and singular or dual and balanced by an "interior" masculinity. Second, it differs in "how far" to the exterior they "push" that interior femininity—or how "far" that interior femininity "pushes [itself]" to the exterior. Drawing on their biographies, their narrative productions, and interested uses of their individual histories, *raerae* go to significant lengths to distinguish themselves, both discursively and performatively, from *māhū,* as well as from the other queer identity categories circulating in the Islands today. In my conversations and inter-views with *raerae* I would often, by way of wrapping up our conversation, ask what was the most important thing other people should know about them. By far the most common response they gave me was, "Not to confuse us with *māhū.*" (The second most common response was "to accept us—that would be good.") Additional evidence for the vital importance *raerae* attri-bute to distinguishing them from *māhū* is also found in Bauer (2002, 103), who entitles one of his chapters, "Ne pas confondre *mahu* et *raerae*" (Don't confuse *māhū* and *raerae*).

Queer Histories and the Politics of Modernity

The dynamics analyzed in this chapter provide insights about the uses of history in relation to the politics of modernity. First, the strategic use of history to represent *māhū* as "traditional" is as thoroughly steeped in the politics of modernity as are all the criticisms of *raerae* as "not traditional." The very discourse on "tradition" not only hinges on a contrast with the present but also operates through an objectification of "culture" that, as other scholars have analyzed, is one of the hallmarks of colonial modernity (see Mani 1998; on the Pacific, see Keesing and Tonkinson 1982; Keesing [1989, 1991] in dialogue with Linnekin [1990, 1991] and Trask [1991]).

Yet, at the same time, the discourse on tradition in the Islands in recent years has also been forged in relation to France's ongoing "civilizing mission" in the Islands, a particularly potent discourse in this French colony, where the "civilizing mission" has been a central prop for the rationalization of continuing French rule. It must also be contextualized in an ongoing cultural revitalization movement that has sought to reclaim Polynesian "tradition" as a site of cultural pride—in a direct counter to France's "civilizing mission." In the process, this movement signifies *māhū* as a vital and legitimate component of that proud history.

Second, *raerae* uses of history in the form of life stories and life narratives are accounts that draw on the politics and projects of modernity for their authority. I have been particularly struck by *raerae* representations of themselves as queer gender subjects—in particular, by their accounts of the pathway they traverse en route to *raerae* identification and the femininity "inside" that pushes "out." Such representations articulate quintessentially modernist discourses of sexuality. In such discourses, sexuality is sited as an "interior" property of the "I" speaking subject as well as a property of individuals (Foucault 1990). At the same time, it is equally striking that *raerae* route such modernist sexual self-constitution through gender, "feminizing" themselves both to express their sexual desires and to incite the desires of "real" men. In so doing they both deploy and reaffirm the Polynesian logic of the heterosexual matrix and render themselves recognizable and meaningful in terms understood by themselves and, they hope, by other Polynesians.

Third, and relatedly, the ways in which *raerae* consume and seek to embody modernist gendered fantasies may also speak to a desire among them for the modern as an alternative to, and perhaps as an escape from, locality (see also Besnier 2002). In this respect, a desire for the modern as the relevant signifying framework may be a desire for a modernity in which, unlike in the local form of modernity, *raerae* are not marginalized or maligned, not prevented from securing respectability and, indeed, not exiled from local structures of status and prestige. Rather, it is a modernity in which they are to be admired and rewarded, perhaps even accepted, as beautiful and valuable sexual and gendered subjects.

Finally, I have been using "the politics of modernity" to encapsulate an analytical approach to modernity that positions it as a set of discursive resources. Particularly positioned subjects draw on these resources, constitute, and understand themselves in relation to and through those discourses, in widely varying ways (see Besnier 2011). Yet I suggest that one of the conclusions to draw from this contemporary contest over legitimate queer identities is that the politics of modernity—meaning the uses subjects make of the discourses of modernity—are taken up and forged in dense dialogue with the uses of "history," such that "history" and "modernity" are made meaningful in the present, not only in relation to each other, but evidently in and through each other.

Acknowledgements

An earlier version of this paper was presented at the 2005 American Anthropological Association annual meetings in the invited session, "Bringing the Past (Back) into the Present: Exploring the Present Tense in Queer Lives." I thank the session's co-organizers, Mary Gray and Bill Leap, for motivating me to develop this analysis; my copresenters for their thought-provoking contributions to my thinking on this subject; and the especially engaged audience for the lively discussions. The revised version has benefited from the comments of colleagues, among whom I especially want to thank Doug Glick. Finally, I thank both Kalissa Alexeyeff and Niko Besnier for their thoughtful comments and feedback and for inviting this submission.

Notes

1   My use of the term "Polynesians" (Fr. *Polynésiens*) for people indigenous to the Society Islands follows local self-naming preferences and practices, and I alternate its use with my own abbreviation of Society Islanders, "Islanders." The English adaptation of *Polynésiens* used in this chapter thus does not refer to all peoples of the culture area of Polynesia (i.e., Samoans, Tongans, Hawaiians, etc.). The more common term scholars use for people of the Society Islands, "Tahitians," has been the object of indigenous critique (Raapoto 1988), in part because, as I have argued elsewhere, it effaces Islanders' place-based identifications and the centrality of island of origin to Islanders' senses of themselves (Elliston 2000).

2   All translations from the French and *reo Ma'ohi* Tahitian languages are mine. There were no discernible patterned differences in language use between *māhū* and *raerae* speakers. Although rural Islanders are more often fluent in both the French and Tahitian languages, both rural and urban Islanders under the age of about sixty-five speak French, and the ethnographic interviews that form the basis of this chapter were conducted primarily in French. That said,

even when speaking French most Islanders use *reo Ma'ohi* Tahitian words and formulations as part of their speech, which I have included in the text and translations.

3   Because *raerae* focus their critical discourse on male-bodied *māhū*—and not at all on female-bodied *māhū*—this chapter focuses exclusively on male-bodied *māhū*. For an ethnographic analysis of female-bodied *māhū*, see Elliston 1999.

4   Levy's specific argument was that the "similarity of much male and female role behavior" (1971, 17) in Society Islander social life makes it difficult for Polynesian men to become properly masculine, and that Polynesians' (covert) solution to this problem is the *māhū*, which Levy terms "a feminine role-playing male" (12). In an argument rather startling to contemporary readers for its reductionism—of Polynesian men's intelligence and of the meanings to *māhū* of their lives—Levy wrote in his widely cited essay that the *māhū* has "persisted" in Polynesian villages so that men have a "highly visible and exclusively limited contrast, implying for other men in the village 'I am a man because I am not a *māhū*'" (12).

5   According to some *māhū* I've worked with, in recent years the one-sidedness of these sexual relations has begun to open, such that there is more, or at least occasional, sexual reciprocity.

6   *Māhū* have emphasized to me that interfemoral sex has been a much more common sexual practice in their sexual repertoires than anal sex. See also Levy (1971, 1973) for substantially similar accounts of the young men (*taure'are'a*) going "to visit the *māhū*" for sex.

7   As one of the manuscript reviewers commented, this Polynesian *māhū*'s statement, "one lives in a neighborhood [*quartier*], so in a given neighborhood there's a *māhū*," could be interpreted as support for Levy's (1971, 1973) spatial quantification and distribution of *māhū* as "one *māhū* in each village" (1971, 12). However, I would argue that such an interpretation was not what the Polynesian speaker intended. Rather, the narrative frame this *māhū* set when he began by stating "one lives in a neighborhood" was designed to emphasize the familiarity that develops out of residential propinquity and that forms the foundation for young men seeking out a *māhū* they know, in a society where residential propinquity is one of the bases not only for friendship and mutual aid but even for kinship itself. Indeed, in opposition to the "one *māhū* in each village" assertion, the *māhū* I quote in this section concludes by referring to "another [*māhū*] who may come into the neighborhood" as being at a disadvantage in attracting *taure'are'a* precisely because the new *māhū* is not known to them. As a final point of clarification, across my research in the Society Islands the only constancy in the number of *māhū* living in any given village or neighborhood (*quartier*) is that it varies: in some villages and neighborhoods there are no *māhū* at all, in others there are two *māhū*, in others one *māhū*, and in some there are three or more *māhū*.

8   For American and other Western readers schooled in the ideologies of mutuality and reciprocity that characterize contemporary Western sexual cultures, such an account may raise questions of what *māhū* derive from such one-sided interactions and what motivates their involvement in relationships with young men who will never reciprocate, either sexually or emotionally. However, the Western emphasis on mutuality and reciprocity, as well as its associated ideology of "intimacy," is both a historically recent and uneven development in Western societies: the anthropological (and historical) record is thick with accounts of other ways of organizing sexuality and producing meaning through it. Indeed, analyzing the wide variation in sexual cultures is one of the more interesting areas of contemporary scholarly investigation, as the present volume demonstrates.

9   While this chapter focuses on male-bodied *māhū*, the coherence of the "heterosexual matrix" for the organization and meaning of sexual desire informs Polynesian women's understandings of sexual subjectivity as well. Polynesian women understand their sexual desires for men as "natural" and stemming from their status as women: women desire men. And, analogously to the male-bodied *māhū* discussed in this chapter, female-bodied *māhū*, who engage in men's labor practices and comport themselves "in the manner of men," understand their sexual desires for women in relation to their self-definition as "half-man, half-woman": their sexual desires for women emanate from their "half-man" side.

10   In relation to the emergence of the term *raerae* in the 1960s, one other theory of the origin of the term is offered in Bauer (2002, 101). While Bauer has only one source for this theory, and I have not yet found additional evidence for it, it is plausible given the odd etymological status of the word *raerae:* Bauer recounts rumors of the existence of a well-known, well-liked, and celebrated *māhū* who lived in Papeete from the late 1950s through the 1960s and who went by the name Raerae. One of the older *raerae* whom Bauer interviewed told him that Raerae had been a very colorful *māhū* who was known throughout Papeete, the implication being that this feminized *māhū* could have been the namesake for the innovated linguistic term.

11   However, and rather unusually from a cross-cultural perspective, because of their association with sex work, *raerae* have taken up the labor-practice dimension of sex work as a centrally meaningful part of *raerae* queer gender identifications. It is a labor practice that, for them, is fundamental to the legitimate acquisition of the specific queer gender identity "*raerae.*"

12   The *raerae* critique of *māhū* as hypocrites and cowards invites the question of whether this critique draws on some dimensions of Western global queer discourse or on modernist discourses of sexuality more broadly and, if so, to what extent *raerae* might be turning to that alternative discursive framework in their projects of self-constitution. Charges of "hiding" one's "true" sexual

nature certainly seem to be invested in a modernist economy of the self, pace Foucault (1990).

13   Less commonly, a *raerae* exemplifies her feelings of difference in terms of finding pleasure in trying on her female relatives' dressier clothes and shoes. While such accounts (situated as the founding moment of queer identification) have been relatively rare thus far in my research, they may signal the beginnings of a shift in, or the expansion of, the viable frameworks for *raerae* self-understandings. If this were to become more commonly the case, it would further deepen the articulations between the meanings (including self-understandings and identifications) of *raerae* and capitalist market relations and consumption.

References

Académie Tahitienne—Fare Vāna'a. 1999. *Dictionnaire Tahitien—Français. Fa'atoro Parau Tahiti—Fārani.* Papeete, Tahiti: Académie Tahitienne—Fare Vāna'a.

Alexeyeff, Kalissa. 2000. Dragging Drag: The Performance of Gender and Sexuality in the Cook Islands. *The Australian Journal of Anthropology* 11(2): 97–307.

———. 2009. *Dancing from the Heart: Movement, Gender and Cook Islands Globalization.* Honolulu: University of Hawai'i Press.

Altman, Dennis. 1996. Rupture or Continuity? The Internationalization of Gay Identities. *Social Text 48* 14(3): 77–94.

Bauer, François. 2002. *Raerae de Tahiti: Rencontre du troisième type.* Papeete, French Polynesia: Haere Po Tahiti.

Besnier, Niko. 1994. Polynesian Gender Liminality through Time and Space. In *Third Sex, Third Gender: Beyond Sexual Dimorphism in Culture and History,* ed. Gilbert Herdt, pp. 285–328. New York: Zone Books.

———. 1997. Sluts and Superwomen: The Politics of Gender Liminality in Urban Tonga. *Ethnos* 62(1/2): 5–31.

———. 2002. Transgenderism, Locality, and the Miss Galaxy Beauty Pageant in Tonga. *American Ethnologist* 29: 534–566.

———. 2011. *On the Edge of the Global: Modern Anxieties in a Pacific Island Nation.* Stanford, CA: Stanford University Press.

Bligh, William. 1792 [1789]. *A Voyage to the South Sea, Undertaken by Command of His Majesty, for the Purpose of Conveying the Breadfruit Tree to the West Indies, in His Majesty's Ship the Bounty, Including an Account of the Mutiny on Board the Said Ship.* 2 vols. London: George Nicol.

Butler, Judith. 1990. *Gender Trouble: Feminism and the Subversion of Identity.* New York: Routledge.

Edwards, Edward, and George Hamilton. 1915. *Voyage of the H.M.S. Pandora, Despatched to Arrest the Mutineers of the "Bounty" in the South Seas, 1790–1791.* Ed. Basil Thompson. London: Francis Edwards.

Elliston, Deborah A. 1999. Negotiating Transnational Sexual Economies: Female *Māhū* and Same-Sex Sexuality in "Tahiti and Her Islands." In *Female Desires: Same-Sex Relations and Transgender Practices across Cultures,* ed. Evelyn Blackwood and Saskia Wieringa, pp. 232–252. New York: Columbia University Press.

———. 2000. Geographies of Gender and Politics: The Place of Difference in Polynesian Nationalism. *Cultural Anthropology* 15 (2): 171–216.

———. 2005. "Butterflies of the Night": Queer Gender and Consuming Desire at Tahiti. Paper presented at Duke University (March 24), invited by the Center for LGBT Life, Department of Anthropology and Women's Studies.

Foucault, Michel. 1990. *The History of Sexuality: Vol. 1, An Introduction.* Trans. Robert Hurley. New York: Vintage Books.

Henningham, Stephen. 1992. *France and the South Pacific: A Contemporary History.* Honolulu: University of Hawai'i Press.

Keesing, Roger M. 1989. Creating the Past: Custom and Identity in the Contemporary Pacific. *The Contemporary Pacific* 1(1/2): 19–42.

———. 1991. Reply to Trask. *The Contemporary Pacific* 3(1): 168–171.

Keesing, Roger M., and Robert Tonkinson, eds. 1982. Reinventing Traditional Culture: The Politics of Kastom in Island Melanesia. *Mankind.* Theme Issue 13(4).

Linnekin, Jocelyn. 1990. The Politics of Culture in the Pacific. In *Cultural Identity and Ethnicity in the Pacific,* ed. Jocelyn Linnekin and Lin Poyer, pp. 149–173. Honolulu: University of Hawai'i Press.

———. 1991. Text Bites and the R-Word: The Politics of Representing Scholarship. *The Contemporary Pacific* 3(1): 172–177.

Levy, Robert I. 1971. The Community Function of Tahitian Male Transvestism: A Hypothesis. *Anthropological Quarterly* 44(1): 12–21.

———. 1973. *Tahitians: Mind and Experience in the Society Islands.* Chicago: University of Chicago Press.

Mageo, Jeannette Marie. 1992. Male Transvestism and Cultural Change in Samoa. *American Ethnologist* 19(3): 443–459.

Mani, Lata. 1998. *Contentious Traditions: The Debate on Sati in Colonial India.* Berkeley: University of California Press.

Montillier, Pierre. 1999. *Te reo Tahiti 'api: Dictionnaire du tahitien nouveau et biblique.* Papeete, Tahiti: STP Multipress/Pierre Montillier.

Oliver, Douglas L. 1974. *Ancient Tahitian Society.* 3 vols. Honolulu: University Press of Hawai'i.

Raapoto, Turo A. 1988. *Mā'ohi:* On Being Tahitian. In *French Polynesia,* ed. Nancy J. Pollock and Ron Crocombe, pp. 3–7. Suva, Fiji: Institute of Pacific Studies, University of the South Pacific.

Rallu, J.-L. 1991. Population of the French Overseas Territories in the Pacific, Past, Present, and Projected. *The Journal of Pacific History* 26(2): 169–186.

Trask, Haunani-Kay. 1991. Natives and Anthropologists: The Colonial Struggle. *The Contemporary Pacific* 3(1): 159–167.

Wilson, James. 1799. *A Missionary Voyage to the South Pacific Ocean, Performed in the Years 1796, 1797, 1798, in the Ship Duff, Commanded by Captain James Wilson.* London: T. Chapman.

CHAPTER 3

"Hollywood" and the Emergence of a
Fa'afafine Social Movement in Samoa, 1960–1980

Reevan Dolgoy

Whenever a *fa'afafine* would come to town,
they would always look for Hollywood.

A fa'afafine *reminiscing about the 1970s*

This chapter traces the development of a *fa'afafine* social movement in Western Samoa from the early 1960s to the mid-1980s. The forces and events that led to the transformation of *fa'afafine* (pl. of *fa'afafine*) remain part of an ongoing and still fluid process. The early *fa'afafine* networks produced a number of organizational structures in which forms of collective activity continued to be reproduced. These include *fa'afafine* involvement in sports, notably netball (a team sport akin to basketball, associated with women, and played in former British colonies) and in the organization of drag-queen pageants from 1983 on. But no institution was more important to the early development of *fa'afafine* identity politics than a particular tailor shop and the people who were associated with it, on which this chapter focuses.

These activities were not politically agitating or confrontational, strategies that are anathema to most *fa'afafine*, but rather promoted a "politics of recognition" (Taylor 1992), which involves the projection of a new notion of identity and solidarity, and the collective desire to be more included in a changing social system that was seen to be both relevant and of value. This politics depended as much on local cultural factors as it did on global transformations (see Good, this volume). It has a history that, as Fox (1991) would theorize, is still an ongoing process. Theirs was a fluid, gentle, esteem-based movement in the collective behavior tradition, the emergence of which was locally managed and bounded. It was based in part on personal biographies, local leadership models, and the availability of new spaces and motifs that decades of contact with the world system and independence from New Zealand had opened up for all Samoans.

As mentioned, this chapter will explore one particular space that became pivotal to the development of the *fa'afafine* as a collective entity in Samoa, a tailor shop in the Saleufi district of Apia, the capital of independent Samoa, which became known as "Hollywood." It is an example of the kind of role that havens, sites, and free spaces play in social movement activity (Melucci 1989; Evans and Boyte 1992; Gamson 1992; Herbst 1994; Fantasia and Hirsch 1995; Taylor and Whittier 1995).

The Origins of Hollywood

Hollywood and the *fa'afafine* movement started with a network of friends who eventually became tailors. They occupied the Hollywood space from the mid-1960s until 1978. One individual remembered *fa'afafine* tailors in Samoa as early as the 1940s. The first anyone could remember by name was called Nancy. She is remembered as a person who was feminine but who did not cross-dress. Nancy was by many accounts a popular tailor whose clientele included elite members of the pre-independence part-Samoans (*afakasi,* or "half-caste") as well as highly placed Samoans. Through her contact with this elite, Nancy had access to venues that other Samoans did not. She was occasionally invited to the Returned Servicemen's Association (RSA) Club, which restricted its membership to high society, as was the norm in colonial Samoa. Nancy died in the mid-1960s, having first turned her shop over to a younger *fa'afafine* friend named Toma.

The tailors at the Saleufi venue developed an excellent reputation for their work. They had many clients from all walks of life. They were also very sociable and had established networks in both the *fa'afafine* and the general community in Apia. As a result of these associations and the tailors' skills, Hollywood, which acquired its name around 1968, soon became more than a tailor shop. It became a meeting place for friends of the group, other urban *fa'afafine,* and rural *fa'afafine* who visited town. It also became a "salon" for other Samoans both male and female, somewhat analogous to alternate social spaces in prerevolutionary Paris (Herbst 1994). In particular, women who appreciated the workers' talents as designers brought their tailoring to them, while at the same time enjoying their company. Women who had argued with their husbands could also be found there to find solace. Other women were networked to Hollywood through kinship ties.

How did the space get named "Hollywood"? The most consistent explanation is the following: "Like we look at the movies and say to ourselves, 'Oh this is where all the actresses [are] from.' So we called the place Hollywood" (Moli). Another possibility is that the name came as a result of *fa'afāfine*'s obsession with the movies. Many of them would regularly attend the Tivoli Theatre, a short walk from Hollywood.

The Tivoli Theatre was Apia's all-purpose venue for movies, weddings, boxing tournaments, and the annual New Year's ball. When the Hollywood *fa'afāfine* attended the cinema, they would mix with all levels of Samoan society. They sometimes sat as a group in the balcony. Some *fa'afāfine* "girl names," like Anita, Mitzi, and Sophia, are said to have been appropriated from the names of actresses who were in the films or of characters from films that showed every week. One of the Hollywood group's first protégées recalls:

> So Sunday's always their movie night . . . if there's a movie that's like a musical or something where an actress is . . . very much involved . . . those are the kinds of movies they always go [to] . . . like if there's an actress that comes with a lot of nice makeup, dresses. They wouldn't go to war movies. [They preferred] singing, musical types of movies. (Moli)

There can be little doubt that the appropriation of the name Hollywood had to do, in part, with the glamour that these individuals espoused and with which they wished to be associated (see Elliston, this volume). It also, in a sense, defined their niche in terms of the novel feminine forms of display with which they were identified in town.

By the late 1960s, two of the four original tailors had moved overseas. Once the emigration dust had settled, only Anita and Lesa remained as the principals at Hollywood, a space that they would occupy for more than ten years. Anita, who, as we shall see, had remarkable leadership qualities, had by her mid-twenties matured into a capable and astute individual. Although she was younger than Lesa, a state that would normally lower one's rank in the generalized Samoan gerontocracy, due to her talents and maturity, Anita became the primary leader of an emerging *fa'afafine* collective that had begun to take form by the late 1960s.

The Hollywood *fa'afāfine* were perceived by some to be both "outrageous" and fun. They appropriated outside cultural forms that referenced the fashion and adornment of Western women. The Hollywood space allowed them to ignore some Samoan norms of dignity in ways that were endearing to some observers, if not to others. From Hollywood they networked into the general community, volunteering to help others and participating in community projects like talent contests.

One of the clients of the Hollywood tailors discussed the Hollywood space and its social purposes:

> And that's why they stuck together in this little area at Saleufi so as they could all sort of back each other up . . . so to speak, or get each other's support. . . . Because I know they all used to congregate there and the more I think about it now, the more I can still see the building, the tiny little building and little rooms and each one had their own little, it was like little rabbit hutches you know. . . . Because I know they all used to congregate there. (Fern)

One of the early tailors recalled the eventual transformation of the Saleufi venue from sewing shop to the more consequential space it was to become around 1965:

> Oh (*chuckling in disbelief*). It's amazing. . . . We all lived in there. We started off [by coming] over there in the day and work[ing] and then [went] home at night, g[o]t changed and [went] out [for the evening]. All of a sudden we start[ed] bringing our clothes and all of a sudden we started to live there, and stay there all the time, work and sleep. . . . So my bed was underneath the table where they cut the sewing. That's my bed. Toma's bed was on top of the table . . . and in the room they were using as a sleeping room was Anita . . . and all the young new ones that [came] over there. (Elisa)

Some of the shelves in the shop also served as bunk beds at night. The "young new ones" were the *fa'afāfine* who eventually came to use Hollywood as a kind of "group home" and meeting place over the years, some having left their villages or families. At Hollywood, they came under the influence of older *faʻafāfine,* who helped them to take care of themselves in the newly materialistic world that Samoa was becoming and that they did not entirely understand. The Hollywood leadership had already appropriated the commoditized world of the town and they understood that money meant status. They were urban, relatively well-educated, talented, and somewhat cosmopolitan. They collectively demonstrated conspicuous consumption, as did other urban Samoans.

The Hollywood tailors found self-esteem through their status as paid professionals. As Elisa, describing the 1960s, put it:

> But once we know how to sew and all that sort of thing . . . and we start to do that to earn our money . . . the same as those business people . . . what the hell . . . we've got the same money as them. We go to the bar. They buy their drink, we buy our drinks from the bar, so we don't look for anything from them. We can earn our own livings. . . . If a Samoan person smoked a Salem in those days you'll have a millionaire in those days, and here were [*faʻafāfine*], we all smoke Salems. When we go to a bar, each of us got a packet of Salem[s] in front of us from the bar. We sit on the stool, you know, we said to ourselves "Why not?" Because people always think that we're just roaming the streets, we've got no money, we've got nothing. So let's show them we can earn our money and we can smoke the expensive cigarettes like them.

The early Hollywood tailors were alumni of the Marist Brothers School in Apia. They had grown up in Taufusi district, where a number of Catholics lived. Another *faʻafāfine,* also an *afakasi* alumnus of the Marist school who had her own business but who remained attached to the Hollywood group out of friendship and solidarity, remembers the cohesion that was forming in those days at Hollywood: "They all sort of come there in the evenings and they all sit around, tell stories and then later on they go out and 'patrol,' you know what I mean?" (Leilei). "Patrol" was the pursuit of men and pleasure, a practice that eventually resulted in a poor public reputation and imputations of sex work and thievery for some. In a suddenly independent and transforming society, Apia was open to all Samoans, and Hollywood attracted *faʻafāfine* from all walks of life, both urban and rural. In contrast to village life, which was circumscribed by chores at home, service (*tautua*) to elders, church activities, and sports, openly "patrolling" for men was something new.

The appeal of Hollywood went beyond its influence on the young *fa'afāfine*. A number of Hollywood *fa'afāfine* were well-educated by the standards of the day. In fact, a few were teachers at various stages. For some, a life spent at Hollywood had been weighed against the status of the teaching profession, and often won out. The expression of new sensibilities and identities that Hollywood enabled was far more appealing, and some left the teaching profession to take up sewing and live a less constrained, somewhat more urban lifestyle at Hollywood. In any case, sewing paid better than teaching.

Unlike today, rural Samoa had no *fa'afafine* subculture and few if any bars or hotels. This meant that *fa'afāfine* professionals assigned to remote areas could only come into town once a week at best. One *fa'afafine* described her decision to leave a steady job in a remote area and move to Hollywood:

> I really wanted to come to where my heart was, you know. . . . It's not that I wanted to be a woman. I was a woman. . . . And despite my mum, you know [asking me to] tell [her] of my whereabouts . . . I just ignore[d] it, you know. And when I came back . . . whether she scolded me, [or] told me off or what, I just didn't listen. I [didn't] care. . . . I realized this is my right place. It really satisfied me and I was interested in it and I realized "Oh, this is where exactly I should be." Plus the friendship amongst the members . . . and the understanding. (Marina)

While some *fa'afāfine* of the period were associated with indolence because they had left home and were not supporting their families, some balanced the lifestyle emanating from Hollywood with their commitments to family. A number of the *fa'afāfine* were deeply involved in the economic and social life of their families. One had a number of dependents, many of whom she eventually sent to New Zealand.

Hollywood began to grow in reputation, and the number of *fa'afāfine* who congregated there increased. It was a place that nurtured their transformation from an earlier amorphous form to an emerging new collective form based on their strength in numbers. As increasing numbers of *fa'afāfine* became associated with Hollywood, they began to more publically feminize their appearances or moving about in groups, projecting a new identity and solidarity in town. *Fa'afāfine* who came into town with their families for education or to sell agricultural staples at the market would inevitably end up at Hollywood for a visit. They held barbecues and parties with their friends at an outdoor space behind Hollywood called "the courtyard." These friends included men, women, and couples.

It is difficult to determine the exact number of *fa'afāfine* who were directly involved in or networked to Hollywood. Estimates vary from around thirty or more in the late 1960s to the early 1970s, to fifty or more toward the end of the tenure of the tailors at Hollywood. The numbers would not necessarily include others who would come in from remote areas and just drop in. One individual with an excellent memory remembered thirty-five *fa'afāfine*, recalling many of them by name, who lived in the town area in the mid-1960s and were associated with Hollywood. All of the town *fa'afāfine* and many from the rural areas were part of this network. The Hollywood leaders were individuals to be emulated. They were self-employed, knew the ropes, and exerted a strong influence on many of the rural and young urban *fa'afāfine*.

It is in the early Hollywood period that some *fa'afāfine* became closely associated with sex work and other criminal activities in the town area. Thus Hollywood became a place where impression management would take place and where the *fa'afāfine* would try to address the negative identity imputations of others (McAdam 1994). The Hollywood leaders would admonish the younger ones, "If you go out with a guy, you do not steal his wallet! You do not do anything stupid because it is a small place. The cops will be on you." Although throughout Samoa's recent history some *fa'afāfine* became potential objects of police surveillance, some of their positive associations in the early days were with policemen. Indeed, some policemen patronized the Hollywood tailors. Anita in particular had close ties to the police through friendships. Respondents also mentioned a number of high-status friends, including members of parliament for whom Hollywood was a site they regularly frequented.

Solidarity and Community

There was, however, more to Hollywood than tailoring and erotics. The main purpose of the group was to establish a community based on the production of identity, acceptance, and solidarity. An individual who had become actively involved by the mid-1970s noted:

> It was a group of people with common interests, same values, same problems, so they came together and started up their own family and community, and it was really based around the older *fa'afāfine* who were doing well, especially the self-employed ones in the dress-making industry. So from there they sort of met up with a lot of wider sector of the society you know . . . and it grew. (Tala)

The leaders at Hollywood remained very Samoan in their outlook, their sensibilities, the ordering of their lives, and most certainly in their relations with families and the general community. Thus, a certain worldliness aside, Samoan culture was the context for actions that were both intentional and day-to-day, and through which change was produced. Though Apia provided sites where new display forms could be tried out, these forays were embedded within Samoan social forms.

Hollywood was organized in terms of an age-based hierarchy, as is characteristic of Samoan society. The older *fa'afāfine* expected displays of respect (*fa'aaloalo*) from their younger associates, including those who were part of their extended network. The gerontocracy that prevailed at Hollywood, characteristic of all Samoan families, was one in which the younger *fa'afāfine* served the elders (*tautua*), waiting their turn to graduate to positions of higher responsibility and status. When elders speak, the young listen, and this was the case with the Hollywood *fa'afāfine*. The leadership usually took the initiative both informally and formally and left the younger ones to *tautua* in a fashion similar to a Samoan family.

At the same time, the solidarities between *fa'afāfine* created a kind of associative kinship common in Samoan society:

> Our kind of people . . . we don't think of getting married and have families and that. We are more like our own family. Another *fa'afafine* is our family. . . . The older *fa'afāfine* . . . look after the young ones and try to push the young ones away from the life that we came through and let them go to school and educate themselves for a better future for the *fa'afafine,* you know? (Anela)

What Anela describes is not unlike Weston's analysis of associative kinship among gay men and women in the West (1991). The family atmosphere at Hollywood was a combination of common sensibilities, interests, and problems, emerging lifestyles, and some fundamental elements of the

Samoan family system that most if not all *fa'afāfine* understood. As Anela
noted, they promoted higher goals for some of the young *fa'afāfine,* such
as staying in school. In cases of emergencies or tragedies that befell the
fa'afāfine or their blood relations, the Samoan motif of kinship obligation or
fa'alavelave came into play. For example, upon the death of a family member, the *fa'afāfine* would often gather and participate as kin in the traditional
supportive *fa'alavelave* material exchanges.

The Hollywood group raised funds among themselves for various projects. These resources were used for donations to communities and individuals, for travel to other islands and overseas, for their netball activities,
parties, and for the running expenses of the place. The traditional Samoan
after-church Sunday meal held at Hollywood was also an occasion for
some associates to contribute resources. These informal gatherings would
eventually become part of more formal types of organization, such as sport
events and beauty pageants. Hollywood ultimately became a mobilizing
structure for many *fa'afāfine.*

Furthermore, Hollywood operated as a space for community building
not only for *fa'afāfine* but also for other Samoans. It became known as a
haven for heterosexual women in need of comfort or support:

> Hollywood, too, was a refuge for women when they had their little
> *"misa"* (quarrel) with their husbands. And they found refuge in
> Hollywood. Anita and [others], they used to bring peace to the
> families. They either called the husband or brought the wife back
> to the husband and sort[ed] things out. Or the wife would take
> the older *fa'afāfine* out for a drink in the bars and pour out their
> hearts. (Makerita)

The reasons for these contacts with women were many. The town *fa'afāfine*
like Anita had a history of association with women. Some of their female
supporters who could be found at Hollywood had been friends or associates from childhood. These kinds of associations in this small community
readily carried over into adult life. Some women simply found the *fa'afāfine*
at Hollywood charming, "real," and more interesting than men. For the
fa'afāfine, the relationships with their women friends were equally reward-
ing. They shared intimacies, gentle teasing, and confidences. This convivial-
ity created solidarities that some women and *fa'afāfine* value to this day (see
Good, this volume).

In addition, within the broader structure of Samoan society, *fa'afāfine* and women are associated by ties related to femininity, kinship, and the discourses regarding kinship. Friendships and to some extent affective proto-alliances between *fa'afāfine* and women are in a real sense conducted within the generalized "Samoan family." To recontextualize G. H. Mead (1961 [1934]), women and *fa'afāfine* are generalized kin in a society predominantly organized along kinship lines. By the same token, *fa'afāfine* also become potential allies of women because, though possessing male bodies, they identify themselves with women. Similarly, although they may compete with women, particularly in terms of their participation in labor and in the sexual economy, they are not involved in the latter's repression in either the private or the public sphere.

As mentioned above, another group that developed a particular bond with Hollywood *fa'afāfine* as far back as in the 1950s (when Nancy ran the shop) were elites and the emerging middle class:

> In society in those days the *fa'afāfine* were accepted by the educated people. They loved the *fa'afāfine*. They were always out of the closet with respect to interacting with the educated. That's why they were so popular. They were the people who introduced fashion to women. (Tauvela)

"Out of the closet" in this case does not refer to erotics or identity, but simply means socially attached or accepted. It would be an exaggeration to say that all educated Samoans appreciated them and that all of the *fa'afāfine* were appreciated. But there was a significant sector of elite society who enjoyed, valued, and relied on creative and affective projections that emanated from their shop, be it through tailoring, friendship, education, kinship, or acculturation. These elites would later become an important source of cultural capital through their patronage of *fa'afāfine* beauty pageants and other endeavors.

By the early 1970s, this thriving but still small subculture and its expanded network were about to come out into the open as the larger community in Apia gradually discovered it:

> Then the whole community . . . heard about this. Then they sort of tried to put their ears on the door and, you know, [find out] what's going on and then all of a sudden the *fa'afāfine* appear in town and

all the people . . . just [made] fun of them and then they feel angry, you know. How can the whole community know about this . . . ? All of a sudden the community reacts. (Ioane)

It may have appeared "all of a sudden" in retrospect. It is more likely that the general community's exposure was more gradual as the number of *fa'afāfine* in town increased and cross-dressing became more salient. It is also possible that conservative and less cosmopolitan village Samoans who had migrated to town may have given the *fa'afāfine* trouble.

Although few *fa'afāfine* actually dressed in drag during the day, some increasingly feminized their appearances in public. They wore their *lāvalava* in a feminine manner; had their shirts tailored in a feminine style; plucked their eyebrows, and used mascara and rouge. Some cross-dressed much more dramatically in Apia bars. Some *fa'afāfine* entertainment groups from Hollywood would perform as dancers or singers in various venues and at fund-raising events.

With the *fa'afāfine* phenomenon as visible as it is reported to have been, the negative reaction from some of the urban public was understandable. Many *fa'afāfine* became the butt of jokes, innuendo, teasing, and insults. Whether it was justified or not, they were also inexorably linked to sex work, possibly because they would often be seen in the company of "ladies of the night" in some bars. Some of the early Hollywood *fa'afāfine* were reputed to cruise the docks, looking for sailors.

Anita

Anthony Schwenke, also called Tony, was known almost exclusively as Anita. She was the de facto leader of the *fa'afāfine* in Samoa from the late 1960s to the late 1970s, but her influence was felt well into the early 1980s. Exploring her influence reveals another piece of the puzzle for an understanding of the formation and transformation of the *fa'afāfine*.

Anita was born in late 1942 into a part-Samoan, part-German family. After her mother died, she was raised by a grandmother. Anita remained committed to her family and provided for them materially in many ways. While this is part of the duty of all Samoan children, it is also a way in which *fa'afāfine* in particular have gained and maintained status, esteem, and social worth and have fulfilled their obligations to family. By all accounts, Anita was a "giver." By her early teens, she was exhibiting the creative, mischievous, and socially alert qualities that she was to employ as an adult. She attracted young people of both genders to her circle. She was already recognized as a leader and socializer of *fa'afāfine* and had a reputation as a dependable person who could be relied upon to carry out tasks and projects. Even at an early age it seems she had the ability to network. Anita was well-known for her creativity as well as her ability to manage people through her humor and intelligence.

Anita was described as having a "forward vision." The words "charming" and "manipulative" have also been applied to her. One respondent described her as a "powerful person. She had power," a description that referred to her charisma and influence. In addition to Anita's canniness and "street smarts," it was her warmth, compassion, and sensitivity that were mentioned most often.

Anita was relatively well situated in Apian society. Although she was from a part-Samoan family, she was not part of the highest elite. She lacked a title, but had authority based on a number of qualities. As part of the Catholic community and as an individual with recognized talent and charisma, she was able to make use of her various contacts to call in favors as the *fa'afāfine*'s activities progressed.

At the traditional level, leadership in Samoa is linked to rank and titular status (Shore 1982). Although rank gives one *pule* or authority, to be effective it must be accompanied by qualities such as charisma and ability, and more recently by education and wealth (O'Meara 1990). In town, a more European and non-sacred space than typical villages, a hybrid of leadership styles is possible. Anita had some aspects of high status in the modern sense: she was self-employed, had a good tailoring business, and was from a modest but hardworking part-Samoan family in town.

To the *fa'afāfine* I interviewed, by then in their forties and fifties, Anita was "like a mother." It is the status of "mother" that is at the root of her activism. Through mothering, she was able to accomplish, in this kinship-based society, the affective conditions necessary for an as yet uncrystallized movement. The label "mother" has a number of connotations. One is the qualities of what a mother should be, or what some *fa'afāfine* believed was necessary in a mother. Some *fa'afāfine* report having been particularly close to their mothers. Witnesses to the socialization of *fa'afāfine* report their having been indulged and coddled by mothers or grandmothers (Tcherkézoff, this volume). In contrast, other *fa'afāfine* report having had to endure corporal punishment and conditions akin to servitude in the family.

Anita offered a modified version of the image of the Samoan mother. She extended mothering into the modern sphere by teaching new forms of self-expression, the emergent norms of the *fa'afafine* group at Hollywood, as well as ways in which new displays could be "bricolaged" and maintained. Transformations of the type that *fa'afafine* were undergoing, and the kind of support that Anita offered, contextualized as mothering, provided both acceptance and empowerment in this transforming kinship-based milieu. Anita fed, housed, trained, socialized, and loved many *fa'afafine*, making them feel appreciated. Thus, through example as well as through discipline, a confidence and a stability were instilled in individual *fa'afafine*, which gave them a certitude about their personal and collective qualities and potentials. Ultimately they gained a collective identity that was stabilized by this powerful but gentle individual.

Anita did not necessarily have a soft touch as a mother. She was a strong and occasionally a harsh disciplinarian, and the young *fa'afafine* listened to her. A former sports associate was shocked when the person she thought of as the normally mild-mannered and dignified Anita began to berate one of the younger *fa'afafine* for misbehaving on the netball court. She was known to swat some of them if they got out of hand. Another *fa'afafine* recalled: "[Anita would have] me stay . . . at night-time and work and she'll go to a movie and then [she'd say], 'I want you to finish all this . . . by the time I come back from the movies.' I have to stay and finish all the stuff" (Moli).

Anita did some formal Samoan "mothering" in the traditional sense. She fostered some young *fa'afafine* during her years at Hollywood. One respondent referred to this relationship as adoption, although these arrangements were not formalized with parents. Anita provided for some of the adoptees and most certainly guided them, as she would do for many others who required it. In the 1960s, she adopted a young *fa'afafine* who had left her village due to tensions in the family and, for a few years in the mid-to-late 1970s, she took a group of educated *fa'afafine* under her wing. Anita's former neighbor mentioned that some older *fa'afafine* who now live in New Zealand and who came under her influence in Samoa still refer to themselves as Anita's children. This demonstrates her power and status that still remains in memory, as do the positive effects of her mentoring.

Anita's mothering was also an attempt to help the *fa'afafine* come to terms with the conflicts in which they were involved, either with their families or with the general public. For Oli, whose self-control was limited and who had a propensity to retaliate physically for slights that she received, Anita had the following advice:

> A: Because we're trying to defend [against] the people, because they're always teasing us [in] those days . . . When you walk on the road (street), oh, they're always teasing you, so you know we'll swear [at] them. . . . So we had to watch our mouth because nobody can stop our mouth when we argue with someone, so those kind of things . . . better be good. Good behaviors.
>
> Q: What else . . . ?
>
> A: . . .'specially our clothes.
>
> Q: What about your clothes?
>
> A: Well, when you wear a lady's dress, well, you must act like a real lady and not wear a lady's dress and act like a man. Because I'm telling you we can fight boys. Nobody can beat us, you know, that's us. Because . . . we don't care, well the time for trouble when you're still in ladies' dress, well, you don't care about the dress. (Oli)

More than anything else, Anita attempted to contextualize this new style of *fa'afāfine* within Samoan motifs of respect and dignity that she herself possessed. There can be little doubt that this was an intuitive, yet culturally based, strategy for the demeanor she felt the younger *fa'afāfine* should adopt. Some older respondents in the 1990s also echoed her contention that some *fa'afāfine* could do with a bigger dose of respect and dignity.

Anita also understood the public "audience" very well. She sensed what it would take to convince the general public that a worthwhile human being inhabited the anomalous, feminized persona that some felt the *fa'afafine* represented. She was not a front-and-center political leader, but her "mothering" comprised a powerful politics with respect to socializing *fa'afāfine*, explaining the world to them, caring for them, organizing their activities, creating solidarity, and managing their new identity. This kind of activity was transformational and undoubtedly led to confidence, empowerment, and independence at both personal and collective levels, and helped to establish some *fa'afāfine* as better human beings.

It is important to reiterate that Anita's initiatives throughout her adult life were in many ways affect-based, pre-political, and not necessarily rationalized. They were reactive, based on her feelings of fairness and her good-heartedness, and were undertaken with people with whom she had already formed social bonds. They were situationally specific in the sense that, despite her "forward vision," there seemed to be little idea of where these initiatives might lead, the desire for protection of *faʻafāfine* notwithstanding. Typical of Samoa, it was the personal that became the transformational, perhaps the only workable, motif in a kinship-based affective society for a group like the *faʻafāfine*, who at that time had no role or standing in the traditional Samoan social order other than as men. Fale, one of many *faʻafāfine* who was close to her, summarized Anita's intentions in this way:

> She probably didn't sit down and say, "I'm going to do this to change the world," but what she did was out of her heart and her own contacts. She had a lot of contacts—*faifeʻau* (pastors), government officers. She was invited to government functions like Independence Day parties. She would be invited only for her own works, loyalty to people, how she came across. She was a very interesting person. I wouldn't be talking about her sixteen years after her death if she wasn't the person she was. (Fale)

Anita died in the autumn of 1983. For many, her passing was devastating. She had been traveling throughout the Pacific Islands that year, returning to Samoa in late summer and early autumn to attend the South Pacific Games, when she suddenly fell ill and died.

There is some evidence that her leadership had aspects of greatness, circumscribed by charisma, compassion, and a sense of fairness. Anita may have led many *faʻafāfine* through a Meadian "game stage."[1] She provided a new game, new rules, and a new "ballpark," as well as instructions as to how to play this new game. It was often done in fun and with performative cosmopolitanism, which encouraged *faʻafāfine* to seek her out.

A Gentle Politics of Recognition

Hollywood was a place of refuge for the *faʻafāfine*, a site where a collective identity and new sensibilities emerged. There, *faʻafāfine* were reproducing forms of modernity, aspects of cosmopolitanism, and new expressions of their personae that were appealing to certain segments of the population and undoubtedly confusing to others. Hollywood was also the focal point for solidarity within the expanded *faʻafāfine* community. Some of the urban community found compatibility between themselves and the Hollywood group. The *fa'afāfine*'s ability to organize themselves, as well as to reproduce certain lifestyle forms that some of the affluent or regularly employed could also adopt, was the beginning of a newly found self-respect for some.

The Hollywood *fa'afāfine* promoted a new, somewhat Westernized persona for themselves and others while remaining within the *fa'a-Sāmoa* or "the Samoan way." For many urban townspeople, they became exponents of fashion. Other *fa'afāfine* in the town area became part of this extended network. History and new social spaces, in which urbanization, cosmopolitanism, and consumption, along with the new qualities of social relations that went with them, would allow the expression of a new kind of leadership that could not be found in a traditional village setting. The circumstances of Apia proved essential to these transformations and to the leadership that created them.

Social transformations in emerging societies can have a complex history of their own. *Fa'afafine* emerged in the urban area of Samoa at the end of the colonial period as a fledgling, fluid, esteem-based identity movement. It played out in already established networks, nurtured in part by the structural opportunities that the transformation to independence from New Zealand provided. It was based on a collective identity that was bounded by perceived effeminacy of manners, an erotic preference for men, early references in Samoan family and work-related practices, the reputation of some *fa'afāfine* as entertainers, new opportunities for expression based on importations from the West, and significant leadership. Its collective activities became attached to a lifestyle that was somewhat modern while having a decidedly traditional relationship to Samoan society.

Notwithstanding the potential for continued and perhaps rapid transformation in the future, this chapter has shown that *fa'afafine* transformation is the product of both structure, in the shape of the *fa'a-Sāmoa,* and agency, in the form of Anita's calculated leadership, for example. *Fa'afāfine,* to an extent, have "made themselves" in the manner of E. P. Thompson's (1963) sense of the construction of the English working class. But in Samoa this process has a local configuration: rather than being propelled by a confrontational style, it has consisted of a "gentle politics of recognition."

Note

1   *Editors' Note:* "Game stage" is the term that social theorist George Herbert Mead (1961 [1934]) applied to the process during which children learn to

situate themselves in relation to a "generalized other" and thus learn appropriate behaviors and norms. Dolgoy's point here is that Anita taught other *fa'afāfine* a new and different set of rules that enabled them to embrace a particular social identity, thus encouraging deeper self-development.

References

Evans, Sara M., and Harry C. Boyte. 1992. *Free Spaces.* Chicago: University of Chicago Press.

Fantasia, Rick, and Eric L. Hirsh. 1995. Culture in Rebellion: The Appropriation and Transformation of the Veil in the Algerian Revolution. In *Social Movements and Culture,* ed. Hank Johnston and Bert Klandermans, pp. 144–159. Minneapolis: University of Minnesota Press.

Fox, Richard G. 1991. For a Nearly New Culture History. In *Recapturing Anthropology: Working in the Present,* ed. Richard G. Fox, pp. 93–113. Santa Fe, NM: School of American Research Press.

Gamson, William A. 1992. The Social Psychology of Collective Action. In *Frontiers in Social Movement Theory,* ed. Aldon D. Morris and Carol M. Mueller, pp. 53–76. New Haven, CT: Yale University Press.

Herbst, Susan. 1994. *Politics at the Margin: Historical Studies of Public Expression outside the Mainstream.* Cambridge: Cambridge University Press.

McAdam, Doug. 1994. Culture and Social Movements. In *New Social Movements from Ideology to Identity,* ed. Enrique Laraña, Hank Johnston, and Joseph R. Gusfield, pp. 36–57. Philadelphia: Temple University Press.

Mead, George H. 1961 [1934]. *Mind, Self, and Society.* Chicago: University of Chicago Press.

Melucci, Alberto. 1989. *Nomads of the Present.* Philadelphia: Temple University Press.

O'Meara, J. Tim. 1990. *Samoan Planters: Tradition and Economic Development in Polynesia.* Fort Worth, TX: Holt, Rinehart & Winston.

Shore, Bradd. 1982. *Sala'ilua: A Samoan Mystery.* New York: Columbia University Press.

Taylor, Charles. 1992. *Multiculturalism and the Politics of Recognition: An Essay.* Princeton, NJ: Princeton University Press.

Taylor, Verta, and Nancy E. Whittier. 1995. Analytical Approaches to Social Movement Culture: The Culture of the Women's Movement. In *Social Movements and Culture,* ed. Hank Johnston and Bert Klandermans, pp. 163–187. Minneapolis: University of Minnesota Press.

Thompson, E. P. 1963. *The Making of the English Working Class.* London: V. Gollancz.

Weston, Kath. 1991. *Families We Choose: Lesbians, Gays, Kinship.* New York: Columbia University Press.

CHAPTER 4

Representing *Fa'afafine*

Sex, Socialization, and Gender Identity in Samoa

Penelope Schoeffel

From eighteenth-century accounts of Tahiti by explorers and voyagers to twentieth-century anthropological controversies about Samoa, the sexual customs of Polynesian societies have attracted more than usual interest among Westerners. Representations of Polynesians as peoples enjoying freedom from sexual restrictions have been a source of considerable scholarly debate (for example, Besnier 1994; Freeman 1983; Mead 1928; Sahlins 1981; Tcherkézoff 2004, 2008; Wallace 2003), while more recently there has been considerable popular and scholarly interest in the alleged institutionalization of social roles for transgender males in Polynesian societies.

For example, in policy papers on culture, sexuality, and HIV in the Pacific Islands, the late respected medical anthropologist Carol Jenkins (2005, 2006) wrote:

> The Pacific Islands are well-endowed with traditional gender-variant roles for males, for example, the *fa'afafine* of Samoa, *fakaleiti* of Tonga, *laelae* in the Cook Islands, *mahu* in Tahiti and Hawaii, and others elsewhere. While there is little evidence that these roles have ever had a real sacred nature, it is well documented that these persons were accepted and respected in their communities, and some served as healers. Although it is generally understood that young males often had their first sex with *fa'afafine* (way of a

woman), the sexual aspects of the role did not predominate in the traditional pattern. Some mothers deliberately raised a last-born son as a *fa'afafine* because they were seen as very helpful and valuable to the community. (2006, 9)

Jenkins was not an expert on Polynesia and relied on works by scholars familiar with the region, but her assertions that Polynesians can and do raise boys to be girls, and that transgender is a product of this unusual socialization, echo many scholarly and popular representations of Polynesian sexuality. Underlying these claims are assumptions that sexuality is fundamentally polymorphous and that gender identity is a conscious choice—if not the individual's choice, then that of those around him or her. Such assumptions are consistent with understandings, prevalent in the 1960s and the 1970s, of mutable and acquired rather than innate gender identity. These understandings, for example, led John Money (1968) to advocate gender reassignment for infants with ambiguous or damaged genitalia in the belief that gender identity is not set at birth but is acquired in the course of early childhood socialization. A great deal of research since that time has shown that he was wrong.

Nevertheless, biological explanations about the origins of gender identity still stand on shaky grounds (Jordan-Young 2010) and social explanations are speculative. For example, evolutionary psychologists claim to have discovered correlations between transgender identity in males and birth order, family structure and the attitudes of doting mothers and grandmothers, and the role of uncles in Samoa (Poasa, Blanchard, and Zucker 2004; Vasey and Vanderlaan 2007). While I do not intend to discuss biopsychological or evolutionary arguments about gender identity here, I take as given that gender identity is a complex phenomenon, that there is no conclusive evidence of how it is formed, nor why transgender males are a recognized category of person in Polynesian societies, as they are in Thailand, Laos, and many other Asian societies. Nor do we know why there is apparently no such category among the indigenous peoples of Papua New Guinea, the Solomon Islands, and Vanuatu.

In this chapter I will contest three anthropological representations that propose *fa'afāfine* are a social institution in Samoa that function as negative models for the psychosexual reinforcement of masculinity, or as gender or sexual surrogates.

Three Explanations

Three broad classes of functionalist explanations have been offered for what scholars have perceived to be the institutionalization of *fa'afāfine* in Samoa. The first explanation maintains that this alleged institutionalization reinforces masculine psychosexual development. The second rests on a notion of gender surrogacy and proposes that some boys are socialized to assume women's roles in order to balance the household division of labor when families have a shortage of girls. The third explanation is that some boys are socialized to be sexually effeminate as sexual surrogates. In other words, they take on a female role in sexual intercourse as a substitute for, or alternative to, a biological female, because Samoan girls tend to be closely chaperoned and are generally not available for premarital sex.

Bradd Shore, who conducted fieldwork in Samoa in the 1970s, proposed a version of the psychosexual explanation, arguing that *fa'afāfine* encourage masculine psychosexual development by demonstrating to boys what a man should not be (1982, 209–210). This explanation is a variant of an earlier account that Robert Levy had put forward in the context of a psychocultural analysis of Tahitian society in the 1960s (1971, 1973). As Levy saw it, Tahitian *māhū* played a social, rather than a sexual, role. Levy defined a *māhū* as "a feminine role-playing male," a culturally created social institution that had "persisted from the past" despite extensive cultural transformations because it was "an expressive outlet for men wishing to avoid masculine role playing, and because it serve[d] important covert needs for other members of the community" (1971, 12). In this analysis, the *māhū* role reinforced the masculine one by "providing a highly visible and exclusively limited contrast, implying for other men in the village, 'I am a man because I am not a *mahu*'" (1971, 12). Both Shore and Levy perceived a weak contrast in gender roles in the societies they studied, in contrast to "Western" gender expectations. They thought that, in this cultural environment, masculine identity needed reinforcement; boys needed not only positive but also negative male roles to direct their development of masculine gender and sexual identities (Elliston, this volume). What are the "Western" gender expectations referred by Levy and Shore? They don't tell us, but we may assume they are referring to old-fashioned pronounced masculine and feminine demeanors and appearance emphasized by clothing, hairstyles, and in the case of women, makeup and high-heeled shoes. In the 1970s

Tahitian and Samoan villagers usually wore notably gendered clothing only on formal occasions; their everyday dress was a shirt or T-shirt, worn over a *pāreu* or *lāvalava*. Women rarely wore makeup or high heels. The demeanor of most mature adult men and women was (and still is) not strikingly different from one another, but, and this is a point to which I will return, it was—and still is—the demeanor of *women* rather than men that differs from the generic feminine stereotypes in "Western" society.

In a series of publications, Jeannette Mageo (1992, 1996a, 1996b, 1999, 2008) proposes a more complicated psychosexual explanation. Claiming that *fa'afāfine* were rare in pre-Christian Samoa, she argues that in modern Samoa the *fa'afafine* role has become common because it serves a new social function. The transformative effects of colonialism and Christianity on Samoan culture were profound, and, according to Mageo, as the ancient traditional (and now obsolete) role of the ceremonial virgin (*tāupōu*) was extended from girls of the highest rank to girls of all ranks, girls became increasingly desexualized, allowing *fa'afāfine* to usurp their former sexually performative roles. In this analysis, historical Christian-colonial interventions created new gender dichotomies. Girls were taught to play idealized, missionary-inspired virginal roles in contrast to ancient, but now forbidden, sexual femininities that satirized authority. Mageo invites us to imagine a past in which *fa'afafine*-like hyperfemininities and sexualities were part of the behavioral repertoire of Samoan girls, a repertoire that is both critical and alluring, before such expressions were crushed beneath the weight of Christian morality. New gender dichotomies, she explains, have created culturally embedded psychosexual anxieties that are now mediated by *fa'afafine* performances as well as those of cross-dressing clowns in *fale aitu*, a comedic performing art (see Tcherkézoff, Pearson, this volume). These subversive elements, she suggests, may explain why some Samoan women encourage their sons to be *fa'afafine* if they show such inclination: "Samoan women appreciate the presence of *fa'afafine* because *fa'afafine* have an important role in deconstructing gender dichotomies that disadvantage women" (Mageo 1996a, 618). While American women may regard drag shows as hostile because they ridicule femininity, Samoan women do not experience *fa'afafine* cabaret performances in this way. However, contemporary *fa'afafine* performances in Samoa (for example, the Miss Gay Samoa pageant and weekly *fa'afafine* cabarets) do not parody Samoan women but Western images of hyperfemininities portrayed, for example, in films and magazines (Besnier 1997, 2002; Alexeyeff 2000)—what Elliston (this volume) astutely terms the "global femme." It is thus not surprising that Samoan women generally do not see *fa'afafine* performances as hostile.

Yet Mageo does not provide evidence to support her historical account of gender transformation (Schoeffel 1998, 161) and analyzes the cultural meaning of the performances she describes (from texts recorded and translated by Sinavaiana 1992) mistakenly as parodies of gender, rather than as parodies of the social pretensions and *Pālagi* (white, foreign) affectations adopted by some Samoans. Mageo has also proposed a gender surrogacy argument, maintaining that in Samoa a boy may be brought up as a girl when there are few girls in a family (1992, 450). This argument is the most entrenched explanation in popular representations, which generally assert that Samoans select boys to be raised as girls because boys may not do "girls' work." An acquaintance of mine in the tourism industry in Samoa told me that many tourists enjoy *fa'afafine* cabaret performances and told her they had heard Samoans sometimes bring boys up to be girls. Indeed, some Samoans believe that this might be so, although in my own discussions of this subject with Samoan friends and relatives, none have ever been able to give me an example based on their own experience.

Douglass Drozdow-St. Christian, who conducted fieldwork in Samoa in the 1990s, proposes a sexual surrogacy explanation. He claims that "socialization into the *fa'afafine* status can be initiated by a parent, usually the mother, or chosen by the individual himself" (2002, 30). In this analysis, *fa'afafine* fulfill a social function by introducing young men to penetrative sex without the multiple social complexities associated with the illicit nature of premarital heterosexual sex. In Samoa, he continues, "it was expected that boys will have some homosexual sex in adolescence. . . . The *fa'afafine* is the legitimate sex partner of young men learning about sex [because] . . . in some ways the *fa'afafine* allows young males to learn about appropriate sexual relations with women, since only *fa'afafine* should engage in passive anal sex" (2002, 155). According to this analysis, Samoans have three distinctive sexes: men, women, and *fa'afafine*, the latter being a "temporary sex" abandoned later in life. Dozdrow-St. Christian considers that Samoans have no fixed gender roles; boys may choose to become either *fa'afafine* or men, and *fa'afafine* usually become men eventually through normative marriage and reproduction. His understanding, which he bases on his informants' narratives, is that elderly and middle-aged *fa'afafine* only exist because in recent times some have clung to being *fa'afafine* past the age in which they could realistically be sexual surrogates (2002, 97, 155).

Masculinity, Sex, and Gender

In contesting these three representations of *fa'afāfine* as negative models for the psychosexual reinforcement of masculinity, or as gender or sexual surrogates, I will first consider the proposition that the institutionalization of transgender males reinforces masculine psychosexual development. Though the gendered division of labor and norms governing sexuality have all been subject to considerable change since Samoa first entered into sustained interaction with the West in the early nineteenth century, cultural ideals of masculinity and femininity from the pre-Christian past continue to permeate beliefs about gender and sexual behavior and cultural notions of transgender identity in contemporary Samoa. Until very recently, Samoans did not admit the possibility of homosexual attraction or preference. Sexuality for both men and women is framed within powerfully erotic notions of male dominance and the conquest and impregnation of females. Homosexuality was only culturally conceivable between two men if one adopted the social and sexual demeanor of a female (Schoeffel 1979; Tcherkézoff, this volume). To explain why this is so, I will outline some fundamental cultural principles that underpin Samoan notions of gender.

Gender relations in Samoa operate within two distinct domains: siblingship and conjugality. The category of siblingship is informed by *feagaiga*, which, in this sense of the word, is a cultural metaphor contrasting ideal qualities of dignity, restraint, and sacredness with natural activities associated with sex, warfare, fishing, hunting, and planting (Schoeffel 1979, 1995, 1998, 1999, 2005). In this sense, *feagaiga* aligns sisters with culture and brothers with nature. However, there is no *feagaiga* between a husband and wife—their relationship belongs to nature, and it is serviceable for sex, procreation, and production. The metaphorical context of *feagaiga* assigns two gendered roles to adult women. As sisters and members of their own 'āiga (descent group), a woman's status and formal authority increases with age. As sisters, girls and women are referred to as *tama'ita'i* (ladies) or *teine* (girls) and even middle-aged women may be referred to as *teine* in this context. As wives in their husband's 'āiga, women are outsiders, and their status is derived from and subordinate to their husband. Their social influence rises only in relation to his. The *feagaiga* requires a brother to protect and provide for his sister; a sister is required to honor her brother with her chaste and dignified conduct (Schoeffel 1995). Neither of the most honored cross-sibling roles is available to *fa'afāfine*, who occupy an ambiguous space within the idealized *feagaiga* of brother and sister. Although in the village setting *fa'afāfine* do the work of adult women, they are not members of the village women's committee or the *aualuma o tama'ita'i* (the association of daughters of the village), nor are they counted among the *aumaga* (the association of untitled sons of the village), even though they are biological males. This aspect of social structure is the main source of *fa'afāfine*'s moral abjection and social marginalization (cf. Besnier 2004, 304 for Tonga).

Fa'afāfine are defined primarily by their demeanor and, to a lesser extent, by the social roles they emulate or adopt, but not by their sexuality. In this respect, I agree with Shore and Levy to the extent that transgender males provide psychosocial reinforcement for masculine roles. This proposition rests on the observation that Samoan society provides a weak contrast in gender roles compared to "Western" gender expectations. Indeed, in daily rural village life, most adult women do not exhibit a demeanor that would be defined as feminine in most Western societies (but nor do adult women in most rural peasant societies), and the workaday dress of men and women is similar if not identical. What is missing from this analysis is a consideration of the way in which masculinity is valorized. Popular modern representations of the masculine ideal appear on T-shirt designs showing heavily muscled and tattooed men in belligerent poses, while other local media representations depict stalwart orators holding their staves and flywhisks in commanding postures, or, more recently, players for the Manu Samoa national rugby team have posed fiercely and heroically on the field. Such images are popular in Samoa and adorn most of the T-shirts sold in the Apia flea market. They are even more popular as emblems of national identity among Samoans in the diaspora. The only equivalent valorization of femininity excludes mature women, who are expected to behave with dignity and modesty and without feminine affectation. If women are valorized, it is as adolescent girls, iconicized as alluringly virginal but forbidden *teine muli* (virgin girls). When they are represented on T-shirts and other items of popular culture, they are portrayed in ceremonial headdresses (*tuiga*) seated before a *tānoa* (kava bowl) preparing *'ava* (kava) for the chiefs. In a more modern manifestation, they are decked out in flowers and the national costume, as demure contestants for the title of Miss Samoa, for example.

Shore is correct that *fa'afāfine* provide negative instances of masculinity. Especially after reaching adolescence, boys who do not exhibit expected manly demeanor are likely to be ridiculed as *fa'afāfine*, whether or not they are inclined to adopt a transgender identity. But it is their demeanor, rather than their role, that is scrutinized in this way. Samoan masculine norms are captured in Besnier's apt description of masculine ideals in Tonga as sustained by: "highly constricting codes of hypermasculine identities and performances of virility, which are in turn related to rank; a highly controlled emotionality; a competitive orientation . . . a disdain for home bound and aesthetic pursuits, and ambivalence towards intellectual ones, little overt concern about body image after early adulthood; [and] friendship networks grounded in exclusively male circles" (2004, 306).

Boys whose personality, behavior, or sexual orientation makes them feel unable to demonstrate a desirable attitude of masculinity are likely to be labeled—whether accepted or resisted—as *fa'afafine*. To be *fa'afafine* is to prefer the company of women, to be interested in things that girls and women are more likely to be interested in, and, in adult life, in many cases, to eschew masculine roles in favor of feminine ones. For example, a talkative, outgoing, charming little boy, the only son and the pet of his two older sisters, was mocked as a *fa'afafine* and severely reproved by his father for being effeminate. A retired middle-aged meat worker, a deacon in his church and the holder of a prestigious *matai* title, was considered *fa'afafine*, although he did not cross-dress. He had a chatty, outgoing manner and his closest friends and regular companions were women of his own age. It was this notion of effeminacy that defined him as *fa'afafine* rather than the fact that he was unmarried and childless. In contrast, a taciturn and industrious farmer of my long acquaintance was never called *fa'afafine* despite his unexplained celibacy—he had never married or had children. Similarly, an elderly, dignified, and masculine holder of high chiefly title was not considered *fa'afafine* even though he never married, which was highly unusual for a man of his status.

Gender and Socialization

I will now consider the widely held belief that *fa'afāfine* are socialized as gender surrogates in the household division of labor. Mass migration to New Zealand, Australia, and the United States, as well as increasing urbanization, has exposed Samoans to evolving Western understandings of gender and sexuality over the past fifty years. However, the modern middle-class Western ideal that childhood is a special time in which children are given central importance in the family still has limited currency among Samoans, although it is gaining ground in privileged families as they have fewer children and increasingly see a child's education as a means to upward mobility. Most accounts of socialization in Samoa indicate that Samoan children from the age of about four or five years until puberty are expected to serve their elders, to help around the house and household compound, fetch and carry, take care of babies and younger children, serve food, and eat only after their elders have eaten, at least on formal occasions (Shore 1982; Schoeffel 1979). In the tasks assigned to it, the gender of a preadolescent child is a secondary consideration to its age. There is no "boys' work" or "girls' work" for children, although most, if they have a choice, choose gendered tasks performed by their older same-sex siblings and other relatives. Boys are circumcised at the hospital without ceremony, usually between the ages of five and ten years, but the procedure makes little difference to their status or role.[1]

After puberty, a gendered division of labor is strongly emphasized. Ideally, "feminine" work is lighter, cleaner, and performed inside the house, while "masculine" work involves heavier and dirtier tasks performed outdoors. But, for most families in rural villages, the gendered division of labor is more of an ideal than a reality. The imperative is to keep adolescent girls under the surveillance of adults or spying eyes of younger children. Boys are most likely to do farm work or perform other tasks outside the village and the household compound, while girls are most likely to do housework. Household composition is the most decisive factor in the allocation of work. For example, in a household with which I have a long association, there were eight boys and six girls in the 1970s. The older children were mainly boys. From the age of about seven until they were adults, the boys did most of the "feminine" household work—cleaning, washing, carrying water, ironing and mending clothes, collecting seafood at low tide, sweeping the house, and soothing babies by carrying them around. They also did the "masculine work"—cutting firewood, making fires, preparing the ground oven, boiling the staple foods, feeding animals, collecting coconuts, and helping to plant, weed, and harvest crops. During school holidays, all the older children collected coconuts and carried them to the copra drier at a village store to pay for their school fees. The younger children were mainly girls and had an easier time than their elder brothers.

However, in two neighboring households, the older children were all girls, and they did both "feminine" and "masculine" tasks; the teenage girls in these families were praised by older women in the village for working on the family farm and preparing the ground oven, thus placing service to their parents above conformity to the ideal roles of girls. The only task that they never performed was spear fishing or climbing coconut trees to harvest nuts. The only "feminine" task that a boy in female-deficient households would not do is plaiting sleeping mats and ceremonial fine mats (*'ie tōga*). *Fa'afāfine*, however, will perform both of these tasks, although in the past, some of my informants insist, they would not have made fine mats. It is not role that defines the *fa'afafine*, but demeanor and preferences. In the setting I describe above, there was a youth aged about nineteen whom others called *fa'afafine*. He lived in a household that had no shortage of girls to perform "feminine" tasks or boys to perform those defined as "masculine." Like the boys in the female-deficient household, he did all gendered tasks required of him, but what identified him as *fa'afafine* in the minds of his family and community, and perhaps in his own mind, was his evident preference for the work and company of girls and women.

At this point, we might consider the question: If transgender males are indeed a Samoan institution, why aren't transgender females? If boys are socialized to do girls' work, why not the opposite as well? Transgender females are not a widely recognized category of persons in Samoa, although the term "*tomboy*" has gained currency since the 1960s to stigmatize some women (Tcherkézoff, this volume). I have heard this term used in more sophisticated urban circles to disparage certain unmarried women in a derogatory manner intended to imply that these women are lesbians. I have also heard it used teasingly of girls who behave roughly or are unkempt. While awareness of the possibility of woman-to-woman sexuality and transgender females has trickled into public consciousness from overseas with returning migrants and the increasing importance of mass media, it is generally considered to be something unlikely to occur in Samoa and, if it does, is vehemently disapproved of. In the 1970s, I knew of only one woman who was referred to disparagingly as *fa'atama* (boyish), and this only on the occasion when she was fined by the village council for verbally abusing someone else. She was in her forties and unmarried—a brisk, unusually slim women who wore her hair short instead of long in a bun, as most women did at that time, and did boys' and men's work (in a household with no shortage of boys and men), such as tending to ground ovens and planting. However, she was by no means the only older woman in the village who conformed to that description, although she was the only unmarried and childless one. When the village council fined her, she was instructed to act in a more womanlike manner.

Generally, older women can transgress gender boundaries more freely without risking being stigmatized. Although some men may express resentment, many older women exercise a commanding presence in their families, hold titles and, in some villages, sit in on the village council. They may take on roles generally considered unfeminine, such as becoming market gardeners, traders, or executives and managers in government and business. Adherence to norms concerning gendered roles and behavior becomes increasingly less important for women as they age. Older women can joke together salaciously and transgressively and also engage in sexual satire. One woman of my acquaintance was renowned for her clowning in the *fiafia* (entertainment) held after meetings of her village women's committee. Her routine mockingly mimed sexual intercourse and reduced her audience to tears of laughter every time she performed it.

Fa'afafine and Sexual Surrogacy

As I have demonstrated, *fa'afāfine* are defined by demeanor and preferences rather than by the roles to which they are socialized or have chosen for themselves. Problematically, and in the face of considerable evidence to the contrary, Drozdow-St. Christian defines *fa'afafine* as "a third transient sex . . . transient because *fa'afafine* for the most part become male by their late 20s or early 30s" (2002, 155). Being *fa'afafine* may possibly be transient for many youths, but as there are a great many middle-aged *fa'afāfine,* it is evident that, for many, the identity is lifelong. In contemporary Samoa since the 1970s, *fa'afāfine* have established their own urban subculture and community associations (Schmidt 2003; cf. Dolgoy, this volume).

Drozdow-St. Christian asserts that "there is no *conventional prohibition* against casual homosexual sex" (2002, 151) and that "[i]t is generally expected that boys will have some homosexual experience in their adolescence and *soa* partners [i.e., age mates who are circumcised or tattooed together] can also be sexual partners . . ." (2002, 152; my italics). While Drozdow-St. Christian may have ethnographic evidence of such practices, there is a great gulf between what is considered legitimate, conventional, or even tolerated on the one hand and, on the other, what is unspoken, illicit, and very furtively—although no doubt commonly—practiced. When I first conducted fieldwork in Samoa in the 1970s, I could only discuss sexual matters (apart from with my Samoan husband) with the nurses serving as public health and family planning advisers who assisted me with my research. This is because sexual matters of any kind may only ever be alluded to in jokes and humorous innuendo, and are otherwise shrouded in silence and secrecy. The nurses I spoke with denied that homosexuality, in the sense of sex between normatively gendered men, could exist in Samoa under any circumstances (Schoeffel 1979). They were convinced that a Samoan male person would never sexually penetrate another male person, but agreed that it was possible that a masculine male person would penetrate a *fa'afafine* (because they were not considered male)—not out of sexual preference, in their opinion, but because of lack of sexual access to a woman. I tried to challenge this assertion. For example, in one interview, my nurse informant told me that, in her village, a schoolteacher (who had never been considered *fa'afafine*) had been dismissed from his post for engaging in a sexual act with a teenage boy who was not considered *fa'afafine* either. I suggested that this must have been an example of a male person desiring to have sex with another male person. My informant admitted that perhaps it was, but explained it as a unique aberration; she had heard that the dismissed teacher had a deformed penis, too small to have intercourse with a woman, and so his sexual frustration led him to try to have sexual relations with a boy. It seemed likely to me that this was a post hoc rationalization, an attempt to explain a situation that was otherwise unthinkable in terms of prevailing beliefs, and her account resembles the "somatic" explanations, common throughout the Pacific Islands, that attribute non-heteronormative desire to physiology.

My point is further illustrated by the Samoan government censor's ban on the film *Milk* in April 2009, much to the surprise of foreign observers who considered Samoans "tolerant" of "sexual diversity." The film represents intimate partnerships between two normatively gendered male persons. The censor was correct in his judgment that it was likely to shock many Samoans, but this was not, as some Western commentators thought, because Samoans are devout Christians. Heterosexually explicit mainstream films have not been banned in Samoa, nor have films depicting promiscuity, adultery, and rape. The objection to *Milk* was more cultural than moral.

Overt association between *fa'afafine* and homosexual practices has only very recently entered public discourse in Samoa. Since 2008, the Samoa Fa'afafine Association (Samoa's prime minister is their patron) has called for the revocation of laws that criminalize sodomy and female impersonation. In 2011, the Samoa Law Reform Commission announced that there might be a review of both sodomy and adultery laws under the 1921 and 1961 Crimes Ordinance. The announcement provoked expressions of outrage by several church groups as well as private citizens, who expressed the opinion that decriminalization of homosexuality and adultery was against God's laws and would undermine the moral fabric of society and Samoan culture. In August 2011, letters to the editor of the *Samoa Observer* raged back and forth between advocates of criminalization laws—with some referring to *fa'afāfine* as perverts who have chosen a life of sin—and members of the *fa'afafine* community and others calling for understanding and tolerance and observance of Samoa's constitutional endorsement of human rights. It was subsequently announced in the *Samoa Observer* (September 21, 2011) that the laws would not be revoked, apparently because, although rarely if ever enforced, these laws reflected the moral principles of a Christian country.

Samoa is a land of ostentatious Christian piety, where the constitution declares that Samoa is "Founded on God." Most speeches employ biblical allusions; prayers precede all formalities; and most villages have at least one large church (more often two or three), a pastor's house, and a church hall. Most people attend several church services on Sundays, usually clad in white garments. But though Samoans profess Christian belief in the ideals of premarital chastity and marital monogamy, there is a certain cognitive dissonance about ideals of morality and masculinity. Male adolescents and younger men are generally conceptualized as, and perhaps even tacitly encouraged to be, predatory sexual beings lacking self-control, from whom women must be on guard and protected, particularly unmarried women who want to keep their socially valued reputations for virginity. An unpublished study conducted in New Zealand on Samoan male attitudes toward sexuality and reproduction (Anae et al. 2000) includes a number of interviews with older Samoan men born and socialized in Samoa who admitted that they had fathered children out of wedlock and declared their belief that for men the quest for sexual experiences with as many women as possible is a biological necessity, an inevitable behavior beyond their control. A typical statement cited by an older man was:

> *[O] lagona o le soifuaga e le mafai ona aveesea, o le natura o le tagata,*
> *e iai ona lagona i tulaga fa'apea, i le age ua tatau ona fai lagona ia.*
> "[T]hese are natural feelings, which are hard to resist, even at this
> age." (Anae et al. 2000, 73)

Drozdow-St. Christian's representation of *fa'afafine* has a certain validity insofar as the Samoan template of sexuality defines penetration as masculine and receptivity as feminine. Historically, sexual penetration was celebrated as the epitome of masculine power, explicit in myths of the divine ancestors of all Samoans featuring Pili, the phallic eel (or lizard) penetrating Sina, the daughter of heaven (Krämer 1994 [1902], 587). Sexually explicit songs were sung at marriage festivities in celebration of aristocratic fertility, extolling the shedding of hymeneal blood after the penetration of virgins and the act of procreation, the ejaculation of semen, the quickening of the womb, and the conception of a child (Moyle 1975). The term *usu*, which can be glossed as "called" or "courted" but implies "conquered" in this context, is used in the standard formula of Samoan genealogies to indicate the primacy of sexual union; for example, "*sa usu* Tui Manu'a *ia* Sina"—"Tui Manu'a conquered [had sexual intercourse with] Sina" (Milner 1993 [1966], 304). The fetishization of defloration persisted long after it was abolished as a chiefly marriage rite (Freeman 1983, 244–249). The conquest of virgins is a thrilling sexual challenge for young men, one to be boasted about to other young men—unless the object of the conquest is to take the conquered girl as wife (Isaia 1999, 142). Christian teaching on sexual morality in Samoa lays more emphasis upon word than deed, and masculinity is covertly associated with considerable sexual latitude. The sexual template of conquering masculinity and submissive femininity leaves no space in the mainstream Samoan cultural imagination for the acceptance of male-to-male sexuality, but it does allow the possibility of male to male-as-female sexuality.

Conclusion

In this chapter, I have contested functionalist explanations offered for the perceived institutionalization of *fa'afāfine* in Samoa. The assertion that the institutionalization of transgender males reinforces masculine psychosexual development is contradicted by the aggressive socialization of Samoan boys to conform to ideal norms of masculinity. Some effeminate males may play the role of sexual surrogates, taking on a female role in sexual intercourse that is consistent with the cultural template of masculine conquest and penetration and feminine submission and receptivity. Sex between a masculine male person and a *fa'afafine* would not be considered by either of the partners as a homosexual act. However, it is highly unlikely that any family would socialize their sons for such a role. *Fa'afāfine* are not primarily identified by their sexuality or their roles, but by their demeanor. Nor is there any evidence to sustain the proposition that some boys are deliberately socialized to assume the role of women or girls to balance the household division of labor when families have a shortage of girls. I have shown that the social expectations of children and youth prioritize service to their elders over conformity to ideal gender roles. Children and adolescents will do almost all gendered tasks if they are required to do so, irrespective of their sex.

Suppose that it were possible for mothers to deliberately socialize their sons to become *fa'afāfine* or to elicit transgender identities in enough men to provide psychosexual encouragement for the development of culturally approved masculine identities. The question must then be asked: Why, in so status-conscious a society as Samoa, within the parameters of cultural notions of gender and sexuality, would any parent encourage a son to embrace a status lacking the most honored or admired aspects of adult masculinity and femininity? Children are discouraged from attention-getting behavior through mockery and teasing. Although some parents might find it cute in very small boys, in my observations little boys are likely to be mocked for "girlish" behavior. Samoans usually show little concern about the gendered behavior of young children, but when they approach puberty, effeminacy is usually discouraged or punished, especially by fathers. I have never known of a woman who welcomed effeminacy in her son, although most women are considerably less hostile to effeminate demeanor in their sons than men are.

Fa'afāfine are tolerated by most people in Samoa, especially by their families once it is accepted that they will not be deterred from their behavior. They are regarded with affectionate amusement by some—but by no means all—women and ridiculed by most men (despite the fact that, and perhaps because, many have sex with them). For a male to be *fa'afāfine* is to be, in a sense, disabled in relation to Samoa's gendered ideals, and it is pushing the boundaries of Samoan cultural dynamics to suggest that *fa'afāfine* are recognized as a "third sex." Although many *fa'afāfine* are considered to do feminine work better than girls and women, and may be admired for their skill, men who conform to cultural ideals of masculinity remain the ideal sons of Samoa.

Acknowledgments

Thanks to Malama Meleisea, Judith Huntsman, and Kalissa Alexeyeff for their helpful comments on early drafts of this paper; I am particularly grateful to Niko Besnier and Kalissa Alexeyeff for their editorial contribution to the final draft.

Note

1   Cross-culturally, circumcision is often interpreted as an affirmation of masculinity, and it no doubt serves this purpose in Samoa. However, it produces a nature–culture distinction consistent with the binary worldview encapsulated in the ancient notion of *feagaiga*—foreskins are associated with animals, so the removal of the foreskin may serve to transfer a boy from the natural to the cultural domain.

References

Alexeyeff, Kalissa. 2000. Dragging Drag: The Performance of Gender and Sexuality in the Cook Islands. *The Australian Journal of Anthropology* 11(2): 97–307.

Anae, Melani, et al. 2000. Report of Research on Samoan Male Attitudes to Reproductive Health. Unpublished manuscript, University of Auckland.

Besnier, Niko. 1994. Polynesian Gender Liminality through Time and Space. In *Third Sex, Third Gender: Beyond Sexual Dimorphism in Culture and History*, ed. Gilbert Herdt, pp. 185–328. New York: Zone.

———. 1997. Sluts and Superwomen: The Politics of Gender Liminality in Urban Tonga. *Ethnos* 62: 5–31.

———. 2002. Transgenderism, Locality, and the Miss Galaxy Beauty Pageant in Tonga. *American Ethnologist* 29: 534–566.

———. 2004. The Social Production of Abjection: Desire and Silencing among Transgender Tongans. *Social Anthropology* 12: 301–323.

Drozdow-St. Christian, Douglass. 2002. *Elusive Fragments: Making Power, Propriety, and Health in Samoa*. Durham, NC: Carolina Academic Press.

Freeman, Derek. 1983. *Margaret Mead and Samoa: The Making and Unmaking of an Anthropological Myth*. Cambridge, MA: Harvard University Press.

Isaia, Malopaʻupo. 1999. *Coming of Age in American Anthropology: Margaret Mead and Paradise*. Los Angeles: Universal Publishers/uPUBLISH.com.

Jenkins, Carol. 2005. *HIV/AIDS in the Pacific*. Manila: Asian Development Bank.

———. 2006. Male Sexuality and HIV: The Case of Male-to-Male Sex. Background paper produced for the conference Risks and Responsibilities: Male Sexual Health and HIV in Asia and the Pacific International Consultation, New Delhi, September 23–26, 2006.

Jordan-Young, Rebecca M. 2010. *Brain Storm: The Flaws in the Science of Sex Differences*. Cambridge, MA: Harvard University Press.

Krämer, Augustin. 1994 [1902]. *The Samoa Islands*. Volume I. Trans. Theodore Verhaaren. Honolulu: University of Hawaiʻi Press.

Levy, Robert I. 1971. The Community Functions of Tahitian Male Transvestites. *Anthropological Quarterly* 44: 12–21.

———. 1973. *Tahitians: Mind and Experience in the Society Islands.* Chicago: University of Chicago Press.

Mageo, Jeanette Marie. 1992. Male Transvestism and Cultural Change in Samoa. *American Ethnologist* 19: 443–459.

———. 1996a. Samoa, on the Wilde Side: Male Transvestism, Oscar Wilde, and Liminality in Making Gender. *Ethos* 24: 588–625.

———. 1996b. Spirit Girls and Marines: Possession and Ethnopsychiatry as Historical Discourses in Samoa. *American Ethnologist* 23: 61–82.

———. 1999. *Theorizing Self in Samoa: Emotions, Gender, and Sexualities.* Ann Arbor, MI: University of Michigan Press.

———. 2008. Zones of Ambiguity and Identity Politics in Samoa. *Journal of the Royal Anthropological Institute* 14 [n.s.]: 61–78.

Mead, Margaret. 1928. *Coming of Age in Samoa: A Psychological Study of Primitive Youth for Western Civilisation.* New York: William Morrow & Co.

Milner, G. B. 1993 [1966]. *Samoan Dictionary.* Auckland: Polynesian Press.

Money, John. 1968. *Sex Errors of the Body.* Baltimore: Johns Hopkins University Press.

Moyle, Richard M. 1975. Sexuality in Samoan Art Forms. *Archives of Sexual Behaviour* 3: 227–247.

Poasa, Kris, H. Ray Blanchard, and Kenneth J. Zucker. 2004. Birth Order in Transgendered Males from Polynesia: A Quantitative Study of Samoan Fa'afāfine. *Journal of Sex and Marital Therapy* 30: 13–23.

Sahlins, Marshall. 1981. *Historical Metaphors and Mythical Realities: Structure in the Early History of the Sandwich Islands Kingdom.* Ann Arbor: University of Michigan Press.

Schmidt, Johanna M. 2003. Paradise Lost? Social Change and Fa'afafine in Samoa. *Current Sociology* 51: 417–432.

Schoeffel, Penelope. 1979. Daughters of Sina: A Study of Gender, Status and Power in Samoa. Ph.D. diss., Department of Anthropology, Australian National University.

———. 1995. The Samoan Concept of Feagaiga and Its Transformation. In *Tonga and Samoa: Images of Gender and Polity,* ed. Judith Huntsman, pp. 85–106. Christchurch: Macmillan Brown Centre for Pacific Studies.

———. 1998. Review of *Theorizing Self in Samoa: Emotions, Genders, and Sexualities,* by Jeannette Marie Mageo. *Oceania* 71: 161.

———. 1999. Samoan Exchange and "Fine Mats": An Historical Reconsideration. *Journal of the Polynesian Society* 108: 117–148.

———. 2005. Sexual Morality in Samoa and Its Historical Transformations. In *A Polymath Anthropologist: Essays in Honour of Ann Chowning,* ed. Claudia Gross, Harriet D. Lyons, and Dorothy Ayers Counts, pp. 63–69. Auckland: Department of Anthropology, University of Auckland.

Shore, Bradd. 1982. *Sala'ilua, a Samoan Mystery.* New York: Columbia University Press.

Sinavaiana, Caroline. 1992. *Clowning as Critical Practice: Performance Humor in the South Pacific.* Pittsburgh: University of Pittsburgh Press.

Tcherkézoff, Serge. 2004. *Tahiti 1768: Jeunes filles en pleurs: La face cachée des premiers contacts et la naissance du mythe occidental.* Papeete: Au Vent des Îles.

———. 2008. *"First Contacts" in Polynesia: The Samoan Case (1722–1848): Western Misunderstandings about Sexuality and Divinity.* Canberra: ANU E-Press.

Vasey, Paul L., and Doug P. Vanderlaan. 2007. Birth Order and Male Androphilia in Samoan Fa'afafine. *Proceedings of the Royal Society for Biological Sciences* 274: 1437–1442.

Wallace, Lee. 2003. *Sexual Encounters: Pacific Texts, Modern Sexualities.* Ithaca, NY: Cornell University Press.

PART II

Performing Gender

CHAPTER 5

Living as and Living with *Māhū* and *Raerae*

Geopolitics, Sex, and Gender in the Society Islands

Makiko Kuwahara

This chapter concerns two transgender categories, *māhū* and *raerae*, as they are deployed in different ways in the two major centers of the Society Islands, Tahiti and Bora Bora. The differences between the categories on the two islands are both surprising and significant, in that they highlight the specific and divergent effects of the interactions of local engagements with global and neocolonial forms, in this particular case tourism and the French military, on sexuality and gender. My analysis of sexual difference on the two islands within the same polity animates a comparative perspective that underlines the importance of historical and geographical specificity for an understanding of the ways in which sexual identities are crafted. While the analysis provides another instance of globalization triggering an efflorescence of gendered and sexualized identities and practices, it also highlights the importance of local dynamics in giving particular meaning to these new identities and practices. In other words, the "frictional relation between geopolitics and embodied desires" (Patton and Sánchez-Eppeler 2000, 3; cf. Tsing 2004) gives rise to not only global homogeneity but also new forms of difference. These differences require us to question more closely what the "local" actually means in analyses of globalization and to track in close and concrete terms local variations of global forms.

Earlier in this volume, Elliston provided a detailed account of gender politics in French Polynesia and of the historical trajectory of the two terms used to describe transgender individuals, *māhū* and *raerae*. As she has shown, *māhū* have been visible as family and community members since the pre-contact period. Early European voyagers' logs and early ethnographic accounts introduced Tahitian *māhū* into the Western colonial imagination (Bligh 1789, 2:16–17; Levy 1973; Morrison 1935, 238; Mortimer 1791, 47; Wilson 1799, 156). In contrast, the term *"raerae"* emerged much later to refer to people who wear female clothing and makeup, and sometimes engage in more extensive modifications of the body, such as hormone treatment and sex-reassignment surgery.

Today, however, perceptions of *māhū* and *raerae* differ between Tahiti and Bora Bora because of the different economic, political, and sexual neo-colonial relationships forged on these two islands. As Elliston (this volume) notes, people on Tahiti tend to differentiate *māhū* from *raerae* by regarding the former as "traditional" and "culturally authentic" and the latter as "new" and "culturally inauthentic." They generally consider *māhū* to be good advisers and caretakers in communities. *Māhū* are considered "traditional" in the sense that they are believed to have always existed. One example is a scene in a local documentary entitled *Mahu, l'efféminé* (Corillion 2001) that depicts the appointment of a prominent *māhū* to the judging committee of the annual Heiva Arts Festival, presented in such a way as to emphasize that *māhū* have always played an important social and cultural role in the performing arts. *Māhū* establish and maintain their social status by differentiating themselves from *raerae,* who, as *māhū* and others on Tahiti view them, are Western-style transgender individuals, engage in sex work, and are immoral and inauthentic. The social marginalization of *raerae* on Tahiti is caused not only by their identificational aspirations and their occupation, but also by their often fraught relationships with both family members and French people.

On Bora Bora, in contrast, the designation of *māhū* as traditional and authentic and *raerae* as new and inauthentic does not apply; both are integrated and valued within their families and in the tourist industry. In contrast to Tahiti, Bora Bora does not have military bases, and the islanders' main contact with the outside world is through tourism, particularly high-end tourism. So although *raerae* on Bora Bora are seen on the streets at night interacting with tourists in ways that may be considered very similar to sex work, they are not labeled as sex workers. Indeed, many *raerae* on Bora Bora claim that they have sexual relationships with foreigners for pleasure and not for money. It is significant that most foreigners are European and American, and *raerae* and others claim with pride that these tourists visit Bora Bora to seek sexual relationships with *raerae* because they are internationally famed for their sexual prowess.[1]

As I will show, in both places perceptions of *māhū* and *raerae* as either traditional or new, and the associated positive and negative evaluations to which they are subject, are shaped by the kind of labor they undertake and their engagement with family and community. Of course, this distinction is ideological, and some transgender people on Tahiti and Bora Bora adopt the terms situationally, moving between the categories according to context and across their life course.

A comparison of *māhū*'s and *raerae*'s relationships to families, communities, and workplaces on Tahiti and Bora Bora sheds light on the complexity of gender and sexual identity formation, as well as on the role that globalization and neocolonial relations have on the construction of the categories. Gender and sexual identity are intertwined with national and island identity, and people's political and economic positions within a global system inform their intimate experiences.

Tahiti and Bora Bora Compared

The Society Islands and surrounding island groups became a protectorate of France in 1842, a French overseas territory in 1946, and a French Overseas Collectivity in 2004. This means that France still controls French Polynesia, and many Polynesians view this control as a neocolonial and unwanted presence. The ethnic composition of the population has changed in the course of colonial history and consequent political shifts. Today, Polynesians, the indigenous people of French Polynesia, make up 66 percent of the population. Europeans (*Pōpaʻa*), who comprise 12 percent of the population, are predominately French people (*Farani*) who reside in French Polynesia for a few years working as government officials, teachers, and military personnel. Asians (*Tinito*) make up 5 percent of the population and *"Demis,"* people of mixed Polynesian, European, and Chinese descent, constitute 17 percent. Employment, income, and status differences tend to operate along racial lines. Most French people work in high-level public service positions, are well-paid, and have access to generous benefits. People of Chinese decent tend to work in commerce and in the black-pearl industry. *Demis* also hold prestigious jobs of high visibility in politics, finance, and the tourist industry.

French Polynesia consists of five archipelagos: the Society Islands, the Tuamotus, the Gambier Islands, the Austral Islands, and the Marquesas. People living in each archipelago have their own language and culture, but everywhere French is the official language and lifestyles have been strongly influenced by French culture and, increasingly, by other "global" forms from America and Asia. A wide range of products imported mainly from France but also from Australia and New Zealand are sold in French chain super-markets like Carrefour. The French television station Canal+ presents not only French but also American soap operas and Japanese anime.

The incursion of global forces has had different outcomes in each island group, depending on geographical accessibility and the political and economic role played by each group. As Elliston has shown earlier in this volume, two key events were particularly influential in reshaping the overall context of life in French Polynesia, including sexuality and gender iden-tity: the opening of Fa'a'a International Airport in 1960 and the estab-lishment of the Centre d'Expérimentation du Pacifique (CEP) for nuclear testing in 1962. With the rapid economic development French Polynesia underwent throughout the 1960s and 1970s consequent upon these events, an increasing number of military personnel and tourists began to visit the territory and spurred the development of a sex industry.[2] Visitors sought sexual relationships not only with women but also with *māhū*. It may have been around this time that the term "*raerae*" came into use. The exact origin of the term is not known, but Robert Levy (1973, 140) suggests that it was the nickname of an early *māhū* sex worker. In addition, military personnel and tourists began introducing Western gay and lesbian cultures to Tahiti, giving *māhū* and *raerae* further options for fashioning the presentation of their gender and sexuality. When *raerae* worked for or had close relation-ships with French men, people on Tahiti considered *raerae* to be complicit with the forces of globalization and neocolonialism particularly associated with the CEP and military bases, and negatively stereotyped them.

Tahiti and Bora Bora have a large concentration of both *māhū* and *raerae,* mainly because of employment opportunities and the attractions of an urban lifestyle. Like many other young people, they move from their home islands seeking higher education and employment. Half of French Polynesia's 267,000 inhabitants live on Tahiti, and it is the political and economic center of the islands. Tahiti is connected to the outside world through Fa'a'a International Airport and several ports, which harbor fish-ing boats and luxury cruisers. All important government offices, tourism facilities, and shopping strips are located in Papeete, the capital. The con-centration of military personnel, seamen, and tourists in Papeete supports a lively entertainment district with many restaurants, bars, and nightclubs. The inhabitants of Papeete and its peripheries lead more urbanized life-styles than the inhabitants of other districts.

With a population of 8,930 (Institut de la statistique de la Polynésie Française 2010), Bora Bora is located 230 kilometers from Tahiti and can be reached by air or sea. With its dramatic volcanic landscape surrounded by a beautiful lagoon, Bora Bora is the second most popular tourist destination after Tahiti. Tourism generates employment in hotels and restaurants, safari tours, island tours, water sport activities, dance shows, and spas, and in the black-pearl and craft industries. Approximately 196,496 international tourists visit French Polynesia annually, mainly from the United States, Japan, France, and other European countries. In 2005, Bora Bora had 103,500 tourist arrivals, with fourteen hotels that provide 1,005 rooms and have a capacity for 2,296 people. Tahiti has 143,533 tourists visit annually, with ten hotels with 1,253 rooms and a capacity of 2,745 (Service du Tourisme 2006).[3]

Although Tahiti has the largest number of tourist arrivals, most tourists consider it merely a transit point to Bora Bora, Moorea, or Rangiroa. Both Bora Bora and Tahiti are considered very touristic islands, although travelers in search of more "authentic" cultural experiences prefer the Marquesas and Austral Islands. Bora Bora's tourism industry targets the luxury market, offering exclusive resorts and top-class facilities. The development of tourism is one significant impetus for many *māhū* and *raerae* to move to Bora Bora and Tahiti. Mainstream Polynesians consider *māhū* and *raerae* as being good at foreign languages, skilled at customer service, and careful in their self-presentation, characteristics that are well suited for work in the tourism industry.

Identity Politics: Race, Gender, and Sexuality

Characterizing Pacific Island categories of non-heteronormative gender as "transgender" or "transsexual" is potentially problematic, because these Western categories do not capture the subjectivity and identification of transgender individuals in the Pacific (Alexeyeff and Besnier, this volume; Alexeyeff 2008, 2009; Besnier 1994, 1997; Roen 2006). In addition, Pacific Island gender categories may be intertwined with other forms of identification such as race, national histories, and regional histories (cf. Jackson 2009). As the material presented here shows, in French Polynesia, the terms *māhū* and *raerae* imply not only gender and sexuality but also *la culture ma'ohi* or "Tahitian culture," which is embedded in social structures and relationships that are historically and geographically specific not simply at the national level but at the level of specific islands.

Polynesians establish and demonstrate their identity in various ways. First, they foreground a sense of belonging to the land, which ties them to their ancestors, on whom they base their claims to indigenous rights to the land in the contemporary neocolonial context (Elliston 2000; Kahn 2000, 2011). Indeed, this relationship to the land is the foundation of the Polynesian extended family structure that connects people to the land and their ancestors. Within the extended family and across families, relatives are expected to provide mutual material support as well as take care of children and the elderly. Polynesians consider these strong family relationships to be a significant aspect of their culture, and one that indexes the central values of *la culture ma'ohi:* sharing, generosity, and community and place-based orientation.

Second, Polynesian identity is constructed through language and by the revival of "cultural" activities such as dancing, singing, playing musical instruments, tattooing, canoeing, and craft making (Kuwahara 2005; Saura 2009; Stevenson 1992). These activities have not been practiced continuously since the pre-European contact period. In fact, many (e.g., dancing and tattooing) became prohibited at the time of Christianization and had not been popularly practiced until the cultural revitalization movement of the 1980s. The cultural revitalization and construction of *ma'ohi* identity was led by Henri Hiro and Duro Raapoto, talented theologians and poets, and was followed by the creation of national cultural institutions: La Maison des Jeunes—Maison de la Culture (for theater, performance, and other cultural activities) was established in 1970; l'Académie Tahitienne (language) and le Musée de Tahiti et des Îles (archeology, anthropology, and history of the islands) in 1974; Conservatoire Artistique (dance and music) in 1978; and le Centre des Métiers d'Arts (art and crafts, particularly sculpture on wood, stone, bone, and mother-of-pearl) in 1980. Traditional styles have been researched, revised, and incorporated into contemporary forms of cultural activities by dancers, musicians, artisans, and teachers who studied seventeenth- and eighteenth-century European sources. A sense of continuity with older forms of cultural production is considered important both by its practitioners and by local audiences. At the same time, new forms that demonstrate individual artistic talent and global influences have also developed within a broadly "traditional" aesthetic format.

Cultural revitalization and anticolonial sentiment have meant that Polynesians view France and French people who live on Tahiti ambivalently. Since first contact with Europeans in the eighteenth century, intermarriage between Polynesians and French, as well as other Europeans and Chinese, has increased, and many households have mixed racial backgrounds. Many Polynesians also have French, Chinese, or *Demi* friends and colleagues at school and work, and rarely express anti-French sentiments openly. On the one hand, French men and women, as well as *Demi,* are often considered to be more intelligent, richer, and more beautiful. Polynesian women may say that they prefer having a French partner because Polynesian men hit their wives when they get drunk. The absence of physical violence and the prospect of social and economic mobility make French men especially attractive. At the same time, the Polynesian independence movement often protests the French presence on Tahiti, but less so on other islands like Bora Bora. In everyday contexts, some Polynesians also complain that "the *Farani* (French people) have taken our work" and that "it is difficult to work with *Farani* because they are too mannered," meaning too formal and patronizing. Increasingly, the value attributed to ma'ohi identity has led to some Polynesian women saying they will marry only a Polynesian husband and to their treating French men with contempt (Saura 1998, 98).[4]

It is in this context that Tahitian *raerae* are often considered "new," "artificial," and *"Pōpa'a"* by mainstream Tahitians. *Pōpa'a,* the term used to describe white people, here also refers to the French-inflected West and is often used interchangeably with the designation *Farani.* Mainstream Tahitians see *raerae*'s involvement in sex work and desire for sex-reassignment surgery as signaling a Western-style sexuality that, together with their adoption of *Pōpa'a* styles of clothing and comportment, helps to construct them as an allegory of the destructive impact of foreigners—particularly the French—on ma'ohi values. Because the term *"raerae"* has negative connotations on Tahiti, *raerae* often choose to refer to themselves by the French term *"l'efféminé"* (cf. Elliston, this volume). For mainstream Polynesians and *raerae* themselves, *l'efféminé* embodies nontraditional and cosmopolitan signs of transgender identity, but it is a far more neutral term than *raerae.*

Polynesian attitudes toward neocolonialism and global forces color their relationships with non-Polynesians, particularly the French. Although many pursue Western, consumer-oriented lifestyles and have non-Polynesian friends, spouses, or relatives, they also emphasize revitalized forms of *la culture ma'ohi* and a *ma'ohi* identity in the context of the ongoing political struggle for independence. These tensions are particularly evident on Tahiti, and they shape the way transgender identities are defined; *raerae* are categorized in derogatory terms such as "culturally inauthentic" and "new" and different from *māhū*, who are positively evaluated as "culturally authentic" and "traditional."

Living as *Māhū* and *Raerae* on Tahiti and Bora Bora

It goes without saying that *māhū* and *raerae* lead diverse lives, but it is equally true that, in all contexts, their lives are informed by the complex interface of global and local forces, making for a lived reality that is invariably more complicated than the stereotypes applied to them. With these qualifications in mind, I now present two examples of the contrasting lifestyles and identifications of *raerae* and *māhū* on Tahiti and Bora Bora in order to illustrate the arguments I have made hitherto.[5]

On Tahiti

Cindy lives in a Papeete flat, which she shares with her roommate Vanessa, located above a grocery shop run by a Chinese-Tahitian family five minutes' walk from The Pool Bar, where she is employed as a waitress.[6] This is a place where locals, military personnel, and tourists play pool and drink. On weekends, bands play local music and people enjoy dancing. Both Cindy and Vanessa consider themselves *efféminé*, but others refer to them as *raerae* (and I use this term throughout for the sake of simplicity). When I visited their flat one day in 2006, Cindy and Vanessa were in the living room. Vanessa was holding her swollen foot over a bucket and rubbing it with an ice cube. "What happened?" I asked. She grimaced and explained that the night before she had been standing on the side of the road with some friends when several Tahitian men drove past, shouting and laughing at them. Vanessa and her friends shouted back, but got frightened when they turned around. The men ran over Vanessa's foot before driving off. Although terrified, both girls ("*filles*" is a term *raerae* often use to refer to themselves) did not view the event as unusual, as *raerae* often experience this kind of verbal abuse and physical violence on the streets.

"That's why I don't like Tahitian men," Vanessa explained. "They are mean, they are violent." "What about French men?" I asked. Vanessa was striking looking, with large breasts and blond hair; she had been crowned "Miss Piano" a few years back. She had a French patron who gave her money, bought her dresses, and had paid for her breast-enlargement surgery. "They are kind. They are more open-minded and understanding of people like us. Normally, Tahitian men are nice but once they drink they change," Cindy added, pulling her *pāreu* (sarong) up above her breasts in the manner of a Tahitian woman. Cindy had also had French boyfriends—six of them in total over the course of her life. They were all military personnel and all had left Tahiti after completing their tour of duty. She did not want to have a French boyfriend again, because he would only leave and break her heart. She also doubted that she would be able to find a nice Polynesian boyfriend, because they were often nasty to *raerae*.

Cindy was slim and attractive as well. Numerous professional photographs of her adorned the walls of her room, and Vanessa's room was similarly decorated. In the portraits, they wore elegant evening dresses and theatrical makeup. Cindy used to take hormones but stopped because it made her gain weight. She did not have breast implants, nor had she had sex-reassignment surgery, and she did not plan to have either in the future. She was quite happy with her physical body. Next to the television set was a photograph of herself as a young man in military uniform. Cindy had enjoyed her military service, extending it to twenty-four months. She would show me numerous photographs of herself and friends, both *raerae* and French men, burned onto a compact disk.

Those who practice cross-dressing and body modification are often obsessed by their changed bodies and are particularly interested in photos of themselves, as was the case with Cindy and Vanessa. Cindy was only one of many *raerae* on Tahiti and Bora Bora who showed me photos of themselves during my fieldwork before their change from male to female. Moreover, those who used to wear women's clothes and makeup and now wore men's clothes showed me photos of their female appearance in the past, bringing to mind the point that "[p]hotography is prized not for its ability to capture lived experience but for its capacity to create 'memories' markedly different from the goings-on of everyday life" (Adrian 2003, 10).

Cindy was from an island in the Tuamotu group. Her father had died when she was still young and she had been brought up by her grandmother. After her military service, she settled in Papeete, as she enjoyed the urban lifestyle and felt it would be a better environment for her to experiment with women's clothes and makeup and with her sexuality. She had worked at the Pool Bar since the age of twenty-two. After watching a Bollywood movie on a DVD that she had borrowed from a *raerae* friend, Cindy and I left the flat, dropping by the shop downstairs to buy a packet of cigarettes. "Ciao Ciao!" she called out to the shop staff as we left, in a display of linguistic cosmopolitanism. Her voice was so loud that everybody in the shop heard her. She walked off with an exaggerated hip sway, all eyes on her.

When I visited Cindy again in the summer of 2008, I was surprised at how crowded the flat had become. Many of her and Vanessa's friends were now also living there. In the living room there was even a large black dog. "Don't worry! She likes all girls. Only girls!" Vanessa and her friends were preparing Vanessa's costumes for l'élection de la Miss vahine-tane, a popular beauty contest for *raerae* held at the Club Med on Bora Bora. In Cindy's room, three girls were watching the DVD of the previous year's contest. One of them, aged sixteen, was also a candidate in the contest, which would be held the following week, and everybody was excited about helping her prepare. The friends had moved into Cindy's flat because they were *fiu* or "fed up" with living in their parents' houses. They would move out of Cindy's flat when they became *fiu* living with their friends. Many *raerae* in Papeete lived together in a similar arrangement. I occasionally saw relatives and woman friends visiting them, but generally these *raerae* kept at a distance from their relatives if the latter did not accept them.

In August 2009, I went to Cindy's flat again but found it vacant. As I wandered outside, the neighbor came out and told me that they had recently moved out, but she did not know where they had gone. So I went to Cindy's workplace. As it was only five p.m., the bar was quiet. A couple of locals were playing pool and a few girls were drinking beer at the bar. Cindy was not working that shift, but her colleague gave me her new phone number, and I called her. She had moved on her own to a one-bedroom flat with a combined kitchen–dining room. She told me she didn't feel lonely, as her friends often visited and sometimes stayed with her. Vanessa had gone to live in France, where she depended on friends who had been living there for a long time. Cindy didn't know when or whether she would come back. I asked her if she also wanted to move to France, but she said she probably wouldn't because she liked Tahiti. She didn't want to return to her home island either, because she would be bored living there—there were only beaches and fish, no nightclubs or friends. Cindy was well connected to other *raerae* on Tahiti, but detached from her family and communities on her island.

On Bora Bora

When I started research on Bora Bora in 2006, I asked people what they thought the differences were between *māhū* and *raerae* and was often surprised to hear them say, "They are the same." On one occasion, I was introduced to a Japanese woman who had many *māhū* and *raerae* friends. Having worked as a hairdresser in Japan, Chiho was now a wedding organizer for Japanese couples, setting hair and doing makeup for Japanese brides who had come to get married on Bora Bora. She often offered advice and support to her *raerae* and *māhū* friends about makeup and hair. As there were no weddings scheduled, Chiho took me to her friends' houses. On the front patio, a straight Polynesian couple in their fifties, their son, and Roana, a friend of the couple, were playing bingo. "Come and play with us! Do you know how to play bingo?" the mother of the family said. Roana, unemployed at the time, was in his late twenties. Chiho said people around him identified him as a *māhū*. When I asked Chiho what this meant, she replied that it was because he was quiet but not overly *"efféminé"* and usually dressed in men's clothes, on this day a T-shirt and short pants. He often spent time with the family, sometimes sleeping over for days at a time, a common practice among younger people without children or partners of their own (Kuwahara 2005).

After a few hours a car drove up, and Tina, one of the daughters of this household, came back from the hotel where she worked as a receptionist. Tina, also in her twenties, was identified as a *raerae* by herself and people around her. She changed from her cotton island-print dress into a *pāreu,* tying her long dark hair into a bun as she came out on the patio to join us. In contrast to Roana, Tina was loud and vibrant. She said to me, "You know, I have a lot of Japanese tourists at work. I like them. They are a little shy but friendly. I always introduce myself to them as a Tahitian *okama* ("effeminate man" in Japanese) and they all laugh. Then they want to have their picture taken with me." Tina said she loved talking to people, especially those from different countries, and so loved her work at the hotel.

Roana's and Tina's comportments could not have been more different. Tina oriented herself to the world at large, and her identification as *raerae* signaled this orientation. She adopted a Western name and a flamboyant manner, and she artfully combined this cosmopolitanism with an island-style flair. In Tina's view, her job in the tourism industry placed her in a sophisticated and vibrant circle of different people, cultures, and sexual subjectivities. Roana, on the other hand, was what you might call a typical *māhū*: unassuming and shy with strangers, "traditional" in the sense that he did not overemphasize his female qualities. It appeared to me that, in the idyllic semi-urban setting of Bora Bora, these two transgender categories coexisted unproblematically.

Of course, life is never that simple. On her next day off, Chiho took me to another friend's house, who on our arrival was working on a sewing machine in his little front yard. Heinui, in his thirties, was wearing a T-shirt and had a *pāreu* wrapped around his waist, although he occasionally wore a woman's dress and makeup. Heinui had received a diploma in tourism and used to work in hotels, but at the time of my research he was working as a dressmaker. Heinui said he grew up in a large family to whom he was still very close and who lived nearby. His eldest brother, however, was a *raerae* and had had a difficult time, especially with his father. Having undergone sex-reassignment surgery, this brother moved to New Caledonia, where he lived with a male partner. Heinui explained that when he was born his parents were already old, so they were not as tough on him as they had been on his brother.

Heinui was raising another brother's ten-year-old daughter. He had been taking care of her since she was born and she called Heinui *"Maman."* When her friends pointed out to her, "But he is a *Papa*," Heinui explained to them, "I am a 'person' who cannot be just *papa* or *maman*." Heinui said he was neither man nor woman but a parent for the girl. Heinui had been teaching his daughter that, in order to be respected, she must first respect others, something that his own parents had taught him. The daughter was staying at her biological parents' place at the time of our visit. Heinui said she often stayed with them, as they lived close to Heinui and they were part of the same family.

Dress and Desire

As bodily representation is one of the significant elements that differentiate *māhū* from *raerae*, this section investigates the differences in physical appearance and clothing of *māhū, raerae,* and others between Tahiti and Bora Bora and the extent to which people can be categorized as *māhū* and *raerae* according to their bodily representation.

While many people on Tahiti and Bora Bora differentiate *raerae* from *māhū* by their physical appearance and clothing, the body is not fixed in time or space, but changes over the course of a person's lifetime and across situations. People in French Polynesia, as elsewhere, select clothes according to taste and social norms, which in turn indicate their age, gender, ethnicity, occupation, social and family roles, and place of residence, as well as the situation in which they find themselves. On the different islands of French Polynesia, both male and female children tend to wear similar clothes, usually T-shirts and short pants, until they reach the stage of life called *taure'are'a,* "adolescence," the transition from childhood to adulthood (Kirkpatrick 1987; cf. Schoeffel on Samoa, this volume). From then on, physical differences between women and men become more clearly marked through clothing. At home, women wear a T-shirt, trousers, or a *pāreu,* which can be wrapped either around the waist or above the breasts, sometimes over trousers. Young women may wear a T-shirt and short pants in daily life. On more formal occasions, such as church services and weddings, women wear a *robe* that resembles a Hawaiian *mu'umu'u,* usually made of brightly colored cottons printed with floral motifs. They also usually wear shoes, a necklace made of flowers, seeds, shells, or black pearl, and a flower headdress. Long hair represents femininity for Polynesians, so most Polynesian women wear their hair long, although some on Tahiti patronize hair salons to have their hair styled and cut short. Men generally wear a T-shirt and pants at home and at work, while some wear a *pāreu* around their waist at home. On formal occasions, they wear a shirt, long pants, and shoes, as do those who work in the hospitality industry or the civil service. Short hair is the common style among Tahitian men, but dancers, musicians, and artisans will often grow their hair long. Today, tattoos are popular among both men and women. Men tend to wear larger tattoos on visible parts of the body, while women often wear small animal or figurative designs on their backs or around the ankles or the navel (Kuwahara 2005).

In short, clothing, hairstyle, and other body ornaments mark gender more distinctively in formal situations than in casual ones. Gender difference is prominent in adolescence and adulthood, but less so in childhood and old age. "Polynesian" ethnicity and *la culture mā'ohi* is also affirmed by wearing a *pāreu,* a *robe,* long hair, tattoos, and flower and shell ornaments.

These gendered patterns of dress also apply to *māhū* and *raerae* sartorial choices on both Tahiti and Bora Bora. *Māhū* tend to wear men's clothes, such as a T-shirt and pants, on casual occasions and, on formal ones, a shirt and trousers. They often wear a flower headdress and necklace, which are considered feminine. *Raerae* also wear a *pāreu* or T-shirt with short pants at home but tend to wear a *robe* when they go out. *Raerae* have long hair or short-styled hair and wear makeup. Some have a small animal or a flower tattoo. Some have had breast-enlargement surgery, which is available only in clinics on Tahiti.

Sex-reassignment surgery is not available in French Polynesia, so some *raerae* go to the United States or Thailand to have it done. For example, while living on Tahiti, Rose searched the Internet for information on sex-reassignment surgery in a Thai hospital and took a month-long holiday there to undergo it. She was very satisfied with the results, which she said demonstrated the skills of Thai surgeons; and also the costs were lower than in other places. *Raerae* also use hormones to make their skin smoother and to enlarge their breasts. However, some, like Cindy, avoid hormones because they make them gain weight. *Māhū* do not undergo breast-enlargement surgery, do not take hormones, and do not wear women's dresses and makeup. The physical distinction between *māhū* and *raerae* becomes obvious when they reach *taure'are'a*, but is less marked when they become older.

Gender differences and personal styles as expressed through clothing choice are more marked on Tahiti than on other islands including Bora Bora because of the availability of a wider selection of Western and local clothing. On both Tahiti and Bora Bora, French and American fashion magazines can be purchased that portray the latest Western fashion trends, makeup, and hairstyles. These materials also shape *raerae* fashion choices, and if certain clothes cannot be bought, *raerae* and *māhū* who work in design, dressmaking, and hairdressing make copies.

As popular tourist destinations, both Tahiti and Bora Bora provide *raerae* the opportunity to meet tourists sporting the latest international fashions. Fashion styles that Polynesians associate with Western transvestites or sex workers have also long been present in French Polynesia. In Papeete, high boots, pin-heels, miniskirts, and tight-fitting evening dresses have become de rigueur for *raerae*. They have access to these clothes and makeup when travelling abroad, usually to France or the United States, or they make requests of friends who travel to these places. Many *raerae* on Tahiti and Bora Bora are also curious about the fashions of transsexuals overseas. *Raerae* living in France send their friends back home photos and newspaper articles of transsexual contests held in France and Thailand.

Some *raerae*, but not *māhū*, participate in annual transgender beauty contests such as l'élection de la Miss vahine-tane (*vahine:* "female"; *tane:* "male") on Bora Bora and l'élection de la Miss Piano, organized by Piano Bar on Tahiti. These contests attract much public attention and are hugely popular among the general population, and the candidates and winners are featured prominently in the media (cf. Alexeyeff 2009 on Rarotonga;

Besnier 2002 on Tonga; Presterudstuen, this volume). The winners live with the honor, and sometimes the notoriety, for the rest of their lives.

Although the body generally marks gender and sexuality, to categorize a person as *māhū* or *raerae* just on the basis of bodily presentation is problematic because gender comportment is not static over the course of a lifetime or across situations. For example, David, who is in his late forties and works in the tourism industry on Tahiti, wears the company's male uniform when at work and a leather jacket and gold necklace when he goes out. He used to wear dresses and makeup when he was young, but changed because he found it difficult to maintain a slim female figure as he grew older. In contrast, when Lily began working at a municipal office on Tahiti, she wore male clothing and short hair, but then gradually began wearing a woman's shirt with long pants, long hair, and light makeup so as to allow her colleagues to get used to it. Even within the space of one day, as in Cindy's case, *raerae* may transform their physical appearance several times.

On Tahiti, the stereotypes of *māhū* as "traditional" and "Polynesian" and *raerae* as "new" and "Western" are partly based on the physical contrast between *raerae*, who may alter their bodies, and *māhū*, who do not. In reality, whether or not they have undergone sex-reassignment surgery, *raerae* as well as *māhū* dress differently at work, at home, and for nights out, just like heterosexual men and women. On both Tahiti and Bora Bora, they often wear women's clothes and makeup when they are young, but stop doing so when they grow older. Many try to be glamorously made up when they go out at night but wear unisex clothing when they are relaxing at home or shopping in the neighborhood.

As for the relationship between *la culture mā'ohi* and *raerae*, people on both Tahiti and Bora Bora respect talented dancers, choreographers, or costume designers even if they take hormones, enlarge their breasts, and/or wear women's dresses and makeup. These talents are taken into consideration before gendered bodily representation, but in some cases appear more conspicuous with *raerae* physical appearance.

One significant difference between sartorial styles on Bora Bora and Tahiti occurs in the tourist industry. On Tahiti, *māhū* and *raerae* are usually required to wear men's uniforms, while on Bora Bora they are usually allowed to wear women's uniforms. This says much about the negative and often defining perception of *raerae* on Tahiti as sex workers and morally tainted individuals. On Bora Bora, tourists think that *raerae* are evidence of the broad-minded and exotic sensuality of French Polynesia and, in terms of the local population, *raerae* are integrated in, if not always accepted by, family and the community at large.

Family Matters

In addition to the body, gender and sexuality are inscribed onto interpersonal relationships, the most important of which in Polynesian society are kinship relations. According to the 2007 census, one out of five households, or one-third of all French Polynesians, consist of three or more generations (Institut de la statistique de la Polynésie Française 2009), a figure that reflects the fact that family relations play a significant part of everyday life in the islands.

Despite the tendency of families and relatives to be dispersed among the islands or around the globe, Polynesians still maintain close relations. Each member of the family plays a role that properly locates him or her in the family and the community. Polynesian identity is largely determined through one's family relationships. For *māhū* and *raerae* on both Tahiti and Bora Bora, whether or not they are accepted by their extended family is very important. While *māhū* tend to have good relationships with their family, *raerae* on Tahiti struggle because of their more obvious displays of sexual preferences for men and their involvement in sex work. According to Louisa Maiterai, director of Te Ti'ama o te Arii Vahine o te Po, an association founded on Tahiti in 1995 that is concerned with *raerae* and *māhū* mental and physical health issues, *raerae* as young as thirteen have been known to have left home because they were not accepted by their family. A commonly heard story on Tahiti is that *raerae* are kicked out when their fathers find out that they are wearing women's clothing and makeup, which stands in stark contrast to fathers' acceptance (but not necessarily approval) of *māhū*. Mothers, in contrast, generally stand by *raerae*, who often keep in touch with their mothers and siblings. After they leave home, *raerae* may sleep under bridges or in the bush before moving in with their *raerae* friends or cousins who understand their situation and support them. Their immediate need for income often impels them to work at nightclubs or work the street. Sometimes, older *raerae* whom they meet at clubs or in the street take them under their wing. Ange, a young *raerae* on Tahiti, considers it appropriate and safe for a young *raerae* to go out to Piano Bar with a more senior *raerae*, who will announce to everybody, "She is my daughter, so don't be nasty to her," thereby conferring the senior's protection and incorporating the younger *raerae* into a family structure (see Dolgoy and Ikeda, this volume).

Raerae on Tahiti sometimes move temporarily into their friends' flats even when they have not been kicked out of their homes, as in Cindy's case. Particularly for those who have left their family, friendships are important because friends can provide material and emotional support. Most *māhū* and *raerae* on both Tahiti and Bora Bora form close friendships not only with other *māhū* and *raerae* but also with women and some "straight" men.[7]

On Bora Bora, many *raerae* as well as *māhū* are accepted by their families and live with them. Some households may include several *māhū* and *raerae* relatives. As is the case in Tina's house on Bora Bora, *raerae* and *māhū* friends may frequently visit particular families and are treated by them like family members. Some *raerae* may not opt for extreme forms of body modification because of the concern that their families might disapprove. For example, Hina on Bora Bora confessed to me that she wanted to take hormones and undergo sex-reassignment surgery but could not bring herself to do it because her adoptive parents would disapprove.

There is another form of kinship that figures prominently in the lives of *māhū* and *raerae* on both Tahiti and Bora Bora, namely *fa'a'amu*, the transfer of children from biological parents to foster parents, usually the child's grandmother, uncle, or aunt, or a close friends of the parents. *Fa'a'amu* differs from Western-style adoption in that children often go back and forth between the biological and foster families and belong to both (Hooper 1970). Parents also form fictive kinship ties with one another through the children. *Māhū* often become *fa'a'amu* parents of their nieces and nephews, as they are considered good at bringing up children. Because boys are sometimes teased by their friends for having a *māhū* parent, some *māhū* prefer to bring up girls, who are less likely to be teased. *Māhū* who are *fa'a'amu* parents are regarded as performing an important family role.

Polynesian Transgender Politics

Throughout this chapter, I have mapped the key differences between *māhū* and *raerae* on Tahiti and Bora Bora. General differences are attributed to dress style and comportment, family and community involvement, and labor. On both islands, *māhū* are considered as a "traditional" and "culturally authentic" transgender category and *raerae* as "new" and "culturally inauthentic." But while people on Tahiti view the connection between *raerae* and modernity negatively, on Bora Bora this is not the case, as the conjunction between the two terms is not as politically and morally charged, and "culturally inauthentic" *raerae* are incorporated into and locate themselves within local familial and community "traditions." In other words, when comparing the two islands, the interaction between global and local forces has had specific and divergent effects on the development and classification of transgender categories within the nation-state.

Many *māhū* and *raerae* choose to live and work on Tahiti and Bora Bora, as they are the most populated islands in French Polynesia and are considered the gateways to the territory. Like many young people, *māhū* and *raerae* move to urban centers for employment, excitement, and the opportunity to socialize with like-minded people. Both islands are "plugged into" global information flows, fashion trends, and medical procedures, and are far more accessible than less urbanized islands. Yet while both Tahiti and Bora Bora are subject to Western and global cultural forces, the delineation between *māhū* and *raerae* is far more marked on Tahiti, where *"raerae"* is a term uttered contemptuously and is associated with sex workers to the extent that *raerae* avoid using it to refer to themselves, instead using the term *"efféminé."* On Bora Bora, the differences in physical presentation and comportment of the two categories are clearly marked, and yet people believe that there is little difference between *māhū* and *raerae* in terms of their role in the family and the broader community. Rather than having negative connotations, the term *"raerae"* is associated with individuals who have excellent social skills and are glamorous and talented.

While the classification of *māhū* and *raerae* in terms of physical characteristics, work, and family relationships operates in relation to individuals' everyday strategizing, these categories emerge as unstable and shifting. On Tahiti, for instance, a public servant I knew, who was taking hormones and had undergone breast-enlargement surgery, wore a dress and lived with her family. She is considered a *raerae* in terms of her body characteristics but a *māhū* in terms of work and relationship with her family, and she herself is unsure of which category she falls into, preferring to think of herself as neither *māhū* nor *raerae.* So those who are successfully employed or take on significant family roles (such as that of *fa'a'amu* parents) or cultural roles (such as those of dancers, choreographers, and costume designers) are considered *māhū* and are distinguished from those who work at nightclubs or as sex workers even if they dress and act like *raerae.*

Polynesians' evaluations of *māhū* and *raerae* highlight the need to consider issues of sexuality in the context of broader national histories of colonialism and contemporary neocolonial relations. On Tahiti, there is marked political tension between Polynesians and the French, as Papeete is the administrative and military center of French Polynesia. *Raerae* who actively imitate "foreign" clothing, makeup, and comportment, and who make their living being intimate with foreign men, have come to symbolize all that is wrong with contemporary life. Tourism and sex work are viewed as important consequences of globalization; the former enhances the economy and the latter offends public morals. This affects the way Tahitians distinguish *māhū* from *raerae,* associating the former with allegiance to families and "traditional" Polynesian culture, the latter with "new" immorality and social independence.

The differences between Tahiti and Bora Bora in terms of the classification of *māhū* and *raerae* also remind us that these national histories cannot be read as proceeding in the same manner, and along the same course, in all islands of the nation-state. For, as we have seen, *māhū*'s and *raerae*'s relationships with non-Polynesians differ markedly on the two islands. On Bora Bora, most non-Polynesians are tourists who are not only French but other Europeans, Americans, and Japanese. So, while *raerae* on Bora Bora may engage in sex work, this is not framed within exploitative neocolonial relations as on Tahiti but as part of a cosmopolitan economy of pleasure. Both the "local" and the "global" thus need to be investigated in order to fully comprehend sexual identities and practices in the contemporary era.

Acknowledgments

The material I present here is based on fieldwork conducted on Tahiti and Bora Bora in 2006, 2007, 2008, and 2009. I acknowledge research funding from the Toyota Foundation in 2007 and 2008 and from Kinjo Gakuin University in 2009. I thank Chiho for her support during the research in Bora Bora, and Bruno Saura for giving me direction and encouragement. I also thank Deborah Elliston for her invaluable advice and suggestions, and Niko Besnier and Kalissa Alexeyeff for providing important feedback and spending an enormous amount of time editing my chapter. Finally, I thank the *māhū* and *raerae* with whom I worked for spending a lot of time with me and telling their stories.

Notes

1   Kulick (1998) notes that *travesti* in Brazil make the similar claim that they perform sex for pleasure and fame, and not for money. In both cases,

the explanation provides an alternative to hegemonic categorizations of transgender as sex workers.

2   The sex industry on Tahiti is said to have developed as a result of the provision of commodified sex to foreigners. Before that time, the provision of sexual services in return for money and other commodities operated on a more ad hoc basis.

3   In total, French Polynesia has fifty hotels consisting of 3,383 rooms and a capacity of 7,928 (Service du tourisme 2006).

4   Although my analysis here does not cover the dominant representations of the Chinese in French Polynesia, it is worth mentioning that they are often the target of racial discrimination but at the same time considered intelligent and hardworking, which explains their success in business.

5   In contrast to Tahitian, French, the language I spoke with people during fieldwork, marks gender differences in pronouns. Participants use French pronouns in the following anecdotes to assert their gendered identification.

6   All names are pseudonyms. The historical present refers to 2006–2009.

7   I use the term "straight" men here to mean those who have sexual relationships mostly with women. They may of course have had sexual relations with *māhū* and *raerae*. There is to my knowledge no Tahitian term to describe a "straight" man; men are simply called *tane*.

References

Adrian, Bonnie. 2003. *Framing the Bride: Globalizing Beauty and Romance in Taiwan's Bridal Industry.* Berkeley: University of California Press.

Alexeyeff, Kalissa. 2008. Globalizing Drag in the Cook Islands: Friction, Repulsion, and Abjection. *The Contemporary Pacific* 20: 143–161.

———. 2009. Dancing Sexuality in the Cook Islands. In *Transgressive Sex: Subversion and Control in Erotic Encounters,* ed. Hastings Donnan and Fiona Magowan, pp. 113–130. New York: Berghahn.

Besnier, Niko. 1994. Polynesian Gender Liminality through Time and Space. In *Third Sex, Third Gender: Beyond Sexual Dimorphism in Culture and History,* ed. Gilbert Herdt, pp. 285–328. New York: Zone.

———. 1997. Sluts and Superwomen: The Politics of Gender Liminality in Urban Tonga. *Ethnos* 62: 5–31.

———. 2002. Transgenderism, Locality, and the Miss Galaxy Beauty Pageant in Tonga. *American Ethnologist* 29: 534–566.

Bligh, William. 1792 [1789]. *A Voyage to the South Sea, Undertaken by Command of His Majesty, for the Purpose of Conveying the Breadfruit Tree to the West Indies, in His Majesty's Ship the Bounty, Including an Account of the Mutiny on Board the Said Ship.* 2 vols. London: George Nicol.

Corillion, Jean Michel, dir. 2001. *Mahu, l'efféminé.* Documentary, France 3 RFO (52 min.).

Elliston, Deborah. 2000. Geographies of Gender and Politics: The Place of Difference in Polynesian Nationalism. *Cultural Anthropology* 15: 171–216.

Hooper, Antony. 1970. Adoption in the Society Islands. In *Adoption in Eastern Oceania,* ed. Vern Carroll, pp. 52–70. Honolulu: University of Hawai'i Press.

Institut de la statistique de la Polynésie Française. 2009. *Famille en chiffres.* Papeete: Institut de la statistique de la Polynésie Française.

———. 2010. *La Polynésie en bref 2010.* Papeete: Institut de la statistique de la Polynésie Française.

Jackson, Peter. 2009. Capitalism and Global Queering: National Markets, Parallels among Sexual Cultures and Multiple Queer Modernities. *GLQ* 15: 357–395.

Kahn, Miriam. 2000. Tahiti Intertwined: Ancestral Land, Tourist Postcard, and Nuclear Test Site. *American Anthropologist* 102: 7–26.

———. 2011. *Tahiti beyond the Postcard: Power, Place, and Everyday Life.* Seattle: University of Washington Press.

Kirkpatrick, John. 1987. *Taure'are'a:* A Liminal Category and Passage to Marquesan Adulthood. *Ethos* 15: 382–405.

Kulick, Don. 1998. *Travestí: Sex, Gender and Culture among Brazilian Transgender Prostitutes.* Chicago: University of Chicago Press.

Kuwahara, Makiko. 2005. *Tattoo: An Anthropology.* Oxford: Berg.

Levy, Robert. 1973. *Tahitians: Mind and Experience in the Society Islands.* Chicago: University of Chicago Press.

Morrison, James. 1935. *The Journal of James Morrison, Boatswain's Mate of the Bounty, Describing the Mutiny and Subsequent Misfortunes of the Mutineers, together with an Account of the Island of Tahiti,* ed. Owen Rutter. London: The Golden Cockerel Press.

Mortimer, George. 1791. *Observations and Remarks Made during a Voyage to the Islands of Teneriffe, Amsterdam, Maria's Islands near van Diemen's Land, Otaheite, Sandwich Islands, . . . in the Brig Mercury Commanded by John Henri Cox, Esq.* London: Printed for the Author.

Roen, Katrina. 2006. Transgender Theory and Embodiment: The Risk of Racial Marginalization. In *The Transgender Studies Reader,* ed. Susan Styker and Stephen Whittle, pp. 656–665. New York: Routledge.

Sánchez-Eppler, Benigno, and Cindy Patton. 2000. Introduction: With a Passport out of Eden. In *Queer Diasporas,* ed. Patton Cindy and Benigno Sánchez-Eppler, pp. 1–14. Durham, NC: Duke University Press.

Saura, Bruno. 1998. *Des Tahitiens, des Français, leurs représentations réciproques d'aujourd'hui.* Tahiti: Christian Gleizal.

———. 2009. *Ma'ohi Tahiti.* Pirae, French Polynesia: Au Vent des Îles.

Service du tourisme. 2006. *Statistiques de fréquentation touristique 2006*. Papeete: Service du tourisme.

Stevenson, Karen. 1992. Politicization of *La Culture Ma'ohi:* The Creation of a Tahitian Cultural Identity. *Pacific Studies* 15: 117–136.

Tsing, Anna L. 2004. *Friction: An Ethnography of Global Connection*. Princeton, NJ: Princeton University Press.

Wilson, James. 1799. *A Missionary Voyage to the South Pacific Ocean, Performed in the Years 1796, 1797, 1798, in the Ship Duff, Commanded by Captain James Wilson*. London: T. Chapman.

CHAPTER 6

Transgender in Samoa
The Cultural Production of Gender Inequality

Serge Tcherkézoff

This chapter deals with the difficulties involved in describing or even evoking the sociocultural paths followed by Samoan *fa'afāfine* and *tomboys*. Both labels were invented and both social categories are constructed from a heteronormative discourse—mainstream Samoan discourse and some academic literature. From these perspectives, *fa'afāfine* are persons whose families and neighbors characterize them as boys at birth but who, later in life (usually in late childhood or early adolescence), are said to act "in the way of women" (*fa'a-fafine,* the plural of the term being *fa'afāfine*). However, they never introduce themselves as *"fa'afāfine,"* but by their own given names. If queried about their gender, they reply that they are "girls."[1]

The chapter broaches another gendered category, which few in mainstream Samoan society are willing to talk about openly—that is, girls or women who are said to be born as girls but who come to be viewed as acting in the way of men at roughly the same stage in life as when boys become *fa'afāfine*. There are two differences between them and *fa'afāfine.* First, they don't claim to be of the other gender: they assert that they are girls, not boys. Second, there is no straightforward Samoan term that designates them as being "in the way of boys or men." When Samoans refer to them, they use various circumlocutions (e.g., "exhibiting the behavior of boys or men") or, more pithily, the English borrowing *"tomboy."* I italicize this word to indicate the particular meaning it has in Samoa.

This contrast between *fa'afafine* and *tomboy* is not just a matter of terminology but runs deeper, in that Samoans born as boys who act like girls have at their disposal a much broader range of identificational practices than Samoans born as girls who act like boys. The contrast is obvious in everyday public behavior, but it is sharpest in the context of the pursuit of fulfillment of sexual desire. The contrast also colors affective relations between non-heteronormative individuals and their families. Under the superficial symmetry between boys who act like girls and girls who act like boys (or the adult equivalents) lies a profound asymmetry—indeed a sharp social inequality—which has yet to receive any analytic attention in writings about gender and sexuality in Samoa or elsewhere in the Pacific Islands. And this asymmetry works directly to the detriment of *tomboy*s.

Instead of attempting to "define" *fa'afafine* and *tomboy* in the context of Samoan gender configurations, I investigate the claims that *fa'afafine* and *tomboy*s make about their own identity and how others talk about them and engage with them. Thus I place the term "transgender" in quotation marks, as it is not a self-characterization but a term that only emerges in discourse *about* them, usually of an academic nature. When used in the heteronormative discourse, it runs the risk of focusing attention on how mainstream Samoan and outside observers view the *trans*-formation of *fa'afafine*'s and *tomboy*s' identity at birth and later in life. Such a discourse about transformation in gender is part of the wider difficulty inherent in gender studies, which constantly must guard against presupposing a universal sex-gender binary opposing male to female and men to women, and then evaluating the extent to which gender and sexual manifestations in each specific society "fit" this binary model or, on the contrary, are "trans-," "liminal," and so on.[2]

Talking about *Fa'afafine* and *Tomboy*s

As many other authors have explained, the word *"fa'afafine"* is made up of a very common and polysemic prefix, *fa'a-*, which in this case can be translated as "in the way of," and the noun *fafine* "woman." The latter is to be understood in the restricted sense that it has come to take on in Samoa (at a time that I am unable to identify), namely to refer to a potential or actual female sexual partner. When speaking Samoan, however, *fa'afafine* assert that they are *teine*, "girls," or *tama'ita'i*, "ladies." In thirty years' worth of fieldwork in Samoa, I have never heard anyone say about her- or himself, "I am a *fa'afafine*" (although the situation may be different for Samoans in the diaspora).[3]

For these reasons, instead of *"fa'afafine,"* I use the term *"fa'ateine"* and the feminine pronoun to refer to them, although this choice is a prescriptive rather than a descriptive one. Ideally, one would also forego the prefix *fa'a-*, because they say that they *are* girls (or ladies) and not just *like* girls. For sake of distinguishing non-heteronormative persons from normative females (*teine*), however, I will stick to the prefixed version of the term.

In the early 1980s, Aiono Dr. Fanaafi Le Tagaloa, a highly respected Samoan scholar and founder of Samoan studies at the University of Samoa, whom I am proud to consider as a mentor throughout the 1980s, told me, "You should not use the word *'fa'afafine,'* it is not really Samoan, it postdates contact with Europeans; the old Samoan word was *'fa'ateine.'* "There is no evidence of this term in early European narratives, but then there is no evidence either of a word *"fa'afafine,"* and thus this linguistic chronology remains open to discussion. But her remark does suggest the fact that, for a number of *fa'ateine*, the term *"fa'afafine"* carries connotations that they strongly reject. Because of the narrow meaning of the Samoan word *"fafine,"* namely a female person within a potential or actual sexual relationship, *"fa'afafine"* gives the misguided impression that the *fa'ateine*'s life is entirely centered on matters of sex. The fact that some Samoan scholars think that the word *"fa'afafine"* is a neologism is also symptomatic of the feeling that the category is a product of modernity, particularly as it now manifests itself to mainstream society (e.g., through the display of fashion and in dance shows). These feelings are echoed elsewhere in the Pacific (Alexeyeff 2008, 2009; Besnier 2002, 2004, 2011; Grépin 1995, 2001; Good, this volume; Elliston, this volume).

The term *"tomboy,"* in contrast, has a rather different configuration. It is obviously a borrowing from the slightly old-fashioned English word, which itself has a complex linguistic history, and which has come to refer to a girl who behaves in a manner that observers consider "boy-like." Although it is unclear when it entered the Samoan vocabulary, today the term has a precise meaning: a girl or woman who acts like a man in contexts where "strength" (*mālosi*) is particularly central to the definition of manhood. This concept encompasses a wide range of connotations, such as the capacity for hard physical work, in olden days the ability to win wars, to be good at competitive sports, and to be sexually successful. During my fieldwork in the 1980s, the term *"tomboy"* did not necessarily imply sexual attraction to girls, whether "straight" girls or other *tomboy*s.[4] Today, however, it does have this connotation. Contemporary mainstream Samoan interlocutors sometime use the borrowed term *"lisipia,"* "lesbian," as their world is increasingly penetrated by global discourses that identify people in terms of the object of their sexual desire.

When I attempted to avoid the borrowed term *"tomboy"* in my conversations with Samoans, I ran into problems: any attempt I made to attach the prefix *fa'a-* ("in the way of") to a variety of words denoting male humans (e.g., *tamaloa,* "adult man," *tama,* "boy, young man," or *tane,* "man as husband, male") either remained unintelligible to Samoan interlocutors or were interpreted literally to refer to someone or something that was somehow "man-like" in a temporally and contextually bounded way. Evidently the word *"fa'afafine"* has no straightforward antonym.

This asymmetry is significant beyond lexical concerns. The fact that *"fafine"* has sexual connotations gives the word *"fa'afafine"* unequivocally sexual connotations. Who can be sexually "like a woman" other than women? Only those born as boys and who later behave "like women" in that they are available for sexual relations with men where they take the insertee role. Theoretically possible terms like *"fa'atamaloa"* to refer to the opposite category do not have any sexual connotations, because the term *"tamaloa"* (and others like it) has no such connotations. This asymmetry touches upon a much wider asymmetry—the fact that in Samoa men can be "men" without being sexual beings, whereas that possibility is far less readily available to women.

The absence of non-borrowed terms for *tomboys* may also be related to their lack of ideological and practical visibility. Some heteronormative Samoans, for example, maintain that *tomboys* "are not part of our custom" (*aganu'u*). Similarly, visitors to Samoa may never see or hear about *tomboys* (there are no shows organized by *tomboys,* for instance), while they will immediately notice the presence of *fa'ateine* in such highly visible contexts as families, shows, and sports.[5]

Western Discourses about *Fa'afāfine*

Since Western or other discourses are silent about Samoan *tomboys,* my discussion of Western representations of non-heteronormative Samoans focuses exclusively on *fa'ateine.* Despite sustained criticism, Western media continue to represent Samoan *fa'ateine* and equivalent categories elsewhere in the Pacific Islands as "homosexuals." If we assume that homosexuals are people who are erotically attracted to one another, then *fa'ateine* cannot be thus characterized because they never express an erotic desire for one another, and in fact are emphatically adverse to it (cf. Schmidt 2001), and this erotic aversion appears to be sustained even in more cosmopolitan regions of the Pacific Islands, such as the Cook Islands (Alexeyeff 2008, 2009). *Fa'ateine* are only sexually interested in those they called, in the 1980s, a *"mata,"* a Pig Latin inversion of the word *"tama"* (boy, young man), which refers to a "straight" man but implies that he could have sexual relations with a *fa'ateine*.

Another very common idea in the Western imagination is that Samoan families that do not have enough girls forcibly bring up one of their boys as a girl. This particular mythology has widespread currency and has been repeated over and over again across media, countries, authors, and times. "*Fa'afafine* play a useful role in the family," asserts a documentary made for television, "their muscular body provides help. . . . In the past, when there were not enough girls in the house, parents would raise one boy as a girl" (*National Geographic* 2007). Yet, over decades of fieldwork, I have never seen a case of such a practice, nor have I heard of one, even when I queried people with whom I was very close. In fact, no family in Samoa would impose on a child the enormous difficulties associated with life as a *fa'ateine,* which vastly outweigh whatever any advantage a family would derive from a *fa'ateine*'s labor contribution (cf. Schoeffel, this volume).

In their eagerness to "explain" the presence of *fa'ateine* in Samoan society, Western observers have provided a number of other functional-ist accounts. One is based on the assumption that society must provide "counter-models" of normative behavior and selfhood. In a society in which the ideal type of boyhood and young manhood is so sharply defined by "strength," particularly as it is visually inscribed in the body's muscularity, this ideal type is difficult to achieve for most boys, and effeminate boys provide an ideal counter-model against which other boys can define them-selves (Shore 1981, 209–210). It is true that Samoan society does set a high standard for the visuality of "strength" in young men's bodies, and that this "strength" (*mālosi*) is an overdetermined concept in Samoan culture. But the exact sociological and cultural operations of the "counter-modeling" that society so desperately would fabricate remain completely obscure, particularly in terms of the material and psychological "costs" to families and individuals.[6]

Another functionalist argument evokes the contradiction between two normative ideals concerning sexuality in traditional Samoa. One demands that girls remain virgins until marriage, while the other prescribes that young men be as sexually active as possible to demonstrate their masculine "strength." *Fa'ateine* would provide a solution to this normative contradiction by offering sexual services to young men "as if" they were girls. But here again, the logic falters. The fact is that *fa'ateine*'s relationships with "straight" men present a power imbalance, for as *fa'ateine* view these relationships as both sexual and affective, straight men approach them in much more utilitarian fashion, at least in their overt representation. Thus, in addition to providing sexual satisfaction, a *fa'ateine* provides material gifts to her straight lover, which inverts the normative representation of heterosexual courting, in which a boy offers gifts to the girl in the hope that in turn she will offer him the ultimate gift of her virginity (an imbalance that Besnier 1997 has documented in some detail for Tonga and that is echoed elsewhere in the world, e.g., Kulick 1998 on Brazil). Negative reciprocity suffuses the relationship between a *fa'ateine* and a straight man, and thus the specter of exploitation looms large in the life of *fa'ateine*. But to posit negative reciprocity as an explanation for the presence of *fa'ateine* in Samoan society is based on a highly uncritical understanding of the constitution of social relations.

The *Fa'ateine*'s Mother

When a young male child displays behaviors that appear to emulate his sisters', however briefly and sporadically, particularly a predilection for women's household work and dancing in the female style (*siva*), it does happen that his mother (or other elder female relatives) encourages these behaviors. This encouragement may be playful (particularly in the presence of others), but in other cases may be sustained. It is important to note that these dynamics do not constitute a matter of upbringing but rather a reaction to a child's actions, and they certainly do not support the tired old myth about parents "bringing up boys to be girls" in order to balance out a gendered division of labor (see Schoeffel, this volume).

What motivates a child to engage in such behavior is very difficult to assess, although it is suggestive to note that certain dynamics in Samoan society may encourage the perception that a boy is "like a girl" in the universal context of the unstable nature of gender assignation in adolescence. This perception may originate with a general discomfort with a male physique perceived as lacking the "strength" that is so central to Samoan male identity. Whether this deficiency is associated with a physical impairment or simply with a spindly physique, or anything in between, it quickly becomes the object of mockery. I have witnessed situations in which a skinny boy engaged in activities that elicited compliments rather than teasing, such as his performing the female solo part of a *siva* dance, whose graceful and delicate choreography showcases femininity, a performance that mother and sisters would applaud vigorously while also finding it humorous.

Such situations engender ambiguity. While the mother and her daughters greet such performances approvingly and may even encourage them, the father and his sons will at best consistently mock them or, at worst, will beat the child up in an effort to instill some sense of gender into him. In either case, the effect will be to encourage the child to seek the company and approval of his mother and sisters—the exact reverse of what male relatives intend. But the opposite scenario can occur with equal ease: the mother's spontaneous reaction of treating the child as a girl can lead the child to reject this gender assignation with increasing assertiveness when he is old enough to do so. Last, all intermediate possibilities are attested: the "*fa'afafine* assignation" may be to the boy's liking for a while or for certain purposes, but then he grows up following a normative path, getting married and having children, none of whom will become a *fa'ateine* if he can help it; or, even worse, in some cases he will join the ranks of fathers who have no interest in trying to understand what can take place in their sons' psychology during adolescence.

The sociological question that emerges from all this concerns the mother: What motivates a Samoan mother to find pleasure in witnessing her son taking on a non-normative gendering and even in some cases encouraging it? Samoan mothers often express regret that, once they reach adolescence, their sons begin to live beyond the realm of both their authority and their affection, and in this respect fathers and mothers have an asymmetrical relationship with their male children, as fathers do not see their relationship with their sons as following such a path. This regret suggests the possibility that some mothers may unconsciously seek to keep their sons close to them by treating them like a girl.

This hypothesis finds some support from an excursus into kinship terminology. Samoan fathers' children are termed "*atali'i*" if male and "*afafine*" if female, terms that remain constant from birth to adulthood. Gender is central to these kinship terms, which are unequivocally distinct, nonreciprocal, and absolute. In other words, they correspond precisely to "son" and "daughter" respectively in European languages. In contrast, a mother's children, called *tama*, are undifferentiated with reference to gender, although it is possible to add an adjective to the term *tama* to specify gender (*tama tama*, "son"; *tama teine*, "daughter"). This gender-neutral basic terminology applies to collateral descent: a man can refer to his sister's child as *"tama sā,"* literally "sacred child" (although this term is now outdated), but the term is gender-neutral. The basic term *"tama"* therefore always refers to a woman's child.

The gender-neutral terms that mothers use to refer to children thus contrast with the obligatorily gendered terms that fathers use, suggesting that children's gender is potentially interchangeable for mothers but not so for fathers. These observations resonate with the fact that mothers easily accept *fa'ateine* sons, while fathers do not accept any gender crossing.

The *Tomboy* Child's Family Relations

Although mothers may indulge their young sons to engage in *fa'ateine* practices while fathers never do, neither mothers nor fathers encourage *tomboy* tendencies in their daughters. Parents never provide any affective compensation for girls' *tomboy* behavior and on the contrary only deplore it. Yet one finds *tomboy* girls in a not unsubstantial number of Samoan families.

As in the case of *fa'ateine*, young girls who fail to live up to the standards against which they are measured, in their case that of the ideal young Samoan girl, may be drawn to self-identify and be identified as a *tomboy*. Parents and siblings encourage this identification, although in this case in negative fashion. These dynamics may be only obliquely related to gender. In one case that I witnessed in the course of my fieldwork, when a baby girl was born, everyone around her marveled at the fairness of her complexion, an iconic sign of beauty in Samoa, as in the rest of the Pacific.[7] As she grew up, however, she displayed a pre-*tomboy* comportment by spending a great deal of time outdoors, thus violating the expectation that girls stay indoors and take responsibility for household chores, which also ensures that their complexion is not affected by the sun. The child in question grew "black," said her relatives, and she became the butt of her parents' and siblings' ceaseless teasing: she was told she was an ugly duckling. Not surprisingly, the girl's behavior increasingly became that of a *tomboy*, behavior she seemed to cultivate, and later in life she became bisexual.

Another case concerns two sisters close in age. One had a light complexion and pleasant features, for which she was complimented from a young age; the other, with a dark complexion and a puffy-looking face, was mocked, and calling her names became a family habit. One became the object of boys' assiduous courting and engaged in exclusively heterosexual practices, while the other became a *tomboy*, with an aggressive demeanor, and eventually exclusively engaged in sexual relations with other women, surreptitiously while she remained in Samoa but more openly once she emigrated overseas.

There is thus a sharp contrast between the affective relationships that *faʻateine* and *tomboy*s maintain with their families. While the rejection of the *faʻateine* by her father and brothers certainly provides grounds for a multitude of psychological problems, she finds herself included by her mother and her sisters, sometimes even coddled, but at least never rejected. Nonetheless, this tension between rejection and approval never colors the *tomboy*'s relationships with her close kindred. I have seen a father good-naturedly teaching his daughter to throw a good punch, but these games are not sustained, and the father quickly changed from stating, "All my children, daughter included, must know how to defend themselves," to mocking and then becoming angry at the same daughter for being too openly *tomboy*.

The socialization of a *tomboy* is far from easy. She asserts herself as a girl and others consider her to be one. For her brothers, she remains a girl for the purpose of one of the most fundamental norms of Samoan (and other Western Polynesian) culture—brother–sister avoidance once they reach adolescence. But her relationship with her brothers is fraught: they brush her off and scold her if seniority entitles them do so. With her sisters, there is competition and jealousy, and she is put down by her sisters' ability to perform difficult feminine tasks, such as plaiting fine mats (even if she does it just as well as they do). She gains no prestige, only mockery, for her ability to perform heavy physical tasks. In contrast, the *faʻateine* asserts that she is a "girl" and thus, exempted from abiding by brother–sister avoidance, is free to socialize with her sisters, who encourage her self-identification as a *faʻateine* and provide her with a role model to emulate.

The *tomboy*'s inability to find a place and a role model in the family has serious consequences. In cases I have known, she exaggerates her *tomboy* identification and may become the school bully constantly punished for beating her classmates to a pulp. Even if she performs well academically, she remains unconvincing in the eyes of her close kindred, because for them the studious girl is by definition self-effacing, demure, bookish, and obedient. Boys are not expected to be diligent, but the *tomboy* is considered to be worse than the worst of boys. As a result, she receives little support in her studies, as neither her family nor her teachers have any faith in her academic abilities. This socialization to an aggressive, confrontational, and independent self is reminiscent of Nancy Chodorow's (1978) classic feminist psychoanalytic account of the oppositional socialization of boys in Western (middle-class) society, but it is all the more poignant in that it takes place in a society that places so much emphasis on sociality.

Coming of Age as a *Tomboy*

Things come to a head with the awakening of sexual desire. A *tomboy*'s sexuality is subject to less surveillance than those of her heteronormative sisters because her parents believe (erroneously) that she has no interest in boys. Paradoxically, it is the parents who consider her "transgender," failing to see her as a girl and to hear her assertions that she is a girl. As a result, she can find herself embroiled in sexual activity much more easily than her closely supervised and frequently admonished sisters, and may find herself pregnant at a young age.

The result is dramatic. Under normal circumstances, a daughter who becomes pregnant out of wedlock is a source of crushing shame for parents and brothers. This shame and the resulting anger it arouses are even greater in the case of *tomboy*s, as family members see the *tomboy* daughter as having doubly "deceived" them. While parents and brothers are expected to prevent all daughters and sisters from being interested in boys, in *tomboy*s this attraction is an abomination. Was she "feigning" *tomboy* behavior in order to mislead those responsible for her? Not only is her comportment "ugly" (*mātagā*) on a daily basis, but she also brings untold shame onto her close relatives by demonstrating to all and sundry that she has fooled them.

One case narrated to me in detail, while perhaps extreme, illustrates the general ideological landscape that surrounds such situations. When the *tomboy* gave birth to a girl, her mother took the baby away from her and banished her to live with cousins on another island of the Samoan archipelago—the culmination of a sense of rejection and abandonment in the tomboy daughter, who would later talk about her baby girl in tears. Sent overseas, she turned to the bottle and became a butch lesbian; but her violent behavior consistently put off potential lovers or made relationships short-lived.

Another asymmetry between *fa'ateine* and *tomboy*s is the fact that the former cultivate sociality with one another in such contexts as fashion shows and sports, while the latter do not. In fact, they are prevented from doing so because the sight of congregating *tomboy*s immediately evokes in the minds of others the suspicion that they are sexually involved, whereas *fa'ateine* seen together arouse no such suspicion, as sexual attraction between them is unthinkable. This contrast is indeed tragic: one category elaborates a sociality that others (particularly young women) not only approve of but even seek out; the other category is composed of despised individuals or couples—and this in a society in which the basic units of sociality are neither individuals nor couples, but families, age cohorts, clubs, and so on.

In the Samoan diaspora (primarily in New Zealand, Australia, Hawai'i, and the continental United States), when *tomboy* couples live together, their lives remain difficult. Parents and friends display little patience for them, refusing to visit or receive them. "What have I done to be thus punished by God?" asks a mother of her *tomboy* lesbian daughter. The *tomboy* may be blamed for her parents' illnesses, and decades into adulthood siblings continue to hate her for the shame that she has brought upon the family. Rarely do such strong feelings surround the presence of a *fa'ateine* in a family.

Fa'ateine who have migrated sometimes establish significant relationships with a partner—if the relationship is long-term, the partner is in all likelihood a Westerner. When the *fa'ateine* visits her family back in the islands or in other diasporic communities, she is unlikely to bring her partner along, choosing to travel alone or in the company of other *fa'ateine*. Her visit will be a delight to her mother, aunts, and sisters, who will have looked forward to spending lively and animated evenings gossiping and telling "women's stories" (often of a salacious nature). Most *fa'ateine* are consummate conversationalists, cultivating the art of being both brilliant and amusing, not unlike the specialists of the local traditional theatre or *fale aitu*, who in fact often appear on stage impersonating *fa'ateine* (Pearson, this volume).

But if a migrant lesbian *tomboy* visits her family with another woman, the situation is very different. Everyone immediately will assume that they are a couple, which is frequently the case, because lesbian *tomboy*s do not seek each other's company simply for the sake of sociability. In the situations that I have witnessed, everyone looks ill-at-ease. Such visits are brief and focus on sorting out family matters. They will not be punctuated by the animated conversations and gales of laughter throughout the evening that characterize the sociality of adults with *fa'ateine*.

Now to the issue of children. Few *fa'ateine* who remain so in adulthood have children in their charge. In contrast, few adult *tomboy*s are without children (at least in the diaspora), but this fact is consistent with Samoan mainstream ideologies of gender: since *tomboy*s remain women, a desire to have children is fundamental to their identity. How they acquire children varies: in one case, a *tomboy* was married heterosexually while she was still young and had children, whom she kept when she and her husband separated and she entered into a relationship with another woman; in another case, a *tomboy* had sex with a man with the explicit purpose of getting pregnant while she was between same-sex relationships. As she lives in the diaspora, the *tomboy* mother is considered to be a single mother with children (she does not officially declare her same-sex relationship) and thus qualifies for substantial government assistance. But problems emerge in the relationship between *tomboy* mothers or couples and their children, particularly boys, stemming from the attitude of the rest of the immediate and extended family—friends, fellow church members, and so on—who find every opportunity to express their pity for the children of a mother living in shame. As a result, it is not uncommon for young children of *tomboy* mothers to run away from home.

The title of this section of course evokes Margaret Mead's famous study of adolescence in Samoa (Mead 1928). Mead did not take into account transgender youth, but any discussion of Samoan past and present norms of sexuality must refer to her views of Samoan adolescent norms. Her understanding of Samoan sexuality was obviously shaped by stereotypes of Polynesian "free sexuality" that the Western world had nurtured since eighteenth-century contacts with Tahiti, which was not at all applicable to Samoa, whether in the 1920 or later. Though her published work presented a picture of "free love" during adolescence, her own field notes (partially published in Orans 1996) reveal that this was not the picture she actually witnessed. Ironically, these notes also reveal that, while claiming to present the perspective of adolescent girls, Mead was in fact strongly influenced by a Samoan male discourse that asserted, and continues to do so today, that boys have easy sexual access to girls (Tcherkézoff 2001). Indeed, Mead's notes bear witness to the depth of the contradiction between the norms imposed on female adolescents (preserving virginity until marriage) and those imposed on male adolescents (the ideal type of a strong "warrior" whose strength allows him to perform physically demanding work but also to "conquer" in sport and sex). This apparently was the normative context in the 1920s and certainly is the case today.

Normative Gender and Sexuality

But the contrast is not only between two gendered norms. Dynamics of gender in Samoan society are better understood in terms of a contrast between two systems of social relations than in terms of two genders (Tcherkézoff 1993, 2003). In one system, which I term the "realm of light" (in a cosmological, social, and everyday sense—i.e., the realm of the visible), the dominant social relation is the brother–sister relationship. In a traditional village, everyone is related to one another through this cross-sibling relationship, even though the village is made up of unrelated extended families or *'āiga*, as the ceremonial groups of "sons" and "daughters of the village" are said to be in a brother–sister relationship. This is the world of the *aganu'u fa'a-Sāmoa* or "Samoan custom" (literally, the "essence of the community living in the Samoan way"). The other system of social relations that makes up gender is the realm where humans are just "living creatures" or *mea ola*. There, humans and animals are considered to be somewhat alike, particularly with respect to sexuality. This realm is situated outside of *aganu'u* and away from visible village life, and there one finds only "males" and "females" (as opposed to men and women). This is where the term *"fafine"* finds its meaning—that is, woman as defined in terms of the contrast between male and female, and thus in terms of potential or actual heterosexual union. Whatever form it takes, human sexuality is located in this realm of "living creatures," and thus outside of the family and village life in its visible form. A striking illustration is the fact that, according to Samoans of whatever age or gender, making love is something "that you do not do in the house, but outside"—the house, being a place where rank and genealogy are rooted, is not a "private" space but a "meeting" place, even if people sleep inside it at night.

In every situation in which men and women are defined as male and female, what emerges is *inequality* between a "stronger" and a "weaker" sex, categories that resemble those that operate in Western societies. Activities like flirting and premarital sex express male domination, and so do aspects of the wedding ceremony (Tcherkézoff 2003). The characteristics ascribed to either sex emerge from their respective essentialized "natures."

But in the realm of the socially visible, the "community" (*nu'u*) is peopled by three metaphorical categories of gendered humans: "chiefs," who can be men or women and are in a certain way outside of gender distinctions; their "daughters," that is, all girls and women belonging to the families of the village (excluding exogamous wives); and the latter's "brothers," that is, all untitled boys and men. Inequality also emerges here, but of an opposite kind: daughters, as "sacred sisters," embody the brother–sister relationship. Men are only defined as "brothers" in relation to women.

Practically speaking, this sharp distinction between sister–brother hierarchy and male–female inequality means that, in most matters relating to rank and titles, genealogy, and land, women as "sisters" have a very strong say and often can impose their views. They can do so because they are "sacred" (Schoeffel 1979; Tcherkézoff 2008b). Their superiority is based on "respect," or *fa'aaloalo*, ultimately backed by supernatural sanctions. But as soon as we revert to the realm of males and females, inequality is only backed by "strength"—that is, male strength.

This in turn informs the path of life-stages for boys and girls. These dynamics are encapsulated in a traditional song that accompanies men's ritual tattooing, which states that the destiny of males (*tane*) is to be tattooed, while the destiny of females (*fafine*) is to bear children (Tcherkézoff 2003: 408). Tattooing was the ritual transition to a life of strength: the boy became a member of the youth of the village, ceremonially called "the strength of the community," ready for hard work as well as courting girls— ideally with the end point of marriage, but also for the purpose of masculine competition over the number of conquests. The girls, of course, were expected to remain virgins until they were married.

Within this ideal binary world, there was and is no place for transgender. *Fa'ateine* can be "as if" sisters, but they will never marry. *Tomboys* do not follow boys' life path: they will never be tattooed with male designs and their physique and demeanor will never make them into any kind of "conquerors of virgin girls."

Fa'ateine, Tomboys, and Sexuality

This normative system has one major consequence for both *fa'ateine* and *tomboys*, at least as soon as they are viewed as potential or actual sexual partners. They are then both trapped within this realm, outside visible customary village life, locked into a world of sexuality under the sign of male domination. This ultimately explains many of the difficulties they encounter in their pursuit of sexual desires, as well as the asymmetry between them.

Heteronormative sisters and brothers know to leave sexuality outside the realm of visible village customary life, away from the household and the village, in order for it not to spoil the social categories "sister" and "brother." Thus, before marriage, sexual relations must remain hidden, and they continue to be so in certain ways even after marriage: in public, husband and wife comport themselves like brother and sister, avoiding physical contact and any allusion to sexuality.

What happens, then, to the *fa'ateine*? In the visible context of village life, her identity operates essentially without difficulty when she takes part in group activities with girls and contributes her labor as a girl in her household, together with her sisters. Within the household, however, her father and brothers fail to consider her as a daughter and sister respectively, and this is where she becomes the object of affective, verbal, and sometimes physical violence. More serious problems emerge in regard to sex, because in the realm of "living creatures" to which sexuality must remain confined, only heterosexual relations are thinkable. If two men engage in sexual relations, the mainstream discourse holds that one of them (and only one) must be "in the way of a (sexual) woman"—a *fa'afafine;* they cannot be "homosexual." While many people today know what these terms mean overseas, they also state that there is no Samoan equivalent and that the practice "does not exist in Samoa." Sex between two male-bodied persons is heterosexual, in that one is "straight" and the other "in the way of a woman" (and pleasure is thought to be located only in the first party, for better or for worse). Heteronormativity is maintained, and perhaps even reinforced.

In actual practice, however, things are more nuanced. While the norm in sex (either oral or anal) is for the *fa'ateine* to take the insertee role and the "straight" man to take the inserter role, the reverse sometimes takes place (cf. Besnier 1997 for Tonga). Some *fa'ateine* explicitly reject the possibility of sex-reassignment surgery, arguing that they may lose sexual sensitivity as a result. Yet the affective dynamics of the relationship are circumscribed by a heteronormative order, in that, whatever actually takes place during sex, the *fa'ateine* lives as a *teine* and is thus trapped in the heteronormative order—indeed, she is only attracted to straight men, an attraction that is both sexual and affective. Her dreams of settling down with him as a couple remain in the realm of impossibility in Samoa itself, as straight men dream of finding the right woman (both the object of his affection and the proper choice for kinship politics). Relations between straight men and *fa'ateine* remain temporary, which for the *fa'ateine* spells out affective loneliness. While many in Samoa maintain that straight men have sex with *fa'ateine* only when nothing else is available, the situation is more complex in that they may develop an affective attachment to *fa'ateine;* but there is no room within the confines of Samoan society to permit this attachment in the form of a stable and open relationship (cf. Besnier 2004 for Tonga).

Heteronormative hegemony applies equally, although more severely, to women's same-sex relationships. The negativity with which parents respond to *tomboy* behavior in daughters is itself the consequence of that hegemony. If half-hidden sexual play between same-sex female adolescents is common currency in Samoa as in many other societies, this laissez-faire does not apply to adults. No group of women is defined by sexual nonconformity and there is no vocabulary with which to talk about it. The very idea of a sexual relationship between women is thus disallowed by hegemonic ideology, and the lack of terminology in the Samoan language to describe it is another sign of its repression. Finally, a lesbian *tomboy* who may have a *fa'ateine* brother will find no comfort there, as the latter strives to be assimilated with her heteronormative sisters; and together, the *fa'ateine* brother and her sisters will not welcome their sister *tomboy*.

A couple can only consist of a woman and a man. While in mainstream representations a man can conceivably "act like a woman" sexually, neither heteronormative nor *fa'ateine* Samoan discourse admits that a woman can really take on a male sexual role. While mainstream Samoans believe and state that some *tomboys* seek to have sex with "straight" girls, the possibility arouses great embarrassment in people of all ages and genderings. To seek a sexual relationship of whatever kind with a woman makes the *tomboy* appear as a *fafine*, a woman defined by her sexual activity.

Status Asymmetry, Gender, and Heteronormativity

In contrast to a male-bodied person who claims to be a girl and sexually "acts like a woman," a female-bodied person cannot claim to be "like a boy/man" who seeks female sexual partners. When a woman is sexually active (through marriage or otherwise), she can only be a *fafine* and cannot claim to be "like" another category of sex or gender.

This asymmetry is already striking at the time of adolescence. A boy risks losing status by appearing not to be masculine enough and thus to be labeled *"fa'afafine,"* while a woman risks losing status by becoming the target of gossip to the effect that she has lost her virginity before marriage and thus be labeled *"fafine"* (Schoeffel 1979; Shore 1981; Schmidt 2010). For both genders, the negativity is located with the female and in sexuality. This in itself says a great deal about male domination in Samoan society.

Terms like *"fa'atamaloa"* cannot be made to imply a same-sex female sexuality because the word *"tamaloa"* (and others like it) denotes a male adult without any connotation of sexuality. Men's gendering can thus be defined without any reference to sexuality, while this is not the case with women's gendering. The resultant ideological asymmetry between the genders also generates an asymmetry between them as sexual categories and, above all, in the way in which women and men become sexually active beings: when they do so, boys are not confined in a category and thus can take on various personae; whereas girls encounter a restriction of who they are once they pass the point of no return—namely, the loss of their virginity.

A strong sign of this asymmetry is the fact that, in Samoa, there is no concept of "male virginity." In practice, the first time a boy has sex is a non-event. What concerns him is to convince his friends that he has already had sex with girls even if it is not the case. In the cultural representation of his body, the first time he has sex with a girl is no different from numerous other occasions on which the simulation of sex takes place—through masturbation, sexual games between male cousins, fondling a girl without penetration, or sex with a *fa'ateine*. In contrast, the representation of female virginity is marked by a rich vocabulary and, in former times, by a striking ritual—namely, the public manual defloration that was part of the marriage ceremony, performed on the village green when the girl was from a high-ranking family, otherwise inside the house.

In conclusion, the dominance of the heteronormative order in sexuality that reigns in Samoa leaves little room for the sexual paths that *fa'ateine* and *tomboys* sometimes seek to follow. Male dominance in all matters sexual generates a particular asymmetry between the two "transgender" categories, very much to the detriment of *tomboys*, which in turns generates inequality.

Notes

1   This chapter is a revised version of a paper presented at a conference organized in Canberra and Nouméa in October 2011, cosponsored by the Australian National University, the ANU center of the École des hautes études en sciences

sociales, and the Centre des nouvelles études sur le Pacifique of the University of New Caledonia. I thank Niko and Kalissa for encouraging me to develop the materials on *tomboy*s and for their tremendous work on editing my "Frenglish."

2   For a critique of this approach in a Samoan context, see Tcherkézoff (1993, 2003, 2008a, 2008b: 319–321). For a comparative perspective, see Tcherkézoff (2011), where I discuss recent critiques by French sociologist Irène Théry.

3   This situation, however, has changed since the creation, in the first decade of the new millennium, of identity-based associations such as The Samoa Faafafine Association and SOFIAS: Sosaiete o Faafafine i Amerika Samoa. As we shall see, the word "*fa'afafine*" was and still is seen as conveying morally negative meanings. Inverting its value and claiming it as a marker of pride is a recent phenomenon. It emerges in relation to earlier global networks, such as The United Territories of Polynesian Islanders Alliance (UTOPIA), "started in San Francisco in 1998 to support the Polynesian gay, lesbian, bisexual and transgender community" (http://www.utopiahawaii.com).

4   The English word "straight" has become part of the Samoan lexicon. It is applied to women and men whose gendered labor contribution and reputed sexual desires conform to what is expected of her/his sex assigned at birth.

5   Global commentaries about Samoa reflect this lack of visibility: while a Google search using the key words "Samoan fa'afafine," "Samoan transgender," or "Samoan effeminates" returns dozens of results, not a single one is obtainable for "Samoan *tomboy*s" or "Samoan girls who act like boys."

6   Levy's (1971, 1973) famous analysis of *māhū* in Tahitian villages is a variant on the same theme (Elliston, Alexeyeff and Besnier, this volume).

7   The aesthetic valuation of fair complexion predates contact with the West and is thus not the result of the internalization of a colonial racism (see Tcherkézoff 2008a, 121–122 and many others).

References

Alexeyeff, Kalissa. 2008. Globalizing Drag in the Cook Islands: Friction, Repulsion, and Abjection. *The Contemporary Pacific* 20: 143–161.

———. 2009. *Dancing from the Heart: Gender, Movement and Cook Islands Globalisation.* Honolulu: University of Hawai'i Press.

Besnier, Niko. 1997. Sluts and Superwomen: The Politics of Gender Liminality in Urban Tonga. *Ethnos* 62: 5–31.

———. 2002. Transgenderism, Locality, and the Miss Galaxy Beauty Pageant in Tonga. *American Ethnologist* 29: 534–566.

———. 2004. The Social Production of Abjection: Desire and Silencing amongst Transgender Tongans. *Social Anthropology* 12: 301–323.

————. 2011. *On the Edge of the Global: Modern Anxieties in a Pacific Island Nation.* Stanford, CA: Stanford University Press.

Chodorow, Nancy. 1978. *The Reproduction of Mothering: Psychoanalysis and the Sociology of Gender.* Berkeley: University of California Press.

Grépin, Laure-Hina. 1995. Tikehau: Des paradoxes sociaux autour de l'adolescence masculine contemporaine dans un atoll de Polynésie française. Masters thesis, École des hautes études en sciences sociales.

————. 2001. L'adolescence masculine aux Tuamotu de l'Est aujourd'hui—Le Taure'are'a: Contradictions et transformations d'une catégorie sociale traditionnelle. PhD diss., École des hautes études en sciences sociales.

Kulick, Don. 1998. *Travestí: Sex, Gender and Culture among Brazilian Transgendered Prostitutes.* Chicago: University of Chicago Press.

Levy, Robert I. 1971. The Community Functions of Tahitian Male Transvestites. *Anthropological Quarterly* 44: 12–21.

————. 1973. *Tahitians: Mind and Experience in the Society Islands.* Chicago: University of Chicago Press.

Mead, Margaret. 1928. *Coming of Age in Samoa: A Psychological Study of Primitive Youth for Western Civilisation.* New York: William Morrow & Co.

National Geographic. 2007. Taboo: Sex Change. http://www.youtube.com/watch?v= EronVtKYr0c (accessed March 2012).

Orans, Martin. 1996. *Not Even Wrong: Margaret Mead, Derek Freeman, and the Samoans.* Novato, CA: Chandler & Sharp.

Schmidt, Johanna. 2001. Redefining Fa'afafine: Western Discourses and the Construction of Transgenderism in Samoa. *Intersections* 6. http://wwwsshe .murdoch.edu.au/intersections/issue6/schmidt.html (accessed March 2012).

————. 2010. *Migrating Genders: Westernisation, Migration, and Samoan Fa'afafine.* Farnham, Surrey, UK: Ashgate.

Schoeffel, Penelope. 1979. Daughters of Sina: A Study of Gender, Status and Power in Western Samoa. PhD diss., Australian National University.

Shore, Bradd. 1981. Sexuality and Gender in Samoa: Conceptions and Missed Conceptions. In *Sexual Meanings: The Cultural Construction of Gender and Sexuality,* ed. Sherry Ortner and Harriet Whitehead, pp. 192–215. Cambridge: Cambridge University Press.

Tcherkézoff, Serge. 1993. The Illusion of Dualism in Samoa: "Brothers-and-Sisters" are not "Men-and-Women." In *Gendered Anthropology,* ed. Teresa del Valle, pp. 54–87. London: Routledge.

————. 2001. Is Anthropology about Individual Agency or Culture? Or Why "Old Derek" is Doubly Wrong. *Journal of the Polynesian Society* 110: 59–78.

————. 2003. *Fa'aSamoa, une identité polynésienne (économie, politique, sexualité): L'anthropologie comme dialogue culturel.* Paris: L'Harmattan.

————. 2008a. *First Contacts in Polynesia, The Samoan Case (1722–1848): Western Misunderstandings about Sexuality and Divinity.* Canberra: ANU E Press.

————. 2008b. Hierarchy Is Not Inequality, in Polynesia for Instance. In *Persistence and Transformation in Social Formations,* ed. Knut Rio and Olaf H. Smedal, pp. 299–329. Oxford: Berghahn.

————. 2011. La distinction de sexe, la sociologie holiste et les Îles Samoa: À propos du livre de Irène Théry, *La distinction de sexe, une nouvelle approche de l'égalité. L'Homme* 198–199: 333–354.

CHAPTER 7

Re-Visioning Family

Māhūwahine and Male-to-Female Transgender
in Contemporary Hawai'i

Linda L. Ikeda

> A way of life can be shared among individuals of
> different ages, status, and social activity. It can yield intense
> relations not resembling those that are institutionalized. It
> seems to me that a way of life can yield a culture and an ethics.
> To be "gay," I think, is not to identify with the psychological
> traits and the visible masks of the homosexual but to
> try and define and develop a way of life.
>
> *Foucault, "Friendship as a Way of Life"*

This chapter explores a particular network of transgender individuals in Honolulu, Hawai'i, and the ways in which they construct family and other communities of belonging. Though only a minority of these individuals identify as gay, Foucault's comments tap into the potentiality of "a way of life" over circumscribed modes of being and sexuality, as well as the inventive "self-fashioning" that appears to be central to transgender family making, at least in particular times and places. Both these features of creative development and self-definition are evident in this Honolulu community.

For all its creativity, however, the self-fashioning of transgender life has remained largely invisible to outsiders, though several have documented other, often more sensational, aspects of their lives, including transgender residing in urban Honolulu. Matzner (2001), for example, photographed and interviewed several prominent *māhūwahine* (male-to-female transgender) as part of an oral history project; Owens (2005) directed a controversial documentary entitled *Downtown Girls: The Hookers of Honolulu* and used candid interviews and hidden-camera footage to record the lives of transgender prostitutes; and Xian (2001) covered both *māhū* and drag queens in her documentary on colonization, sexuality, and homophobia in Hawai'i. The mainstream media have also paid little attention to transgender and their ordinary lives, including their family formations, though they remain quick to cover the titillating—such as transgender involvement in sex work, the drug trade, and other illegal or risk-taking practices (e.g., Gulya 2008).

As a result, we have information about the novel and the "spectacular" (Namaste 2000), but little understanding of transgender individuals and their everyday lives, particularly with regard to practices of survival and belonging across societies and historical times. Furthermore, we have little understanding of the formation and importance of family for the transgender, as well as other forms of relatedness.[1] In this chapter, I have two aims: first, to shed light on female-identified transgender in their making of community and family in contemporary Honolulu and, second, to challenge the sensational—that is, impoverished and bleak accounts as well as those that have been glamorized, exoticized, or sexualized—in favor of the ordinary and the "everyday" (Smith 1987).

The Photovoice Project

The data for this project were partially comprised of photographs taken by sixteen camera-wielding study participants. These photographs served as springboards for narratives, which I collected in the course of four focus groups conducted in the city and county of Honolulu in the fall of 2007.[2] These narratives, including the verbal and photographic, illuminate particular positionings rather than set or static identities. The narratives also serve to situate individual stories within broader cultural and historical trajectories: "Identities are the names we give to the different ways we are positioned by, and position ourselves within, the narratives of the past" (Hall 1989, 225).

All sixteen participants self-identified as *māhū, māhūwahine,* or female-identified transgender (sometimes referred to as "TG"), with fourteen living as women and two as men (self-identified as "butch queens").[3] Of the sixteen participants, ten self-identified as Hawaiian or part Hawaiian and six as Pacific Islander (mainly Samoan) or mixed Pacific Islander and other ethnicities. The average age of participants was thirty-three; all but one were residing with a partner, family members, or friends or in a residential facility, such as a "clean and sober" house for recovering substance abusers. Though only one had completed college, 18 percent held an Associate's degree (granted after two years of tertiary education or training) or its equivalent. The average income (for the 81 percent who were employed) ranged from US$800 to US$3,833 a month.[4]

The community leader who was charged with recruitment for the project was heavily involved in drag pageants and similar events, which led to recruitment of others involved in drag performances. The resultant emphasis on pageants and drag shows, however, should not be misread as representative of the broader transgender or even local *māhūwahine* community, as many transgender in Hawai'i have no interest in pageants or the stage.[5] Also, while all of the participants (excluding the butch queens) had engaged in some degree of medically assisted gender transitioning—including hormonal therapy, surgery, implants, and silicone injections—their identification as transgender preceded these body modifications. Further, most participants did not view transitioning as a change from male to female or vice versa so much as a shift to a desired place "in between" or even beyond gender binaries (cf. Feinberg 1996).

In this sense, the very terms that define the participants—that is, "*māhūwahine*" and "transgender"—are inadequate and found wanting. While all self-identified as transgender and as Native Hawaiians or Pacific Islanders in some contexts, they also felt that these terms did not encompass the whole of their identifications. (On the problematics of terms in general, see Alexeyeff and Besnier, this volume.) Some, for example, referred to themselves as "transgender," a term consistent with the classification used by government agencies and in medical discourse (e.g., the US Centers for Disease Control and Prevention, medicine, and psychology), and thereby used by local nonprofit organizations. At the same time, many have turned to the traditional terms *māhū* or *māhūwahine*, though the former remains associated with slang and derogatory use (and sometimes with gay men) and the latter is often viewed as applying primarily to those of Native Hawaiian ancestry (Morgan 2010).[6]

At other times, participants referred to themselves as "women," "queens," or "gurls" (or, in the case of two participants, "butch queens"). For the purposes of this project, however, they were classified as *māhūwahine* (male-to-female transgender). This problematic concession, juxtaposing an indigenous term with a Western understanding, arguably served to privilege the Western understanding and render the "alternative" indigenous understandings unintelligible, except in translation or as borrowings (Valentine 2007).[7] The working definition adopted here, then, is that the categories *māhū* and *māhūwahine* exceed Western male/female binaries and the category "transgender," as well as any identity that is limited to a single gender.

In addition, the terms differ with regard to historicity; both "transgender" and "*māhūwahine*" are contemporary terms in contrast to the term "*māhū*." This is significant, as the latter is generally viewed as holding traditional meaning, thereby providing a historical trajectory for the acceptance of contemporary non-heteronormative Hawaiians. Briefly, Native Hawaiian academics and historians have documented that *māhū* were given a specific place in traditional Hawaiian society for their healing skills, their ability to simultaneously occupy both male and female spaces, and their talent in *hula* and *mele* (chanting and song), among other attributes. According to this view, with colonization and the spread of Christianity, this status became eroded (Kameʻeleihiwa 1999).[8]

Subsequently, with the influence of Western psychology and its pathologizing theories of sexuality, *māhū* became conflated with transvestism, transgenderism, homosexuality, and inversion, adding to this loss of status (Morgan 2010). In short, the imposition of a Western gender binary and reliance on a framework of identification based on sexual rather than social practice have left *māhū*—as neither men or women, nor homosexuals—without a place on the social map (Besnier 2004; Gopinath 2005; Namaste 2000). It is this condition of social and institutional negation, if not "erasure," that necessitates the development of new ways of life and community and family making (Foucault 1997; Muñoz 1999).

Queer Affect

Participants expressed a sense of placelessness, often as a result of hegemonic categorizations of their sexuality and the negativity provoked by their non-heteronormative identities (figure 1). For instance, when asked why they thought this photovoice project was necessary, participants variously stated that: "[Transgender] has something to do with bad, you know, something with sex. The straight people would come by us and they grab their husband and they say, 'Take a look.' And the husband would give that smirk to us, you know what I mean? . . . and they think . . . [we] have to do with something nasty; that, you know, like we're . . . in the gutter; . . . our lifestyle is just pure gutter."

As these comments suggest, outsiders (i.e., non-transgender) may perceive *māhūwahine* as deviant, sick, or criminal. The desire to challenge these misperceptions, linked to media portrayals of *māhūwahine* as drug-abusing street prostitutes and HIV carriers, motivated the project participants to share their accounts and me to record them.

Although it was the initial intent of the study to focus on positive aspects of collectivity and kinship (in part, as a counterpoint to negative representations), it became impossible to disregard the pain and marginalization that surfaced in participants' accounts. Listening to recordings, one can hear (even more clearly than in the original narrations) the long pauses in attempts to regain composure, the faltering, the hurried tale, the subtle but perceptible changes in tone—so difficult to render on the page. Even more difficult to tease out and convey, their grief, hurt, remorse, and other feelings were often mingled with conflicting sentiments—for instance, shame entangled with gratitude. Eventually, I came to understand the pain expressed by participants as both complicating the project and speaking to and underscoring its necessity.

To understand why and how *māhūwahine* families are formed and to capture the complexity and depth of their feelings, I turned to Love (2007) and Muñoz (2009), who detail the productivity of melancholia in general and sadness in particular as impetus toward action or activism, and as a link

FIGURE 1

Melancholia

to the past. (Similarly, Crimp [1989] argues for the utility of mourning and its place in social action.) This expanded notion of sadness serves two important functions: "It lays bare the conditions of exclusion and inequality and . . . gestures toward alternative trajectories for the future" (Love 2007, 29).

Consistent with this understanding, the sadness expressed by project participants appeared to be related to exclusion from both heteronormative and homonormative society. As an example, many current LGBT political goals in Hawai'i, and more generally in the United States (e.g., the legalization of same-sex marriage and the repeal of the "Don't Ask, Don't Tell" provisions in the military) leave them even further marginalized as what some have called "other others" (Shankman 2010). The sadness was also related to the participants' family histories, which arguably motivated their shaping of "alternative trajectories" through new kinship choices, though they retained a deep respect for ancestors and (blood) elders and concern for children—that is, for the past and future generations. Even more, I came to understand Love's notion of an alternative trajectory as tied to the emergence of hope—an element that, however intangible, helped to transform their acts of caregiving, and even family making, from task or performance to a "promise for tomorrow" (Muñoz 2009).

Attention to negative affect also sheds light on identity construction and family making in relation to wider cultural politics. As Gopinath (2005) argues, transgender individuals represent the epitome of the hypervisible—that is, the sensationalized and spectacular—leaving them unintelligible to dominant culture. The result is a condition of (im)possibility, of loss, absence, and negation, and of relentless acts of contestation and struggle in the effort to simply survive (also Halberstam 2005; Namaste 2000). Yet, it is this very condition that Muñoz (1999) links to processes of identity creation and collectivity, serving, as it does, as a social location of commonality and thus a foundation (figure 2).

Family Matters

Many participants described significant relationships and enduring ties to a range of collectivities—including biological families, partners, and children; adopted and traditionally fostered (*hanai*) relatives; and chosen or drag families (e.g., those created through involvement in drag shows), as well as people with whom they worked (figures 3 and 4).

In reference to biological families, one common narrative was that of struggle and rejection, often prompted by an initial coming out or move toward transitioning. In many cases, these initial difficulties prompted them to run away or to be exiled by the family. After an initial period of distress and strained relations, however, many participants managed to restore a connection to their families. Given their young age when these troubles occurred, their schooling, and consequently employment and housing opportunities, had often suffered. One participant spoke of her coming out as a strain on her family and a disappointment to her mother, at least at first:

> And me coming out, being a TG, me coming out to her, my family, was kinda hard 'cause I was the first one, out of six kids, and it was kinda a big shocker to my family seeing me coming out in drags because, you know, I was a boy, had girlfriends, . . . played sports and when I said that I wanted to be *māhū*, [Mom] was the first one that I actually go confided, and she was in shock and . . . my relationship with my family . . . was . . . kinda strained . . . ; they never understand why I chose to be rebellious, why I chose to, you know, run towards the streets, why I chose not [to] be the good kid that she wanted me to be.

FIGURE 2

Supporting a drag sister

FIGURE 3

Family of origin

FIGURE 4

Blended family

Others shared similar experiences, such as this participant (at the time of the focus groups, in her mid-thirties), who spoke of being disowned and her family's shame, expressed particularly by the men—noteworthy in its contrast to accounts of traditional Native Hawaiians' alleged acceptance of *māhū:*

> You know, no father wants his son to be *māhū* but like I told them, like I think I haven't seen them for almost like seven or eight years, I kinda just left the family; my father already told me he disowned me, um when my grandfather died . . . ; he's pure Hawaiian; . . . and my dad said you're not a part of this family; . . . you're not welcome around the family, and . . . I had to do a lot of soul-searching to find myself.

In light of these difficulties, accounts of blood relations who remained loyal to participants, especially in times of hardship or struggle, were the subject of particularly cherished memories. For instance, one participant who had been in trouble with the law spoke movingly of her father overcoming his shame and visiting her in jail:

> My father would always come down, when I was in prison, my father came to visit me every single weekend. . . . That was when my father actually saw me for the woman that I was . . . and even though it might have been shame-faced [embarrassing] to come to the prison or shame for him to have somebody from the family be in prison, he stayed by me and made sure I was always taken care of.

Still, for other participants, grandmothers emerged as particularly important, consistent with the strong emotional bonding of grandmothers and their grandchildren that is commonplace in many Polynesian societies (figures 5 and 6). One, for example, explained that it was her grandmother who paved the way for others in her family to accept and support her:

> My grandmother, being the matriarch of the entire family, being the person who um . . . (*pause*) . . . pulled the whole family together, she supported me; my God, she's the one . . . , that's how the whole thing came together, the whole entire family had to accept me. She bought me clothes, she bought me my girl clothes; . . . she didn't

understand but she knew that's what I wanted and she supported everything that I wanted.

Participants also shared many stories and pictures about the importance of siblings, even when their acceptance was lacking in enthusiasm or less than wholehearted (figure 7). Speaking of her brother, one participant said:

My brother, you know, no matter what, he introduced me as S. [initial of her given "boy" name]; to this day he still introduced me as S. "This is my brother, S." He accept[s] me for what I am but, in his eyes, I'll always be his brother.

Another participant, in contrast, spoke of her sister as more inclined toward acceptance:

This photo is . . . of my mom and my sister, my younger sister and um . . . (pause) . . . Me being TG affects my sister for sure 'cause now she has a sister. Before she had two brothers but now she has an older brother and she calls me her sister.

FIGURE 7

Siblings

Acceptance and rejection, then, emerged as key themes running throughout the narratives. Though acceptance was more forthcoming in some families than others, all participants spoke of the importance of finding some recognition, if not approval, of their transgender or *māhūwahine* identity. Along these lines, one participant, whose family was Christian, explained a "compromise" on the part of some her family members:

> They are all accepting except for the name part; they address me by my last name which is M. [initial] and they will not call me by my legal first name [a female name] because they feel that in their religion, you cannot do that; but the sisters will call me, "oh, sis," and my brother-in-law and them, they don't care; they'll call me sis and by my girl name.

Another participant described a reunion with her family after a long period of separation during which she transitioned from male to female presentation. Though her family was initially shocked, they were quick to reach acceptance. A photo of a reunion sparked the following:

> When I went up there, they totally wasn't ready (*laughter*); they totally didn't know; they knew through errors [rumors] but they never seen and when I went up there, they were like "Oh, wow," you know, . . . adjust to the change so . . . this was our . . . family reunion; this [is] my *ohana* [family].

Participants also spoke of strong bonds with their adopted or *hanai* family members. This latter family form, related to a traditional Hawaiian practice that creates ties beyond those of blood, often takes place through mutual agreement and without legal backing, akin to fosterage practices found throughout the Pacific Islands (Marsh 2004; cf. Kuwahara on Tahiti, this volume). In the following narrative, the *hanai* relationship was informal and related to the significance of the caregiving provided to the participant's mother:

> This is [my mother's] church buddy, and I consider her family because . . . when I go to work she knows, she keeps contact with me with appointments; she's there to feed my mom when I cannot. She's precious, so I adopted her . . . because she's been with my mom for so long she's just, um, just like a sister; . . . I adopted her, like my sister.

In other cases, *hanai* relations had been formalized legally. One participant, for instance, legally changed her last name from that of her biological family, who had disowned her, to that of her *hanai* sister:

> So the pictures that I chose . . . of my *hanai* sister . . . she's my sister because when I first came out and my family . . . disowned me and I didn't have a place to go, she was the one who . . . took me in; come with me . . . she opened up her house to me.

Several also spoke of their work families, viewed as especially significant in light of the difficulties routinely faced by *māhūwahine* in obtaining decent and secure jobs. These work families were important not only because of the amount of time spent together but because of the values they shared with participants and their encouragement and support.

Caring for Kin

Many of those involved in the project engaged in practices that might best be understood as creating a "genealogy." I use this term not to reference biological connection but to signal various activities that build, support, and enhance families—such as caring for children or the elderly (covered later in the chapter), and the staging of drag shows or pageants. Genealogy also encompasses efforts to spare younger generations the pain and hardship related to the "catastrophes and losses" experienced by the current or former generations (cf. Muñoz 1999).

Many participants spoke about their involvement in caring for elders and children. While this might have been a function of their age (as members of the "sandwich generation"), this role was also expected of them, given their transgender or *māhūwahine* status: "So that's why a lot of *māhūs* are the chosen ones . . . we're the thin line between love and hate because sometimes our straight families are not a family; they get so caught up in things . . . [but] it's not really about them. It's really about the children, you know. That's where we're always connected to, the caregiving thing; that's the life of a *māhū*. We're chosen."

Similarly, with regard to elders, several spoke of caring for their ill or aging parents or grandparents. This participant described a situation of caregiving for her mother that was supposedly shared among the siblings but in fact fell most heavily upon her. The sentiment expressed, however, was not one of resentment but of worry: "This woman is eighty-seven years old. I love her with all my heart; her memory is fading and it's fading at a rate where she could get one minute [of lucidity, or even of life] and it's hard for me because I have to work . . . I have to watch her, make sure she takes her medication, she eats."

Another participant described a "sister" who was caring for and entertaining her grandmother (figure 8):

> I took this picture of S. and her grandmother in her . . . living room. . . . She was putting on her drags and she would come out from down the hallway with music blasting and she would come spinning down . . . and, you know, performing for her grandmother who, you know, has a hard time hearing, has a hard time seeing. But she was laughing, she was cracking up every time she [S.] came out from around the corner; . . . and S. was . . . posing for her and asking her how she looked. Do you love it?

Several participants spoke also of raising children, sometimes from birth. In one case, these children had been born to a biological sister who

FIGURE 8

Do you love it?

had lost custody of them due to drug use and incarceration; in another case, to a biological sister who had been killed in an accident; and in a third, to a female long-term partner. For those who had raised or helped to raise children, their gender identity was posed as creating little conflict with their parenting role: "Well, with my kids [aged nine, eleven, and fourteen] they really don't consider me as a TG. They might know I'm a TG, but the subject doesn't really come up. . . . I know one day I would have to talk to them about it, but as for now I can only say that my kids see me as their mama; I'm not even called a TG or a *māhū* aunty, I'm just their mama. Um, so they have accepted me as a certain way. . . . I had them all as baby, yeah, from birth." Similarly, for another participant: "We're actually really close; . . . and me being transgender, they've all come to know me being *māhū* at a different stage and time in their lives; it's always been in front of them; it's never been hidden."

In addition to caring for children, many participants provided for their biological as well as their chosen families. One participant, at the time just out of high school, spoke of her efforts to help supply money and food to her mother and sister. In addition to material care, participants provided for their biological and chosen families emotionally, working to ensure their safety and well-being. Describing a drag son, another participant shared that:

> He was going through some stuff; his family kicked him out because he was a gay boy and they didn't want anything to do with him and so I took him in and I told him, you know, one day your family gonna take you back; you just take some time to let all of this process. And then one day I . . . made him call his parents . . . and they . . . cried and they asked to see him so I took him to go see his family and . . . (*pause*). It's all good now and . . . that's how I became close with his parents.

Drag Families

Another type of family that participants created was the drag or chosen family. While drag families can involve support for nascent drag queens in terms of helping them cultivate talents and a particular look (including grooming of the body, face, and hair, and costume selection), they may also involve more general support, such as the provision of food and shelter.

While this can take the form of people living together in the tradition of the ball houses, houses in Hawai'i can also be formed among people who live separately yet are unified under a particular queen mother or other leader, or through their involvement in nightclub drag shows or pageants. These drag families emerged as an extremely significant form of connection:

> Because some of us, we can get isolated by our "real" families . . . so we tend to make a whole new family with our friends, you know what I mean. And we take it to a whole new level . . . with this drag family, you know what I mean? So it's . . . for our peace of mind and our well-being; . . . it's . . . to make our self-esteem a whole lot better, to face society and its cruelties and ridicules . . .'cause their ignorance we face every day.

Similarly, participants highlighted the significance of their "sisters" (sometimes part of their drag family, sometimes not), whose acceptance and support could mean the difference, in some instances, between life and death. While this support was usually psychological or emotional, it could also be material—for example, involving money, food, or shelter:

> This one right here [pointing to a person in a photo] is J. . . . At the time meeting her we was into the scene of fast money and stuff so we didn't really meet on positive terms but it was pretty fun (*laughter*); but she's been there for me, too. For me right now, she's like my sister, she's my godmother, she's my aunty.

And from another participant:

> If it wasn't for them I think I would have . . . committed suicide. . . . I don't know, I woulda done the worst of things to me . . . but they were there to pick me up when I was at my lowest, and my family . . . when I moved from my family, trying to transition, understanding what *māhūwahine* was about; that was me, those were my sisters.

Others entered drag families in response to loss, sometimes related to tragedy or death:

I heard a lot about drag families and when I was first brought into a drag family it was by my first queen mother . . . and it was the perfect timing for me because . . . when I first met her, my real mom had passed away and I needed that female figure in my life and she was it.

This feature of providing support emerged as a key theme, with almost all the participants having served as a mentor to a younger person in the process of coming out or transitioning. Although this relationship was often informal, it was sometimes made official or public by way of a title and role, with many serving as a drag parent while being drag-parented themselves. Also, the same individual could serve as a drag father to some and a drag mother to others. One participant, a *māhūwahine,* explained it this way:

So for a lot of my kids, they look at me as a mother and a father figure; to some, their mother, to some who already have mothers, I'm their father figure, and it's funny because I actually possess [both] those qualities, you know—[as] the mother, I'm very nurturing and loving, but as the father, I'm very strict and . . . sometimes a disciplinarian.

Given their embracing of both sides of the gender binary, any participant could potentially serve as a drag father or mother to either drag daughters or sons. As an example, another participant, also *māhūwahine,* stated: "Because she doesn't have a drag mother and, with all due respect, she's a sister of mine . . . but, um, she looks at me [in] another light, which would be another parent. Instead of being a mother, I'm like a father and she calls me 'Pops.'"

So again, we see a *māhūwahine* "sister" taking on the role of a drag father, which might entail the provision of housing and other material support, alongside emotional and other care often designated as "male."

Furthermore, butch queens (participants with male presentation) were also involved in drag families and pageants, whether as performers, assistants, or supporters. One butch queen (figure 9), incidentally also a housemother (or family leader, responsible for the well-being of her drag sons or daughters who, in this instance, did not share a common living space) stated:

For these two [*pointing to people in a photo*] . . . we have this very special bond and relationship because of what we went through growing up, you know, that I'm [considered] a gay man but they also know I'm a butch queen. I mean I was an entertainer and they stood up for me when I was in an abusive relationship, when my back was against the wall, when I questioned whether or not I wanted to be a transgender, and they've been there for me through a lot of these issues that I've been through, some things that I never even talked to my sisters about.

Most commonly, though, drag children were taken in to be groomed as performers, an act that can also be understood as caregiving. One participant described preparing her drag daughter for the stage and grooming her to increase her chances of finding a significant other (figure 10):

That's K., it took me a long time to (*pause*). This one actually put me through a lot because, you know, I wanted her to be better, yeah, and it was like, I guess all her relationships she's been in . . . really I don't know what brought her down, whatever, so I tried my best, I don't know. I put her on hormones. I wanted to help groom

FIGURE 9

An evening out

her. I wanted . . . to dolly up somebody. I wanted to put silicone in them and let them look really fishy [feminine] and stuff like that. I wanted to help her.

This narrative highlights attempts to feminize a drag daughter, not only to provide her with a more recognizable and socially acceptable "feminine" appearance, but also to increase her odds of attracting a man (a goal of many *māhūwahine*). In this case, the drag daughter had struggled with finding a suitable male partner and was losing hope for a relationship. The narrator's note of frustration was in recognition of the inadequacy of her efforts; she knew that no amount of "dollying up" could truly remedy the situation.

Participants also spoke of sharing their "drags"—that is, their costumes and accessories—with the children in their households, both as a learning experience and as part of a caregiving role. In this narrative, "drags" does not refer to cross-dressing but to *über*-feminine dressing with glitter, false lashes, high heels, and the like: "So I've been with this family for, like I said, ten years so I've watched her grow up from a tiny little girl . . . and she loves being in drags and getting her hair [done] and all of that."

Similarly, another participant spoke of sharing her "drags" with her children, in this case, through face painting for Halloween (figure 11):

FIGURE 10

Drag parents

"Last night I was just going to take my babies trick-or-treating but then my middle boy decided that he wanted to go and . . . when I was painting him [his face], his brother was saying, . . . 'Oh mama, could you make me a mask, too?' . . . So I ended up [painting] both of my sons."

Finally, being a drag parent and having drag children were viewed as related to genealogical inheritance—that is, the passing down of character traits, or even of physical characteristics or style. One participant described her photograph in these terms: "The previous picture that you've seen . . . that's her queen daughter, and I think in her queen daughter you can see a lot of traits in this mother right here." In response to this remark, those familiar with both the queen mother and the daughter laughed, recognizing the physical and personality traits that they shared despite the absence of genetic relatedness. What stood out here were not the particulars of the shared traits (which may well have been "undesirable") so much as the knowledge that they were being "passed down."

FIGURE 11

Halloween 2007

New Ways of Doing Family

For participants who had been stigmatized, harassed, ostracized, and otherwise shunned, family, however conceived, was a critical place of support and refuge. Family, in fact, remained as one of the few constants in the face of ongoing drawbacks and challenges: "We have families just as any normal people [do] and, um, everyone has their own different mindset on TGs and I believe that, in the end, families are going to be there for who you are and what you are and I believe we're no different from anybody else."

A key theme running throughout the narratives was the role that family, particularly chosen family, played in shaping participants' identity as *māhūwahine,* along with ensuring their well-being and sense of belonging. Conversely, participants played an important role in shaping their families, especially their families of origin, providing them with new insights and understandings about gender and sexuality. Here, a participant talks about her biological family:

> So that's what it taught my family, to be very accepting and very open, to open your mind and really that's what it would take, especially for a lot of local families, because once you are born male into the family you have all of these stereotypes for what you need to be as a male and sometimes you need to open up your mind and allow different concepts to form.

In addition, many believed that exposing children to different ways of being would result in the kind of world that would allow for a wider range of gendered options (and sartorial choices). Here, a participant describes an interaction with her toddler niece (figure 12):

> When it comes to them, when I won Universal [pageant], [my niece] had my crown, so I have picture of her with, you know, me holding the crown on top of her . . . because drags is kind of what I share with them; I mean . . . they come into aunty's closet and they see all this shiny, shiny stuff . . . and it's obviously not what mom has in her closet or grandma so I . . . share my drags with them to, you know, bring them into my world a little bit, educate, [help them to] understand.

In short, participants expressed a sense of hope for future transgender and other marginalized groups, related to efforts to instill change in the mindset of young people today.

Lessons Learned

Melancholia, related to trauma and loss, can be closely tied to the formation of collectivities and the creation of new forms of belonging and affective ties. Kinship, and collectivity in general, can develop in response to melancholia (inclusive of hardship, especially as related to loss of status). This can serve to bring people together and offer a common understanding and shared mission—for instance, the aim of sparing the younger generation from the harms endured by transgender today.

The potential of pain as impetus or fuel for social obligation is highlighted by these narratives, demonstrating how this particular network, like others similarly situated, has managed and continues to manage through "a susceptibility to pain and a sharing of a hope for its future alleviation" (Holt

FIGURE 12

Sharing drag

1997, 103). Stated differently, shared identity among the participants was related to a social positioning rather than to anything intrinsic, with a key feature being one of exclusion from mainstream society, whether hetero-normative or homonormative.[9] Rather than succumbing to the ill effects of this exclusion, however, this network of individuals has managed to band together so as to work toward a "better tomorrow."

Reading these understandings of the function of sadness and melan-cholia alongside the narratives of project participants, we can better appre-ciate family making and its connection to futurity recognized, not as "an end, but an opening" in its allowing for the "potentiality of the quotidian" (Muñoz 2009, 91). From the vantage point of melancholia (encompass-ing a range of losses), one can better assess the obstacles to a manageable life in the present—a present, in this case, surely marked by postcolonial effects. Particularly for *māhū* who traditionally held positions of status and pride, the mere knowledge of a different past can provide hope for an improved tomorrow, encouraging steps toward the envisioned future. These steps—for Muñoz "utopian kernels" (1999, 25)—make for an altered sense of time, linking yesterday with today and today with tomorrow, thereby expanding the scope of possibilities and breathing new life into the ordi-nary and day-to-day.

Beyond, and possibly related to, their survival today and hope for a more desirable tomorrow, the collectivities and family formations brought to light by the study participants were likely facilitated by cultural practices common to Pacific Islanders. To elaborate, the family making described by participants may be a contemporary example of ball-house culture, which may be more readily accommodated by the local Pacific Islander or host culture as compared to mainstream US culture.[10] Even this accommoda-tion, however, has not been sufficient to wholly safeguard the study partici-pants from the harms of conventional misunderstandings, such as the view of sexual minority individuals as insular beings capable of relations that can only mimic those of "real families" (Weston 1991, 212).

Yet this group of individuals has not succumbed to this marginalizing negation, possibly because their struggles make family particularly critical to their very existence and possibly on account of their strong ties to the past, whether related to descent and bloodlines or to ties beyond. Their hope, put simply, is for broader freedoms and acceptance, if not for them-selves, then for those who will follow. This is what the narratives and images arguably offer—a unique glimpse into a conscious disidentification borne of a particular grief, rooted in a particular cultural knowledge and pride (however borrowed or shared), and tightly fixed on future potential.

Acknowledgments

Many thanks to Ann Rosegrant Alvarez, Peter Mataira, Lana S. Kaʻopua, Meda Chesney-Lind, and Susan Hippensteele, all of whom took a chance on me through supporting and helping to shape the initial study. Thanks also to Niko Besnier, Kalissa Alexeyeff, and the anonymous reviewers for their receptivity and careful critical readings, to Reid Uratani for his remarks on an earlier draft, to drag mother/sister/friend Maddalynn S. Sesepasara for assisting me with entry into the community, and to all the study participants for their candor and courage. I remain indebted.

Notes

Epigraph. Foucault 1997, 138.

1   Exceptions can be found in the work of historians George Chauncey (1994) and Eric Garber (1989), among others, who describe the drag balls of Harlem in the 1920s and 1930s, now understood as the origin of the ball houses that began to develop in the 1970s and 1980s. See also Livingston 1991; Valentine 2007.

2   Photovoice is a participatory research method developed by Wang and Burris (1997), combining a grassroots approach to photography with social activism or efforts to affect social change. See also Carlson (2006) on photovoice and the usefulness of strategies from visual anthropology.

3   *"Māhū"* is a term than can include female-identified men as well as male-identified women, while *"māhūwahine"* refers specifically to the former. While butch queens are different from *māhūwahine* in terms of physical presentation, they are arguably similar in terms of (some degree of) female identification. In this study, I included self-identified butch queens, understood as transgender individuals who identify as women but present themselves as men for social, economic, or political reasons.

4   According to the US Census Bureau (2007), the per capita monthly income for Honolulu County in 2006 was $2,368. While some participants talked about work, no questions were posed as to the exact nature of this work and the source of their income. It is of interest, however, that the participant with the highest income and educational level presented as male (a butch queen)—a presentation that likely spared this individual the discrimination and setbacks routinely suffered by more physically obvious sexual minority "others."

5   Downtown Honolulu, where the study was conducted, has long served as a gathering place for transgender—a history that can readily be traced back at least to the Glades Nightclub, where many transgender performed from the 1960s to the 1980s. Much of the earlier history, however, from the time of colonization until this period, has gone undocumented or has been hidden. (See Kameʻeleihiwa, 1999 for the historical context; Matzner, 2001 for contemporary accounts.)

6   Carol Odo and Ashliana Hawelu (2001), affiliated with the nonprofit organization Kulia Na Mamo, have described *māhūwahine* as a recently coined term of empowerment among the transgender in Hawaiʻi. This term signifies a range of male-to-female (MtF) transgender identities and coincides with the Hawaiian cultural renaissance that began in the 1970s.

7   The study was part of a dissertation project in social work (Ikeda-Vogel 2008), a discipline strongly influenced by psychology. This connection to the university required that the study adhere to Western understandings, despite its focus on a primarily indigenous population and despite the locale.

8   Native Hawaiian historian Lilikalā Kameʻeleihiwa (1992) references the *ʻaikane,* or kept male lovers of high chiefs. Though the (often bisexual) *ʻaikane* should be distinguished from the *māhū,* both are supposed to be viewed as acceptable identities that held important roles in traditional society.

9   See Duggan (2003) for a discussion of homonormativity and its ties to consumer culture as well as, more generally, Duberman (2002) on social exclusion and the potential radicalizing power of transgender.

10   While this suggests that *māhū* are more readily accepted within Polynesian cultures, this small and localized qualitative study cannot be generalized to make that claim. At the same time, several have documented an openness among Native Hawaiians (and other Pacific Islanders) toward gender and sexual diversity, pre-contact (e.g., Kameʻeleihiwa 1999) and contemporarily (e.g., Matzner 2001; Xian 2001). Also, from an LGBT rather than a cultural standpoint, others have documented the strengths and enduring qualities of chosen (e.g., Weston 1991) and ball-house families (Butler 1993).

References

Besnier, Niko. 2004. The Social Production of Abjection: Desire and Silencing among Transgender Tongans. *Social Anthropology* 12: 301–323.

Butler, Judith. 1993. Gender Is Burning: Questions of Appropriation and Subversion. In *Bodies That Matter: On the Discursive Limits of "Sex,"* pp. 121–140. New York: Routledge.

Carlson, Elizabeth D. 2006. Photovoice as a Social Process of Critical Consciousness. *Qualitative Health Research* 16: 836–852.

Chauncey, George. 1994. *Gay New York: Gender, Urban Culture, and the Making of the Gay Male World, 1890–1940.* Chicago: University of Chicago Press.

Crimp, Douglas. 1989. Mourning and Militancy. *October* 51: 18.

Duberman, Martin B. 2002. *Left Out: The Politics of Exclusion: Essays 1964–2002.* Cambridge, MA: South End Press.

Duggan, Lisa. 2003. *The Twilight of Equality: Neoliberalism, Cultural Politics, and the Attack on Democracy.* Boston: Beacon Press.

Feinberg, Leslie. 1996. *Transgender Warriors: Making History from Joan of Arc to Dennis Rodman.* Boston: Beacon Press.

Foucault, Michel. 1997. Friendship as a Way of Life. In *The Essential Works of Foucault 1954–1984,* ed. Paul Rabinow, pp. 135–140. New York: New Press.

Garber, Eric. 1989. A Spectacle in Color: The Lesbian and Gay Subculture of Jazz Age Harlem. In *Hidden from History: Reclaiming the Gay and Lesbian Past,* ed. Martin Duberman, Martha Vicinus, and George Chauncey, Jr., pp. 318–331. New York: Penguin.

Gopinath, Gayatri. 2005. *Impossible Desires: Queer Diasporas and South Asian Public Cultures.* Durham, NC: Duke University Press.

Gulya, Lisa. 2008. The Evolution of Transgender Media Coverage. *Utne Reader,* March 27; http://www.utne.com/2008-03-27/Media/The-Evolution-of-Transgender-Media-Coverage.aspx (accessed December 2011).

Halberstam, Judith. 2005. *In a Queer Time and Place: Transgender Bodies, Subcultural Lives.* New York: New York University Press.

Hall, Stuart. 1989. Cultural Identity and Cinematic Representation. *Framework* 36: 68–81.

Holt, Robin. 1997. *Wittgenstein, Politics, and Human Rights.* New York: Routledge.

Ikeda-Vogel, Linda. 2008. Re-Visioning Family: A Photovoice Project with Transgenders and Their Families in Hawai'i. PhD diss., School of Social Welfare, University of Hawai'i at Mānoa.

Kame'eleihiwa, Lilikalā. 1992. *Native Land and Foreign Desires: Pehea Lā E Pono Ai? How Shall We Live in Harmony?* Honolulu: Bishop Museum Press.

———. 1999. *Ka Le'alea o nā Kupuna,* Traditional Hawaiian Sexuality, A Celebration of Life: Ni'aupio, Punalua, Po'olua, Aikane and Māhū. Paper read at Building Bridges with Traditional Knowledge II: An International Summit Meeting on Issues Involving Indigenous Peoples, Conservation, Sustainable Development and Ethnoscience, Honolulu.

Livingston, Jennie (director). 1990. *Paris Is Burning.* Buena Vista Home Video (78 min.).

Love, Heather. 2007. *Feeling Backward: Loss and the Politics of Queer History.* Cambridge, MA: Harvard University Press.

Marsh, Rebecca. 2004. Shortcomings in American Adoption Policies and a Hawaiian Alternative. *Hohonu: A Journal of Academic Writing* 2(2); http://hilo.hawaii.edu/academics/hohonu/writing.php?id=28 (accessed May 2012).

Matzner, Andrew. 2001. *'O Au No Keia: Voices from Hawaii's Māhū and Transgender Communities*. [s.l.]: Xlibris.

Morgan, Dan. 2010. Are Mahu Youth Safe in Hawaiʻi's Schools? *Honolulu Weekly*, Nov. 24.

Muñoz, José Esteban. 1999. *Disidentifications: Queers of Color and the Performance of Politics*. Minneapolis: University of Minnesota Press.

———. 2009. *Cruising Utopia: The Then and There of Queer Futurity*. New York: New York University Press.

Namaste, Viviane K. 2000. *Invisible Lives: The Erasure of Transsexual and Transgendered People*. Chicago: University of Chicago Press.

Odo, Carol, and Ashliana Hawelu. 2001. *Eo na Māhū o Hawaiʻi:* The Extraordinary Health Needs of Hawaiʻi's Māhū. *Pacific Health Dialog* 8: 327–334.

Owens, Brent (director, producer). 2005. *Downtown Girls: The Hookers of Honolulu*. HBO documentary/America Undercover (53 min.).

Shankman, Steven. 2010. *Other Others: Levinas, Literature, Transcultural Studies*. Albany: State University of New York Press.

Smith, Dorothy. 1987. *The Everyday World as Problematic: A Feminist Sociology*. Toronto: University of Toronto Press.

US Census Bureau. 2007. State and County Quick Facts. Data derived from Population Estimates, American Community Survey, Economic Census; http://quickfacts.census.gov/qfd/states/15000.html (accessed December 2011).

Valentine, David. 2007. *Imagining Transgender: An Ethnography of a Category*. Durham, NC: Duke University Press.

Wang, Caroline, and Mary Ann Burris. 1997. Photovoice: Concept, Methodology, and Use for Participatory Needs Assessment. *Health Education and Behavior* 24: 369–387.

Weston, Kath. 1991. *Families We Choose: Lesbians, Gays, and Kinship*. New York: Columbia University Press.

Xian, Kathryn, and Brent Anbe (directors). 2001. Ke Kulana He Māhū: *Remembering a Sense of Place*. Documentary (67 min.), VHS. Kathryn Xian, Jaymee Carvajal, Brent Anbe, and Connie Flores, producers. Distributed by Zang Pictures, Honolulu.

CHAPTER 8

Men Trapped in Women's Clothing
Homosexuality, Cross-Dressing, and Masculinity in Fiji

Geir Henning Presterudstuen

This chapter explores the processes of gendered self-identification among non-heteronormative ethnic Fijian men in contemporary Fiji. Although these men perform masculinity in diverse ways, they all display an ambiguous relationship to Fijian traditional notions of gender and masculinity as normative concepts. This highlights the often complex relationship between individuals' experiences of gendered identities and culturally specific, dominant notions of gender.

A striking aspect of the relatively new Fijian urban scene, which has emerged in tandem with the growth of tourism and of a local entertainment industry, is the increasing visibility of men who self-identify with and openly play out non-heteronormative gender identities. Often derogatorily referred to as *qauri*, which was translated to me as "poofter," "fag," "gay," and "homosexual," they are a conspicuous presence throughout urban Fiji, predominantly as entertainers in special events, as employees in the service industry, as partygoers in the nightclub scene, as well as sex workers along the increasingly busy entertainment strips in Fiji's major urban centers.

Like many terms used to describe non-heteronormative men throughout the world, the terms that refer to non-heteronormative Fijians change tone and meaning depending on the context and on who is using them. The same terms may vary from being an outright abusive label shouted by drunken nightclub patrons or intolerant passersby to a term signifying self-awareness and pride when appropriated by gay activists and non-heteronormative men themselves. Furthermore, none of these labels can be unproblematically used as collective descriptive terms. Popular contemporary terms in the Western world, like "gay" or "queer," presuppose the universal nature of Western heteronormativity and gender binary, and are thus often inadequate to describe circumstances outside the European and American cultural sphere. Similarly, many local terms describing non-heteronormative gender identities, both in Fiji and elsewhere, are often capriciously used and understood, and commonly blur the division between gender and sexual identities. This fact was prominent during my fieldwork, as my respondents used a mixture of local and imported terms when identifying themselves and conceptualizing their gender identities. Throughout this chapter I have consequently endeavored to describe respondents according to their own self-identification.

For the purpose of this discussion, it is thus useful to divide my non-heteronormative respondents into three distinct categories. First, transvestites, a group comprised of male-bodied performers who permanently undertake feminine gender performances and wear women's clothing. Second and equally prominent are *qauri*, whom I refer to here as "queens," a title my respondents often used to self-identify, in an obvious reference to Western notions of effeminate gay masculinities. They usually fulfill social roles or jobs stereotypically associated with female responsibilities such as cleaning, hairdressing, and dressmaking, and often sport markedly feminine hairstyles and sometimes modest makeup, but refer to themselves as men and dress in a gender-neutral or masculine-coded way—for instance, in tight-fitting jeans and T-shirts or brightly colored shirts—and act out in a more androgynous way than transvestite genders. The final group, a largely invisible minority in Fiji's public scene, consists of non-heteronormative men who dress and act "straight," but privately and sexually identify themselves as "homosexuals," sexually desiring more effeminate *qauri* or other masculine men. However, as most respondents somewhat embraced the local term *qauri* as a collective description of all male-bodied, non-heteronormative persons, I will use this as a value-neutral collective noun when distinguishing between non-heteronormative and heteronormative persons.

The research material for this chapter was collected in and around the three major centers of Fiji: Suva, Nadi, and Lautoka. Importantly, all my respondents defined their ethnic identity as indigenous Fijian. My discussion will thus disregard other forms non-heteronormative performances in contemporary Fijian society, including Indo-Fijian and *kai loma,* or people of mixed Fijian and European ancestry. Research on non-heteronormative sexuality in these other groups, which is needed to contextualize the material I present here, remains to be conducted.

Historically, *qauri* in Fiji were comparable to other "third-gender" categories prominent elsewhere in the Pacific Islands (Besnier 1994). Hence, despite the fact that many of my respondents in urban Fiji, both *qauri* and non-*qauri*, treated gender liminality and hyperfeminine men as a natural part of everyday life, they failed to acknowledge the existence of masculine non-heteronormative men. Indeed, dominant Fijian discourses about gender and sexuality often construct *qauri* as a homogeneous group of male-bodied but femininity-performing people referred to as *vakasalewalewa*, similar to Samoan *fa'afafine* and Tongan *fakaleitī*. However, rather than being viewed as a distinct third group outside the male–female gender binary, the dominant Fijian discourse today positions contemporary *qauri* as something akin to male transgender or biological males performing hyperfemininity.

A key argument in this chapter is that the contemporary community of *qauri* in Fiji is in fact multifaceted and that the urban scene comprises different groups of non-heteronormative men whose gendered self-identification varies significantly. Crucially, many of my *qauri* respondents rejected the *vakasalewalewa* label, which literally means "men behaving like women," as "constrictive," "old-fashioned," and ultimately inadequate to describe their respective gender identities as male-bodied agents desiring sex with other men (see also Teaiwa, this volume). Thus, while many men experience relative acceptance for non-heteronormative practices traditionally associated with the social role of *vakasalewalewa*, others struggle to find a social space for more masculine displays of non-heteronormativity, highlighting that the apparent acceptance of a particular type of *qauri* often conceals a systematic persecution of other forms of non-heteronormativity.

Gender Liminality and Third Genders in Pacific Island Cultures

A key aspect of Fijian *qauri* as a collective group, then, is that it frames an extraordinarily varied group of social performers whose relationships to Western concepts of sex and gender are complex and ambiguous. As such, they are comparable to other non-heteronormative identities in Pacific Island cultures that frequently are simplified as "third gender." In her discussion of gender in the Cook Islands, Kalissa Alexeyeff argues that *laelae*, a "category of feminized masculinity that is common throughout the

Pacific," refers to a great number of different practices and identity traits, from "women trapped in men's bodies" to presumably heterosexual men with female friends and white-collar jobs, to cross-dressers, and to boys wearing men's clothing, lipstick, and female jewelry (2008, 147). Particularly striking is the construction of *laelae* as a sexual category: "A key difference between *laelae* and Western homosexuals is that self-identified *laelae* sexually desire straight men, not other *laelae*. *Laelae* I spoke to found the idea of having sexual relations with another *laelae* as largely incomprehensible and likened it to sleeping with someone of the same sex. Straight men who have sex with *laelae* are not considered, and do not consider themselves, to be homosexual" (2008, 147). Fijian *qauri* are understood in much the same way, in terms both of their gender identity and of their sexual desires. One of my non-*qauri* respondents once explained to me that, when they went out on the town, some of his friends from university days would "always go for the *qauri*" rather than girls, without implying or suggesting that these men were motivated by homosexual desires. Rather, as another respondent suggested, *qauri* were more readily "available for sex" and sexual encounters with *qauri* were "less complicated" than getting involved with women. These practices are in line with known practices in Samoa, where it is commonplace for boys who go to bars and clubs and find no willing girl to allow transvestites to take them home without being considered queer or homosexual (Mageo 1992, 449–450). It also accords with the widespread practice of French Polynesian men to seek sexual gratification from the local *māhū* prior to settling down with a wife (Elliston, Kuwahara, this volume).

More than anything, however, these statements highlight the significant point that same-sex encounters do not necessarily determine gender or sexual identity in Fiji. All my *qauri* respondents argued that it was purportedly common for "straight" men to seek sexual encounters with other biological males, something that finds support in a study suggesting that "there are generally no obvious differences between straight men who like to have sex with other biological men versus those that never would [in Fiji]" (Bavington et al. 2011, 25). This is perhaps neither a typically Pacific Island phenomenon nor a particularly "modern" occurrence. In fact, the understanding of sexual relationships as organized according to a strict binary oppositional structure of hetero- and homosexual desire appears to be a fairly recent creation in all societies of the West, as it is well documented that many men throughout history "neither understood nor organized their sexual practices along a hetero-homosexual axis" (Chauncey 1995, 65).

In the Pacific Islands, these dynamics must also be understood in relation to cultural constructions of the self, which often differ from Western constructions. It is gender, rather than sexual identity, that "is given ontological priority" (Alexeyeff 2000, 297), and gender liminal identity is mainly defined in terms of the role played in social life and expected contribution to the collectivity, not in terms of inner personal desires (Alexeyeff 2008; Besnier 1994). To equate traditional notions of gender liminality with a Western understanding of gayness and homosexuality is consequently an oversimplification, although it is beyond doubt that, at least in Fiji, the modern appropriation of "third gender" as "homosexual" is in use in society at large and deployed by individuals who self-identify as such.

For my heteronormative Fijian respondents, the gender category of *qauri* is thus generally associated with some level of "feminine appearance" or what many of them labeled cross-dressing or "transvestism." While I will argue that this categorization is largely inaccurate as it ignores the multitude of gender performances that challenge the dominant gender and sexual norms present on the urban scene, it does reflect the fact that most *qauri* who openly self-identify as and perform non-heteronormativity do so by displaying physical appearances and attires that are identified as "feminine" or "girly."

Furthermore, the focus on cross-dressing highlights the extent to which dominant discourses in Fiji narrowly associate all non-heteronormative identities with the traditional notion of *vakasalewalewa,* a concept that today is often understood as equivalent to transgenderism (Bavington et al. 2011). Naturally, this blurs the distinction between gendered and sexual identities that has underpinned much of the historical and academic discourse about non-heteronormativity in the Pacific Islands.

Historical records of early colonial Fiji were generally silent on the presence of non-heteronormative gender identities, and no European sources mentioned *vakasalewalewa,* or any other "third-gender" category, as an institutionalized part of premodern Fijian society, as elsewhere in the Pacific (McIntosh 1999, 6–7; Levy 1971; Robertson 1989; Watts 1992). Neither were the brief early descriptions of ritualized homosexuality and practices of sodomy between kinship groups (Seeman 1862, 161–162) linked to specific gender identities or sexual categories.

Despite their absence from early colonial records, Fijian *qauri* are conspicuous elements of the contemporary urban scene in Fiji, and as Mageo points out for Samoa, it is not plausible that these "sprang full blown, like

Venus rising from her oyster shell" in today's setting (1996, 588). Indeed, there was a general consensus among all my respondents that *qauri* occupied a social position in premodern Fijian society, albeit perhaps a more marginal one than in other Pacific societies, and that this social role was consistently coupled with a sexual desire for men.

This transhistorical conceptualization obviously helps explain the very visible presence of cross-dressing and strikingly effeminate men in contemporary urban Fiji. At the same time, however, it poses some interesting questions about the relationship between traditional gender liminality and more modern expressions of queerness or gayness, as well as how these labels can blur the distinction between gendered and sexual categories. Hence, a central theme that I will focus on for the remainder of the chapter is how many of my contemporary *qauri* experienced pressure to conform to this traditionally condoned third-gender category as a consequence of their sexual desires.

The very visible presence of cross-dressers and effeminate men in the Fijian urban scene is thus not necessarily evidence of widespread tolerance of non-heteronormative men per se, but may in reality hide a structural violence implicit in the emphasis on *qauri* as a strictly social gender role. In fact, the predominance of references to cross-dressing and the *vakasalewalewa* role in dominant discourses about non-heteronormative men may be a Fijian example of how "the apparent tolerance of homoeroticism in many non-Western cultures disguises the reality of persecution, discrimination, and violence, which sometimes occurs in unfamiliar forms" (Altman 2001, 23).

An example of these dynamics is how dominant Fijian discourses about gender emphasize that *qauri* traditionally served a social function in village Fiji that was implicitly asexual. Many contemporary *qauri* explained that this historical construction remains a defining principle for the social expectations of non-heteronormative men in many village settings in rural Fiji. Two *qauri* I interviewed, Eroni and Eli,[1] explained that life within the traditional boundaries of the village and their *mataqali* (the most important kinship and landowning unit in most of Fiji, comprising a few smaller family units, or *tokatoka*) generally was free from persecution or scrutiny on the explicit condition that they "did not do anything" of a sexual nature in the village. Eroni elaborated on this by explaining that he frequently was reminded about these rules by traditional or religious authorities, who made it clear to him that the acceptance of his gender identity came with the condition that he could not "seek out . . . or demonstrate" his "sexual lusts" for other, presumably "straight," boys in the village.

This construction of *qauri* as asexual is in obvious contrast to the way in which heterosexual men's sexuality is construed in traditional Fijian discourse about gender, sexuality, and identity. Fijians consider men, particularly if they have been drinking alcohol, to possess an inherent drive for sexual contact, and this is amply borne out by observation (Toren 1994). This contrast serves to underline the distinction between "real men" and *qauri* as belonging to two different gender categories. Interestingly, however, Eroni further explained that this social censorship of his sexuality only forbade him, as *qauri*, to initiate sexual contact or "be sexually active," implying that it was perfectly acceptable, indeed expected, for him to be on the receiving end of "real men's sexual initiatives," because "receiving a man's sexuality is what *qauri* [do]."

Most *qauri* thus appear to have an implicit sexual license to satisfy unmarried men but not to fulfill their own sexual desires. As such, they carry out a sort of exaggerated feminine sexual role (young women do not have the same license to provide sexual favors to unmarried men). What is more, dominant Fijian discourses on gender also construct this sexual role to be the defining aspect of *qauri*'s gender identities. This suggests that the perceived acceptance of non-heteronormative men's overt displays of femininity in public in effect reproduces Fijian notions of heteronormativity through a repression of *qauri* men as sexual agents. I will explore these ideas by taking a more careful look at the most visible representation of *qauri* in contemporary Fiji—namely, drag contests through which men display embellished and stylized public displays of female sexuality on stage.

Drag Shows as Public Performances of Gender Liminality

Drag shows and beauty contests involving male-bodied cross-dressers play an accepted part in numerous prominent public events such as fundraisers and festivals, as well as more private occurrences like wedding celebrations. These events are of course not specific to Fiji but are commonplace in many societies, such as Samoa and American Samoa (Mageo 1992; 1996), the Cook Islands (Alexeyeff 2008), the Philippines (Remoto 1995; Johnson 1997), and Tonga (Besnier 2002). A striking aspect of these events in Fiji is their relative ubiquity and mainstream popularity. Often part of mainstream cultural festivals, such as the week-long Suva Hibiscus Festival,

Nadi Bula Festival, or Lautoka Sugar Festival, they frequently draw more than a thousand spectators.

When I attended the fittingly named "Priscilla Night" of Nadi's Bula Festival in July 2009, the show started with a set of dance and lip-synched numbers. Most performers were relatively young men of slender appearance, identified by the audience as *qauri,* carefully dressed up in hyperfeminine and ostentatious clothing and hairstyles or wigs, mimicking highly sexualized female performers as they are presented in Western popular culture—what Elliston (this volume) aptly terms the "global femme." The suggestive dancing, set to soundtracks by prominent Western female entertainers such as Britney Spears, Beyonce, and Madonna, was sexually explicit and included vigorous simulations of oral sex and other forms of sexual intercourse. Following these preliminary entertainment numbers, most performers took part in a highly stylized beauty contest characterized by a humorous tone bordering on the raunchy. The contestants posed in different costumes, answered questions about their personality traits, and competed in a talent section. Hosted by a local cross-dressing celebrity, the interview sections focused on seemingly arbitrary topics, such as "What are your special talents?" and "What do you most like to eat?" The expectation was that the responses be at least somewhat sexually suggestive.

The answers that the mock-misses provided generally followed from the theme of the initial performances and included obvious allusions to same-sex acts. "Special talents" included "horse riding," "pole dancing," "ball sports," and "water sports," and contestants listed both "lollipops" and "big meat" as being among their favorite foods. At one point, the contestants were asked to explain which animal they would want to be if they had to choose one, and the answers comprised an impressive hodgepodge of sexual allusions: pussycat, woodpecker, swallow, clam, crab, mouse, electric eel, horny bull, and a humpback whale ("or anything with a blowhole") were favorite choices.

The practices that these jokes insinuate are somewhat of a taboo in other contexts in Fiji (where "sodomy" remained criminalized until 2010), but the pageants were valued as comedic entertainment. The audiences responded with encouraging exclamations and gestures, wolf whistles, loud laughter, and enthusiastic ovations. These reactions reflected the common sentiment among my urban Fijian respondents that cross-dressers are socially accepted only in contexts that emphasize uninhibited entertainment and mockery of social conventions.

However, the drag shows may also take on more complex meanings, and I argue that a basic premise for their mainstream success is that performers assume particular hyperfeminized characters that are often devalued in dominant Fijian discourses about gender. As personifications of "loose" or hypersexualized women, *qauri* on stage act out negative models of proper girls and implicitly link this behavior to a foreign cultural sphere. Indeed, by mimicking Western female artists' sexually explicit and exuberant stage performances, these Fijian cross-dressers serve at once to demonstrate the intrinsic immorality and inappropriateness of the "European way" and play out the negative role models that Fijian girls should not try to emulate.

Hence, the contemporary social of role of *qauri* largely operates within the dominant heteronormative context, where they are positioned as immoral "girls" who transgress accepted gender conventions. This is despite the fact that many *qauri* I came across self-identify as men who transgress masculine conventions through their sexual practices. In fact, though contemporary *qauri* are far from a homogeneous group, a key finding in my research was that many of them experienced problems relating to the traditional notion of *qauri* and the cross-dressing paradigm they often felt "forced into." This highlights the potential hidden violence implicit in dominant Fijian discourses about *qauri,* and for the purpose of the remaining discussion I will return to the typology I outlined earlier.

Cross-Dressers, Queens, and "Very Straight" Men

The cross-dressing performances that I discussed in the previous section are more or less the only aspects of non-heteronormativity that have become part of mainstream Fijian society. It is perhaps not surprising, then, that the *qauri* who take part in these events are not all transvestites on a regular basis or engage in cross-dressing outside these pageants. There are, in fact, many performers who would generally reject the equation of transvestism with non-heteronormativity and who subscribe to a variety of other, more masculine, gender identities. Participation in the non-heteronormative mainstream was not an uncomplicated exercise for these performers, however, as they often had to struggle to fit into events rigidly based on dominant Fijian discourses about *qauri* as intrinsically hyperfeminine. In general, the different stage performances were relatively uniform in that they emphasized hypersexualized feminine performances, and contestants put much effort into creating an appearance that exaggerated stereotyped images of Western womanhood, in a similar fashion to drag queens in the urban West. This generally included particular manipulations of the body, such as waxing away body hair or tucking away genitals, retraining the body to walk and gesticulate in feminine ways, wearing wigs, artificial breasts, makeup and female clothing, as well as voice manipulation. However, on two separate occasions, I witnessed performers who, by deliberately defying some of these conventions, created a *qauri* performance that exposed the gender mimicry and thus challenged the view of *qauri* performers as models for inappropriate females.

The first was a performer who, though wearing heavy makeup and high heels, performed a number that the audience perceived as more masculine than feminine. Entering the stage to the strains of a heavy Western rock tune rather than the customary dance remixes or pop songs, the contestant sported a short, masculine Mohawk and a tight-fitting leather suit instead of a dress, and wore no artificial breasts. The dance routine was arguably sexually suggestive but lacked the overt references to the stereotyped sexual receptivity. Instead, the performer flexed his arm muscles and caressed his body in time to the rhythm of the music, seemingly playing out an androgynous or gay male persona. After the performance, parts of the audience were silent and the response lacked the vigorous enthusiasm afforded the more conventional performers. While few in the audience appeared to take offense or openly dislike this alternative display, many expressed confusion about the nature of the performance.

The second example, which took place on a different festival night, was more dramatic and proved to be a transgression of norms that, at least temporarily, startled the audience completely and elicited negative comments suggesting that the performer was "missing the point" of the event. From the outset, the performer appeared to be following the conventions of the contests with a full drag appearance and exaggerated feminine mannerisms. During the dance routine, however, he lifted his skirt to unveil tight underpants in which his semi-erect penis was clearly visible to the audience, before he went behind some of his co-performers and simulated sodomizing them, emphasizing a male, active sexual role that was considered out of place in an event showcasing *qauri* as hyperfeminine.

These two performances were merely two out of approximately thirty official drag performances I witnessed, and the only ones that seemed deliberately to challenge the conventional representation of *qauri* in these settings. However, they are worth noting, as they reflect the fact that the traditional

Fijian notion of *qauri* as equated with transvestism and hyperfemininity does not exist undisputed in contemporary Fiji. In effect, it appeared that these mock beauty pageants, which served as the only socially accepted events where gender liminality was celebrated, potentially might be seen as contested spaces where competing non-heteronormative identities could use the spotlight to lay claim to their position in the larger social field.

The performer in the first example openly expressed these ideas in a brief conversation with me on the night of his performance. By creating a performance that transgressed the idea of *qauri* as a third gender or "women in men's bodies," he wanted to reflect the notions that Fijian gays were "all different, and should be allowed to be different . . . not only dress up to fit some stereotype." These comments arguably reflected a conscious effort on his part to position his performance as an ideological statement challenging dominant notions of non-heteronormativity in Fiji and were possibly based on a more Western "gay" identity. The performer identified himself as a "gay activist" based in Suva, where he was part of a small but "politically aware" group of students who entertained contact with similar movements in Australia and New Zealand (George, this volume). His testimony reflects the complexity of the gay scene that was developing in Fiji and was by no means an isolated case. In fact, when one moved away from these stylized, public displays of transvestism, it became obvious that many Fijian *qauri* actively sought to downplay overtly feminine personas and to construct new gay identities more in line with Western and perhaps globalized understandings of sexual orientation and gender performance as separate entities.

It is now undisputed that sexual identity is established and "read through appearances that are gendered" (Hutson 2010, 221; Han 2009; Kessler and McKenna 1978) and that gay subjectivities are often communicated through clothing and bodily attire, which mark the bearer as non-heteronormative, be it through gender bending or the exaggeration of gender stereotypes (Ingraham 1994). Tight-fitting clothing, moreover, is often found to be associated with a distinct gay style and seen as a way to mark a distinction between homosexual and heterosexual masculine appearance (Barber 2008; Hutson 2010). For some of the respondents who referred to themselves as "queenie" but still wanted to maintain a masculine identity, the adoption of such Western-style clothing also became a way to express gayness "without becoming a woman." Sefanaia Waqabaca, subject of a feature interview in the *Fiji Times*, exemplifies this category: "With his short styled bleached blonde hair, jeans, tee-shirt and a scarf, Sefa says he wouldn't be caught dead in a skirt or dress for that matter. And he doesn't go by some chic nickname either" (Taylor-Newton 2010). Despite deliberately distancing his persona from that of his contemporary transvestites, Sefa describes himself as "a feminine or gay . . . in the sense that he walks, speaks, and acts like a woman," something he has always done and feels is not his choice, "but something in [him]" (Taylor-Newton 2010). Hence, while gayness is equated with femininity and "acting like a woman," many Fijian gay men, like Sefa, have no intention of being, becoming, or appearing like a woman, thus defying the traditional notion of *vakasalewalewa.*

In fact, while most *qauri* men I interviewed and spent time with in Suva, Nadi, and Lautoka (Fiji's three largest urban centers) had long hair, wore tight-fitting clothing, applied some makeup, and displayed mannerisms that could be defined as feminine, they generally stated their aversion to being defined as "lady-boys" and lamented the fact most Fijians held the view that "all gay men are [like] women." Eroni explained to me that he had not always acted as feminine as he did now but had gradually taken on a more "girly appearance" as he grew up: "As a boy I was maybe more quiet and . . . maybe weaker than the other boys, but it's not like I didn't get on with boys. It was later, when I knew I was a poofter, I got more girl friends and got into makeup and things . . . but it's not like I need it, need to do it, I mean." He later elaborated, explaining that Fiji villagers "don't really understand or accept gay men" but considered any deviation from the masculine norm as "girly behavior . . . only suited for girls."

While such divergence appeared to be frowned upon in general, there was a precedence for men "who went all the way," meaning those who embraced femininity to act and dress like girls and perform girls' tasks locally, in their own as well as in other surrounding villages. While this was "too much" for Eroni, he explained that he had started spending more time with girls and acted "more girly" as he grew older and was then labeled a *qauri,* until he was almost completely excluded from "men's activities" in the village because he was "a poofter": "I didn't play rugby anymore . . . and [did] no work in the land, like farming. . . . [W]hen I got older I was never offered a *bilo* [coconut-shell cup used to serve kava] or invited for grog [i.e., kava] sessions . . . till all I did was girls' work, like catching mussels, sweeping, and things."

Acting "like a poofter," then, was something Eroni adopted in order to fit in with the role assigned to *qauri* in the village and not something he understood as inherent to his identity. Indeed, the ascribed non-heteronor-mative identity in this particular village was so closely related to "acting like a girl" and doing women's chores that Eroni appeared to feel compelled to act more girly and perform tasks appropriate for a woman. In addition, he had gradually started to grow his hair longer and style it in more feminine ways, to use makeup "such as rouge and eyeliner," to grow his nails longer and occasionally paint them, and to buy women's jeans because they had a "tighter fit."

Similar dynamics were evident in Hosaiah's account of his experience. Hosaiah is a transvestite who at the age of thirty-three now dresses per-manently as a woman and lives his life "wholly as a woman" but maintains that this had never been her preferred option—it "just happened like that." Hosaiah, who now often uses the name Sera and is a sex worker in one of the major urban tourist centers of Fiji, explained that he had grown up being a "tough muscle boy" who enjoyed playing rugby and "hanging with boys" in rural Fiji, though he had been "totally homosexual, total gay" and had many sexual liaisons with "straight boys and men," which eventually forced him to leave his native village. His sexual identity was seen as being incompatible with village life, leading him to migrate to the urban centers of Fiji—a pattern noted as common among young gay men worldwide who try to orient themselves toward places and professions "in which it is pos-sible to imagine that they will benefit from a greater degree of tolerance, or, at least, which will enable them to live out their sexuality more easily" (Eribon 2004, 31).

Yet Hosaiah went on to add that he had soon come to the realization that even in urban Fiji it eventually became "impossible [for him] to be gay and man" because "taking sex from other men means Fijians think you should be a girl." Over the last ten years he had gradually moved toward becoming what he labeled "a full drag queen," dressing, acting and talking like a woman while doing "women's work," such as catering and clean-ing in the tourist industry, and later becoming a sex worker. He had also shed more than twenty kilos in order to look more slender (i.e., in line with a feminine cosmopolitan aesthetic), taken great care to shave his legs, arms, and chest on a regular basis, and trained himself to "act and walk" like a woman.

Hosaiah, then, provided another example of a *qauri* who had been pushed into acting like a woman because of his sexual proclivities, indi-cating that, while being openly feminine and sexually receptive was not socially accepted as part of any man's behavior and indeed was detrimental to one's status as a man, "acting like a woman . . . as a typical village *qauri*" provided at least some form of refuge from the most dramatic forms of social sanctions.

Still, for Hosaiah, this new gender identity did not come easily and did not appear to correspond to his idea of self or personal identity. For men like him, the choice was generally between suppressing their sexuality in its totality and being forced into heterosexual living arrangements or acting out a life as a flamboyant feminine persona, despite the fact that they "felt like a man" and "got along with men . . . like[d] what men do." For Hosaiah, who had "gone all the way," this had been a dramatic life change; he said that he often felt like a "man trapped in women's clothing."

Both Eroni and Hosaiah had retrained their bodies to correspond more successfully to the traditional notion of *qauri* as hyperfeminine, both in action and appearance, but at the same time they adopted a modern Western sense of their own gender identity, which was determined by sexuality rather than gender performance. In fact, Hosaiah asserted that he had permanently adopted his alter ego, Sera, only in order to more easily live out his sexual life as a passive, receiving gay man, although he had to struggle to come to terms with his embodied womanhood.

Both these cases support assumptions that the subjective experience of a gendered self is "shaped through bodily decoration" in contradictory ways (Schrock et al. 2005, 323; Bartky 1990; de Beauvoir 1953). In order to discipline their bodies to express and embody more feminine personas, both Hosaiah and Eroni managed to pass as *qauri* in a traditional sense and, despite their expressed aversion to doing so, started to view themselves as and actually to feel "more girly." Their experience demonstrates the "emotionally ambiguous path" that cross-dressing requires one to travel, with its evocation of myriad conflicting feelings about subjective identity and social position (Schrock et al. 2005, 323). For Hosaiah, these contradictory ideas and emotions about his own persona were experienced as a feeling of inauthenticity that lay at the core of his identity, and he frequently made distinctions between his "real me," Hosaiah, and his "put-on" persona, Sera.

Of course, there were also respondents who found the feminine gender role easier to deal with, and who articulated the view expressed by *Fiji Times* interviewee Sefa, namely, that being feminine was both intrinsic to one's personality and inalienable from a gay sexual identity. For example, Nasoni and Paul were both in their early twenties and inhabited the typology of "queens," a label they used to refer to themselves in my and others' company. They frequented a popular nightclub in one of Fiji's largest urban centers, together with a group of female friends, because they "liked the scene and enjoyed dancing." They both wore subtle makeup (Paul more so than Nasoni), some jewelry such as bracelets or anklets, and tight-fitting clothes that emphasized their slender bodies in a way that made them fit certain Western images of a particular type of modern gay man.

In contrast to Eroni and Hosaiah, Nasoni and Paul did not view their feminine demeanors as unnatural or trained behavior but as who they were, despite the fact that they defined themselves as men. Paul argued that he was "both masculine and feminine," but that different character traits were played out in various contexts: "I work and live as a normal man, a normal gay man . . . but when going to the club or hanging out with my "sisters" I like to . . . like, gay it up, just be a poofter and play the role, you know." For Paul, to be a "poofter" was about playing out a part of his own identity without inhibitions in an appropriate context, not a negotiation of his masculinity in order to fit in. Indeed, Paul did not have any problems reconciling the idea of acting in effeminate ways with being a proper man, as he understood them as two aspects of his identity.

Hence, while respondents like Eroni and Hosaiah had felt compelled to retrain their body to become more like a woman in order to fit better into the cultural logic in which gayness was traditionally constructed in Fiji, Paul and Nasoni adopted a markedly different notion of what it meant to be gay and how that impacted on their masculinity. Put simply, Paul and Nasoni appeared to identify with what Altman calls a "global gay identity," "no longer considered an expression of 'really' being a woman in a man's body (or vice versa), but rather as physically desiring others of one's own gender without necessarily wishing to deny one's masculinity/femininity" (Altman 2001: 26). At the same time, by "gaying it up" and conforming their behavior to the stereotypes of what a *qauri* is when going out on the nightclub scene, Paul and Nasoni subjected themselves to the censure associated with being a non-heteronormative man in Fiji, something they sought to negate by "only having *qauri* or poofter friends" or "go[ing] out with girls." Consequently, they were not particularly successful in maintaining their social roles as men and being treated as men by their peers, but encountered a social stigma similar to that experienced by their more effeminate or permanently cross-dressing fellow *qauri*. While Paul played out his masculinity and was "a normal man" in his working life, he later

confided to me that his job as a tour host for an adventure company was one
he shared with "only girls" and that it was a profession often associated with
women and effeminate men. Similarly, Nasoni explained that, while he felt
like a man and acted like one, he was no longer playing rugby, as "it didn't
feel right . . . with the other boys, because he experienced their disapproval
and rejection."

For these respondents, adopting a Western-style gay identity that
emphasizes masculine homosexual practices did not necessarily pay off,
as it provided little assistance in gaining acceptance among fellow Fijian
men. On the contrary, Eroni explained that the closer his performance and
appearance came to those of a woman, the more he played up to the traditional notion of *qauri,* the easier he fitted into the social structure of
village and kinship. In fact, when I asked him directly if he had ever been
the target of negative comments in the village when acting in feminine
ways, he claimed that all the comments he received were "from tourist types
of persons."

For many homosexual men, overemphasizing effeminacy in public
emerged as a way to negotiate a gender order in which masculine non-heteronormativity was rejected as "un-Fijian and unnatural," although a "third
gender" had at least a liminal status. Taking on a hyperfeminine gender
performance appears to have safeguarded them from abuse, violence, and
prosecution, especially given that sodomy was still illegal in Fiji at the time.

The third type of non-heteronormative men whom I came across during my fieldwork I label "invisible gays." Noa and Simon were both in their
late twenties and held skilled positions in the white-collar bureaucracy following their university education. (Noa had spent five years studying in
Melbourne, and Simon had received prestigious scholarships to complete
his studies at the University of the South Pacific in Suva.) While they both
understood themselves as having exclusively homosexual desires, they did
not describe themselves as *qauri,* nor did they see themselves as deviating
from the traditional male gender role beyond meeting other men for casual
sexual liaisons. Noa claimed he did not have "a feminine bone in [his] body"
and drew a clear distinction between femininity and homosexual desire:
"I just have urges, sex and all that . . . for men, which has nothing to do
with how I behave, talk and that . . . I don't wanna be less of a man just
because of what type of sex I have, you know." Simon expressed similar
sentiments, pointing out that he had not been willing to let his "sexuality determine [his] person[ality]." In practical terms, this meant dressing

in standard men's clothing, having short-cropped curly hair, maintaining well-built defined bodies, and generally presenting themselves in a manner in line with the gender expectations associated with Fijian men. However, their professional background and relatively privileged socioeconomic situation enabled them both to craft an appearance that was more carefully maintained and focused on fashion than was common for Fijian men.

For Simon, this included wearing relatively expensive brands of business shirts, ties, and designer suits, luxuries that most Fijian men cannot afford but something that he considered a necessity because of his work. Noa displayed a more casual—and distinctly Western—style of clothing, including board shorts, jeans, and T-shirts sporting Australian labels. They were both obviously embarrassed when I suggested that such a relative awareness of taste and fashion and the willingness to spend considerable amounts of money on clothes were often associated with many middle-class gay men in the Western world (Martin 1993; Bantjes 2007).

Due to their study and work lives, Noa and Simon had both left their remote villages in their teenage years, something which, according to Simon, made them "quite independent from their family" and had instilled in him "a quite relaxed" relationship with traditional social protocol. Though he still considered himself proud of his Fijian ancestry and chiefly descent, in actual fact he only sporadically visited his native village, and then mainly for significant events such as "funerals and weddings." For Noa, who had spent time in Australia and had many relatives overseas, some traditional notions were overshadowed by a "more modern . . . you know, educated" understanding of the world, to the extent that he rejected many aspects of Fijian tradition: "You realize, you know, that Fijians need to change too . . . it's not like Fijians get everything right, just look at the government, the prisons and stuff . . . tradition is no good except as a building brick, something we always keep referring back to without being ruled by it."

In these expressed attitudes there are obvious parallels to Teaiwa's work on non-heteronormative Fijians living in Great Britain (this volume). Distance from Fiji, geographical but also ideological, enabled one of her respondents to "feel comfortable and safe, not only in living his identity, but also, ironically, in not having to be 'flaming' in order to express himself as a sexual minority." What is obvious from this example is that frequent and more consistent contact with modernity and non-Fijian cultural spaces provides Fijian *qauri* with richer possibilities in understanding their sexual and gendered self-identities beyond the constraints of traditional notions of *vakasalewalewa* or *qauri*. For Simon and Noa, these dynamics were associated with coming to terms with engaging in homosexual practices and reconciling their own self-identities with what they perceived to be the core values of Fijian society. They both defined themselves as devout Christians and regularly attended church, something they considered a key aspect of Fijian society, but rejected many "stereotypes and prejudices" prevalent in dominant Fijian discourses. In short, they perceived "pride, respect, and integrity" as the key components of what it meant to be Fijians and did not consider that their same-sex desires and practices conflicted with these principles. Their main sexual relations were casual flings, often with tourists or business visitors whom they met via Internet sites and chat rooms, or with effeminate or cross-dressing *qauri*. Noa named a particular establishment in Suva where he would frequently go to "pick up" without fearing detection.

These men considered discretion and anonymity paramount. Simon explained that he preferred his homosexuality to remain a personal matter, for fear of what its associations with the larger *qauri* community would mean for his professional life and standing in the wider community, and also because he considered sexuality "a personal thing" that he did not want to "demonstrate to the world." That these two "invisible gays" sexually desired men and frequently engaged in sexual encounters with what they understood to be "traditional *qauri*" but did not desire female sexual partners made their relationship to conventional Fijian gender norms especially ambiguous.

On one level, Noa pointed out that it was hardly uncommon for Fijian men to receive sexual gratification from cross-dressing *qauri,* and thus it was hardly the defining aspect of his identity. On the other hand, both Noa and Simon occasionally took on receptive sexual roles in both oral and anal sex with *qauri* and non-Fijian men. This, coupled with their homosexual exclusivity, made them, in Simon's words, "like girls in bed," a recognition that undeniably made it difficult for them to sustain a self-identification as what they labeled the "Fijian definition of real men," which as we know foregrounds heteronormative sexuality and domination over women.

What is more, this engagement with modern gay culture is arguably more accessible, in both practical and ideological terms, to representatives of the urban middle-class like Noa and Simon than it is to Fijians of more limited means, who are subject to traditional as well as material restraints to a much greater extent. As educated professionals, Simon and Noa have been able to establish their lives independently of the traditional and social hierarchy within which less privileged Fijian *qauri* are shaped and have access to social spaces where they can play out different social roles. The ability to distinguish sexual closure from a social gay identity is thus intrinsically linked to the privileged position of urban middle-class subjects with access to Internet dating sites and other social spaces where homosexual encounters can be arranged.

Qauri, Hyperfemininity, and Sexual Repression

While it is clear that the Fijian system of gender differentiation has historically operated with a more complex categorization than the Western gender binary, the visibility of *qauri* in Fiji does not necessarily suggest greater acceptance of non-heteronormative gender displays and in fact calls into question the analytic usefulness of the very notion of "acceptance." The seemingly homogeneous group of labeled *qauri* does in reality cover an array of different gender identities; most of them draw upon different aspects of masculinity in order to construct their masculine identity. For many, their presentation of self differs significantly from the public persona they enact in a society that remains largely belligerent toward non-heteronormative men, particularly those who do not display characteristics in line with the dominant understanding of *qauri* as hyperfeminine. Most informants displayed an ambiguous relationship to what they considered masculinity, at once drawing upon it to understand and define their own life situations and seeing it as a culturally constructed category from which they were largely excluded.

What is more, some men embraced, both on stage and in everyday life, the gender performance of cross-dressing that does not disrupt the alignment of sexuality with gender. Although these gender strategies often came at considerable personal cost, particularly for men who did not self-identify as feminine *qauri*, it protected many non-heteronormative men from social exclusion from the village system. This appears to be based on the fact that Fijian gendered discourse has considered the presence of a third-gender category a historical reality, which consequently fit into the margin of the traditional ethos of Fijianness and gender performances.

Other men attempted to juggle their gender performances according to context and appeared to draw successfully upon traditionally condoned notions of masculinity to create masculine performances in some situations, while adopting more liminal or feminine gender performances when they considered it appropriate. This strategy was perhaps most obvious in the group of invisible gay men whom I described in the last section. A core problem for these men was the unavailability of a gendered identity within which they could reconcile their sexual practices with their masculine identity. The *qauri* traditionally remains socially and sexually defined as an entirely feminine gender category that functions to fill the female role in situations where this is impossible or undesirable for female-bodied subjects. While this role certainly provides a safe space for some non-heteronormative men, namely those who embrace femininity with relative ease, it remains both socially unavailable and undesirable for many male-bodied homosexual men. This highlights the fact that narrowly defined "traditional" gender identities may be experienced as both exclusive and constrictive to actual gender performers. Moreover, their ubiquity in contemporary society, which often has been interpreted as widespread tolerance for homoeroticism and alternative gender behaviors, can hide more complex systems of structural violence and sexual repression.

These social differences are often patterned on an urban/rural and social class divide. Urban middle-class Fijian men are able to remain closeted and thus claim a larger part of the patriarchal dividend through their heteronormative public performances, while less privileged non-heteronormative men are often forced to accept and perform subordinate masculine roles in accordance with traditional social expectations of Fijian *qauri*.

Note

1   Throughout this chapter I use pseudonyms to refer to my respondents.

References

Alexeyeff, Kalissa. 2000. Dragging Drag: The Performance of Gender and Sexuality in the Cook Islands. *The Australian Journal of Anthropology* 11: 297–307.

———. 2008. Globalizing Drag in the Cook Islands: Friction, Repulsion, and Abjection. *The Contemporary Pacific* 20: 143–161.

Altman, Dennis. 2001. Rupture or Continuity? The Internationalization of Gay Identities. In *Post-colonial Queer: Theoretical Intersections,* ed. John C. Hawley, pp. 19–42. Albany: State University of New York Press.

Bantjes, Rod. 2007. *Social Movements in a Global Context: Canadian Perspectives.* Toronto: Canadian Scholars' Press.

Barber, Kristen. 2008. The Well-Coiffed Man: Class, Race, and Heterosexual Masculinity in the Hair Salon. *Gender and Society* 22: 455–476.

Bartky, Sandra Lee. 1990. *Femininity and Domination: Studies in the Phenomenology of Oppression.* New York: Routledge.

Bavington, Ben, Niraj Singh, Dipesh S. Naiker, Marcus N. Deo, Metuisela Talala, Moji Brown, Rishi R. Singh, Sanjay Dewan, and Simione Navokavokadrau. 2011. *Secret Lives, Other Voices: A Community-Based Study Exploring Male-to-Male Sex, Gender Identity and HIV Transmission Risk in Fiji.* Suva, Fiji: AIDS Task Force of Fiji.

Beauvoir, Simone de. 1953. *The Second Sex.* Trans. H. M. Parhsley. London: Cape.

Besnier, Niko. 1994. Polynesian Gender Liminality through Time and Space. In *Third Gender: Beyond Sexual Dimorphism in Culture and History,* ed. Gilbert Herdt, pp. 285–328. New York: Zone.

———. 2002. Transgenderism, Locality, and the Miss Galaxy Beauty Pageant in Tonga. *American Ethnologist* 29: 534–566.

Chauncey, George. 1995. *Gay New York: Gender, Urban Culture, and the Making of the Gay Male World, 1890–1940.* New York: Basic Books.

Eribon, Didier. 2004. *Insult and the Making of the Gay Self.* Trans. Michael Lucey. Durham, NC: Duke University Press.

Han, Chong-suk. 2009. Asian Girls Are Prettier: Gendered Presentations as Stigma Management among Gay Asian Men. *Symbolic Interaction* 32: 106–122.

Hutson, David J. 2010. Standing OUT/Fitting IN: Identity, Appearance, and Authenticity in Gay and Lesbian Communities. *Symbolic Interaction* 33: 213–233.

Ingraham, Chrys. 1994. The Heterosexual Imaginary: Feminist Sociology and Theories of Gender. *Sociological Theory* 12: 203–219.

Johnson, Mark. 1997. *Beauty and Power: Transgendering and Cultural Transformation in the Southern Philippines.* Oxford: Berg.

Kessler, Suzanne J., and Wendy McKenna. 1978. *Gender: An Ethnomethodological Approach.* Chicago: University of Chicago Press.

Levy, Robert I. 1971. The Community Function of Tahitian Male Transvestism: A Hypothesis. *Anthropological Quarterly* 44: 12–21.

Mageo, Jeannette M. 1992. Male Transvestism and Culture Change in Samoa. *American Ethnologist* 29: 443–459.

———. 1996. Samoa, on the Wilde Side: Male Transvestism, Oscar Wilde, and Liminality in Making Gender. *Ethos* 24: 588–627.

Martin, Richard. 1993. The Gay Factor in Fashion. *Esquire Gentleman* 1 (Spring 1993): 135–136.

McIntosh, Tracey. 1999. Words and Worlds of Difference: Homosexualities in the Pacific. Sociology and Social Policy Working Paper Series, 3/99. Suva, Fiji: Department of Sociology, University of the South Pacific.

Remoto, Danton. 1995. *Seduction and Solitude.* Manila: Anvil.

Robertson, Carol E. 1989. The Mahu of Hawaii. *Feminist Studies* 15: 312–326.

Schoeffel, Penelope. 1979. Daughters of Sina: A Study of Gender, Status and Power in Samoa. PhD diss., Department of Anthropology, Australian National University.

Schrock, Douglas, Lori Reid, and Emily M. Boyd. 2005. Transsexuals' Embodiment of Womanhood. *Gender and Society* 19: 317–335.

Seeman, Berthold. 1862. *Viti: An Account of a Government Mission to Vitian or Fijian Islands in the Years 1860–61.* Reprint. Cambridge: Macmillan & Co., Colonial History Series No. 85, 1973.

Taylor-Newton, Ruby. 2010. Please Don't Judge Us. *Fiji Times Online,* March 21, 2010 (accessed April 10, 2012).

Toren, Christina. 1994. The Drinker as Chief or Rebel: Kava and Alcohol in Fiji. In *Gender, Drink and Drugs,* ed. Maryon McDonald, pp. 153–173. Oxford: Berg.

Watts, Raleigh. 1992. The Polynesian *Mahu.* In *Oceanic Homosexualities,* ed. Stephen O. Murray, pp. 171–184. New York: Garland.

CHAPTER 9

Two Sea Turtles

Intimacy between Men in the Marshall Islands

Greg Dvorak

It is a rainy afternoon in Jaluit Atoll in the Marshall Islands, and the lagoon's surface is textured with a fine turquoise upholstery of raindrops, the horizon obscured by gray mist. Under the aluminum awning of a small house next to a giant breadfruit tree, I sit with a small gathering of Marshall Islander men, drinking extra-sweetened instant coffee and enjoying *bwe-bwenato,* the Marshallese pastime of "talking story." A middle-aged man named "Billy" clears his throat, sips from his Styrofoam cup, leans back (in one of those ubiquitous white plastic lawn chairs that one finds even on the tiniest of Marshallese Islands) and begins to tell his tale.[1] Reflecting his many years spent in America, he speaks to me in English mixed with Marshallese words, in an accent that sounds no different from that of a native speaker of the Midwest United States:

> Oh, it's been raining for weeks here this season. Just a couple weeks ago we were out fishing in this weather, a whole bunch of us. We were looking for the biggest sea turtle we could find, so we could have a big feast for a *kemem* [a first birthday party] for my nephew. We searched and searched in the rain, and we went out by that bird island where we go sometimes to find the bigger turtles or hunt for coconut crabs. Ah, we were just about to give up when, all of a sudden, this gigantic turtle comes up to the surface to breathe. So we surround it and the guys jump into the water to catch this big beast and bring it up onto one of the boats. But

then I notice there's another turtle attached to it under the water, and it's holding on tightly to its shell, like they do when they mate. These turtles are totally locked on each other, totally in love, totally doing it with each other. But they've both got long tails—so it's obvious to everyone that they're both males! I sat there up on the boat scratching my head because I'd never seen two male turtles going at it like that with each other, but we saw it with our own eyes, and anyway we knew we were gonna have a gigantic feast!

The next day when we started preparing the turtles to cook them, the priest came around. He looked at me very seriously and said, "So how did you catch two big male turtles like this at the same time?" And I told him, "well, it was easy—they were making love!"

The priest, he gets upset and looks at me like I'm joking, and says, "That's impossible! That kind of thing's not supposed to happen and you know it—you must be making this up!"

But I told him, "Hey Father, it looks like gay marriage has finally come to the Marshall Islands. It's about time we accept it!"

Billy winks at me after a long chuckle, looks out at the sea, and nods with a pleasant certainty as he turns back to the group, "Well, I guess the priest didn't like what I had to say, but hey, Marshallese turtles seem to have a different opinion!"

Violence and "Liberation"

I prelude my chapter in this volume about Oceanian genders and sexualities "on the edge" with this anecdote to draw attention to how local discourses about sexuality, like anywhere in the world, operate in conversation within interwoven local contexts and global discourses. This is especially true in the Marshall Islands—now an independent republic freely associated with the United States but saturated for centuries by Spanish, German, Japanese, and American missionization, militarization, and colonization. Billy's tale thus weaves together ancient Marshallese fishing knowledge with religious morality and contemporary international politics.

The story derives its humor from the collision of these contexts and discourses—not from the surprise of finding two amorous male turtles locked in a "homosexual" embrace, but from Billy's encounter with the priest. In this narrative, the priest's inability to reconcile the fishermen's tale with his moral vision, and the punch line—Billy's tongue-in-cheek advocacy of marriage equality—actually serves as a Marshallese mockery of Western responses (both liberal and conservative) to sexuality between men. Though Billy and the other fishermen were intrigued to find two male turtles engaged in intercourse, they themselves made no fuss about this; in fact, they saw the catch as a fortuitous blessing.

The mockery implicit in Billy's story underscores the deep ambivalence I have felt in debating whether or not to contribute a chapter to this volume: Does this discussion matter more to the community in which it is situated, or to a Western audience preoccupied with its own, often Orientalist, desire to frame and categorize gender and sexuality? By publishing in an English-language volume likely to be read mainly outside the Marshall Islands, am I not just smuggling "gossip" to the metropolitan academy without contributing to the communities for whom these issues are most relevant? I agree with Niko Besnier that ethnographic writing is just as political a medium as gossip, and that it is not meant to represent a whole society to its readership but rather to "establish a *connection* between societies and audiences" (Besnier 2009, 27; my italics). Still, there are many in Marshallese society for whom the themes of this book may seem to be a uniquely Western fascination, if not completely pointless in a Marshallese context. For instance, in response to some of my initial inquiry about this project, one Marshallese friend in the islands responded by saying:

> Why would anyone bother to [write] such a thing? While that might hold high merits, it does not make much sense, at least for us in the tiny Marshall Islands. . . . We're still recovering from World War II, and thereafter, from missionizing aftermaths, to say the least—and now we're trying to be eventually economically independent and be productive globally. We have more on our plate than our resources and islands can handle, let alone time to be debating about how we think about homosexuality!

On the basis of the above comment, one might presume that the topic is avoided locally partly as a consequence of both colonial and religious epistemologies and partly out of the urgency to survive amid the global economy. Given the intensity of colonial influence in the Marshall Islands in the nineteenth and twentieth centuries, it is easy to speculate that the judgments of early Christian missionaries, followed later by the mores transmitted through German, Japanese, and American educational systems, have overwhelmed or silenced precolonial indigenous discourses. This comment resonated with my observation that there is little open discussion in Marshallese or other languages about same-sex relations between men or women in the Marshall Islands, or even in the region known as "Micronesia" in general.

In terms of social scientific research, the topic of homosexuality has been addressed, albeit scantily, in another Micronesian context. *Truk: Man in Paradise* is an American ethnographic survey conducted over seven months in 1947 that attempts to inventory "the process of personality development" in immediate postwar Chuuk by looking at the areas of childcare, adolescence, sexuality, marriage, and adult life (Gladwin and Sarason 1953, 20–21). The authors touch briefly upon same-sex relationships between Chuukese youth, pointing out that when friendships get too close, friends of the same sex who might otherwise be deemed as "logical partners in homosexual relations" in other societies are perceived instead as "brothers" and "sisters," as having more like a sibling relationship (283). Arguing that the likelihood of "homosexual tendencies" is thus minimized in Chuukese society, the authors tactfully relegate the possibility of homosexuality to a fleeting stage of sexual development and foreclose any further contemplation of same-sex intimacy. Although the project was obviously researched rigorously and meticulously, clearly these particular questions lay beyond the frame of the authors' inquiry. Conducted via multiple psychological testing models and methodologies, the research also seemed more interested in depicting an overall general picture of the island than it was in relating Islanders' own individual voices about lived experience.

Aside from these marginal allusions to Micronesian homosexuality in academic literature, or Internet blogs alluding to perceptions of Marshall Islander gender ambiguity that I found written in their respective languages by American or Japanese volunteers in the Marshall Islands, I was unable to find much in the way of written material that seriously addressed this topic in the Marshall Islands context. Curious about the deeper reasons behind this local silence or ethnographic ambivalence, I finally raised the issue frankly with a Marshallese elder, who thought about it for a moment and then, smiling wisely, retorted: "Maybe it's not that we don't want to talk about this stuff; it's that we don't need to. Maybe we just take it for granted, unlike you Americans. Maybe we've just gotten it all figured out!"

As this elder suggested, the lack of discussion perhaps indicated that Marshall Islanders simply took same-sex relations so much for granted that they were not worth discussion, description, or contemplation. The elder continued by likening the issue to a simple matter of preference, in the way that one talks about personal taste for one food over another. "Maybe people think it's funny you like red fish when everyone else eats blue fish," he explained, "but that's the extent of it. The topic gets very boring after a while. We don't make a big deal about this kind of stuff. You guys do," he said, again poking fun at my Americanness in even raising such a topic in the first place.

Following such logic, even asking the question about homosexuality in the Marshall Islands, in its very problematization of same-sex love as particular, may reveal more about the unstable twenty-first-century contextual framework of the questioner than it does about the subject itself. Here, it is important to be mindful also of the critique made by Tom Boellstorff, who questions "the social scientific obsessions with finding the 'right words' to label 'things' assumed to exist in the social world independent of the observer":

> Claiming that concepts like "homosexual," "sexuality," and "gender" fail to explain non-Western realities misleadingly implies that the concepts are adequate in the West. It confuses modes of argumentation, mistaking interpretive frameworks for authoritative typologies. It also makes it difficult to examine how what Geertz terms "concepts put together in the West" are increasingly "put together" in non-Western contexts prior to the ethnographic encounter. (Boellstorff 2005, 8)

I agree that such "Western" categories or frameworks are highly inadequate and arbitrary wherever they are applied, especially when deemed to be somehow superior, but it is also important to keep in mind how the inherent othering in the ethnographic encounter has a tendency to create a binary between the observer and observed; for Marshallese and other "non-Westerners" also participate in creating and reproducing these frameworks themselves. In the post-independence era of the Compact of Free Association with the United States, Marshall Islanders are highly mobile and cosmopolitan; they enjoy unrestricted migration to and from the United States, and over twenty thousand Islanders have settled in communities from Hawai'i to Arkansas.[2] There are now Marshallese citizens who have grown up studying in North American schools without even learning their ancestors' language or customs, and many model their lives on the norms of the Americans among whom they live. There is, arguably, sometimes no clear line to be drawn between "Western" or "Marshallese" logic. Actually, for Islanders who have migrated across the seas for thousands of years and encountered visitors upon their reefs from all around the world, this boundary has always been blurry.

A Marshallese educator friend in Majuro Atoll pointed out that while in many respects considerations of same-sex desire may once have been a matter of "blue fish versus red fish," the Marshall Islands is globalizing, as information flows freely into the islands through the Internet and other means, and Islanders increasingly migrate back and forth to the United States. As more and more young Marshall Islanders grow up with American education and popular media they are beginning to model their identities and behavior after Americans, sometimes also adopting homophobic values as their own. Part of this, she explained, comes from Marshallese moving into conservative, evangelical Christian communities in the United States.[3] Anti-homosexual sentiment, she emphasized, sometimes leads to hatred and even violence.

The problem of homophobia (and the problems of violence it perpetuates) in the Marshalls and other islands is apparently what compelled Micronesian Seminar, a Jesuit research institute in Pohnpei, to devote the July 2006 issue of its *Micronesian Counselor* pamphlet series to the topic "Homosexuality in Micronesia."[4] Authored by Scott Nicloy, head of the Salvation Army Mission in Pohnpei, the pamphlet is a rare gesture for a Catholic institution like Micronesian Seminar (or the Salvation Army for that matter). Yet, despite its bold title, it is little more than a generic message that might as well have been written for an American audience of a bygone era. It treats homosexuality as therapists or clergy might have done in 1960s America, presenting it as a chronic and vexing mental condition that needs to be tolerated or endured, but certainly not acted upon or celebrated. The pamphlet is written in a spirit of sympathy toward sexual minorities, but Nicloy clarifies that churches and pastors ought to "support and promote traditional concepts regarding marriage and family throughout Micronesia," conceding that "it is not necessary to wound and to destroy people who are struggling with same-sex orientation issues" when doing so (Nicloy 2006, 18). But even Nicloy's notion of "traditional concepts" here is clearly referring to a Western, Christian practice of marriage that is not understood or practiced in the same way in Micronesian communities, especially in legal terms. Implying that Western notions of matrimony and family are "traditional," whereas homosexuality is an unavoidable but nonetheless troublesome, negative, and certainly nontraditional aspect of life, Nicloy writes that "you are more than your sexual orientation. Whether you are gay or straight, your positive qualities as a person outweigh your negative" (Nicloy 2006, 9–10). The pamphlet concludes with a plea to accept gay, lesbian, and bisexual people in "Micronesian society as a whole": "They are, after all, your sons and daughters, and in some cases, your husbands and wives, your mothers and fathers. Many of them are struggling with same-sex orientation issues in pained tortured silence that you may know nothing about; because the horror of growing up gay is the horror of having a secret that you do not understand, and you are afraid to tell anyone for fear that they will not love or respect you anymore" (Nicloy 2006, 18).

It is puzzling why a pamphlet published by one of the Micronesia region's leading research institutions, albeit a Jesuit organization, dwells on the supposed "horror" of growing up with same-sex desires without acknowledging indigenous contexts wherein such desires might not have been deemed "horrifying" to begin with. Indeed, same-sex relations, as well as transgenderism, were likely widely practiced and accepted by many precolonial local Pacific Island communities. More important, the pamphlet's preoccupation with "the homosexual" as a social category reproduces a dated, American discourse of sexuality that disavows contemporary indigenous notions of relationships between members of the same sex. Though the intention appears to be liberatory—to help Islander readers accept and tolerate various sexual orientations—the very invocation of the categories "gay," "lesbian," or "bisexual" without mentioning local terms, concepts, traditions, or histories effectively denies and silences Islander subjectivity.

As Joseph Massad writes about European works on the sexuality of Arab societies, "There is nothing liberatory about Western human subjectivity including gays and lesbians when it does so by forcibly including those non-Europeans who are not gays or lesbians while excluding them as unfit to define or defend themselves" (Massad 2007, 42). In some ways, it could be argued that the growing sense of "homophobia" in Micronesia that Nicloy attempts to quell is only exacerbated by this very disavowal or ignorance of local practices and understanding in favor of a Western view of sexuality, with all its cultural baggage.

The decision to write this chapter arose from my desire to look past this mire of Western terminology and open up space for a productive conversation that pays attention to local lived experience without relying on Western labels or constructs. It is not my intention to reinstate a utopian vision of premodern "Marshallese sexual freedom" or somehow to "liberate" Marshallese "sexual minorities" from the clutches of colonialism and globalization. After all, such politics are already familiar territory for all Islanders who experienced the invasion of their lands and seas and hearts over the past several centuries. Not only did US forces most recently claim to "liberate" Marshallese and other Micronesians from Japanese militarism during the Pacific War and swiftly recolonize them into American militarism;[5] the same could be said for a postwar "liberatory" politics of universal sexual rights that imposes Western values and judgments about sexuality, love, and private personal relationships on island populations. This is therefore more a chapter about some of the unique dimensions of friendship and intimacy between men in the Marshall Islands than it is about issues of identity, an approach that falls in line with this edited collection's shift from identity to practice. Though I can only hope to sketch out some suggestions for reconsidering these themes, hopefully this can inspire future discussions that will have the potential to transcend American hegemony in this part of Oceania.

Throughout this project, I consulted with various Marshallese and non-Marshallese men and women for their feedback and insights, but I interacted primarily with a group of three Marshallese men who were willing to share their views and personal experiences candidly, on the condition of anonymity.[6] Out of these three, I had the most extensive discussion over the course of a year with an individual in his sixties who was educated in both the Marshall Islands and the United States and to whom I will refer as "Robert." The following pages are written in conversation mainly with Robert and supported or contrasted with insights from other participants as well.

Life without Closets

"There's no language in Marshallese for the imported word 'gay,'" explains Robert. "Culturally the word doesn't make any sense unless it is spoken within a Western context, and most people do not use it this way anyway, because they lack the understanding or knowledge to do so." Although younger people use this word when speaking English in some cases, and of course the concept comes up in American films (which are watched on DVD players even in the most rural atolls of the Marshall Islands), the idea of assuming an identity or being labeled based on one's sexual preference is unfamiliar. In the context of Billy's story of the two sea turtles, the term "gay" serves as a frame for the storyteller to make a commentary on a uniquely foreign, American way of seeing things.

Although there is no local word to describe exactly what the English word "gay" typically suggests, there is a social category or identity in the Marshalls that often gets confused with this Western construct. The word *kakōl* refers to men who live within the circle of women and generally assume women's roles, often decorating or carrying their bodies in (often extremely subtle) feminine ways, or wearing items of women's clothing. In general, *kakōl* tend to prefer "masculine" men (though they sometimes date each other), and they are integrated into their atoll communities by assuming responsibilities and holding social positions identical to women. This term has been awkwardly translated into English as "hermaphrodite" or "eunuch," but the *Marshallese–English Dictionary* also lists the word "hybrid" to indicate some of the deeper origins of the *kakōl* term (Abo et al. 1976, 129).[7]

Although it is beyond the scope of this study to ascertain when the exact term *kakōl* first came into its contemporary usage, the word is believed to have premodern origins, and gender liminality in the Marshall Islands is by no means a recent phenomenon. One photograph taken by Marshallese-Portuguese photographer Joachim deBrum in the early 1900s shows four men standing somewhat alluringly in feminine poses with their arms wrapped around each other, their hair neatly groomed and decorated with matching white flowers.[8] I resist drawing a facile parallel between *kakōl* and transgender counterparts in other parts of Oceania, but two of the individuals with whom I spoke, who had traveled widely in the Pacific Islands, suggested that *kakōl* were positioned in their respective communities on terms similar to those of *fa'afafine, fakaleitī, laelae,* or *māhū.*

Perhaps because of the visibility of *kakōl* in the Marshalls, non-Marshallese, such as overseas volunteers or the Americans who work at the vast US military installation on Kwajalein Atoll, tend to notice them and postulate their own theories about Marshallese sexuality. Typically they draw upon erroneous but typical stereotypes—conflating transgenderism with sexual orientation, viewing *kakōl* as "gay men," or presuming that all

Marshallese men who engage in intimate relations with other men are *kakōḷ*. For instance, a Japanese overseas volunteer I spoke with drew an analogy between *kakōḷ* and the Japanese derogatory term *okama*, a word often used to describe cross-dressing television personalities. She also went on to conflate *kakōḷ*, *okama*, and gay as "exactly the same thing."[9] On her blog, an American volunteer makes a similar conflation of sexuality and transgenderism when she uses the terms "homosexual" or "openly gay" to describe what might more accurately be understood as the widespread and visible social position of *kakōḷ*:

> Homosexuality, particularly among men, is widely accepted in the RMI, despite strong Christian influence. Per capita, I would think there are more openly (and I mean openly) gay men in Majuro than in many major U.S. cities (San Francisco excluded). To explain that a man is gay, a Marshallese person will simply point to his or her own upper arm, stating matter-of-factly "he has the woman bone." Guess that takes care of any debate over nature versus nurture.[10]

This blogger seems to presume that "openly gay" is the same as "being biologically male but living in the manner of a woman," thus revealing her inability to differentiate between gender and sexuality. Though indeed Marshall Islanders may refer to "the woman bone" in the context of *kakōḷ*, the notion of masculine men who prefer other masculine men as being romantic and sexual partners is another matter altogether.[11] Referring to such Marshallese individuals as "gay," whether describing *kakōḷ* or men who prefer men (or even the public health label "men who have sex with men," or MSM), is not completely accurate.

The blog continues to theorize that same-sex relations between women in the Marshalls are either accepted or just ignored, and that Marshallese married couples turn a blind eye to each other's sexual dalliances with members of the same sex in the interests of procreation and the pressure to have children. When I shared this blog with the Marshallese men and women I talked with for this project, they disagreed with this essentialist generalization in every respect. Several of them pointed out that romances between women in the Marshalls were no less common than those between men, and all cited examples of bitter dramas and jealousy when a partner in any committed relationship had sex outside the relationship, whether it was with someone of the same sex or not. The unmarried men with whom

I spoke also emphasized how they proudly took care of their nieces, nephews, and others' grandchildren, just as people of any sexual proclivity or gender do when they do not have children of their own. Particularly in the Marshall Islands, where the birthrate is high, and where the children of one's siblings are all considered to be as important as one's own biological children, these men insisted that they felt no pressure to produce their own children in the first place.

Between Marshallese men, however, friendships and romantic relations with *kakōḷ* are more often perceived as relations with a woman than with a man, and this has to do with gender identity rather than sexual orientation, as Robert explains:

> I've known and been in situations . . . where a very masculine guy, even a married one, is known to be exceptionally close to a *kakōḷ*, which is not that uncommon and is really no big deal among ourselves in the Marshall Islands. . . . But the funny thing is that when this guy brings his *kakōḷ* friend into a men's circle, there is usually a rather "uncomfortable" atmosphere here and there, not because we suspect they're having a so-called "gay" relationship with each other (which would be accepted anyway), but more so because the situation is the same as if only one woman were among us. This tension would be resolved instantly if there were "another" woman on board, because the effeminate guy would probably be more comfortable hanging around with her rather than with the men (at least this is the usual case). Any Marshallese man can attest to this reality. But the relationship between these two guys in itself is no big deal. This "gay" issue as it is in the West just does not make sense in Marshallese culture.

While it may not make much sense in "Marshallese culture," some Marshallese also use the term "gay" themselves in contradictory ways, often with the connotation of *kakōḷ* rather than of a man who partners exclusively with other men. I discovered a complex illustration of this sort of conflation in a YouTube video of an encounter between Marshallese soldiers working for the US Army and a group of Afghan villagers in Kabul.[12] The video, taken by two Marshallese soldiers on a special operations antiterrorism mission, is a rare glimpse of two non-Western groups trying to make sense of the awkward term "gay" in English. As the

Marshallese cameraman pans across the group of Afghan men, he lands upon one of them who appears somewhat effeminate, and who has decorated his fingernails. Curious about what this means, he strikes up a cultural conversation with the translator. "Why does he have fingernail polish on his hands?" the Marshallese soldier asks. The Afghan translator pauses for a long while and then hesitatingly explains that the man's hands are painted with henna decorations usually only appropriate for women, but that "the gay men, the gay people" use these as well. "So he is one of them?" asks the Marshallese soldier, giggling. "Yes, he is," replies the translator. "Hi, Gay!" the soldier says to the man, who shyly waves back at him. There is a protracted silence as the group chuckles and the soldier pans his camera over the crowd of villagers again, but then the conversation resumes, with no further mention of the topic.

This exchange is significant on a number of levels that extend beyond the scope of this project, but it is worth exploring the role of the military in shaping local representations and interpretations of gender and sexuality. In one respect, the very act of serving with the US military imposes American stereotypes and categories upon soldiers from multiple cultural backgrounds. I am tempted, for example, to explore the performativity (Butler 1993) of American hegemonic masculinities by Marshallese men in the US Army, as I have in an earlier project (Dvorak 2008; compare Teaiwa, this volume). In another respect, as I will revisit later, some same-sex affairs between Marshallese and American men have received attention from the war to the present, especially in locations like Kwajalein Atoll, where there is a consistently large population of civilian contractors and military staff from the United States.[13]

We could also interpret the confusion of typologies here through translation—indigenous terms for transgender identities being conflated, roughly and inaccurately, into the English word "gay." Boellstorff's concept of "dubbing culture" is useful here: "To 'dub' a discourse is neither to parrot it verbatim nor to compose an entirely new script. It is to hold together cultural logics without resolving them into a unitary whole" (2005, 58). Of course, Marshall Islanders make sense of American hegemonic cultural values on their own terms and through their own encounters.

Younger generations in the Marshallese diaspora use the very same terms or concepts that their American contemporaries might use to describe same-sex relations or identities based on sexual orientation; yet this "dubbing" process is informed by a Marshallese worldview as well. As

Robert comments in response to this YouTube video, "If this was in the Marshalls, this soldier would be super careful not to offend another man, much less a woman." The above exchange in a Kabul market is a good example of "cultural dubbing" that shows how often the term "gay" is used to describe such transgender identities, even by non-native English speakers. Inside and outside the Marshall Islands, I have also heard some bilingual Marshallese speakers attempt to "dub" the term *kakōļ* as "gay" when speaking to non-Marshallese, but this of course fails to express the uniquely gendered space—and the roles and responsibilities—of *kakōļ*, while it also elides the existence of relationships between men in the Marshall Islands that are not tied up in identities based on gender and sexuality.

"'Coming out' is also a very foreign concept in the Marshalls," adds another interviewee. "Came out of what, and into what?" asks Robert. "'Closet' is a Western concept—we never had closets or drawers in the old days; everyone slept in the same room, a reality still true in most parts of the Marshalls. Everything and everyone was out in the open—everyone worked and lived together. We, in the Marshalls, are always among one another inside and outside, we identify ourselves, for one, [through] blood connection and everything that has to do with where we came from. So 'coming out' makes no sense to us."

Yet what happens when these different paradigms meet in contemporary globalized spaces? "Jeb," a twenty-five-year-old Marshallese man, reflects on his experiences of coming to terms with his desire for other men amid conflicting American and Marshallese cultural norms. He describes having a series of girlfriends but never really being interested in having a more serious commitment with anyone until he had an experience with a man. Working as one of the roughly one thousand Marshallese laborers at the military base on Kwajalein, Jeb lived on Ebeye islet among Marshallese family and friends, but during the day he worked among Americans, watched American television, surfed the Internet in his office, and played basketball every afternoon with his American colleagues. He was also friendly with a lesbian American supervisor who was open about her relationship with her partner.

Interestingly, Jeb felt inclined to follow a more American paradigm and "come out" as a "gay man" on Ebeye, where he felt upset that he wasn't meeting any friends who understood his feelings. This did not go as well as he had hoped when he revealed to a close friend his preference for men while they were drinking. He describes that his friend shocked him by laughing at him and "outed" him as "gay" to other friends, who collectively ostracized him for a while, and even punched him in the arm on one occasion when they happened to be out drinking in the same bar. Jeb speculates in retrospect that it was because his "macho" friends might have interpreted his confession as a proposition for sex, or even simply as a big joke. Their reactions may also have been caused by the stigma they attached to the notion of "gayness" and, moreover, to the whole idea of "coming out" in the first place. *Kakōḷ* do not "come out," but are visibly effeminate and occupy a space in society that is widely understood. However, men who are not transgender but openly identify themselves in the Western sense as "gay" do not fit into an established Marshallese category, and so their status is ambiguous and potentially problematic.

Meanwhile, although it does happen occasionally, bullying itself is uncommon in the Marshall Islands. There, bullying one person, adds Robert, is essentially bullying that person's whole family or clan, and the bullied person may often turn out to be a member of one's own clan due to intermarriage. This is especially true in the case of *kakōḷ*, who are usually protected against violence by their family and friends. Jeb concedes that what he experienced amounted more to an instance of friendly ridicule than outright bullying, but he was traumatized by it nonetheless.

After spending several weeks on his own and suffering intense loneliness and self-doubt, Jeb decided to socialize with some of the *kakōḷ* who lived near him on Ebeye, thinking that perhaps he would feel more comfortable in their company:

> I was so amazed when I first went out with them. . . . Because the way they talked was better than any man I have known. All they ever talked about was nice things like traveling a lot when they don't even work. They talked about purses, earrings, pearls, you name it. I thought it was fun at first.
>
> All the *kakōḷ* surrounded me and asked if I was a *kakōḷ* too. I said, "Just because I hang out with you it doesn't mean I'm one of you!" So then they asked me, "Do you like guys, though?" And I said, "Yes, sometimes." So I went out with them to drink, and we drank so much I didn't know where I was. One of the *kakōḷ* hugged me and asked me to go do something in his room. I went with him but only because I wanted to go to sleep, and then all of a sudden I realized he was taking off my clothes and trying to have sex with

me. So I got up and ran and ran and ran. I've never felt so lonely and scared in my whole life.

Jeb thus consulted *kakōl* as part of his own "coming out" experience, and this, in turn, seems to have helped him to clarify his own gender position and orientation in *opposition* to them. It is also worth considering how the *kakōl* in this scenario might have been interrogating Jeb about his sexual orientation out of their desire to engage as women in a "heterosexual" encounter with a "straight" man.[14] Still, *kakōl* ultimately took on a negative role in Jeb's experience, as he perceived their advances with anxiety and felt physically repulsed by the idea of having sex with effeminate men. At the same time, Jeb also acknowledged that the popularity he enjoyed among *kakōl* gave him more confidence to pursue his desire for more masculine men, and it terrified him that he himself might become a *kakōl* if he succumbed to their seduction. He spoke of his longing to be able to meet up with a "real man," and to enjoy a "real gay relationship," which, he concluded, was not possible in the Marshall Islands. At one point he also dated a gay American employee on Kwajalein, but this relationship completely fell apart when he lost his job as a part of military budget cutbacks and was no longer able to access the base.[15]

In time, Jeb's friends began to talk to him again, and, not surprisingly, one of them even confessed his own interest in other men. But the trauma of his experience and the loneliness he felt, combined with the desire for better employment and companionship, led Jeb to move to Honolulu, where he eventually partnered with an American man. He continues to identify himself as "gay," and insists that he could never live in the Marshall Islands again.

Although Jeb's experience demonstrates in some ways the awkwardness of becoming an adult in the Marshalls, let alone anywhere in the world, it is especially reminiscent of the narratives of sexual minorities in the United States grappling with their own sexual orientation. It also resembles the stories of young men who identify as "gay" in the United States who struggle in rural communities until adulthood, when they move to urban centers, with the military playing a particularly important, if ironic, role in this process (Bérubé 1990). Situations like this call attention to the flows of global power, urbanization, militarism, and the huge influence that American discourses have on young Marshall Islanders, but they also show how incongruous and illegible the "gay" and accompanying "coming out" constructs can be in Marshallese social circles.

Sacred Bonds

There is in fact plenty of space for intimacy between men in the Marshall Islands within the framework of close friendship and bonding. Several of the people with whom I spoke emphasized that Marshallese social bonds enable and encourage all men to befriend each other deeply and to experience a special, powerful kind of closeness with each other that is honored and valued by their families and communities. "I even have a difficult time with the term 'love between men,'" says Robert, "since this exists among men even without sexual relations or feelings in the Marshall Islands. . . . An American may have male 'friends,' for instance, without feeling any 'love' for them; but in the Marshalls, *iakwe* is practiced when one breathes. *Iakwe* and love do not have equivalent terminology or connotation, this is for sure! The former goes far, far beyond romantic connotations."

Iakwe (also spelled *yokwe*) is an everyday Marshallese greeting, which also conveys the meaning of "love for you."[16] It is used commonly to say "hello" at all times of the day, much like the Hawaiian *aloha.* The term has a much deeper meaning, however, that expresses a sense of compassionate, universal love imbued with empathy and respect. For example, the same word can also express extreme sorrow and sympathy about a death or loss, such as when elders reflect on painful memories of the enormous loss of life during the Pacific War. *Iakwe* is thus a kind of loving that holds together all the constituents of the social fabric of an atoll community (see, e.g., the description of the comparable Micronesian concept of *fago* in Ifaluk Atoll described in Lutz 1988).

Yet *iakwe* is not sufficient to describe what two individuals share when they engage in a close relationship. Long-term intimate relations between two people of the same sex can carry a special kind of significance without being stigmatized. In fact, of the participants with whom I spoke for this project, none of the unmarried men in relationships with other men said that they were subjected to any social disapproval for not marrying a woman and having children, and several of them added that they were often envied for having more freedom to devote energy and resources to the people they really cared about, including distant relatives and friends.

"These loving relations between two people of the same sex are definitely not 'taboo,' as many people presume," explains Robert. "They are simply sacred grounds, just like the intimate relations between men and women of the opposite sex." That which is forbidden or "taboo," after all, is often really also sacred, powerful, and special in the sense that it is off-limits to ordinary people, inaccessible to but a privileged few. Moreover, in the unique environment of small islands and atolls, private relations, and the very notion of privacy itself, are sacred and special because of the very fact that most time in one's life on small coral atolls like the Marshalls is so communal, life being spent with the rest of one's family, clan, and friends. Robert continues:

> There's really no such thing as "private" in Marshallese culture. The closest word I can come up with is the word *jolet*, a valuable "gift" which even money cannot buy, and even the highest chief is not allowed to ask for in exchange; it could be a thing, promise, person, concept, land, piece of cloth, jewelry, child adoption, legend, potent medicine, and so on. Second, the word *jolet* we use here implies something strictly between two persons, but then when two persons share these "sacred" spaces and moments—like being super intimate with each other—it does not stop there at all. . . . What I'm getting at is that if two men become intimate and publicly "close," the ultimate results are such that all of it brings everyone closer: the two become on "the same level," which has a host of ramifications (for example, their children will treat one another as fellow siblings; mothers will treat one another as if blood sisters; and so on).
>
> And, third, "bedroom" implies privacy, but Marshall Islanders do not have a concept of a private "bedroom" where you sleep by yourself. Hey, everyone sleeps in a dwelling with everyone else.

We could compare this to Kalissa Alexeyeff's (2008) notion of an "open secret" in her discussion of same-sex relations in the Cook Islands. Yet, Robert's point here is that such encounters or intimate moments between men are not secretive in the sense that they would be stigmatized if they were known; rather, they are kept out of public view because privacy itself is such a precious commodity. The deeper dimensions of romantic relationships between men are thus "hidden in plain sight"—it is understood that such intimacy exists, but people respectfully choose to look the other way out of respect for the sacredness of mutual privacy. If this privacy is breached, Robert adds, the consequences are rarely more than an embarrassing tense moment of being "caught":

If two guys got caught having an intimate encounter, for instance, it would be considered not "shameful" but just "unfortunate"; for such moments are precious time and space between two persons. Boys and men in these circumstances are more likely to chuckle among themselves more out of the surprise of being "caught in a private act," and not really because of any guilt or shame about what the act itself was. I've experienced this situation ever since I can remember as a kid. So where do these "sacred moments" happen or take place? Anywhere and everywhere; they happen in places everyone else uses or shares, even in fishing expeditions and on canoes. Sometimes "we" just "know" they happened, or that there was a high probability that they have happened, or perhaps they happened, or it doesn't matter at all.

That being discovered in an intimate embrace or sexual act would result in little more than an uncomfortable "chuckle" is certainly not the norm for all Marshallese men, however. Some of the men with whom I spoke suggested that they were met with an attitude of homophobia or disgust from both men and women in reaction to such moments, much like the reactions Jeb experienced when he "came out" to his friends. Yet, ordinarily such relations are not framed in a context of shame or abnormality; they are simply not meant to be expressed in the open.

*Jerā*ship: A Marshallese Paradigm

In Marshallese, one usually refers to intimate friendships between two men or two women as *jerā*, with an implication similar to "my best friend." Marshall Islanders use this term to describe any close relationship with one special person of the same sex (as compared to relationships with the opposite sex), usually with no implications of romantic love or sexual intimacy. "*Jerā*ships" (for lack of a better term in English) can be formed by any two people of the same sex, though my intention here is to focus on the unique implications of such relationships between men. Robert elaborates:

These *jerā* relations among men are one aspect of the world I grew up in, and they seemed so natural among all of us; I believe the lack of these kinds of close relationships is the reason men in the West say they feel incomplete when they are not as interconnected with the men around them. These relations are so sacred and they were practiced by all my older brothers, my own Dad, and just about all my uncles. Many women in my family also had *jerā* relations with other women, but this was far more commonly practiced among men.

*Jerā*ships can also involve romantic love, though this is not typically inferred, as the concept is quite broad. It is appropriate, for example, to refer to another person's dear male friend (regardless of whether he might be a "lover," "partner," "boyfriend," or just a "best friend" or "soul mate") as "your *jerā*" (or, more precisely, "*jerām*").[17] It is a widely used term that covers a large semantic field, and for this reason some of the Marshallese men I spoke with about this project emphasized strongly that *jerā*ship is usually just a form of male bonding without any romantic or sexual nuances.[18] Indeed, it is common for many men to have both a *jerā* and a wife; likewise, it is acceptable for men with no romantic interest in women or marriage to have only a close relationship with his *jerā*, if he has been fortunate enough to find such a friend. Nevertheless, the most important implication here is that one's *jerā* is an ultimate endearment, an extension of oneself. This kind of connection between two people is widely considered a treasured and sacred gift or *jolet*, which is "so sacred that its blessings can only bounce back to everyone in sight and in blood," according to Robert.[19]

When one adopts someone to be one's *jerā*, it is even customary to introduce him or her to one's family just as one would when choosing a partner of the opposite sex. This may be done formally or informally, but making the effort to give an official introduction of one's *jerā* to siblings, parents, and relatives is the norm. Such relationships can even be prearranged, or at least encouraged, by two different families who are friends and wish to deepen their own bonds by pledging their children to each other. In a formal context of chiefly relationships, this has also been the case, as is described by former First Lady of the Republic of the Marshall Islands, Emlain Kabua. She writes about her relationship with her late husband, Amata Kabua, the first president of the Marshall Islands: "Even before we were born, our families had pledged Amata Kabua and me to each other. They planned if we were of the same sex, then we would be *jerā* (best friends). If we were of the opposite sexes, then we would marry" (Loeak, Kiluew, and Crowl 2004, 73).

This is not to say that *jerā* relationships are interchangeable with marriage; there is, however, a parallel with marriage in that *jerā*ship weaves families together across lines of power and land. Robert compares it to the traditional practice in the Marshall Islands of cousins marrying and having children together. These cousins are known as *ri-lik,* an in-group term that literally means "a behind person," in contrast to someone who is seen as being on the same level. In the matrilineal Marshallese clan system, land arrangements and rights pass through women (see Tobin 1953, 1958; Mason 1968; Kiste 1974).

Robert brings up the example of the Marshallese proverb *"Ieb jel tok, Ieb jel lok,"* which refers to two baskets woven of coconut fronds and filled with a bounty of food—one that faces toward oneself and one's family and one that faces outward to all other people. Used in the context of a newborn baby, he explains that this proverb implies, "If it's a boy, he will be a fortune to others; if it's a girl, it will be a fortune to us." This expression refers to the practice in the Marshall Islands of the groom relocating to the family of the bride, taking with him all of his skills and blessings and thenceforth following his wife and her family's decisions.

In the Marshall Islands, where the land of each islet in an atoll is divided and measured perpendicularly from ocean to lagoon-side in parcels (*wāto*), island inhabitants do not live in one centralized village, but rather in dispersed settlements on their own ancestral land of inheritance. In such a context, with the need to expand one's family, populate one's land, and survive resourcefully in one's *wāto,* being limited to marrying only one's first cousins presents a challenge. Many of the men with whom I spoke surmised that *jerā*ship was thus a way for men to affiliate between families independently of the matriline as a complementary practice to marrying one's *ri-lik,* designed over the centuries as a means of survival in harsh atoll environments. Entering a *jerā*ship with another man from another clan from another atoll brings fortune and blessings to both families by linking two clans and pooling their resources and specialized knowledge for survival.

Weaving It All Together

The idea of *jerā*ship is steeped in its own profound symbolism and connotations of interwoven brotherly ties, even linguistically. The root word *"jer-"* in *"jerā"* and its variants derives from the word *"er,"* Robert theorizes. *"Er"* is a root word that suggests a sort of protective barrier, cushion, or cover laid down under something, like a tablecloth (*eran tebōḷ*). The branches of coconut palms lined up in a path along a beach from the lagoon's edge to protect an outrigger canoe when it is brought on land for repairs are also referred to as *er*, for example. Robert also makes a strong association with *"jaki,"* woven mats. *Jaki* are seen traditionally as sacred objects imbued with much sentiment. These mats serve three main purposes, and Marshall Islanders weave them specifically for use as a simple floor covering (in which case it is the only kind of mat that can be walked on); a sleeping mat (that can be lifted if one needs to get past it but never walked on); or a funeral mat on which to lay a dead body (intricately woven and decorated).

*Jerā*ship, argues Robert, encompasses all three of these sacred meanings in one way or another:

> "Who is that man?" one may inquire of Alfred's partner. "Oh, *jerān* Alfred"—a person whom Alfred lies on, under, or with, one who looks after Alfred's delicate being and needs and wants, one who is sacred to Alfred (and vice versa), one who is "part of" Alfred, one "who is the same" as Alfred. And the meaning of "one who sleeps with" literally means just that—*jerā* normally sleep in the same mat, room, even the same bed. It's not expected otherwise; the two are expected to be always doing things together throughout their lives, without one single exception. I cannot think of any single issue or activity that these two men cannot do together—everything is assumed and expected.

One's *jerā* is thus like a protective, supportive presence akin to a mat, protecting and nurturing him. Like a *jaki*, he is seen as woven together with his partner, as part of his life in every respect. And, though walking over any person's body or any part of his/her body is highly unacceptable in the Marshall Islands, one does step over one's *jerā* without inhibition, just as one can walk freely over one's closest family members (especially those of the same sex). This indicates just how much a *jerā* is a part of one's inner circle and is an expression of endearment.

My discussions with Robert and the other men who shared their experiences for this project went beyond the definition of this conceptual framework and into the realm of personal "interweavings" and tales of relationships and life experiences far too complex to relate here. I heard many stories about each of their respective partnerships with their own *jerā,* however, and in all respects these sounded like profoundly deep bonds and commitments that were honored and appreciated by all of these men's families. I have, of course, also observed and learned of many more lifelong *jerā*ships between men whose friendships are not romantic but perhaps more fraternal in nature.

In either case, my intention in having this conversation and sharing our ideas in this chapter is to try to destabilize the authority of Western, and particularly American, frameworks of identity politics and sexuality. Marshall Islanders often express ambivalence toward the "liberation" purportedly brought by American forces when they planted their flag on Marshallese shores at the end of the Pacific War; likewise, most of the men with whom I spoke felt ambivalent about the "liberation" promised by the rainbow flag. Acknowledging that their relationships and their lives are anything but oppressed, these so-called liberatory gestures appear pointless, and even aggressive.

So what should we make of those two sea turtles and their transoceanic love affair? Were they really "gay" newlyweds like their American human counterparts? On that rainy day, was Billy not just framing his turtle story in the context of "gay marriage" to tease me, knowing I came from a country where such charged debates transpired? Did the Marshallese fishermen really care about whether they were "gay" or not? After all, what they probably found most entertaining about finding these two entangled turtles was actually not that they both were male but that—locked in their amorous embrace—these turtles had been *caught in the act,* an awkward moment of erotic humor for all parties concerned. And as for the turtles themselves? Somehow I cannot help but imagine them enjoying the intimacy of each other's company as they rode the ocean currents from atoll to atoll, diving deep into the blue and watching the sunset as they surfaced, sharing their every intimate secret with one another—theirs was truly a match made in heaven. For even if they suffered the misfortune of getting caught in the end, no one can doubt that their *jerā*ship brought blessings to the whole community.

Acknowledgments

I wish to express my deepest thanks to all the men and women in the Marshall Islands who so candidly shared their very private experiences and reflections with me throughout this research, and to all my colleagues and close friends who made helpful comments on earlier drafts, including my own *jerā*, Kenji.

Notes

1   I have chosen to protect the identities of all the people who generously participated in this study by deliberately changing personal details that might identify them and at times using pseudonyms to clarify differences between speakers, indicating this by quotation marks.

2   The 2010 figure for Marshallese living in the United States was 22,434, according to Hixson, Hepler, and Kim 2012.

3   Though the original source no longer exists, I recall viewing blog postings on one of the Marshallese diasporic news and community websites available in the late 1990s where the topic of "gays and lesbians" in the Marshall Islands was discussed extensively, resulting in increasingly homophobic responses from Marshall Islanders living in the United States replete with condemnatory interpretations of biblical scripture. The hate language that erupted in this forum was so inflammatory that the entire forum was eventually deleted by the moderator.

4   Micronesian Seminar publishes *Micronesian Counselor* as a public service outreach gesture to communities throughout Micronesia on a wide range of social issues—politics, psychology, health, religion, and various other themes. These editorial pamphlets, devoted to commentary, usually by one author about a single topic, are distributed to public institutions in all of the islands and can be freely downloaded from the Internet.

5   See Dvorak (2008) for an interpretation of how the politics of liberation intersected with the construction of postwar Marshallese masculinities in relation to Japanese and American militarism.

6   Many of the individuals I consulted were somewhat concerned that their families and communities might consider it inappropriate for them to speak out as cultural authorities, *not* out of any concerns about the subject matter itself. In fact, they each felt quite confident in their assertions and were very generous in sharing stories about their own personal experiences with me.

7   Hybridity, in the sense of being both man and woman, may be one way of describing the *kakōḷ* social position, but as Samoan novelist Albert Wendt writes, even the concept of "hybridity," when applied to postcolonial Pacific Islander identities, evokes labels of the "half-caste" or otherwise impure that "smacks of the racist colonial" (Wendt 1999, 411). *Kakōḷ* nonetheless embody a simultaneous in-betweenness and fusion of both male and female attributes while living within the world of women.

8   See deBrum Collection Plate F-81. This collection of early photographs taken by Marshallese-Portuguese Joachim deBrum is held by the deBrum family and the Republic of the Marshall Islands Historic Preservation Office. Though not available for reproduction, it can viewed on a restricted basis.

9   There have been many fine works published in recent decades that describe the origins of these terms and the same-sex sexual traditions of *nanshoku* or "male love" in Japan over the past several centuries (e.g., Schalow 1990; Pflugfelder 1999; McLelland 2005; and Reichert 2006).

10   Excerpted from http://sarahslifeplan.blogspot.com/2010_03_01_archive.html (accessed April 6, 2010).

11   The Marshallese individuals with whom I spoke for this project claimed that they had never heard of this "woman bone" expression referred to by the American blogger.

12   http://www.youtube.com/watch?v=j3n0-yIPCl8 (posted in January 2009, accessed December 8, 2010). As constituents of an island nation freely associated with the United States, citizens of the Republic of the Marshall Islands are eligible to join the United States Armed Forces.

13   Of course, such liaisons likely existed in earlier regimes as well. As I have written elsewhere, Japanese male socialization through *seinendan* men's youth groups, military drills, and other disciplines was a big influence on local concepts of sexuality and gender (Dvorak 2008). Though I have been unable to find any Japanese archival materials that pertain to same-sex relationships specifically between Japanese and Micronesian men during the colonial or war era, one wartime memoir poignantly describes a comparable context. McLelland translated a postwar article written by a former soldier about a loving and erotically charged relationship that took place between that soldier and a young Javanese man in wartime Indonesia who massaged him regularly and sexually pleasured him while he was tending his battle wounds (McLelland 2005, 52–53). Another reference point would be the Filipino film *Markova: Comfort Gay* (Portes 2000), based on the true fact of young Filipino men being raped and forced into being a transgender version of "comfort women" to serve Japanese soldiers during the occupation of the Philippines. Though both these narratives are examples of exploitative or violent relationships between Japanese superiors and colonized locals, they suggest the kind of power that Japanese men had over local men, let alone women.

14   The language of transgenderism in English, with its emphasis on "transitioning" from one gender to the other, fails to account for the ambiguity expressed by *kakōḷ*, who most often position themselves as women in relation to "masculine" men, even while adopting only the subtlest feminine behaviour or style.

15   I interviewed one long-term Kwajalein American resident who had close contact with the Marshallese community of Ebeye and a long-term boyfriend

there in the 1970s until their relationship was discovered by the military leadership. Unfortunately, the US Army's response to this at the time was to terminate the American employee's contract and force him to leave the island immediately.

16   Recently, the word *"iakwe,"* which happens to be composed of homonyms for the words for "rainbow" (*ia*) and "you" (*kwe*), has been romanticized by some Marshall Islanders, who say that the expression, with all its connotations of love, beauty, and admiration, originally meant "you are a rainbow." Elders and other cultural authorities, including Robert, contest the "silliness" of this interpretation, which they argue is merely a modern invention.

17   *Jerā* is the form of the word with a first-person possessive pronoun suffix ("my best friend"), while *jerām* is suffixed with a second-person possessive pronoun, and *jerān* with a third-person pronoun. To avoid confusion, here I am mainly using the first-person form, *jerā*, and my own formation, *jerā*ship.

18   There is of course no way of determining how many *jerā*ships actually involve physical, sexual intimacy, but most of the men with whom I spoke stressed the point that in such a close relationship between two men, there always exists the possibility of such sexual involvement, and it is not uncommon.

19   Here we could compare the idea of "brothers" and "sisters" described in the Chuukese setting (Gladwin and Sarason 1953, 283) as another example of same-sex bonding being incorporated into the family circle, but it is important to emphasize the intimacy and "sacredness" Robert describes here, as well as the sense of loving, potentially romantic partnership.

References

Abo, Takaji, Byron W. Bender, Alfred Capelle, and Tony DeBrum. 1976. *Marshallese–English Dictionary*. Honolulu: University Press of Hawai'i.

Alexeyeff, Kalissa. 2008. "Globalizing Drag in the Cook Islands: Friction, Repulsion, and Abjection." *The Contemporary Pacific* 20(1): 143–161.

Bérubé, Allan. 1990. *Coming Out under Fire: The History of Gay Men and Women in World War Two*. Boston: Free Press.

Besnier, Niko. 2009. *Gossip and the Everyday Production of Politics*. Honolulu: University of Hawai'i Press.

Boellstorff, Tom. 2005. *The Gay Archipelago: Sexuality and Nation in Indonesia*. Princeton, NJ: Princeton University Press.

Butler, Judith. 1993. *Bodies That Matter: On the Discursive Limits of Sex*. New York: Routledge.

Dvorak, Greg. 2008. "The Martial Islands": Making Marshallese Masculinities between American and Japanese Militarism. *The Contemporary Pacific* 20(1): 55–86.

Gladwin, Thomas, and Seymour B. Sarason. 1953. *Truk: Man in Paradise.* New York: Wenner-Gren Foundation for Anthropological Research.

Hixson, Lindsay, Bradford B. Hepler, and Myoung Ouk Kim. 2012. *The Native Hawaiian and Other Pacific Islander Population: 2010.* U.S. Census Bureau, 2010 Census Briefs, C2010BR-12; http://www.census.gov/prod/cen2010/briefs/c2010br-12.pdf (accessed June 15, 2013).

Kiste, Robert C. 1974. *The Bikinians: A Study in Forced Migration.* Menlo Park, CA: Cummings.

Loeak, Anono, Veronica Kiluwe, and Linda Crowl. 2004. *Life in the Republic of the Marshall Islands: Mour Ilo Republic Eo an Majōl.* Majuro: University of the South Pacific.

Lutz, Catherine A. 1988. *Unnatural Emotions: Everyday Sentiments on a Micronesian Atoll and Their Challenge to Western Theory.* Chicago: University of Chicago Press.

Mason, Leonard. 1968. The Ethnology of Micronesia. In *Peoples and Cultures of the Pacific,* ed. Andrew P. Vayda, pp. 275–298. Washington, DC: The Natural History Press.

Massad, Joseph. 2007. *Desiring Arabs.* Chicago: University of Chicago Press.

McLelland, Mark. 2005. *Queer Japan from the Pacific War to the Internet Age.* Lanham, MD: Rowman & Littlefield.

Nicloy, Scott. 2006. *Homosexuality in Micronesia.* Ponhpei: Micronesian Counselor, vol. 62.

Pflugfelder, Gregory M. 1999. *Cartographies of Desire: Male–Male Sexuality in Japanese Discourse, 1600–1950.* Berkeley: University of California Press.

Portes, Gil. 2000. *Markova: Comfort Gay.* Manila: Vagrant Films (97 min.) DVD.

Reichert, Jim. 2006. *In the Company of Men: Representations of Male–Male Sexuality in Meiji Literature.* Stanford, CA: Stanford University Press.

Schalow, Paul Gordon, trans. (Ihara Saikaku). 1990. *The Great Mirror of Male Love.* Stanford, CA: Stanford University Press.

Tobin, Jack A. 1953. *The Bikini People, Past and Present.* Guam: District Administrator, US Trust Territory of the Pacific Islands.

———. 1958. *Land Tenure Patterns in the Trust Territory of the Pacific Islands.* Guam: Office of the High Commissioner, US Trust Territory of the Pacific Islands.

Wendt, Albert. 1999. "Afterword: Tatauing the Post-Colonial Body." In *Inside Out: Literature, Cultural Politics, and Identity in the New Pacific,* ed. Vilsoni Hereniko and Rob Wilson, pp. 399–412. Lanham, MD: Rowman & Littlefield.

PART III

Politics of the Global

CHAPTER 10

The *Fokisi* and the *Fakaleitī*

Provocative Performances in Tonga

Mary K. Good

In the brightly lit hall of the Wesleyan church, just off the main government road that runs across the island of 'Eua, the hired DJ blared one last upbeat Pacific Islands dance song filled with synthesizer trills, hoping to reel in a few stragglers to the night's program. Finally, the deafening volume of the music was lowered and, amid the insect noises from the warm summer night, the leader of the 'Eua Youth Congress took the microphone. The young man gave a brief speech of thanks and introduction to the night's program, then asked the minister of a nearby church to offer an opening prayer.

Following the prayer and a resounding "*Ēmeni!*" (Amen) uttered by all present, the front of the hall was occupied by a quartet of young people in their late teens and early twenties dressed in bright red T-shirts screen-printed with "Break the Silence! For our Future!" and other encouraging slogans, as well as a now globally iconic symbol: the trailing loop of the AIDS ribbon. Two elaborately coiffed and made-up women began a presentation about HIV, AIDS, and sexually transmitted infections (STIs). They were followed by two *fakaleitī*, men who dress and act in a manner similar to women, who took turns providing additional information on symptoms and prevention of the diseases.[1] All four facilitators delivered the information with great skill, deftly referring to hand-printed charts copied from materials provided by a transnational organization and proudly wearing T-shirts that had recently been delivered from the national youth group offices. The rapt audience treated the presenters with a surprising

213

amount of deference and respect, given their loud joking and sexual teasing just a few minutes before during the DJ's musical "crowd warm-up." After the main presentation, the audience split into single-gender groups for "breakout sessions," where the information deemed to be more sensitive in nature could be shared without risk of breaking the rules of respect between classificatory brothers and sisters. After a brief moment of indecision, one young *fakaleitī* joined the group of young women, crouching close to the two young female facilitators, but the latter shooed the *fakaleitī* away and told him to go sit with the young men and the other young *fakaleitī*. The peer facilitators led the groups and fielded questions with confidence, occasionally turning to me or the other youth group facilitator, a male American Peace Corps volunteer, to ask for additional information. Following the meeting, the group gave itself high evaluations for their ability to present the information without experiencing too much shyness and embarrassment (*mā*) and spoke about how well their campaign to empower the island's youth seemed to be going after its initial set of meetings and educational events. Two of the young women, who under normal contexts were often called "*fokisi*" for their purported promiscuity and semiotic markers of questionable morality, while recapping the night's events, attempted to stifle their beaming grins at how well their breakout session had gone.

On many Friday or Saturday nights, a different kind of event sends out a similar musical invitation to the same young people on the island. The single disco on 'Eua blasts its distinctive blend of Pacific dance music and American hip-hop through a neighboring village to welcome revelers. Most of the Pacific Island tunes used to attract them shared the characteristics of what Tongan youth called "remix," a style of music popularized by artists like DJ Darren and involving thumping, quick-tempo percussive beats and electronic synthesizer trills overlaying sped-up tracks of familiar ukulele melodies and multipart harmonies from traditional Samoan, French Polynesian, or Tongan love songs. Decorated with blinking Christmas lights and a spinning disco ball hung precariously from the rafters of the dilapidated warehouse, the disco doubles as a venue for church services on Sunday mornings, the lit-up cross hanging behind the DJ the only sign of this double duty.

Invariably, a smattering of young *fakaleitī* dressed for an evening of excitement can be found among the undulating circles of dancers of all ages. These transgender men who dress and behave in ways that emulate a certain image of femininity command a fair share of onlookers and whispered gossip as they perform dance steps and other moves signaling intoxication. A group of young women, wearing their hair long and loose over their fitted tops, shake and step right along with them. The young women's frequent presence at the disco and their style of dress are some of the justifications others give for labeling them *fokisi,* women who do not live up to local moral standards. The dancers at the disco, ranging in age from approximately five to seventy-five, good-naturedly watch the antics of the *fakaleitī* and their *fokisi* female friends. They will certainly report on the actions of this group in days to come, and possibly even subject the *fakaleitī* and *fokisi* to some teasing and heckling later in the night.

The presence and performances of *fakaleitī* have become infamous in the circulation of information among international travelers to Tonga, and the usual scenes played out at the disco on 'Eua are fairly similar to those seen in other nightclubs elsewhere in Tonga and farther afield in Samoa, where *fa'afāfine* enact similar social identities (Besnier 1997; Mageo 1992; Dolgoy and Schoeffel, this volume). Both *fakaleitī* and the women labeled *fokisi* have become associated with the values and venues of the world beyond Tonga, due in part to their being commonly employed at hotels, restaurants, and other sites associated with foreigners, but also for their real or imagined interest in activities like going to nightclubs, drinking alcohol, and engaging in sexual activities outside the socially condoned realm of marriage. *Fakaleitī* and *fokisi* occupy some of the most marginalized and precarious social positions in Tongan society and, especially in the case of youth in these categories, are vulnerable to physical and other kinds of violence. Yet their positions on the very edge of acceptable behavior also afford them certain allowances in thought and action. Although the range of their power or influence may be somewhat limited, *fakaleitī* and *fokisi* still manage to provoke social change and command center stage through the performance of the very identities that keep them on the periphery.

Because of their perceived threat to "traditional" values and their shared orientation toward transnational media and globally circulating discourses of youth and cosmopolitanism, *fokisi* and *fakaleitī* often develop strong friendships with one another, creating counterhegemonic alliances in spite of the fact that such relationships involve additional social risk taking. Marginalized on the local scale yet eager to become involved in global movements and identities, *fakaleitī* and *fokisi* become willing participants in certain kinds of "modernizing" development projects that have become increasingly visible in Tonga in recent years. No matter what their central focus, these projects arrive in Tonga with a complementary intention to "empower" local youth. Often sponsored by other national governments or transnational development organizations, the projects nevertheless find it challenging to surmount the obstacles of well-engrained Tongan cultural expressions for youth, including the embodied representation of *mā*, an embarrassment or shyness that also indexes respect and deference for specific individuals or particular social contexts. In the context of development work most often available to Tongan youth, the culturally engrained attitudes of shyness in one-on-one interactions with foreigners, a staunch unwillingness to single oneself out from the crowd, and a lack of confidence in showing one's ability to speak English can sometimes collide with the best efforts of foreign aid workers attempting to make their programs "inclusive" and "empowering," concepts to which I will return.

However, many youth who might typically be chastised for behaviors considered overly bold, brash, presumptuous, or arrogant (*fie poto, fie lahi, fie lelei*) welcome the opportunity to interact with (usually younger) foreigners, practice their English, and perhaps even gain knowledge and financial resources. In many cases, transnational development organizations and other NGOs intent on spreading what they see as vitally important information represent avenues for marginalized youth such as *fakaleitī* and *fokisi* to strengthen their bonds of friendship while forging identities that provocatively push the boundaries of Tongan cultural norms and make it possible for them to acquire knowledge regarding global issues and concerns.

Analyzing the case of one particular group of *fokisi* and *fakaleitī* friends on the island of 'Eua, this chapter sheds light on how transgender and "hypersexualized" individuals negotiate their subjectivity and perform their identities in relation to each other. Through their nonsexual bonds of intimacy, *fokisi* and *fakaleitī* youth claim to "empower each other," trading in the rhetoric of the development organizations with which they engage, yet also highlighting the precarious liminal position they occupy as purveyors of globally circulating forms of knowledge in a highly structured local context. The awareness of HIV/AIDS and sexual responsibility that members of this particular youth group dealt with provided a context that was especially fraught with tension for them. "Youth tend everywhere to occupy the innovative, uncharted borderlands along which the global meets the local" (Comaroff and Comaroff 2000, 308); the presentation of information about a disease that is global in scale and necessitates the description of sexual practices not typically discussed in public certainly seems to be situated in such "borderlands." The work meant a nearly constant negotiation of particular subjectivities and power relations cast upon them in both the local and the global contexts in which they became enmeshed. For these young people, local and global were not simply theoretical abstractions but instead real, meaningful sets of people, practices, and knowledge that they had to manage. The meanings of their own sexualities and potentialities, and the ways these articulated with global concerns, emerged through their work, and especially through their continued reliance on the bonds of friendship. Through its focus on friendships between transgender and (non-normatively) heterosexual youth and how these relationships allow the opportunity to explore identities and take actions that reach from a local situation of marginality onto the global stage, this chapter highlights the importance of understanding "the edge" of sexual identities and practices as always connected to a wider plane of social relationships, moral frameworks, local cultural meanings, and global interpretations.

Always on the Move, Always on the Edge: Tonga

Sitting east of Fiji and south of Samoa, Tonga is an archipelago of roughly 175 islands stretching across five hundred miles of ocean from the northernmost to southernmost points, with about fifty of those islands used for continuous human inhabitance. The nation's residents are particularly proud of their standing as the last true monarchy in the Pacific, as well as of the fact that Tonga has never been formally colonized by another nation (although it did maintain a special formal relationship of protection with Great Britain between 1900 and 1970, which on many occasions placed the country in a de facto colonial position). The country is classified as part of Polynesia, and the language is Austronesian.

According to the most recent census figures (2006), there are 101,134 people living in Tonga. Government immigration estimates, social science research, and popular reckonings place the number of Tongans living outside of the nation's borders at about 100,000, although this figure is probably a gross underestimate today (Small 1997; Lee 2003; Lee and Francis 2009). Most Tongan migrants live in New Zealand, Australia, and the United States, although people of Tongan heritage also reside in Japan, England, France, Russia, and other parts of the world for multiple reasons, including schooling, work, sports, and personal desire. An accurate count of the overseas-based population is impossible given the increasing numbers of circular migrants of all ages who leave Tonga for varying periods of time, reside in another country, and eventually return either temporarily or permanently, and because Tongan identity has become somewhat diffuse among new overseas-based generations of Tongan origin. Within Tonga and on the outer islands in particular, a sense of constant movement and flux permeates the social structure, as people leave their towns to travel to the capital, other islands in Tonga, or farther afield, sometimes without specific dates of return.

Along with this constant transnational movement, a heightened awareness to the flows of information and ideas between Tonga and other places is pervasive in day-to-day life. Many Tongans young and old, from all walks of life, engage in a variety of practices that provide them with news— both formal and informal—and information about events and issues in other parts of the world. A constant stream of national news is broadcast from radio sets in houses and places of business, and the national television network broadcasts local news as well as taped segments of the BBC international news channel. Moreover, Tongans take full advantage of communication technologies such as e-mail, online social networking websites, and text messaging to stay in contact with relatives and friends overseas and hear about important activities and ideas not covered by the formal news media. The steady stream of circular migrants also means that relatives, friends, coworkers, and fellow churchgoers return from other places in Tonga or in the diaspora with fresh gossip and news. To a large extent, then, ideas about Tonga, its people, and its culture are shaped in conjunction with and against the backdrop of ideas about the rest of the world, filtered through the lenses of both formal and informal information networks.

As is the case of many other Pacific Island nations, particularly the so-called "MIRAB economies" (those dependent on migration, remittances, overseas aid, and bureaucracy), Tonga depends economically on a combination of local small business and a wide-ranging, bureaucratic civil service, in addition to larger infusions of capital through remittances and foreign aid with considerably greater impact. Unlike Samoa, Fiji, or French Polynesia, however, Tonga's tourism sector is seriously underdeveloped despite government-led efforts to encourage development in this area. While some regional and international visitors pass through the country each year, they do not carry as much weight in the local economy as they do in other Pacific Islands. While most accounts of MIRAB economies in the Pacific focus on the social, economic, and political impacts of unwieldy and unstable dependency on remittances from migrants overseas (Evans 2001; Small 1997), it is also important to note the force of foreign aid in both its governmental and nongovernmental forms. Aid from transnational non-governmental organizations (NGOs) has contributed to Tonga's physical infrastructure and general economy; as this chapter intends to show, in the past few decades, foreign monetary contributions have also had a significant bearing on social organization and cultural change. Along with these investments and engagements in the formal capitalist economy, many Tongans still participate in other, more informal systems of exchange and subsistence, including cooperative labor, reciprocal contributions of traditional items such as mats or tapa cloth for food or material goods, and farming or fishing. The networks of exchange in labor, material objects, and other resources extend from island to island and beyond to diasporic communities in New Zealand, Australia, the United States, and even farther afield, creating one more type of link between Tongan localities and other, global sites.

The island of 'Eua, where I conducted my research, lies southeast of the main island of Tongatapu and is the third largest island in Tonga in both geographical size and population. Tongans consider 'Eua to be an enclave of traditional cultural practices, although it is only a two-hour ferry ride from the densely populated and highly urbanized capital city of Nuku'alofa. While most people still characterize the island's villages as "more traditional" and less developed or industrialized than the main island and other parts of the Pacific, the island's residents do have access to basic services, paved roads, and, increasingly, communication technologies like mobile phones and the Internet. Because of its spatial proximity to the capital, the vast social networks that extend across the islands, and the mobility of its residents, 'Eua is far from isolated from global circuits of information and objects. At the same time, due to its geographical location and reputation for maintaining Tongan cultural values, its villages appear quite literally to be perched on the edge of globalizing processes. 'Eua is characterized locally by a number of seeming contradictions that foreground the peripheral status of life "on the edge" of global modernity. Residents complain it is "too close" to Tongatapu and thereby susceptible to its questionable modern influences, yet they also complain that 'Eua is still a "forgotten outer island."

'Eua is considered to be both a bastion of tradition and the seat of the most easygoing Tongans, who are purportedly unconcerned about cultural norms and rituals. The island's towns grow in population each year yet send off hundreds of residents overseas for work and other opportunities. Given the contradictions inherent in the local experience of global modernity, 'Eua is a particularly appropriate site for research on the many conflicts and ambivalences youth must deal with as they strive to make sense of their lives in a time of rapid change. Notably, the island's ambiguous position as physically close to the main island yet fairly distant in terms of the rhythms of daily life has made it a focus of particular interest to the Tonga National Youth Congress (TNYC) and its international counterparts for distribution of knowledge and skill development programs. These groups see in 'Eua's youth population an ideal testing ground for programs before they set off to outer islands even farther away from the capital city.

'Eua's population, as recorded by the 2006 national census, is 5,206, although local estimates range from 5,000 to 10,000 residents, and the actual number of residents varies greatly depending on the time of year. A staggering 70 percent of residents were under the age of thirty-four in 2006, and 29 percent of the total population was between fifteen and thirty-four, the official boundaries of the category of "youth" (2006 national census data). On the island, estimates put these numbers at about the same level or higher. Many 'Euans spend at least part of the year either on another island for work or school, or overseas in New Zealand, the United States, or (less commonly) Australia. These fluctuations contribute to the sense of mobility and flexibility, particularly among out-of-school youth, who are discursively constructed as the most mobile people on the island.

'Eua has fourteen villages stretching along one main paved government road. 'Ohonua, the largest, acts as the port town and administrative capital and is also home to the government high school. The northernmost village of Houma sits in a remote location near the island's somewhat dilapidated royal residence, while the remaining twelve villages are clustered together along the main road a few miles from the edge of 'Ohonua. In addition to the government high school, which caters to approximately five hundred students from all villages, the island hosts a Wesleyan Church high school with about a hundred students, a small Mormon Middle School, six government primary schools, and a handful of kindergartens and preschools, most of which are run by local churches. Just outside 'Ohonua, on the edge of the neighboring village of Ta'anga, is Hango Agricultural College, a postsecondary technical school affiliated with the Free Wesleyan Church.

While national law and the desires of most parents on 'Eua intend for all young people to complete secondary school and even acquire some tertiary education, school fees, the demands of farm work, and other filial responsibilities all compete with these ideals, and many youth leave school early. They quickly become involved in the daily duties of maintaining households, although some attempt to find work outside of home, either of their own volition or with the encouragement of their parents. If they do not work, the social world of out-of-school youth, especially young women, is often confined to their families and relatives. Many out-of-school as well as un- and underemployed youth who have finished school with an upper-level certificate welcome the opportunity to participate in church, village, and island-wide youth groups or special programs designed for them to interact with peers, meet people from other islands, and potentially develop new skills or abilities that can help them to secure a job in the future.[2]

Gender, Youth, and the Seductions of "Empowerment"

Peer-group facilitators experienced palpable excitement, nervousness, and pride during each island activity they led. A few mentioned to me that they felt proud and grateful to have the "duty" of distributing important information. For several of the participants, this was the first job they had ever held, and most had limited experience being the center of attention and authority as they were at the meetings. These feelings of pride and gratitude foreground some of the ways in which local issues and connections have become deeply connected to global concerns. Beginning in the late 1990s and early 2000s, the Tongan government began to scrutinize the nation's youth with fresh interest and to implement measures that directly addressed the concerns of this ever-expanding segment of the population. The government subsequently provided support for the establishment of the TNYC and, later, created a Ministry of Training, Employment, Youth and Sports. Various government ministries also entered into partnerships with NGOs such as the World Health Organization, the United Nations, and the Salvation Army to identify issues related to youth and conduct studies on these issues. A number of reports and action plans followed, written in the rhetoric of global development discourse, outlining the challenges that youth faced, such as teen pregnancy, alcohol and drug abuse, suicide, obesity, and sexually transmitted infections (STIs). Some of these issues had long been within the range of Tongan youths' life experiences, but they were only identified as "problems" or "challenges" within the context of internationally sponsored projects that were largely framed in Western cultural terms (cf. Adams and Pigg 2005). Youth-oriented efforts at the national level gained renewed energy following the political riots and cata-strophic events of November 16, 2006, commonly referred to by Tongans as "16/11," which were largely blamed on underemployed, disaffected youth in the capital (Besnier 2011, 1–6; Campbell 2008). The peer facilitator training that the 'Eua youth attended was part of this wave of programs that used connections with transnational organizations to combat "youth underemployment," which the TNYC identified as a major issue, but also addressed a global public health issue, linking Tongan youth with other youth and organizations around the world involved in similar work.

Like numerous similar workshops and youth activities conducted over the course of my fieldwork, part of the explicit aim of the peer facilitator training, as stated by local representatives and their transnational organiza-tions, was to "empower" local youth and give them a "voice" in society. As in many parts of the world, in Tonga youth occupy the lower reaches of the status hierarchy and have few opportunities for claiming power and authority except over those younger than themselves (Morton 1996, 130–131, 252). "Empowerment" became one of several terms circulating around the globe along the paths of development projects and foreign assistance, linking particular kinds of youthful action to idealized notions of liberal citizenship and individualized forms of agency (Durham 2007, 102–103).

At the same time as these programs allegedly empower youth and boost their self-esteem, however, they overlook preexisting ideologies of knowledge and authority that limit the distribution of information to those of higher status, who in turn decide who should have access to that knowledge and how. Because of the ways in which peer group facilitators received and distributed knowledge in the island communities, their work on promoting awareness of HIV/AIDS also became an epistemological and moral project. As in the work of HIV/AIDS peer facilitators in other locations of the world (e.g., Boellstorff 2009), knowledge distribution about the spread of a global disease has become tied to ideas about the social appropriateness of *knowing:* who is allowed to know, what they are able to know, and how they come to acquire this information from agents out-side of the conventional framework of authority on the island—informa-tion that is eventually transmitted by people occupying relatively powerless identity categories. The work of communicating information about HIV/AIDS takes on multiple voices and multiple forms of power, expressed within and supported by a network of friends performing counterhege-monic and marginalized identities.

The peer facilitators stood out in the positions of leadership that they occupied not only because of their youth but also because of their particular gender identities. The two *fakaleitī*, each with her own unique performance of this subjectivity, and the young women who were widely perceived as *fokisi* broke away from mainstream, hegemonic, and heteronormative notions of gender identity, using their work as a means of affirming their identities and positions as essential mediators between local and global information flows.[3] In a hierarchical society in which distinctions of titled rank and achieved status continue to carry considerable social and political weight, distinctions in gender identity and roles also arguably remain one of the most important categories of social difference in Tonga (Gailey 1988; Morton 1996, 100; Philips 1994). Ideologies of gender in Tonga and their connections to other social categories such as status, kinship, and religious affiliations play a significant role in the management of everyday social interactions and in the development of culturally specific moral frameworks. The co-construction of gender norms and identities as well as their surveillance and reproduction in Tongan social life are also implicated in the distribution of power, knowledge, and authority. At the same time, transgressions of these gender ideologies and the performance of innovative or contested gender positions provide interesting insights into the boundaries of proscribed norms and the subtle ways in which gender ideologies change over time. *Fakaleitī* represent a quasi-institutionalized, conditionally accepted gender identity that, while tolerated in most social circumstances, is not completely condoned and remains on the margins of mainstream gender sensibilities. *Fokisi,* on the other hand, represent a real or imagined breach of normative feminine behavior and style yet play an important role in defining the acceptable in multiple domains of femininity, such as hairstyle, clothing, language, and movement.

In general, women and men are considered to be structurally opposite, and mainstream discourses about roles and activities reflect this division (Bott 1981; Gailey 1988; Teilhet-Fisk 1991). Within the family, women are considered to be higher-ranking than their brothers, but of lower rank than their husbands. Men command most positions of authority in government and the public sphere and are more powerful than women in most social situations. The historically rooted brother–sister relationship of respect, or *faka'apa'apa*, dictates the morally appropriate conduct for cross-gender sibling relationships and remains one of the most important aspects of Tongan social organization today. While both boys and girls are raised to understand the importance of paying respect to those of higher rank, women are characterized as "naturally" quieter, more demure, and shyer. Generally speaking, cultural norms dictate that women spend more time indoors, preferably at home, and that men are given to being "outside," working on farmland or attending to other public activities. As in other societies of Polynesia and beyond, men are considered to be more mobile, while women are more restrained, passive, and less active. Almost as soon as children can walk, they are socialized into the gendered division of labor as well, where women handle most domestic chores and men perform the "heavier" work associated with the outdoors. As children grow up, enter school, and begin to partake in church activities, common cultural norms attribute superior learning abilities and greater religious devotion to girls, in keeping with ideas about the feminine propensity to stay indoors and quietly accept responsibility and information. Yet many teachers on 'Eua bemoaned the fact that once girls reached puberty they lost interest in their studies and could only think about boys or other social distractions. This period of a girl's life also represents the time when she becomes tightly enmeshed in social networks and obligations to prepare feasts, weave mats, paint tapa cloth, and complete other traditional duties associated with women.

For boys, on the other hand, early adolescence and the time around puberty signals a social separation of young men from the feminine domain of household and family. A disassociation from maternal care and social institutions, in conjunction with contemporary gender norms that dictate masculine impassivity and lack of emotional expressiveness, lead to an experience of young manhood with fewer social support networks than young women have (and often feel constrained by). Particularly within the last few years, as Tonga moves toward an economy that depends more on money than men's traditional agricultural efforts, young men have become increasingly "lost" and disenfranchised. In comparison, young women and *fakaleitī* have far more outlets to provide them with social and emotional support.

Adults begin to demand that young people, once they reach adolescence, take the rules of brother–sister avoidance (*faka'apa'apa*) seriously, highlighting the ways in which ideologies of gender and age categories interact. In the past, in order to avoid contact with adolescent sisters, young men would move out of their parents' homes and begin to spend more time with peers or extended kin in a boys' hut (Morton 1996, 112). This tradition persists into the present, but has recently undergone modification as more families build Western-style houses and consider separate bedrooms adequate for preserving respect. Although cultural ideals dictate that all youth remain chaste until the time of marriage, young women are the objects of particularly close surveillance to ensure the preservation of their modesty. While young men are supposed to respect all women and abide by Christian values, the image of boys as perpetually "naughty" extends to a naturalized assumption that they cannot control their sexual urges, and some amount of sexual experience is taken as a sign of youthful virility. Any sexual joking or interaction between cross-gender siblings, however, is emphatically prohibited, and adolescents are instructed to avoid any situations in which they might even accidentally offend someone within earshot of this person's cross-sex sibling or cousin (e.g., by alluding to the body or to sexual matters). In everyday life, this translates into an assumption that anyone could be a possible classificatory brother or sister, placing restrictions on all communication and action at all times (Philips 2008). For youth living in small villages on outer islands, where extended families have been settled for many generations, the moral framework constituted through the brother–sister relationship can make it difficult to engage in many social events where both young men and women are present, as it is likely that relatives will also be in attendance.

Within the context of these general ideologies of gender, however, the new demands of global modernity have produced areas of possible conflict or even "ideological diversity," in which multiple interpretations of gender norms coexist (Philips 2008). Because they are socialized into behaviors conducive to the educational environment, upper-level high school courses are increasingly dominated by young women, and as a result far more young women than young men seek entry-level professional or civil service employment. At a time when access to capital is becoming increasingly essential for food, school fees, utilities, and other daily necessities, young women make important financial contributions to their families rather than depending on men to support the household. Subtle changes in gender norms extend to religious and leisure activities as well. Many churches, including both newer evangelical denominations and long-standing traditional ones, now offer extensive youth programs including choir groups, retreats, and Bible study, and young men often participate just as enthusiastically as their female counterparts. In addition, the relatively recent increased attention to youth causes has provided increased opportunities for young men and women to interact with each other and even necessitate knowledge of sex and sexuality. However, even programs that explicitly deal with issues of sex attempt to uphold cultural values of sexual propriety, using elaborate euphemisms when necessary and separating youth into gendered groups to discuss sex-related topics.

Breaking molds of ideal femininity and ideal masculinity are youth who identify as or are determined to be *fokisi* and *fakaleitī*. As mentioned above, *fakaleitī* typically take on feminine behaviors and characteristics, although the specific manner in which any one *fakaleitī* chooses to perform femininity can vary dramatically (Besnier 1997). They profess to favor women's work and activities over those of men, often (though not always) choosing to remain at home and help with domestic tasks such as cooking, weaving, and taking care of the house. Young women often enjoy talking to and working with *fakaleitī,* as they are perceived to be outspoken and humorous; they also appreciate the *fakaleitī*'s ability to comment on society in ways the women may be too shy or socially constrained to do on their own (Besnier 1994, 297–298). In terms of style, *fakaleitī* may choose to grow their hair long or wear it in a "Fijian-style" women's Afro, or wear flowers in their hair; they may pluck their eyebrows and/or occasionally wear makeup; and they may wear women's-style clothing all the time or only in certain social situations.[4] In most cases, young *fakaleitī* who choose to wear women's clothing lean toward a more "cosmopolitan" or Western style of feminine clothing, favoring tight jeans, revealing tops, short skirts, or the latest fashion in suits and dresses rather than the styles favored by traditional women in Tonga, such as more conservative long skirts or *pule taha,* a matching shirt and wraparound skirt usually made from the same tropical-printed fabric.

The two *fakaleitī* peer facilitators on 'Eua each expressed their identities in different ways. Twenty-three-year-old Pulu, the older and more outgoing of the two, lived in one of the villages farthest from the main town.[5] While known for his captivating feminine fashion sense at the disco on the weekends, Pulu usually wore masculine clothing on a day-to-day basis, only occasionally donning a long skirt rather than the long shorts or twill wraparound *tupenu* favored by young men. Pulu worked on the family's farmland allotment in a cooperative group with extended kin and friends and would sometimes drink *kava,* a male-exclusive activity, with the young men in the neighborhood. A reputation for drinking massive quantities of alcohol and offering sexual favors to passing men when intoxicated earned Pulu the disapproval of older women and was the object of lively gossip among young women and men.

Nineteen-year-old Heilala, on the other hand, was quieter and shyer, but chose to perform a more feminine identity on a regular basis. Heilala had plucked eyebrows and a medium-length crown of hair combed out in the style of Fijian women, although at times she would opt for more elaborate hairstyles. She usually wore longer skirts and loose yet feminine blouses, although sometimes she sported more revealing clothing when planning for a night out. When not taking part in youth group activities, she stayed at home with her mother and aunt, helping to weave mats and take care of the house. Although they resided in different villages, the two *fakaleitī* in the peer facilitator group were close friends and spent most of the free time during the workshops talking to each other and their *fokisi* friends.

More often than not, *"fokisi"* is a term attributed to others rather than self-selected, although the extent to which a particular woman chooses to embrace non-normative practices or amend her ways to comply with mainstream standards of comportment after being labeled a *fokisi* is an intentional choice. A borrowing from the American English slang word "foxy" to describe a sexually attractive woman, the term *"fokisi"* could possibly have started being used in the 1960s or 1970s following the first waves of circular migration between Tonga and the United States, especially California. The label is usually applied to young women deemed lacking in morality, although the reasons for such evaluation can be difficult to pin down. Adults describe young women as *fokisi* if they behave in any number of ways that go against mainstream gender ideologies: for instance, smoking, drinking alcohol, brazenly talking to young men in public, swearing, dancing suggestively, or being excessively loud or boisterous. Although all women in Tonga pay attention to their appearance, *fokisi* do this to the extreme, wearing provocative fashionable clothing and paying too much attention to the application of makeup or plucking eyebrows. *Fokisi* are also known for wearing their hair loose or in elaborate styles instead of adopting the more conservative, tightly pinned bun favored by other women and considered reflective of a neat, controlled Christian moral identity. In their appearance and in their embodied practices, *fokisi* directly oppose Tongan standards of demure feminine beauty, traditionally epitomized in the *tau'olunga* dancer (Besnier 2011, 133–135). Depending on their profession, young women are sometimes called *fokisi* for holding a job or engaging in other activities that keep them away from home and in the presence of non-kin for extended periods of time.

Perhaps more so than with *fakaleitī*, the appellation of *fokisi* is based on the context in which young women's behaviors are observed and evaluated as well as the frequency with which they occur. For instance, as noted, the ideal young Tongan woman would spend most of her time at home, weaving mats and helping with domestic chores, or at church engaged in religious activities. In actual practice, out-of-school young women spend at least part of their days in less structured activities, finding some excuse to pass by a friend's house or meeting others for conversation on the road as they walk to the shop. In contrast to age-mates who would arrange activities in such a way as to avoid bringing shame to themselves or their families by appearing willfully disobedient or purposeless, *fokisi* might exhibit more enthusiasm for meeting friends outside the home and invite observation through loud conversations and "clowning" behaviors perceived as ostentatious. Likewise, an occasional visit to a nightclub might not earn one the status of *fokisi*, but making it a habitual activity and getting drunk, dancing unrestrainedly, and failing to embody deference and shyness will.

Rather than viewing the label as the deprecating insult and call for behavior modification it is intended to be, some young women choose to embrace the role of *fokisi* and may even exaggerate certain aspects of their personal style to signal their appropriation of the identity. Several young women I knew told me they did not care or did not pay attention to people who meant to offend them or curb their actions by applying the label to them, and cited the fun they had and friends they made as ample reasons for continuing to act in non-normative ways. The young women deemed *fokisi* in the peer facilitator group fell into this category, scoffing at the possibility of eventual punishment by parents and asserting their entitlement to enjoy themselves. One of the young women, 'Ofa, had recently finished school and worked at one of the hotels on the island, which would have singlehandedly earned her a designation of *fokisi* for the long hours worked in the presence of non-Tongans, who presumably exerted a bad influence. However, 'Ofa also gained her reputation for such activities as smoking, sneaking out of the house to go to the dance club, and engaging in semipublic romantic relationships with young men. Soana, on the other hand, came from a family whose members played highly visible, active roles in the Mormon Church and seemed to have earned a reputation for *fokisi* behavior by smoking occasionally, wearing very fashionable clothes and heavy makeup, and hanging out with other transgressive young women. Once the peer facilitation training started, the bond between these young women and the *fakaleitī* was almost immediately evident, providing a unifying social support mechanism throughout the season of presentations and workshops. In their orientations to global youth culture and Western fashion and media, both *fakaleitī* and *fokisi* occupy precarious social positions in Tonga, which paradoxically situates them simultaneously on the edges of mainstream culture and at the heart of the nation's negotiations with ideas and institutions of modernity, development, and globalization.

Friendship and the "Friendly Islands"

Local legend claims that Captain Cook nicknamed Tonga "the Friendly Islands" because of the residents' warm hospitality (while, unbeknownst to him, they were busy plotting the captain's murder), but actual ties of friendship have been downplayed in research on Tonga and in other parts of the world. Perhaps due to the overwhelming attention that kinship and other systems of social organization have received in the study of culture, friendship has remained understudied in anthropology and other social sciences (Allan 1989; Bell and Coleman 1999; Desai and Killick 2010). Even with the increased focus on new forms of kinship (Carsten 2000; Franklin and McKinnon 2001) and other neglected forms of social relations like romantic pairings (Hirsch and Wardlow 2006; Rebhun 2002), friendship continues to be undertheorized and loosely defined, particularly in its unstructured manifestations outside of formalized age-sets or bond mates. Some cite the bias toward studying formal kinship as reflecting an analytic inclination for relationships that can be mapped easily onto larger structures of social organization (Bell and Coleman 1999). But the erasure of friendships from culture reflects an ethnocentric leaning in anthropology to privilege heterosexual norms of dyadic relationships above all other types of social connections.

While not specifically attended to as such, friendship has played an important role in many foundational works of anthropology, especially in the study of youth cultures and social practice. For instance, the friendships that produce and support shared interests, styles, and ways of speaking drive the values and practices of the subcultural groups that Willis (1977) and other Birmingham School scholars studied (Hall and Jefferson 1976). Similarly, ties of friendship are the basis for the formation of "communities of practice" in United States high schools, as linguistic anthropologists have demonstrated (Bucholtz 1999; Eckert 1989; Mendoza-Denton 2008). The intimate connections and shared values of youth groups in these works highlight the ways in which friendships between young people produce and maintain identity, even when not explicitly referred to as friendship. Friendships between young people also form the basis for interactions that constitute and contest overarching mainstream cultural values and practices.

Although friendship has been characterized as a unique kind of social relation because of its "voluntary" or "non-ascribed" nature, more recent approaches have noted that making or keeping friends is not a matter of complete free will, and that context plays a key role in understanding how friendships begin, develop, and end (Allan 1989; Spencer and Pahl 2006). Friendship is also complementary to, rather than contrastive with, kinship, because these two categories often overlap, and certain relatives may choose to spend more time or share more resources with each other than is dictated by cultural norms (Aguilar 1999; Desai and Killick 2010). Friends provide companionship and sociability, but can also act as sources to be called upon for help, for "friendship is not just about liking people, emotional commitment or a sense of worth, important though these are. Friendship is also a resource that we use, to differing degrees, to get through the everyday contingencies of living, further our social and material interests, and help sustain our social identity" (Allan 1989, 50). The locally specific ways of building and maintaining friendships in particular cultural contexts thus deserve further attention (Bell and Coleman 1999; Desai and Killick 2010), as do the ways in which friendship can simultaneously reproduce existing social norms while contesting others (Dyson 2010).

One type of friendship that has received considerable attention in recent decades is the long-standing bond, both sexual and nonsexual, between lesbians and gay men (Carrington 1999; Nardi 1999; Weston 1991, 1998). These friendships resemble and often substitute for family relationships. Research on these friendships, however, has privileged relationships between people of the same gender and the same sexual orientation. Much less attention has been given to cross-gender nonsexual intimate relationships or friendships among gay, transgender, and straight people. One reason for this is that the lesbians and gay men studied in the West form friendships based on shared struggles in coming to terms with their sexuality in a social context where sexual orientation plays a major part in defining identity. Gay men and women in the United States often choose "families" of lovers and ex-lovers (in addition to other homosexual friends) because they can relate best with people who have had similar experiences (Nardi 1999; Weston 1991). This premise of friendship rests on the assumption that all possible lovers of gays or lesbians are also gay and actually do share common sexual histories. This rendering of friendship does not take into account situations of "contrastive" sexuality such as those in Tonga, where the partners of *fakaleitī* claim heteronormative identity and explicitly reject the notion of shared sexual identity or common experience. In societies such as Tonga, where identity is based more on one's orientation to gendered morality rather than sexual identity, friendships between cross-gender gay, straight, and transgender actors may arise more frequently and visibly than in other contexts because of a shared position on the periphery of moral propriety.

In Tonga, youth participate, either voluntarily or involuntarily, in a number of institutional settings that encourage the development of friendships among both kin and non-kin. School, church groups, and other village- or island-based activities provide plenty of time for them to interact with familiar faces and meet new ones. However, Tongans are also socialized from a very early age to view the extended family as very important, and this is reflected in their friendship practices. When I asked them to identify their friends or their best friends, youth would often assert that they were best friends with everyone in the five-hundred-person school or, alternatively, when I replied that this was clearly not the case, would say that they had no friends at all. The youth I interviewed worried that having close friends would distract them from their studies and family responsibilities, as would having romantic partners. Pressures to do well in school and unending household chores often limited the time available to meet with friends and filled youth, particularly young women, with moral ambivalence. However, it appeared that youth also enjoyed spending time with friends who shared their interests and would try to find opportunities to interact with their friends as often as possible. Older youth who had left school early or graduated a few years before had only limited opportunities to interact with friends but clearly enjoyed what little time they were able to spend with them.

Youth tend to interact most frequently with, in descending order, close kin, extended relatives and loosely related kin who often also share church affiliation, immediate neighbors (who may also be very distant relatives), neighborhood or village mates, and finally people from other villages or religious congregations. Ideologies of gender also seem to prevail over age and other kinds of categories, so that it is more common for girls ranging in age from nine to twenty to interact with one another than with boys of the same age. Boys and girls may interact with one another, but the possibility of being mistaken for a romantic couple and the strictures of brother–sister rules of respect hamper casual interactions, particularly in smaller villages. Unless formal activity such as a church performance or village youth group event justifies casual copresence, close nonsexual cross-gender friendships are rare.

Given the cultural context of friendship, then, intervillage activities such as the workshops on HIV/AIDS constitute relatively novel opportunities for out-of-school youth to interact closely with peers whom they may know well. The situation can generate new friendships or further cement existing ones through joint effort and mutual support in times of tension or conflict. In the following section, I demonstrate that the friendships formed in the context of the HIV/AIDS peer facilitator group enabled youth to perform marginalized and socially vulnerable identities by situating the youth within a transnational network of power/knowledge while claiming certain kinds of local social authority.

Provocative Performances and Global Connections

From the very beginning of the first session of peer facilitator training, it was evident that the identities of the *fokisi* and *fakaleitī*, as well as their friendships, would have an interesting impact on the workshop and the work of the group. In order to understand how the identities of these youth and others involved came into play, some background of HIV/AIDS in Tonga is necessary. Unlike its regional neighbor Papua New Guinea, where the rate of infection is high (see Stewart, this volume), Tonga has had only seventeen documented cases of HIV and AIDS to date.[6] Although awareness programs have been running off and on since the 1990s, everyday discourse about the disease is muted, and information about the disease is relatively new to most people. All seventeen cases have been Tongan citizens, most are over the age of twenty-five, and two are reported to have died of AIDS-related complications. Of course, this does not take into account those who are untested and unreported, or non-Tongan visitors to the country, but the country is far from having an AIDS crisis on its hands. It is also estimated that rates of other STIs such as gonorrhea and chlamydia are high and are on the increase (World Health Organization 2008).

In the past, HIV/AIDS awareness efforts were specifically targeted toward *fakaleitī*, creating among the general public a sense that this was a disease of the "other" and thus unlikely to infect heteronormative Tongans (despite the fact that many heterosexual men have sex with *fakaleitī*). In some ways, the recent training seemed to reproduce these views, aligning HIV/AIDS infection with the immoral activities of the "other," although the definition of who was "at risk" had expanded somewhat. In the training materials, the disease was characterized as something coming from outside Tonga, potentially carried not only by *fakaleitī* or foreign homosexual men but also by visiting tourists or other non-Tongans. While many Tongans who go overseas, particularly young men on work visas, might have the opportunity to have sex with these "others" and bring HIV/AIDS or other STIs back home, this was never explicitly addressed (although a few peer facilitators and several presentation attendees pointed out this possibility at various times). *Fokisi* were also implicated in the "at risk" group due to their perceived lack of moral propriety, extending to their interest in interacting with non-Tongans in bars, clubs, and hotels.

The fact that *fakaleitī* were training to be peer facilitators further reinforced the message about HIV/AIDS as merely a disease of the other. Workers from several youth organizations and NGOs stated that *fakaleitī* made the best presenters and peer facilitators, as they were not shy about performing in public, and there were already several *fakaleitī* throughout the country working as peer facilitators. Though *fakaleitī* may indeed have possessed greater skills or the desire to be peer facilitators, it seems that casting them as self-evident choices for this role portrays HIV/AIDS as a problem doubly associated with *fakaleitī* and *fokisi:* they facilitate the presentations, but they are also cast as being most vulnerable to infection.

Yet the *fakaleitī* seemed to have another role to play in the constitution of gendered identities and of participants' relationships to the information presented. In the meetings, a Tongan representative from the sponsoring organization on the main island visited ʻEua to lead the peer facilitator training workshop. This man, Sitiveni, was born on ʻEua but had lived and worked on the main island for several years. While not related to any of the group members, he had ties of kinship in the nearby villages. Throughout the training, he would make frequent remarks about the *fakaleitī*, commenting on their appearances or their need to learn the information, aggressively teasing them in a way that contrasted sharply with his interaction with the rest of the class. While his style of interacting resembled common interactions between heterosexual men and *fakaleitī*, who are of inferior status to heteronormative men, the presence of *fakaleitī* in the peer group training made Sitiveni's own potentially status-threatening position as group leader slightly easier to manage than if all of his trainees had occupied moral sub-jectivities similar to his own. Most Tongans, especially adults, are ambiva-lent regarding information about HIV/AIDS and sexuality, fearing that they may inadvertently violate brother–sister respect or encourage youth to engage in sexual activity. Acting as a teacher placed Sitiveni's own identity and status in a vulnerable position, but his teaching marginalized youth and emphasizing his power over them mitigated the awkwardness of that posi-tion and secured it within the bounds of propriety.

As the group moved on to presenting the information on their own, the youth began to voice the idea that, precisely because they were marginal-ized, they were perfectly qualified to communicate important information, and in fact had a moral duty to do so. Pulu told me on multiple occa-sions that he thought his work on AIDS awareness was important, both personally and socially, because many people thought he had the disease. Everyone thought he had sex and "did dangerous things" because he was a *fakaleitī,* and as a result he felt socially marginalized. Yet he thought that being able to share information was a wonderful opportunity, both to make other people aware of how to be safe from AIDS and also to show them *he knew* how, invoking an epistemological claim and asserting authority. In this way, Pulu acknowledged his marginalized place in Tongan society but also claimed knowledgeable authority. Because of his identity and the particular status that others ascribed to him, he had a special relationship to this knowledge and utilized it not only to help others but also to claim an authoritative space at the center of others' attention.

Similarly, 'Ofa asserted that her own position as a *fokisi* accorded her special status that allowed her to distribute knowledge to those that needed it most, and to do so more efficiently than heteronormative young women would be able to do. Like Pulu, she felt that she had a personal moral duty to participate in the presentations and raise awareness of HIV/AIDS and STIs because she knew some people on the island who had had to deal with infection and its social consequences. She also thought that people would listen to her because she was more like them than teachers or other typical purveyors of knowledge, unintentionally echoing the peer facilitator group's mission.

Throughout the program, 'Ofa and Pulu supported each other, dis-cussing the information and quizzing each other on details in preparation for their public performances. The *fokisi* and the *fakaleitī* youth were com-pletely at ease with each other, helping each other to style their hair and trading pieces of jewelry, common practices among Tongan girl friends. The youth also reinforced each other during the presentations by sharing bits of forgotten information, helping each other set up charts and other props, and importantly, offering an ear to gossip after their performances and the teasing that sometimes followed. As the meetings continued, the *fokisi* and *fakaleitī* youth became increasingly devoted to the project and would frequently reiterate the need to "empower" themselves and others through information.[7] Rather than focusing on their marginalized social status within the larger society or on the adults in the audience who occasionally challenged their rights of authority, the youth formed bonds based on their provocative identities and the distribution of thought-provoking knowledge that connected them to an imagined transnational community of public health workers. While their day-to-day existence was rooted firmly in the local context of small villages on 'Eua, the *fokisi* and *fakaleitī* participating as peer facilitators in the HIV/AIDS awareness workshops could claim a new kind of power through the special edge that, in their view, their marginalized status afforded them in the global fight against HIV/AIDS.

Conclusion

In Tonga and elsewhere, HIV/AIDS is seen as a problem of "the future" (particularly in the case of Tonga, where there are still so few incidences of it), a problem of the sexually uncontained or unconstrained, and a problem of transnational and "modern" scope and standards. All three of these constitutive associations (the future, unconstrained sexuality, and global modernity) are also categories to which youth are aligned in Tonga, and all three carry moral weight and considerable ambivalence, pointing to latent fears of exactly what it means to be Tongan and how this meaning is to be implemented in the current context. The work of youth to distribute knowledge locally about HIV/AIDS further links them to a more transnational stage and forces all Tongans to consider the ways in which the production and circulation of knowledge shapes cultural values and moral frameworks.

Across the Pacific, transgender identity is negotiated and played out in relation to other cultural actors of various sexual identities and social positions. The ethnography I have presented in this chapter demonstrates how particular interactional partners help to constitute the meanings of transgender identity through everyday nonsexual encounters. Through their

work with transnational NGOs, *fakaleitī* and *fokisi* strategically reappro-
priate ideas about their sexuality in order to gain a measure of authority
through association with foreign and transnational knowledge, practices,
and capital. The very marginality of these non-normative gender and sexual
identities helps these agents to convey information perceived to be important from a public health perspective and to create possibilities for broader
cultural changes. Friendships between *fakaleitī* and *fokisi* support the goals
and the actual work of the youth group, making tasks enjoyable through the
heightened sociability of shared activities with friends, and efforts slightly
easier than they would be without the emotional and informational support
of these allies. In their work with the transnational development organization, *fakaleitī* and *fokisi* also acquire new agency through the language of
"empowerment."

However, this language of transnational development has limited circulation locally, calling into question the scope and force of their agency. As
they communicate knowledge through new channels and with new forms
of authority, *fakaleitī* and *fokisi* subtly shift the moral and epistemological
frameworks available to them in 'Eua. Yet, this orientation to a more global
sphere and association with new forms of "risky" knowledge also potentially
provide new justifications for marginalizing them. Non-normative gender
identities in Polynesia are increasingly constructed not only with an awareness of local standards but also through an engagement with global discourses
of gender and sexuality. While *fokisi* and *fakaleitī* remain "on the edge" of
social boundaries, both locally and globally, they still appear to claim a space
at the very center of circulating discourses of sexuality and sexual health. The
edge, in fact, appears to be flexible enough to allow for the creation of new
ways of being for *fokisi* and *fakaleitī* as "empowered" global agents.

Acknowledgments

I respectfully acknowledge the Government of Tonga for allowing this
research to be carried out. I am grateful to the people of 'Eua and especially to the members of the 'Eua Youth Congress HIV/AIDS Awareness
Group for their time, friendship, and thoughtful conversations throughout
my ethnographic research. Thanks also go to the Salvation Army, United
States Peace Corps, and the staff of 'Eua High School for facilitating some
of the events mentioned here. I wish to thank the editors of this volume
for their encouragement of my work. The detailed and insightful comments

of Niko Besnier were much appreciated. Thanks also go to Micah Boyer and Ben McMahan for comments and suggestions on an early draft. This research was supported by the School of Anthropology and the Social and Behavioral Sciences Research Institute at the University of Arizona.

Notes

1   The Tongan word *fakaleitī* translates as "in the manner of women," combining the prefix *faka-*, "in the manner of, the way of, as if," and *leitī*, borrowed from English "lady," but semantically different from other words used for women (e.g., *fefine*, "woman," or the polite *finemotu'a* for an older woman). *Fakaleitī* themselves prefer the term *leitī*, arguing that they are not *like* ladies, they *are* ladies. They also are sensitive to the fact that the first syllable of *fakaleitī* sounds very close to English "fuck," reflecting a consciousness of global modernity and the hypersexualized, immoral place ascribed to them in local mainstream discourse (Besnier 1997, 19–20). Both forms of the term are used here to describe members of this group.

2   Most organizations benefiting youth, such as the TNYC, the Tonga Civil Society, and the local branches of transnational organizations such as the Salvation Army and the US Peace Corps are sensitive to the underemployment of youth as well as to the importance accorded locally to documented verifiable credentials. They thus provide "Course Completion Certificates" to participants in all of their activities, from first-aid programs to workshops on human rights. Youth can then add these certificates to their portfolios and present them to potential employers.

3   The group consisted of ten members in total: two *fakaleitī*, four men, and four women. One of the young men decided not to participate in the presentations after undergoing the training, and one of the young women was hired at a local store immediately after training and so could not attend the presentations. Eventually, one additional young woman joined the group. Within the group, three of the women were labeled *fokisi* by other interlocutors on the island (and sometimes jokingly referred to each other by this term), one man and one woman were unwed parents, one of the men was a relatively recent arrival to Tonga after having been deported from the United States for gang activity, and one of the men was an enthusiastic volunteer in activities that would develop his skills in the hopes of one day migrating to the United States (he subsequently became engaged to a Peace Corps volunteer). The remaining members could be considered more "mainstream" or heteronormative in their identity practices and were generally considered to be upstanding members of their villages and respective churches. Three Peace Corps volunteers (two

women and one man) attended the initial training, but only the male volunteer
ended up participating in the subsequent meetings.

4   Heteronormative men may wear flowers in their hair, and young men
sometimes wear nail polish or light eye makeup as well. Examining hegemonic
masculinity in comparison with *fakaleitī* highlights the cultural specificity
intrinsic to definitions of masculinity everywhere, as well as the ways in which
multiple symbolic practices used simultaneously and in repeated performances
serve to generate particular gender identities (Butler 1990, 1993).

5   All names used in this chapter are pseudonyms.

6   This number is the one most widely used in government and nonprofit
information as well as news media reporting. Several people I interviewed
who worked closely with public health and youth organizations were strongly
suspicious of the veracity of this figure. Various other agencies report anywhere
between five to thirty cases.

7   The English words "empower" and "empowerment," along with a few other
words and phrases such as "pride" and "break the silence," were always used
among group members. These words are closely related to the development of
Western HIV/AIDS awareness efforts that have subsequently moved around
the world and are difficult to render accurately into Tongan.

References

Adams, Vincanne, and Stacy Leigh Pigg, eds. 2005. *Sex in Development: Science,
Sexuality, and Morality in Global Perspective.* Durham, NC: Duke University
Press.

Aguilar, Mario I. 1999. Localized Kin and Globalized Friends: Religious Modernity
and the "Educated Self" in East Africa. In *The Anthropology of Friendship,*
ed. Sandra Bell and Simon Coleman, pp. 169–182. Oxford: Berg.

Allan, Graham. 1989. *Friendship: Developing a Sociological Perspective.* New York:
Harvester Wheatsheaf.

Bell, Sandra, and Simon Coleman, eds. 1999. *The Anthropology of Friendship.*
Oxford: Berg.

Besnier, Niko. 1994. Polynesian Gender Liminality through Time and Space. In
Third Sex, Third Gender: Beyond Sexual Dimorphism in Culture and History, ed.
Gilbert Herdt, pp. 285–328. New York: Zone.

———. 1997. Sluts and Superwomen: The Politics of Gender Liminality in Urban
Tonga. *Ethnos* 62: 5–31.

———. 2011. *On the Edge of the Global: Modern Anxieties in a Pacific Island Nation.*
Stanford, CA: Stanford University Press.

Boellstorff, Tom. 2009. Nuri's Testimony: HIV/AIDS in Indonesia and Bare
Knowledge. *American Ethnologist* 36: 351–363.

Bott, Elizabeth. 1981. Power and Rank in the Kingdom of Tonga. *Journal of the Polynesian Society* 90: 7–81.

Bucholtz, Mary. 1999. "Why Be Normal?" Language and Identity Practices in a Community of Nerd Girls. *Language in Society* 28: 203–222.

Butler, Judith. 1990. *Gender Trouble: Feminism and the Subversion of Identity.* London: Routledge.

————. 1993. *Bodies That Matter: On the Discursive Limits of Sex.* London: Routledge.

Campbell, I. C. 2008. Across the Threshold: Regime Change and Uncertainty in Tonga 2005–2007. *The Journal of Pacific History* 43: 95–109.

Carrington, Christopher. 1999. *No Place like Home: Relationships and Family Life among Lesbians and Gay Men.* Chicago: University of Chicago Press.

Carsten, Janet, ed. 2000. *Cultures of Relatedness: New Approaches to the Study of Kinship.* Cambridge: Cambridge University Press.

Comaroff, Jean, and John L. Comaroff. 2000. Millennial Capitalism: First Thoughts on a Second Coming. *Public Culture* 12: 291–343.

Desai, Amit, and Evan Killick, eds. 2010. *The Ways of Friendship: Anthropological Perspectives.* New York: Berghahn.

Durham, Deborah. 2007. Empowering Youth: Making Youth Citizens in Botswana. In *Generations and Globalization: Youth, Age, and Family in the New World Economy,* ed. Jennifer Cole and Deborah Durham, pp. 102–131. Bloomington: Indiana University Press.

Dyson, Jane. 2010. Friendship in Practice: Girls' Work in the Indian Himalayas. *American Ethnologist* 37: 482–498.

Eckert, Penelope. 1989. *Jocks and Burnouts: Social Categories and Identity in the High School.* New York: Teachers College Press.

Evans, Mike. 2001. *Persistence of the Gift: Tongan Tradition in Transnational Context.* Waterloo, ON: Wilfrid Laurier University Press.

Franklin, Sarah, and Susan McKinnon, eds. 2001. *Relative Values: Reconfiguring Kinship Studies.* Durham, NC: Duke University Press.

Gailey, Christine Ward. 1988. *From Kinship to Kingship: Gender Hierarchy and State Formation in the Tongan Islands.* Austin: University of Texas Press.

Hall, Stuart, and Tony Jefferson, eds. 1976. *Resistance through Rituals: Youth Subcultures in Post-War Britain.* London: Routledge.

Hirsch, Jennifer, and Holly Wardlow, eds. 2006. *Modern Loves: The Anthropology of Romantic Courtship and Companionate Marriage.* Ann Arbor: University of Michigan Press.

Lee, Helen Morton. 2003. *Tongans Overseas: Between Two Shores.* Honolulu: University of Hawai'i Press.

Lee, Helen Morton, and Steve Tupai Francis, eds. 2009. *Migration and Transnationalism: Pacific Perspectives.* Canberra: ANU E Press.

Mageo, Jeannette M. 1992. Male Transvestism and Cultural Change in Samoa. *American Ethnologist* 19: 443–459.

Mendoza-Denton, Norma. 2008. *Homegirls: Language and Cultural Practice among Latina Youth Gangs.* Oxford: Blackwell.

Morton, Helen. 1996. *Becoming Tongan: An Ethnography of Childhood.* Honolulu: University of Hawai'i Press.

Nardi, Peter M. 1999. *Gay Men's Friendships: Invisible Communities.* Chicago: University of Chicago Press.

Philips, Susan U. 1994. Local Legal Hegemony in the Tongan Magistrate's Court: How Sisters Fare Better than Wives. In *Contested States: Law, Hegemony, and Resistance,* ed. Mindie Lazarus-Black and Susan Hirsch, pp. 59–88. London: Routledge.

———. 2008. The Organization of Ideological Diversity in Discourse: Modern and Neotraditional Visions of the Tongan State. *American Ethnologist* 31: 231–250.

Rebhun, Linda. 2002. *The Heart Is Unknown Country: Love in the Changing Economy of Northeast Brazil.* Stanford, CA: Stanford University Press.

Small, Cathy. 1997. *Voyages: From Tongan Villages to American Suburbs.* Ithaca, NY: Cornell University Press.

Spencer, Liz, and Ray Pahl. 2006. *Rethinking Friendship: Hidden Solidarities Today.* Princeton, NJ: Princeton University Press.

Teilhet-Fisk, Jehanne H. 1991. To Beat or Not to Beat, That Is the Question: A Study on Acculturation and Change in an Art-Making Process and Its Relation to Gender Structures. *Pacific Studies* 14(3): 41–68.

Weston, Kath. 1991. *Families We Choose: Lesbians, Gays, Kinship.* New York: Columbia University Press.

———. 1998. *Long Slow Burn: Sexuality and Social Science.* London: Routledge.

Willis, Paul. 1977. *Learning to Labor: How Working Class Kids Get Working Class Jobs.* New York: Columbia University Press.

World Health Organization (WHO). 2008. *Regional Strategic Action Plan for the Prevention and Control of Sexually Transmitted Infections, 2008–2012.* [s.l.]: World Health Organization, Western Pacific Division.

CHAPTER 11

Televisual Transgender

Hybridizing the Mainstream in Pasifika New Zealand

Sarina Pearson

Pacific transgender has long captured the erotic and intellectual imaginations of Western writers and academics. In addition to being liberally exploited as exotic spectacle, gender liminality in the Pacific provides opportunities to interrogate how masculinity and femininity are constructed and performed. It challenges notions of gender's relationship to kinship, status, and sexuality as well as conceiving of transgender as a dynamic phenomenon deeply embedded in tradition but increasingly implicated in modernity. Frequently defined by its incommensurability with Western regimes of sexuality and identity, Pacific transgender is nevertheless increasingly implicated in the West. This is not just because Western idioms, practices, and symbols figure in events such as Tongan *fakaleitī* beauty contests or Rarotongan drag competitions, nor because of the role that Pacific transgender may have played in historical metropolitan constructions of European sexuality, but because Pacific transgender performance is part of the contemporary theatrical and televisual repertoire in "Western" sites such as New Zealand.

Transgender on New Zealand Television

Since the mid-1990s, transgender has become a staple on New Zealand television, particularly, although not exclusively, in comedy. Many comedies featuring transgender, such as *Skitz, bro' Town,* and *The Laughing Samoans at Large,* are explicitly associated with Pasifika.[1] These "Pacific-influenced" shows attract both diasporic Pacific audiences and the multicultural mainstream. In form and comedic sensibility, they owe a significant debt to Samoan *fale aitu,* the Samoan carnivalesque theatrical tradition featuring transvestism in which normative status can be reversed, caricature performed without consequences, and political critique delivered with relative impunity under the guise of satire (Wake 1994; Sinavaiana 1992). This debt reflects the demographic and cultural dominance of Samoans among Pasifika communities in New Zealand. Their signature comedic device is male-to-female drag and, while they manifest continuities with the historical political and gendered dynamics of *fale aitu,* they are also profoundly transformed by their mediation and social context. Pasifika comedies exemplify the dexterity with which Pacific communities hybridize tradition and modernity using both local and transnational repertoires. These shows might be better understood as foregrounding a "*fale aitu* sensibility" rather than faithfully reproducing the traditional theatrical form. Nevertheless, they retain the traditional genre's capacities for social commentary, status parody, and gender inversion, albeit directing these capacities toward new targets.

Transgender in New Zealand televisual comedy is not limited to shows associated with Pasifika. Non-Pasifika New Zealand sketch comedies also make liberal use of gender instability and drag. To date, contemporary *fale aitu*–inspired Pasifika comedies such as *The Laughing Samoans* have been considered as entirely distinct from New Zealand comedic acts such as the twin lesbian, yodeling, country-and-western–singing Topp Twins. The Topp Twins' iconically New Zealand gender-bending comedy is routinely attributed to European comedic theatrical traditions such as British pantomime, but on closer inspection they also bear recognizable traces of Pacific comedic performance. These transgender traces are more than merely coincidental. They suggest that, far from being independent of them, New Zealand popular culture is indebted to Pacific cultures in ways that are rarely acknowledged. Furthermore, an examination of the apparent paradox presented by the Topp Twins and other New Zealand transgender performances through the lens of Pacific identity suggests that Pacific influences on New Zealand cultural formations are not only aesthetic but also substantive.

Reversing Center-to-Margin Orthodoxies

Reigning discursive orthodoxies structuring the production of ethnicity, media, and cultural power in New Zealand historically locate legitimate sources of cultural inspiration in former imperial centers. In 1997, I presented a conference paper about the industrial and symbolic conditions under which Pasifika communities in New Zealand gained visibility on prime-time television. In the course of my analysis, I connected the then popular sketch comedy *Milburn Place* to Polynesian traditions of clowning such as Samoan *fale aitu* through its use of carnivalesque humor and transvestism (S. Pearson 1999, 2005a). *Milburn Place* was set in the South Auckland home of the Semisi family. Much of its comedy revolved around the absurd antics of the family matriarch, Mrs. Sia Semisi, played by male actor Hori Ahipene dressed in a large-flower-print gown, with abundant plastic hair garlands and an ample application of brightly colored lipstick.

After showing a few clips of the show and winding up my presentation, the chair opened the floor to questions and comments. From the back of the room, a gentleman observed that, as far as he was concerned, Sia Semisi and *Milburn Place* could be explained simply as a prime example of pantomime—nothing more, nothing less. The comment has haunted me ever since, not just because at the time I thought he was incorrect. Certainly, upon reflection, features of British pantomime are arguably present in New Zealand television sketch comedy (Ardener 2005) and *Milburn Place* was no exception. But what rankled was the ease and conviction with which he had made his observation. Despite abundant models of cultural dynamism, including cultural flows, scapes, disjuncture, difference, disorganization, encounter, entanglement, and reciprocity (Appadurai 1996; Thomas 1991; Wallace 2003a), the default approach to instances of cultural syncretism and hybridity in New Zealand media studies axiomatically presumes minoritarian response rather than agency.

A significant number of critics and artists have responded to these easy assumptions by chronicling the dynamism of modern indigenous Polynesian political commentary across a diverse array of contemporary Pasifika practices, including fine art (Tamaira 2010; Salmond and Raymond 2008), fashion (Colchester 2003; Raymond 2003; Taouma 2005), popular music (Henderson 1999; Zemke-White 2001, 2002, 2004; Mitchell 2002), theater (Balme 2007; O'Donnell 2007; Fresno-Calleja 2010), and screen production (S. Pearson 2005a, 2005b; Bannister 2008; J. Smith 2008). While the project of claiming Pasifika agency through various expressions of resistance and subversion has been widely undertaken, the fundamental dynamic underlying my interlocutor's comment remains largely unchallenged. The prevailing assumption made by creative, industrial, and policy gatekeepers that minorities react to, rather than engage with or influence the mainstream is not exclusively applied to Pasifika but to New Zealand's visible minorities in general. Migrants of all persuasions are presumed to labor under the implicit understanding that their obligation is to become New Zealanders and that ideally their cultural contributions will be limited to cuisine, costume, and performance. Acceptable forms of hybridity are celebrated when they reinforce identities already perceived as quintessentially New Zealand. Examples include the central (although uneven and ambivalent) role that Pasifika rugby stars play in the national imaginary and celebrations of Pacific theater as evidence of cosmopolitan sophistication (Teaiwa and Mallon 2005).

New Zealand whiteness, in contrast, is considered fundamentally unaffected by minority influence. Despite recent moves to ethnicize it (Spoonley 1995a, 1995b), it continues to enjoy the discursive privilege of invisibility on television. Its largely uninterrogated values constitute the environment to which visible minorities are compelled by the Euro–New Zealand mainstream to respond and adapt. New Zealand televisual whiteness is deemed subject only to influences from centers of former imperial power such as Great Britain, and to a lesser extent from contemporary hubs of popular cultural production such as Sydney or Los Angeles. Hence transgender performances by comediennes Lynda and Jools Topp can only derive from British pantomime's tradition of the principal boy where women take on the male roles. But is this a reasonable assumption in a country where one in four New Zealanders will claim Pasifika and/or Maori descent in less than a decade, and in which Polynesians already wield palpable political influence (Rudman 2010)?[2] As was the case in *Milburn Place*, the answer is not either British pantomime or *fale aitu* but some messy combination of the two. Reversing or complicating orthodoxies that consistently shape conventional narratives about transgender comedic performance offers potentially new ways of looking at the apparent paradox of queer performance and national identity in New Zealand. Shows like *The Laughing Samoans at Large* and *The Topp Twins* owe a clear debt to *fale aitu*.

Fale Aitu

Fale aitu places particular emphasis on performances of gender in general and transgender in particular, providing opportunities to reveal how gender, sexuality, and identity intersect. *Fale aitu* are comedic sketches that periodically punctuate an evening program of Samoan song and dance.

Evidence of *fale aitu* performance prior to European contact is relatively sparse, however, the presence of early historical accounts of clowning traditions resembling this theatrical practice in other Pacific islands suggests that it predates intensive missionization (Looser 2011). The term *fale aitu* translates as "house of the spirits" (Sinavaiana 1992) or "house of ghosts" (Kneubuhl 1987). Well into the twentieth century, everyday Samoan life was richly populated with *aitu:* a pantheon of ancestral spirits who could be benevolent or malevolent but were virtually guaranteed to be capricious and chaotic (Kneubuhl 1987). Lead comedians in *fale aitu* are considered to act in some sense as mediums for *aitu*. Consequently, human actors are not held directly responsible for bawdy, inappropriate behavior or potentially disrespectful criticism. The signature feature of *fale aitu* shows, which are performed by all-male casts, is male-to-female transvestism (Mageo 1992). The meaning of the gender inversion varies depending on whether the transvestite character is played by a comic actor who performs in drag for the duration of the performance or by a *fa'afafine*, who can be thought of as performing gender liminality both on- and offstage. Mageo (1996) analyzes both variants of *fale aitu* as localized responses to the profound changes in gender and status that were enacted by colonial intervention and Christian missionization.

Anxiety about changes in masculinity and associated status are mimicked and mocked in *fale aitu* plots that feature domestic situations. Much to the hilarity of the audience, unruly "wives" defy and undermine their husbands' autocratic authority within the domestic sphere. In addition to plot and subject matter, the formal organization of *fale aitu* mirrors the decline of male status. Mageo observes that Samoan conceptions of gender are governed by a complex system of binary categories in which male and female are mutually constitutive. Therefore, "having a 'wife' who is in fact male decreases the male/female differential by which the category male is defined" (1996, 599). The absence of women in these performances means that, strictly speaking, there were no "real" men either. In *fale aitu*, "the comic playing the wife's role wears a loose, flowered dress and somehow manages to project femininity despite his obviously male physique, mustache, and prominently tattooed biceps. He speaks in a high-pitched voice and occasionally engages in flirtatious exchanges with the audience by wagging a hip or waving coyly" (Sinavaiana 1992, 207).

Mageo (1996) notes that the cross-dressing *fale aitu* wife has been largely supplanted by a *fa'afafine* who parodies and problematizes the figure of the properly chaste marriageable girl. In Samoan systems of identity construction, *fa'afafine* are defined by kinship, labor, and self-presentation rather than Western regimes in which sexuality constitutes a key coordinate. In *fale aitu*, the *fa'afafine* lampoons the role of a virtuous and chaste Christian girl by performing outrageous antics in sexually provocative and suggestive ways. By transgressing the boundaries of appropriate behavior, the *fa'afafine*'s *fale aitu* performance simultaneously mocks and reinforces the proper repressive sexual constraints that apply to young women. *Fa'afafine* may perform like girls in these sketches, but the comedy and satire rely on the audience's apprehension of her gender liminality. *Fale aitu* is therefore an entertaining genre that lampoons values associated with proper masculinity and proper femininity, alluding to latent social anxieties and pressures engendered by colonialism and modernity. While not all scholars of Samoan social systems agree with Mageo's emphasis upon colonialism's impact on gender, her approach nevertheless offers suggestive ways of thinking about *fale aitu* performances and gender.

Fale Aitu Sensibilities on New Zealand Television

The "*fale aitu* sensibility" that emerges in New Zealand television comedy retains transvestism, transgender, and gender parody as its signature trope. It privileges family as central to identity construction, emphasizes domestic relations, enacts narratives of heterosexual romance, and engages in critical political satire. It is largely improvisational, often associated with musical performance and, despite its politically subversive rhetoric, serves to reinforce rather than undermine local hegemonies. I use the term "sensibility" strategically to signal that the dynamic at work is not the deliberate cooptation of minority motifs by a dominant culture, but rather something less deliberate and potentially more osmotic.

The Laughing Samoans at Large

The Laughing Samoans perform transgender and gender parody in ways that closely resemble Mageo's analysis of historic and contemporary Samoan *fale aitu*. Male duo Tofiga Fepulea'i and Eteuati Ete began performing as a live act in 2003 and in 2010 produced a national television series titled *The Laughing Samoans at Large*. Their series features sketches with a series of established characters and musical interludes. Fepulea'i and Ete make substantial use of situational humor in their television show, improvising against nonactors in real locations. This strategy produces seemingly spontaneous performances more akin to live theater than conventional television comedy. In addition to touring extensively throughout New Zealand, across the Pacific, as well as to Australia and North America, they have produced DVDs of many of their live shows, including *Laughing with Samoans* (2003), *A Small Samoan Wedding* (2005), *Off Work* (2007), and *Choka Block* (2011). Their television series includes segments from these earlier live performances intercut with sketches shot especially for television. Ete and Fepulea'i perform a range of comedic characters (not all transgender), but their most popular are the irrepressibly loud, romantic, and impulsive Aunty Tala and her long-suffering niece, Fai. Fepulea'i, who plays Tala, is masterful at physical comedy. He typically takes on the exaggeratedly naïve and unsophisticated characteristics that overseas-born Samoans describe as "Fobby," or "fresh off the boat." Ete, who usually provides the relatively straight foil for Fepulea'i's comic antics, plays the role of more sophisticated, worldly, and cosmopolitan Fai. Both men appear in these sketches in what could be described as "bad" drag (figure 13). They wear ill-fitting wigs

FIGURE 13

Aunty Tala (Tofiga Fepulea'i), Robbie Magasiva, and Fai (Eteuati Ete). Courtesy of The Laughing Samoans.

and excessive amounts of poorly applied makeup. Fepuleaʻi retains his goatee and adopts a falsetto voice punctuated by excessively "girlish" giggling.

Whether Fepuleaʻi and Ete are enacting a relatively straightforward parody of women or performing yet another layer of gender inversion by parodying *faʻafafine* is ambiguous. As neither adopts a *faʻafafine* persona offstage, it would stand to reason that their parody approximates the comic in drag performing a *fale aitu* wife; but the sexually suggestive nature of the Aunty Tala sketches is more reminiscent of the *faʻafafine*'s send-up of proper Christian Samoan girls. Tala's primary focus is on romance, preferably with an All Black rugby player, although she is also preoccupied with global circuits of celebrity, fantasizing about tabloid personalities such as former pop star-turned-fashionista Victoria Beckham and her husband professional footballer David Beckham. Whether the sketches are about a four-star Hawaiian hotel that Tala inherits, a serendipitous gym encounter with All Blacks Jerome Kamo, Maʻa Nonu, and Neemia Tialata, or a trip to London where she plans to launch her career as a pop star and marry a footballer, her pursuit of virile, high-profile men is as relentless as it is comically unseemly.

The Laughing Samoans' comedy echoes Mageo's "zones of ambiguity" where Samoan performers and audiences rehearse, problematize, and place "images of gender and race that circulate in colonial and postcolonial cultures within ironic quotation marks that serve to question these images" (Mageo 2008, 61).[3] Fepuleaʻi and Ete's work similarly places prevalent tropes of Pacific masculinity in scare quotes, effectively invoking continuities with historical Samoan constructions of gender while enacting dynamic transformations in the transnational present. If Samoan conceptions of gender are governed by a complex system of binary categories in which male and female are mutually constitutive, Fepuleaʻi's rendition of Aunty Tala threatens to diminish the masculinity of a highly select male cohort celebrated for their mastery of masculine repertoires, not just in the Pasifika community but in the New Zealand national imaginary. The ambiguity regarding Polynesian All Blacks could be interpreted as a metacommentary on their contradictory status as icons authenticating national myths of multicultural inclusion and egalitarianism in sport on the one hand, and as symbols of the enduring exclusion of Pacific Islanders from New Zealand's national imaginary on the other (Grainger 2008; Starr 1999; Teaiwa and Mallon 2005).

The Laughing Samoans' caricature of *faʻafafine* similarly comments on gender while expressing ambivalence about Pasifika stereotypes circulating in the New Zealand mediascape. For New Zealand audiences, *fa'afafine* are a well-established and often repeated trope. Tala's parody of a *fa'afafine* therefore offers Pacific audiences the possibility of placing transgender in ironic quotation marks, recognizing her as a salient cultural figure and as one of mainstream New Zealand's clichéd Pacific stereotypes of choice. Sketches such as Tala's meeting with Prime Minister John Key (of the conservative National Party), wherein she persistently tries to seduce him, threatens to undermine white masculinity while asserting that even the highest executive officer in the country can play along with comedic transgender, thereby suggesting his apparent open-mindedness about nonmainstream ethnicity and gender.

Despite the complex and layered nature of the Laughing Samoans' gender parody, they are remarkably consistent in placing Samoanness in ironic quotation marks. Fepulea'i's characters typically epitomize "fobbiness." In addition to Aunty Tala, he plays an inept television correspondent called Sam in the Kala TV sketches and a young boy in a series of schoolyard sketches. These characters (and others) express the naïveté and lack of sophistication associated with "fobbies," who are represented by their difficulties with Standard English, chaotically inventive word plays, mispronunciations, and unintentional double-entendres. Ete, in contrast, tends to play the sophisticate. He quietly criticizes Tala's outrageousness and constrains her excesses. In the Kala TV sketches, he operates the camera, directs the segments, and corrects Sam's randomly improvised commentary. On the playground, he teaches his compatriot the finer points of spelling and how to pronounce "ough" words in English. What the Laughing Samoans offer up for their audience's enjoyment is a broad caricature of first-generation Samoans. Fepulea'i's characters are affectionately drawn, but they problematize primordial and diasporic Samoan identity for the pleasure of sizeable transnationally based Samoan audiences in New Zealand, Australia, and the United States who identify with Samoa and at the same time register their displacement from it.

The degree to which specific gender inversions are legible to overseas Samoans is as yet undetermined. Sua'ali'i (2001) observes that traditional gender principles in general remain salient for many New Zealand-based Samoans, in spite of improvisations imposed by the practical necessities of living overseas. Her findings suggest that diasporic communities are well versed in the gender systems Pasifika comedies exploit. For non-Samoan audiences, Aunty Tala sketches provide an instance of transgender performance that is unfamiliar and potentially exotic, but oddly familiar if they have been watching New Zealand television comedy.

New Zealand television has historically made ample use of transvestism as a comedic device, but cross-dressing alone is insufficient to account for an audience's sense of déjà vu. What they may find vaguely familiar are the use of gender parody to produce hegemonically contained sociopolitical critique and the placing of performances of identity in affectionate if ambivalent scare quotes. These characteristics are present to varying degrees in a range of different series, but they are particularly manifest in the Topp Twins' screen performances.

The Topp Twins

The Topp Twins are *Pākehā* lesbian twin sisters from the rural Waikato.[4] For more than thirty years, they have honed a semi-improvised act that includes original country-and-western music, yodeling, and a cast of broadly drawn sketch characters premised on New Zealand archetypes. In the mid-to-late 1990s, the Topps adapted their repertoire of characters for television, producing several seasons of *The Topp Twins*. Since then, they have continued to tour the country and to release music. Most recently they starred in the critically acclaimed and commercially successful autobiographical documentary titled *Untouchable Girls*.

A comparison between the Topp Twins and Samoan televisual transgender performed by The Laughing Samoans may seem unlikely at first glance. There are, however, discernible traces of *fale aitu* sensibilities in the Topp Twins' affectionately gender-bending satirical approach toward New Zealand identity. The Topps satirize both masculine and feminine archetypes. Their most popular sketch personas include dairy farmer Ken Moller from the agricultural Wairarapa region and his best mate, Ken Smythe, a small-town sportscaster. The two Kens invoke New Zealand's rural heartland and nostalgia for New Zealand's settler colonial past in contrast to its urban multicultural present. Bossy "Camp Mother" and her minion "Camp Leader," who run the Happy Valley Camping Ground (the pun on the queer associations of "camp" is entirely intentional) engender similar kinds of sentimentality. The Topps' musical repertoire, country and western, is considered to be an especially redneck and heteronormative genre of popular music.

American recordings by Jimmie Rodgers introduced Australians and New Zealanders to country-and-western music in the 1920s. Initially referred to as "hillbilly" music, the musical genre became closely associated with Gene Autry's cinematic image of the cowboy in the 1930s. By the 1950s, country-and-western music was a well-established cultural phenomenon in Australasia, primarily although not exclusively in rural locales. Whereas country music became closely associated with Australian national identity through artists like Slim Dusty and his repertoire of bush ballads that "evoked the world of the small farmer and of the pioneering struggles of country people" (Smith and Brett 1998), it appears to have remained relatively marginal in New Zealand critically, symbolically, and commercially (Harding 1992).[5] Nevertheless, it has had a substantial grassroots following in New Zealand, with more than two hundred and fifty active country music clubs and several high-profile annual national events. Journalist Braunias writes, "with their monthly shows held at church and memorial halls, their loyal following and their afternoon teas, country music clubs travel like a subterranean river all over New Zealand" (2008, 64). In the New Zealand context, country music epitomizes the particular communitarian sociability and the constraints imposed by dairy farming in particular. Although written in reference to constituencies for country music in Australia, the following observation similarly applies to New Zealand, and particularly to the Waikato, from which the Topp Twins originate.

> It was among the small farmers of the dairying industry that the music held its greatest appeal. They were tied to endless work in relative isolation, yet due to the perishable nature of dairy products, were in areas which were fairly closely settled, and in contact with local towns with marketing and processing establishments. These were the social and geographic prerequisites for the development of the musical form. Furthermore, the romanticized West had a special appeal to dairy farmers. Though they were cowboys of a completely different sort, using different skills to those depicted in the cowboy songs, they were still able to identify the mythologized West as part of the great outside world beyond the farm in which they had a privileged place. (G. Smith 1994, 301)

Country music may have made incongruous and derivative references to "coyotes" and "prairies," but for rural New Zealanders and Australians it nevertheless captured something about their daily experiences on the farm and their self-imagining. The Topp Twins capitalize on country and western's rural masculine associations, juxtaposing it with broadly drawn New Zealand stereotypes to produce gently ironic performances of quotidian sexual and social queerness.

In her discussion of *fale aitu* performances, Mageo argues that the constructions of Samoan femininity were particularly sensitive to colonial pressures. In contrast, the dominant site of symbolic privilege in New Zealand centers on masculinity. Drawing on D. Pearson (2001), Bannister (2005) argues that mainstream New Zealand has historically identified with a model of rural, pioneering, and white masculinity that privileges physical industry over intellect. This model places an absolute premium on a self-sufficiency born out of the country's geographic isolation during the colonial period. "Discourses of masculine homosociality, male autonomy, and independence from the 'feminizing' influences of domesticity, 'polite' society, and imported mass culture have been central to the construction of *Pākehā* cultural identity" (Bannister 2005, 2). "Bloke" masculinity may have initially developed in order to distinguish successive generations of New Zealand settlers from recently arrived British colonizers and long-established indigenes, but the symbolism continues to play a central role well into the postcolonial present. Bannister suggests that the bloke's signification has changed from anti-imperial resistance to the representation of a distinctively localized New Zealand identity in a rapidly globalizing mediascape: the "bloke" now symbolizes rural, "clean and green" New Zealand. His image is deployed both domestically and internationally to produce the locality that has become central to differentiating "brand New Zealand" in the global market.

The Topps' transvestite characters, Ken Moller and Ken Smythe, specifically unsettle New Zealand masculinity. Lynda Topp plays "typical bloke" Ken Moller, while her twin sister Jools performs Ken Smythe, but their performance is less reminiscent of the principal boy in British traditions of pantomime than of Samoan *fale aitu* gender inversion. In their autobiographical documentary, *Untouchable Girls,* Ken Smythe introduces Ken Moller to the audience during a live gig. He announces, "just take a long hard look at him, ladies and gentlemen, that's the sort of man we're turning out in this country and by God, what a bloody—what an icon he is, ladies and gentlemen." At this point, the documentary cuts to a medium close-up of Moller in profile. The audience takes in his bad wig, mutton-chop sideburns, stuck-on moustache, and hand-rolled cigarette fixed permanently between his teeth, and they can't help but recognize that Moller's profile, with its soft jawline and multiple chins, is less than robustly masculine.

Furthermore, when the camera cuts to a long shot taken from the audience's vantage point, they are enabled to contemplate Moller's soft protruding beer belly and register that his ample thighs are wider than his shoulders.

Smythe continues his introduction: "And of course he's a great farmer, brilliant farmer, ladies and gentlemen, he's a, just pure poetry to watch him work a dog, just a beautiful animal handler all the way around, ladies and gentlemen, really." As Smythe refers to Moller's animal-handling skills, Moller unselfconsciously adjusts the fly of his pants and then hitches them up, sending the audience into paroxysms of laughter as it recognizes the gesture from real life, and the joke that Moller is not handling the "animal" in his pants. The legibility of the Topps' "real" gender beneath the dated double-knit polyester suits of varying shades of tan and powder-blue celebrates, denaturalizes, and ridicules New Zealand masculinity. Audiences take pleasure in the performance of the bloke while recognizing that Ken Moller is undercutting the symbol's claim to masculine mastery. On closer inspection, Moller looks suspiciously like a middle-aged woman and occasionally acts like one, indulging in moments of excessively unmasculine sentimentality about his phantasmic erotic obsession (whom he calls the "lady in pink" recognizable to the audience as Camp Mother), his favorite heading dog, and most of all his very best mate, Ken Smythe (figure 14).

FIGURE 14

The Topp Twins: Ken Smyth (Jools Topp) and Ken Moller (Lynda Topp). Courtesy of Diva Productions.

Moller is presented as the archetypal bloke, who is most at home on his farm in the company of other men and distinctly less at ease with women. In contrast, his best mate Smythe is described as a "townie" who, although more socially self-assured, manifests suspiciously effete characteristics. Smythe's hobbies include Japanese flower arrangement (*ikebana*), breeding Burmese cats, and musical theater. Despite or perhaps because of their differences, the two Kens counsel and support each other through their respective foibles. In an episode titled *Waka*, Ken Moller takes Ken Smythe on outdoorsy manly pursuits like fishing along the shores of the Waikato River. While fishing they notice "the lady in pink" rowing a dinghy in the distance. They set out to find her, but unfortunately Smythe is spooked on the way by a herd of pigs in a paddock. He trips and falls down a shallow ravine, twisting his knee. Fixated upon his romantic obsession, Moller is initially dismayed by Smythe's ineptitude but, ever pragmatic, he remains unfazed as he hauls his best mate over his shoulder and resumes his quest for his lady in pink.

Smythe reciprocates Moller's friendship by helping his blokey mate improve his social manners. For example, in an episode titled *Food and Wine,* he coaches him on the finer points of romantic wining and dining. The men stage a mock rendezvous at Moller's house, with Smythe playing the role of the prospective date. Smythe arrives to find Moller in a state of nervous anticipation. Moller thanks Smythe for helping him out, to which Smythe replies: "No problem, what's a mate for, eh? Righty-o, I'll pretend to be the 'lady in pink' and you turn on the charm, Ken." The gender inversion of the ensuing sketch is thus deftly set up. Smythe is Jools Topp playing a man playing a woman. Moller is Lynda Topp playing a man. The sketch is manifestly about Smythe coaching Moller on what to serve for a romantic dinner (not pork sausages), how to decorate his house (move the stuffed boar on the dining-room wall somewhere else), and how to serve the wine (do not open the bottle by placing it between one's thighs and grunting "You bloody mongrel"). But, latently, the casting of the sketches undermines masculinity.

As already noted, in *fale aitu* domestic sketches, the absence of "real women" means that there cannot be any "real men" either, because the categories mutually constitute each other. On their date night, the Kens denaturalize New Zealand masculinity by demonstrating that its distinctive rhetoric can be performed without any "real" men at all. But the Topps' subversion of masculinity is not just a matter of gender inversion. They ridicule it and its attendant emphasis on homosociality by mocking the emotional intimacy that characterizes "best mates" relationships. Smythe's attempt to show Moller how to wine and dine the phantasmic "lady in pink" allows the Topps to explicitly satirize Moller's curiously close homosocial relationship to Smythe. For example, Moller explains to Ken his desire to settle down with the right woman: "I can just see us now, watching the sun set over a beer and walking hand-in-hand through the paddocks. I'd give you a hand over the electric fence." The description sounds suspiciously like the life he now shares with Smythe. Moller might desire a date with the "lady in pink," but his truly intimate relationship is with his best mate.

The Topps' sexuality forms a running subtext throughout their sketch performances, producing critical commentary as well as comedic effect. Their masculine parodies, such as the Kens' mock date, are tolerated and enjoyed because they are performed by women whose queer sexuality oddly authenticates and fortifies the transgender performance. In an interview with Smythe and Moller at their local pub in *Untouchable Girls,* Moller explains: "Ken and myself, we know the Topp Twins, don't we Ken, we don't know them that well.[6] We don't mix in the same circles, but I suppose that, uh, when you look at it basically, the similarity is Ken, that we all go out with women!" There are parallels here between the *fale aitu fa'afafine* performer, who although anatomically male, performs as a straight woman who desires straight men—except in this case the Topps are lesbians who perform the Kens as straight men who supposedly desire women. The desire expressed in both kinds of performances is consistent with heteronormative regimes of sexuality. Audiences understand that, underneath the gender roles performed by the *fale aitu* "women" or the two Kens are latently sexed bodies and sexual desires that are crucial to producing comedic effect.

The Kens may ridicule bloke masculinity, but they also have come to symbolize it. Brady observes, "[t]hrough the characters Ken and Ken, . . . the Topp Twins demonstrate an unquestionable fidelity to discourses of 'New Zealand masculinity' while simultaneously disturbing the gender performance that such discourses might usually effect" (2010, 3). For instance, quite apart from their television appearances, the two Kens emcee major sports events such as rugby matches and have presented prizes for horse racing and for "best bull" at regional A&P Shows. The comedic irony of Moller and Smythe's relationship relies on their audience's ability to recognize gender subversion and lesbian desire.

In *Untouchable Girls,* one of New Zealand's foremost singer-songwriters, Don McGlashan, recounts a particularly revealing example of the slippage that occurs between Ken Moller as masculine parody and Ken Moller as masculine icon. He relays a story Lynda Topp once told him of going as alter ego Ken Moller to Showgirls, a gentleman's strip club near Auckland's waterfront. At the club, she encountered a group of farmers from Tuakau, a rural farming area south of the city, who invited her to their table, where they all proceeded to have a great time, drinking and leering at the pole dancers. McGlashan wonders if the farmers were aware that they were socializing with a gay woman wearing a suit and a stick-on moustache, pretending to be a man. Or did they think that they were having a great time with Ken Moller? More than likely, he surmises, they were thinking, "That's Ken (rather than Lynda dressed up as Ken) and we're all sitting here enjoying naked ladies." Their experience may have been sanctioned in part because, paradoxically, Lynda Topp's sexual orientation effectively authenticates Ken Moller's sexual identity. Like the *fa'afafine*, whose gender identity is feminine and her desires for straight men, Lynda's Ken performance potentially can be read as masculine and interpreted, either through his gender or the performance of her subtextual sexuality, as a desire for women. In short, the farmers could have settled in for the evening with Ken privileging gender and acknowledging lesbian sexuality (to some degree) because they all prefer women.[7]

Paradox and Pacific Conceptions of Identity

McGlashan's bewilderment over the farmers' reaction is far from isolated. *Georgie Girl* is a documentary about Georgina Beyer, a Maori transsexual who became the mayor of a small rural Wairarapa town named Carterton and later moved onto a high-profile career in national politics as a member of Parliament. Peter Limbrick notes that several interviews in this documentary slide uneasily between "rural naïveté" and "blasé sophistication" about alternate sexual practices and gender identities. He cites a comment from an unnamed farmer from Dannevirke, another small town in the same region, as evidence of the potential ambiguity at work. The farmer says, "I'm going to vote for that Georgina Beyer because she's a go-getter and she's a good chap" (2008, 184). While this comment might signal the farmer's inability or refusal to read Georgina Beyer as transsexual, its proximity to a litany of unanticipated attitudes toward transgender in New Zealand's hinterland supports Limbrick's contention that "[t]here is certainly a tradition of vernacular knowingness about transgender identities in New Zealand that, in its paradoxically expressed nonchalance, engages the complexities of gender and public identities as perceptively as anything from the cities" (2008, 186).

The apparently incongruous rural nonchalance to which Limbrick refers cannot be adequately explained by liberal progressive politics. Homosexuality, for example, continues to be significantly discriminated against in urban and rural New Zealand settings.[8] What, then, adequately explains the "long national tradition of implying there is a queer underside to everything and saying nothing more about it" (Wallace 2003b, 67–68)? Is transgender such a non-event that it escapes comment? Or is the silence surrounding transgender more deliberate, as Wallace intimates when she argues that "transgenderism, and the homosexuality it frequently screens, is something all New Zealanders know about without being taught" (Wallace 2003b, 68). Public indifference to transgender in New Zealand's heartland is paradoxical if sexuality is considered an individual's most salient characteristic. But if gendered social roles, performance, and kinship relations are foregrounded (as they are in many Pacific contexts) the apparent paradox potentially diminishes. Perhaps the presence of *fale aitu* sensibilities in New Zealand televisual comedy is symptomatic of more than a purely aesthetic exchange, signaling that reading transgender in New Zealand might owe a partial debt to Pacific conceptions of identity.

Anthropologists and Pacific subjects alike continue to assert that gender rather than sexuality defines identity in many Pacific societies. Gender-liminal individuals such as Samoan *fa'afafine,* Tongan *fakaleitī,* Cook Island *laelae,* and Hawaiian *māhū* derive their identities from kinship relations, gendered forms of work, and self-presentation and subjectivity, rather than whom they have sex with.[9] Analyzing Cook Island *laelae* identities, Alexeyeff writes that, although "there is ambivalence about *laelae* sexuality, *laelae* are simultaneously accepted as members of family groups, and are widely admired for their talents, particularly as dancers, singers, and composers, and their accomplishments at female tasks, such as sewing" (2008, 148). Whereas Western regimes define individuals according to whom they have sex with, same-sex sexual relations in the Pacific "are seen as an optional consequence of gender liminality, rather than its determiner, prerequisite or primary attribute" (Besnier 1994, 300). From the relatively conservative perspective of many of the societies in which they are situated, Pacific transgender identities are recognized primarily in relation to a set of social roles, with little apparent public attention paid to sexual ones.

Western and Pacific gender systems thus tend to be set in contradistinction to each other and are occasionally even described as incommensurable, as is the case in the 1995 New Zealand television documentary *Fa'afafine: Queens of Samoa*. Wallace (2003a) criticizes this documentary for its vociferous assertion that *fa'afafine* cannot be understood in relation to Western categories of sexual identity such as gay, transvestite, transgender, or transsexual. The film demarcates Pacific gender liminality from Western sexual categories by defining the former as traditional and indigenous and the latter as modern and imperial. Wallace's critique is based on this absolute differentiation between traditional and modern identities. She argues that the documentary fails to acknowledge that these systems, while not commensurate, nevertheless have existed synchronously and in close association historically and continue to do so in the present.

Wallace's larger project aims to produce "a gay reading of the Pacific" (2003a, 140) that acknowledges the role that Pacific gender liminality played in redefining "the possibilities for sexual variance in European masculinity" (2003b, 2). She traces sexual influence against the conventional grain from European "metropole" to Pacific "margin," chronicling "the mutually transformative effects of historical encounter on all sexualized bodies of all colonial subjects." My project traces a similar route, from Pacific Islands to the so-called West (in this case New Zealand), but instead of offering a historical gay reading of the Pacific, I argue that contemporary popular culture in New Zealand can be productively read through the lens of Pacific gender. The influence of *fale aitu* on New Zealand television comedy perhaps explains the cultural context in which the Topp Twins make sense.

The key framing device surrounding the Topp Twins' performances on stage as well as throughout their documentary is their unlikely success as national treasures. Like the paradox presented by Georgina Beyer, the Topps seem to operate effortlessly in contexts presumed to be hostile to homosexuality and transgender. In many of their television sketches, they improvise against the backdrop of "real" events. The sketches are shot on location, often at quintessentially New Zealand events such as the national sheep-shearing championships and regional wine and food festivals. Backdrops like these enable them to improvise comically, but also produce a setting in which their incongruity is both acknowledged and disavowed by the participants in the sketch, and by extension the television audience.

For instance, the various women whom Ken Moller attempts to pick up at a wine-and-food festival good-naturedly play along, participating in their own ridicule, despite the fact that they can tell that they are dealing with Lynda Topp with a stick-on mustache, and they most likely know that she's lesbian. Ken Moller is tolerated or perhaps enjoyed by the Tuakau farmers at Showgirls because his gender performance is privileged. The Laughing Samoans enact a similar strategy, through which they exploit the comedic potential of improvised encounters with nonactors. Embedding comedic performances in unstaged settings produces an everyday commonplace effect in which sexuality may be registered but gender performance and social role continue to take precedence.

Pacific conceptions of identity not only privilege gender performance over sexuality, they also emphasize the importance of family in identity formation. The Topp Twins may consistently foreground their lesbianism in their press and in their offstage personas, but their performance of kinship and their relation to family potentially deemphasize their sexuality. *Untouchable Girls* duly acknowledges the Topps' political contribution to the passage of antidiscrimination legislation and their respective long-term romantic partnerships. The documentary, however, bookends these aspects of their lives with a very strong focus on family. In the first half, it establishes the twins' relationship to their parents, Jean and Peter Topp, who acknowledge their initial ambivalence about their daughters' sexuality but swiftly affirm their eventual acceptance of it. We then see them in an audience as part of a supportive and admiring crowd of fans and fellow artists. The Topps also make repeated references to their close sibling bond when describing their decades-long professional collaboration and recounting more recent personal challenges such as Jools' breast cancer diagnosis. The documentary ultimately conveys to its audience that their success lies in their strong sibling relationship, their kinship ties, and their social standing within the broader community. Kinship also operates in their televisual sketches, potentially diminishing (although not disavowing) their sexuality.

Interpreting the Topp Twins' humor according to Pacific traditions of clowning could be read as a homophobic gesture. Wallace argues that, by eliding homosexuality, the documentary *Faʻafafine: Queens of Samoa* teaches its New Zealand homosexual audience an all-too-familiar lesson, in which gender liminality can be tolerated if stripped of sexuality. My argument, however, is not that sexuality is inconsequential and that the Topp Twins make sense only if everyone politely ignores that they are lesbians. Quite the opposite, the Topp Twins are comically successful because their sexuality provides a recurrent subtext to all their performances. Jools Topp's character, Camp Mother, applying sunscreen to a beefy lifeguard at Mount Maunganui on a brilliant summer day is particularly funny because the audience knows that her flirtations are ironic. Similarly, Fepuleaiʻi's advances to rugby star Josh Kronfeld are funny because his advances are similarly sexually misplaced, despite his gendered performance. Gender inversion in comedy reveals that gender roles are significant and that, although unarticulated, comedy's sexual subtext is also important. Performances such as those by the Laughing Samoans and the Topp Twins suggest not only that Pacific and Western New Zealand systems of understanding gender and sexuality are synchronous, but that the systems may be more mutually constitutive than previously acknowledged.

Conclusion

This chapter has documented the influence of Pacific clowning and Samoan *fale aitu* on New Zealand televisual comedy. Tracing the emergence of a *fale aitu* sensibility in Pasifika sketch television series offers the opportunity to reaffirm the role that Samoan performance traditions play in New Zealand popular culture and to consider how these forms reflect cultural continuity and contemporary transformation. *Fale aitu* sensibilities are not, however, restricted to television racially marked as Pasifika. The Topp Twins exemplify many of the characteristics of Pacific clowning. Their sketches satirize gender and national identity, allowing audiences to acknowledge the significance of New Zealand identity while potentially registering their own likely exclusion from its narrowly defined masculinist iconography. *Fale aitu* also offers another lens through which to examine the Topp Twins. While this strategy may seem counterintuitive given the way contemporary New Zealand television and culture in general are understood in relation to minority media, there is evidence of bilateral cultural exchange. If the Topps can be thought of in terms of Pacific clowning, then perhaps they can also be read according to other Pacific schemata, including gender and identity, which are an integral aspect of Pacific clowning and *fale aitu*. The seemingly intractable paradox that the Topps appear to present becomes less so if their gender performances are given preeminence and their sexuality acknowledged but relatively deemphasized. Sexuality certainly matters, but the evolution of New Zealand televisual comedy suggests that the incommensurability between Pacific and Western notions of sexuality, gender, and identity may not be so impermeable after all. Pacific notions of transgender provide a productive conceptual apparatus through which to think through gender liminality, inversion, and comedy in the New Zealand context.

Notes

1   "Pasifika" is used primarily by New Zealand government agencies and educational institutions to denote New Zealand-based Pacific peoples. Perrot describes the term as a "samoanisation of a Portuguese nod to the Latin phrase Mare Pacificum, or peaceful sea, so named by navigator Ferdinand Magellan. In [New Zealand] it has become an umbrella term for everyone living here with traceable Pacific Island heritage" (Perrot 2007).

2   In the 2010 Auckland mayoral race of the newly integrated "Supercity," which incorporates in a single administration a number of previously autonomous cities such as Manukau, Waitakere, and North Shore City, Len Brown's victory was attributed to "a tide of support from Pasifika, Maori and other non-Pakeha voters, both from his South Auckland stronghold and out west as well" (Rudman 2010).

3   Mageo (2008) draws upon Bhabha's (1994) "zones of ambivalence" but makes a strategic departure from his framework. Whereas Bhabha's zone of ambivalence grants indigenes the possibility and limited expression of mockery offered by the contradictory representational regime they are compelled to participate in, Mageo grants indigenes agency to question this regime.

4   Although its meaning is contested, *"Pākehā"* refers to New Zealanders of European descent, and specifically those who trace their ancestry to settlers from Great Britain. The rural Waikato is an agricultural region in the central North Island of New Zealand where dairy farms predominate.

5   Despite the differential status of country music in the Australian and New Zealand public imaginaries, these scenes are intimately linked. The first credible interpreter of American hillbilly music in Australia, who went by the name Tex Morton, was a New Zealander named Roger Lane (G. Smith 1994). In turn, The Topp Twins learned to yodel from listening to vinyl seventy-eights of Australian yodeling stars Shirly Thoms and June Holmes.

6   The joke here is that, although the two Kens are played by the Topp Twins, they are so thoroughly differentiated and developed as characters that they can refer to the Topps as external entities and the audience can enjoy the irony of the Kens presuming to have passing knowledge of the women who actually play them.

7   Bannister (2011) offers another explanation, citing Halberstam (1998) to suggest that female masculinity might be tolerated more in rural New Zealand because there women undertake more manual labor in farming.

8   See, for example, reports of harassment and violence experienced by the lesbian couple Juliet Leigh and Lindsay Curnow, whose rural home has been covered in homophobic graffiti and their outbuildings burned to the ground (Wade 2011).
9   Gender liminality in pre-contact New Zealand society is sparsely documented. Moloney argues that early accounts attributed restrained sexuality to Maori and excessive sexuality to Tahitians, effectively reinforcing Eurocentric notions of "hard" and "soft" primitivism. He writes, "the invisibility of same-sex desire in the ethnographic record for Maori is partly explained by the hard primitivist and Gothic assumptions of European commentators" (Moloney 2005, 45). In contemporary Maori society, individuals who might "otherwise describe themselves as gay, lesbian, transgender, bisexual, and intersexual" (Aspin 2011, 118) increasingly use the term *"takatāpui"* to describe themselves (cf. Alexeyeff and Besnier, this volume).

References

Alexeyeff, Kalissa. 2008. Globalizing Drag in the Cook Islands: Friction, Repulsion, and Abjection. *The Contemporary Pacific* 20(1): 143–161.

Appadurai, Arjun. 1996. *Modernity at Large: Cultural Dimensions of Globalization.* Minneapolis: University of Minnesota Press.

Ardener, Shirley. 2005. Male Dames and Female Boys: Cross-dressing in the English Pantomime. In *Changing Sex and Bending Gender,* ed. Alison Shaw and Shirley Ardener, pp. 119–138. New York: Berghahn.

Aspin, Clive. 2011. Exploring Takatapui Identity within the Maori Community: Implications for Health and Well-Being. In *Queer Indigenous Studies: Critical Interventions in Theory, Politics, and Literature,* ed. Qwo-Li Driskill, Chris Finley, Brian Joseph Gilley, and Scott Lauria Morgenson, pp. 113–122. Tucson: University of Arizona Press.

Balme, Christopher. 2007. *Pacific Performances: Theatricality and Cross-Cultural Encounter in the South Seas.* Basingstoke: Palgrave.

Bannister, Matthew. 2005. "Kiwi Blokes: Recontextualising White New Zealand Masculinities in a Global Setting." *Genders OnLine* 42; http://www.genders.org/g42/g42_bannister.html (accessed June 2013).

———. 2008. Where's Morningside? Locating bro'Town in the Ethnic Genealogy of New Zealand/Aotearoa. *New Zealand Journal of Media Studies* 11(1): 1–15.

———. 2011. Happy Campers: The Topp Twins, Queerness and New Zealand Identity. In *Instruments of Change: Proceedings of the International Association of Popular Music Australia–New Zealand Conference 2010,* pp. 15–19. Melbourne: International Association for the Study of Popular Music.

Besnier, Niko. 1994. Polynesian Gender Liminality through Time and Space. In *Third Sex, Third Gender: Beyond Sexual Dimorphism in Culture and History*, ed. Gilbert Herdt, pp. 285–328. New York: Zone Books.

Bhabha, Homi. 1994. *The Location of Culture*. London: Routledge.

Brady, Anita. 2010. Camp Mothers of the Nation? Reading Untouchable Girls. *Women's Studies Journal* 24(1): 3–13.

Braunias, Steve. 2008. Country and EASTERN. *North and South* 271: 64–71.

Colchester, Chloë. 2003. T-shirts, Translation and Humour: On the Nature of Wearer–Perceiver Relationships in South Auckland. In *Clothing the Pacific*, ed. Chloë Colchester, pp. 167–193. Oxford: Berg.

Fresno-Calleja, Paloma. 2010. Playing (with) Stereotypes in Postcolonial Pacific Theater. *The Journal of Commonwealth Literature* 45(2): 171–188.

Grainger, Andrew. 2008. Pacific (White) Multiculturalism: Rugby, Pacific Peoples and the Egalitarian Myth in New Zealand. In *Social and Cultural Diversity in a Sporting World*, ed. Chris Hallinan and Steven J. Jackson, pp. 141–166. Bingley, UK: Emerald.

Halberstam, Judith. 1998. *Female Masculinity*. Durham, NC: Duke University Press.

Harding, Mike. 1992. *When the Pakeha Sings of Home: A Source Guide to the Folk and Popular Songs of New Zealand*. Auckland: Godwit Press.

Henderson, April. 1999. Gifted Flows: Netting the Imagery of Hip Hop across the Samoan Diaspora. MA thesis, Center for Pacific Studies, University of Hawai'i at Mānoa.

Kneubuhl, Victoria N. 1987. Traditional Performance in Samoan Culture: Two Forms. *Asian Theater Journal* 25(9): 166–176.

Limbrick, Peter. 2008. The Stallion Who Became a Gelding Who Became a Mayor: Georgie Girl. *Camera Obscura* 67(23): 184–193.

Looser, Diana. 2011. A Piece "More Curious Than All the Rest": Re-Encountering Pre-Colonial Pacific Island Theater, 1769–1855. *Theater Journal* 63 (4): 521–540.

Mageo, Jeannette M. 1992. Male Transvestism and Cultural Change in Samoa. *American Ethnologist* 19(3): 443–459.

———. 1996. Samoa, on the Wilde Side: Male Transvestism, Oscar Wilde, and Liminality in Making Gender. *Ethos* 24(4): 588–627.

———. 2008. Zones of Ambiguity and Identity Politics in Samoa. *Journal of the Royal Anthropological Institute* 14 [n.s.]: 61–78.

Mitchell, Tony. 2002. Kia Kaha! (Be strong!): Maori and Pacific Islander Hip-Hop in Aotearoa/New Zealand. In *Global Noise: Rap and Hip-Hop Outside the USA*, ed. Tony Mitchell, pp. 290–305. Middletown, CT: Wesleyan University Press.

Moloney, Pat. 2005. Shameless Tahitians and Modest Maori: Constructing the Sexuality of Pacific Peoples. In *Sexuality Down Under: Social and Historical Perspectives*, ed. Alison Kirkman and Tony Mitchell, pp. 29–46. Dunedin: University of Otago Press.

O'Donnell, David. 2007. Reclaiming the FOB: The Immigrant Family in Samoan Drama. In *New Zealand Theater and Drama in an Age of Transition*, ed. Marc Maufort and David O'Donnell, pp. 307–330. New York: Peter Lang.

Pearson, David. 2001. *The Politics of Ethnicity in Settler Societies: States of Unease.* Basingstoke: Palgrave.

Pearson, Sarina. 1999. Subversion and Ambivalence: Pacific Islanders on New Zealand Prime Time. *The Contemporary Pacific* 11(2): 361–388.

———. 2005a. Pacific Camp: Satire, Silliness and Seriousness. *Media, Culture and Society* 27(4): 551–575.

———. 2005b. Darkness and Light: Dusky Maidens and Velvet Dreams. *Camera Obscura* 58(20, pt.1): 185–207.

Perrot, Alan. 2007. Pasifika—Identity or Illusion. *New Zealand Herald,* Thursday, March 8; http://www.nzherald.co.nz/alanperrott/news/article.cfm?a_id=50& objectid=10455473 (accessed January 30, 2011).

Raymond, Rosanna. 2003. Getting Specific: Pacific Fashion Activism in Auckland during the 1990s. In *Clothing the Pacific,* ed. Chloë Colchester, pp. 193–214. Oxford: Berg.

Rudman, Brian. 2010. Brown Revolution Signals Rise of Hidden Aucklanders. *New Zealand Herald,* October 20; http://www.nzherald.co.nz/brian-rudman-on -auckland/news/article.cfm?c_id=1502866&objectid=10682213 (accessed August 20, 2011).

Salmond, Amiria, and Rosanna Raymond, eds. 2008. *Pasifika Styles: Artists Inside the Museum.* Cambridge: University of Cambridge Museum of Archaeology and Anthropology, in association with Otago University Press.

Sinavaiana, Caroline. 1992. Traditional Comic Theater in Samoa: A Holographic View. Ph.D. diss., University of Hawai'i at Mānoa.

Smith, Graeme. 1994. Australian Country Music and the Hillbilly Yodel. *Popular Music* 13(3): 297–311.

Smith, Graeme, and Judith Brett. 1998. Nation, Authenticity and Social Difference in Australian Popular Music: Folk, Country, Multicultural. *Journal of Australian Studies* 22(58): 3–17.

Smith, Jo. 2008. Postcolonial Affirmations: The Return of the Dusky Maiden in Sima Urale's *Velvet Dreams. Continuum* 22(1): 79–88.

Spoonley, Paul. 1995a. The Challenges of Post-Colonialism. *Sites* 30: 48–68.

———. 1995b. Constructing Ourselves: The Post-Colonial Politics of Pakeha. In *Justice and Identity: Antipodean Practices,* ed. Margaret Anne Wilson and Anna Yeatman, pp. 96–115. Wellington: Bridget Williams Books.

Starr, Lynne. 1999. "Blacks Are Back": Ethnicity, Male Bodies, Exhibitionary Order. In *Masculinities in Aotearoa/New Zealand,* ed. Robin Law, Hugh Campbell, and John Dolan, pp. 229–250. Palmerston North, NZ: Dunmore Press.

Sua'ali'i, Tamasailau. 2001. Samoans and Gender: Some Reflections on Male, Female and *Fa'afafine* Gender Identities. In *Tangata o Te Moana Nui: The Evolving Identities of Pacific Peoples in Aotearoa/New Zealand,* ed. Cluny MacPherson, Paul Spoonley, and Melanie Anae, pp. 160–180. Palmerston North, NZ: Dunmore Press.

Tamaira, A. Marata. 2010. From Full Dusk to Full Tusk: Reimagining the "Dusky Maiden" through the Visual Arts. *The Contemporary Pacific* 22(1): 1–35.

Taouma, Lisa. 2005. "Doubleness of Meaning": Pasifika Clothing, Camp and Couture. In *The Art of Clothing: A Pacific Experience,* ed. Susanne Küchler and Graeme Were, pp. 111–123. London: UCL Press.

Teaiwa, Teresia, and Sean Mallon. 2005. Ambivalent Kinships? Pacific People in New Zealand. In *New Zealand Identities: Departures and Destinations,* ed. James Liu, Tim McCreanor, Tracey McIntosh, and Teresia Teaiwa, pp. 207–229. Wellington: Victoria University Press.

Thomas, Nicholas. 1991. *Entangled Objects: Exchange, Material Culture, and Colonialism in the Pacific.* Cambridge, MA: Harvard University Press.

Wade, Ameila. 2011. Persecuted Lesbians Forced from Home. July 28; http://www .nzherald.co.nz/nz/news/article.cfm?c_id=1&objectid=10741288 (accessed September 28, 2011).

Wake, Jenny. 1994. Funny Place. *The New Zealand Listener,* June 18, pp. 28–29.

Wallace, Lee. 2003a. *Sexual Encounters: Pacific Texts, Modern Sexualities.* Ithaca, NY: Cornell University Press.

———. 2003b. Queer Here: Sexuality and Space. In *Cultural Studies in Aotearoa New Zealand: Identity, Space and Place,* ed. Claudia Bell and Steve Matthewman, pp. 66–83. Auckland: Oxford University Press.

Zemke-White, Kirsten. 2001. Rap Music and Pacific Identity in Aotearoa. In *Tangata o Te Moana Nui: The Evolving Identities of Pacific Peoples in Aotearoa New Zealand,* ed. Cluny MacPherson, Paul Spoonley, and Melanie Anae, pp. 228–242. Palmerston North, NZ: Dunmore Press.

———. 2002. Reverse Resistance: Pacific Engagement with Popular Music in New Zealand. In *Pacific Art Niu Sila: The Pacific Dimension of Contemporary New Zealand Arts,* ed. Sean Mallon and Pandora Fulimalo Pereira, pp. 117–132. Wellington: Te Papa Press.

———. 2004. Keeping it Real (Indigenous): Hip Hop in Aotearoa as Community, Culture and Consciousness. In *Cultural Studies in Aotearoa New Zealand: Identity, Space and Place,* ed. Claudia Bell and Steve Matthewman, pp. 205–228. Melbourne: Oxford University Press.

CHAPTER 12

Same Sex, Different Armies

Sexual Minority Invisibility among Fijians in the Fiji Military Forces and British Army

Teresia K. Teaiwa

In the summer of 2008 and the autumn of 2009, I traveled around England trying to learn what I could about the experiences of Fiji women serving in the British Army (BA) for a research project I was conducting on Fiji women soldiers.[1] Through a network of personal contacts, I was invited to stay with service personnel and their families at a range of army bases in different parts of the country. At one of these bases, I had an uncanny experience while sitting down with my host at her dinner table. As we chatted, we heard the door open and she explained to me that it was her cousin, a corporal in the BA, with whom she shared the semidetached home. She called out to him to join us in the dining room and announced that they had a visitor named "Teresia." The response from the corridor came, "Is that Teresia Teaiwa?" I was caught completely off guard. In came a stunningly handsome, lithe young man with close-shaven hair, whom I did not recognize at all. "Do we know each other?" I asked hesitantly. "Yes!" the young man exclaimed, "You were my lecturer in Foundation at USP!"[2]

Although I pride myself on having a good memory for names and faces, I could not place him at all. It was only with further prompting that I realized that the athletic and indubitably masculine specimen in front of me was once the bleached-blonde, straightened-haired, and overtly camp student I had had in my Laucala campus classroom in Suva, Fiji, thirteen or fourteen years before.[3] In the course of our unexpected reunion and excited conversation, I learned that a family tradition of military service had led

266

him down this path. It became apparent to me that, rather than forcing him to conceal his sexual orientation as one might assume a military culture might do, the BA's policies and the distance from Fiji made him feel comfortable and safe, not only in living his identity, but also—ironically—in not having to be "flaming" in order to express himself as one of a sexual minority. [4] His partner was an Englishman who had just retired (at a relatively young age) from service in the BA officer corps, and although I was told that they were not quite ready to move in together at that time, they were in the process of planning a joint holiday in Fiji.

To fully appreciate the significance of this encounter, it is useful to reflect on how Fiji's national culture is one of stark contrasts and contradictions—some coexisting easily while others are in marked tension. Much has been made by human rights activists of Fiji becoming, in 1997, one of only two countries in the world whose constitutions enshrined freedom from discrimination on the basis of sexual orientation (George 2008).[5] Yet the murder of a prominent humanitarian and Fiji citizen of European descent, John Scott, and his New Zealander partner, Greg Scrivener, in 2001 produced a most astonishing circus of police attempts to prejudice the investigation and cast moral judgment on the deceased pair (Scott 2004; Goldson 2008).

Paradoxically, in 2008, I was able to witness firsthand civilian members of Suva's sexual minority community serving as referees of the Fiji Military Forces (FMF) versus Police netball matches at the two disciplined services' annual Ratu Sukuna Bowl games. What makes it possible for the horrific double murder with homophobic intent of a white couple to be treated without compassion by police, while camp Fijian men were adjudicating in sport over groups that to a large extent determined whether they would or would not be safe in society? What are the various contexts we need to account for in order to understand how intersections of race, class, sexuality, and other social matrices in Fiji produce different effects and meaning?

Is there another country in the world where the head of state (who holds a high chiefly title in the indigenous customary social hierarchy of Fiji and is also a former commander of the FMF) would be feted as the guest of honor and patron of a drag-queen pageant? Fiji's President Rātū Epeli Nailatikau was just so honored in 2010 at the annual Adi Senikau festival, the transgender mirror of the more heteronormative institution of the annual Miss and Mr. Hibiscus pageants. Just prior to the Adi Senikau festival on August 10, 2010, at the 10th International Congress on AIDS

held in South Korea, the same president announced that travel bans preventing persons with HIV from entering Fiji would be lifted (http://www
.unaids.org.fj/). This followed logically from the decriminalization of
homosexuality by military decree announced in February 2010 (Chand
2010). However, *Kaila*, the newspaper insert for younger readers of *The
Fiji Times*, a national daily newspaper over a hundred years old, in 2011
was able to print a feature piece that derided attempts to view transgender
behavior as normal. The author of the article stated: "Morally . . . the only
gender that is 'normal' . . . is our God given gender [*sic*], male or female"
(Serelini 2011, 3). Less than a year later, in May 2012, the Fiji Police
revoked a permit for civil society organizations planning to hold a march
to mark International Day against Homophobia.[6] So although my former
student experienced the BA as affirming of his sexual orientation, some of
the ambivalences and antipathies that portions of society in Fiji have about
homosexuality will no doubt have also traveled with Fiji's military diaspora
to the UK.

The impetus for this reflective chapter arose out of interviews, anecdotal evidence, and my own fieldwork observations among service personnel in both Fiji and the UK between 2008 and 2009. Although my research
focused on the experiences of Fiji women serving in the FMF and BA,
I encountered several servicemen and women who candidly shared with
me their thoughts about and experiences of being a sexual minority in the
military.[7] During this period, for many of them, the memory of a fatal
attack on a Fiji serviceman who had recently completed an overseas tour of
duty was still raw. Everyone who spoke to me about the case described the
deceased as gay and believed that the attack was homophobic in intent, but
none of this surfaced in the media coverage surrounding his death or the
conviction and sentencing of a fellow Fijian for the murder. Quite rightly,
all the reporting emphasized the fallen soldier's exemplary service and the
unprovoked nature of the attack. However, this studious official avoidance
of any acknowledgment of the relevance of sexual politics effectively meant
that the contributions of Fiji's sexual minorities to one of the most elevated
categories of citizenship remained invisible.

I am deeply interested in Fiji's social and cultural complexities and
the problems these present for analysis. I use the term "problem" here,
not so much in the sociological sense, but in the sense that the invisibility of Fiji's sexual minorities in the FMF and BA presents a challenge to
understanding the differential ways in which militarization affects diverse

communities. While there are no official data on sexual minorities in the FMF or sexual minorities from Fiji in the BA, an analysis of the conditions shaping their invisibility is further hampered by the paucity of serious scholarship on same-sex practices and sexual minorities issues in Fiji.[8] Apart from an impressionistic article by sexual minority activists and educators Tora, Perera, and Koya-Vaka'uta (2006), the most significant work in this area prior to the chapters in this book was by George (2008). In that article, George describes and analyses a distinctly hypermasculine ethos pervading the dominant social context that is at once condoned in Christian ethno-nationalist discourse and at the same time serves to limit—if not eliminate—tolerance of most other forms of minority cultural and political expression. While George makes a valuable contribution to the literature, further work is needed to capture the complex layers of tolerance and intolerance that can coexist in Fiji and shape the everyday experience of those who identify as sexual minorities.

I draw on a combination of my personal experience growing up in Fiji, observations I made while conducting research on Fiji women soldiers, and my own survey of recent secondary sources related to same-sex orientation and sexual minorities in Fiji. I present a picture of same-sex issues in relation to military service for indigenous Fijians in the BA and FMF that highlights both the complexities of social and cultural values and concepts at play and the challenges for research in such contexts. In the next section, I lay out some of the cultural and linguistic contexts for identifying and discussing same-sex categories in Fiji. I discuss colloquial terms that have been used to describe individuals with a same-sex orientation and read this alongside major lexicographies. My purpose in this section is to highlight the epistemological challenges to researching and understanding which same-sex terms are relevant and intelligible, and in what ways, to people from Fiji. In short, this section reminds us that the terms we use can determine the levels of visibility and invisibility of same-sex issues vis-à-vis particular audiences.

In the second section, I explore the notion of "different armies." I underline the way in which same-sex orientation has often been cast in heteronormative societies as a difference worthy of naming and othering. Here I draw attention to a link between heteronormative forms of othering and military forms of othering, especially in terms of historical practices of excluding different categories of people from the particular privileges of citizenship bestowed upon military service personnel and veterans. I also compare the

FMF and the BA in terms of their explicit or implicit policies on sexual minorities, pointing to the ways in which different demographic contexts shape the conditions of visibility and invisibility for Fiji's sexual minorities.

In the third section, I reflect more explicitly on the challenges that surround research on sexual minorities under conditions of invisibility. I outline issues of accessibility in relation to military archives and share some of my own experiences of having same-sex issues come up in interviews with servicewomen. Overall, I suggest, the field is wide open for research that will illuminate both the conditions that produce invisibility and the complex stakes of achieving visibility of Fiji's sexual minorities in military service. I offer my thoughts here as someone who has close kin and friends who identify themselves as gay, lesbian, bisexual, transgender, and queer, and as someone who is concerned about how military service becomes invested with the expectations and aspirations of marginalized communities.

Same Sex

Alexeyeff and Besnier (this volume) argue that focusing on difference, categories, and terms as objects of our analyses of non-heteronormativity is less productive than exploring social relations. This section, however, is focused on terms—but not for the purpose of reification. My discussion here attempts to explore both heteronormative and non-heteronormative conditions of social relations in Fiji through a tracing of colloquial terms used to describe non-heteronormative subjects. The section also positions me as a researcher who comes to the topic through particular social and cultural contexts.

Fiji in the 1970s and 1980s provided me with my introduction to sexuality. My own early understanding of social responses to same-sex orientation came from noticing how my peers at school reacted to boys whom they called "poofters" and girls whom they called *"panikeke."* The etymology of the term "poofter" is unclear, but it appears to have been brought to and embedded in Fiji by British, Australian, and New Zealand colonial influences.[9] An indigenous synonym is *qauri,* which is not found in either the standard Fijian–English dictionary (Capell 1991) or the Fijian monolingual dictionary (Tabana ni Vosa kei na Itovo Vakaviti 2005). This word is likely to have been borrowed into Fijian from the Fiji Hindi word *gauri,* meaning "homosexual" or "a male who behaves in a feminine manner" (Geraghty, Mugler, and Tent 2006, 238; see also Presterudstuen, this volume). The term may be used in the following way in colloquial Fijian: *"Raica mada na qauri"* (i.e., "Take a look at that gay guy") or *"Kua ni vāqauri tiko!"* (i.e., "Don't behave like an effeminate man!"). Brison (1999) has observed the latter injunctions, particularly in Fijian children's speech. While there were certainly negative connotations to the term *"qauri"* when I was growing up, in my experience it was often also used as a matter-of-fact descriptor.

Panikeke is a Fijian borrowing of the English word "pancake" and refers to the presumed absence of a penetrative sexual organ in the act of women having sex with women. The term "lesbian" may be mobilized when one is speaking Fiji English to confirm the meaning of *panikeke* (e.g., *"Era panikeke. Kilā? Lesbian,"* or "They are *panikeke*. You know? Lesbians"). While there must have been some pejorative dimensions to the term *"panikeke,"* I personally have not witnessed it being used as an insult. In any case, when I was growing up in the 1970s and 1980s in urban centers of Fiji from Savusavu to Levuka, Lautoka, and Suva, the ambiguous term *"tomboy"* had more currency and cachet among my peers. *Tomboy*-hood was something that we knew most girls grew out of and a few girls never did. However, to say that someone was a *tomboy* had no direct bearing on her sexual orientation, so the term did not necessarily refer to lesbianism (compare Tcherkézoff, this volume, on Samoa).

Even though it appeared to me as a child that there was nothing explicitly sexual in the general behavior of poofters or *panikeke*s, it seemed that it was assumed by many that their respective favoring of the opposite sex's accepted clothes or mannerisms signaled an interest in members of the same sex as potential partners.[10] There were cruder discussions about poofters and *panikeke*s that I occasionally overheard while growing up— although, to be fair, heterosexual activities are still probably the ones discussed in the most vulgar terms in the urban Fiji social circles with which I am most familiar.

It wasn't until I was in my teens in the 1980s that I heard the term *"wādua"* (Fijian for "one string") to describe men who engaged in sexual relations with other men. The impression I got from its usage was that *wādua* were not necessarily poofters. It was just over a decade later, in the 1990s, that "men who have sex with men" or "MSM" began to be used as an analytical unit, especially in association with HIV/AIDS and STD research in the Pacific (e.g., Peteru 2002, 1997). The term *wādua*, however, appears not to circulate as widely as *qauri* today and does not appear in any of Fiji's dictionaries.[11]

Of course, the most dignified of Fijian speakers will use more polite terms to describe transgender and same-sex sexuality: McIntosh (1999, n.d.) makes passing reference to the Fijian term *"vakasalewalewa"* as the equivalent to the more prominent Polynesian categories *fakaleitī, fa'afafine,* and *māhū. Na Ivolavosa Vakaviti* (2005, 759) does not indicate what the origins of *vakasalewalewa* might be, but its gloss is remarkably respectful: *"tiko ruarua vua na gacagaca vakatagane kei na vakayalewa; tagane itovo vakayalewa,"* outlining the identity as one of having two spirits—both masculine and feminine, or being a male who has been assigned feminine duties.[12] *Vakayalewa, dauyalewa,* and *vakamocetagane* are additional terms that might be used to refer to males with feminine behavior or a sexual orientation toward other men; and *vakatagane, dautagane,* and *vakamoceyalewa* to refer to females with masculine mannerisms or a sexual orientation toward other women.[13] Today, these terms may be considered archaic or more reflective of a particular generation's linguistic turns and sensibilities.[14]

It was also when I was in my late teens and twenties in the late 1980s and 1990s that I noticed that the term "gay" had entered popular usage in Fiji to describe same-sex orientation, although in a way similar to other international contexts, it was applied more frequently to men than to women (Smorag 2008). As has been documented elsewhere, the term "gay" signals a kind of politics that may have a high profile in the public imaginary but is not necessarily universally embraced by people with same-sex orientations (Adam, Duyvendak, and Krouwel 1999). Wallace (2003) argues that modern Western notions of sexual personhood, such as those that cohere around the categories "homosexual," "transgender," or "transvestite," owe their historical constitution to early encounters of European explorers in Pacific Island societies where same-sex relationships were treated as normal rather than deviant. She resists positing rigid cultural and historical boundaries between indigenous and "modern" terms and categories of sexual personhood, preferring to see them as co-constitutive of one another (2003, 139; see also Alexeyeff and Besnier, this volume).

It is interesting to note that in the 1990s an NGO taking up the challenge for the first time of directly countering heteronormative biases in Fiji society downplayed gay terminology and put itself forward under the conceptual framework of "sexual minorities" (George 2008, this volume). The focus on "minority" status for individuals, couples, and groups with same-sex orientations allowed the NGO to keep questions of human rights at the center of their activism and gave them the assurance of having recourse to those international human rights conventions that the state of Fiji was party to, deflecting some of the moralistic intolerance based on particular interpretations of the Scriptures in this predominantly Christian nation.

There are a myriad of other terms related to same-sex orientation that, to my knowledge, have had little traction in Fiji English. Many of these are derogatory, although some have been rehabilitated and reclaimed in international gay pride movements (see Smorag 2008). "Queer" terminology, while popular in places like the United States, has recently gained some currency among sexual minority activists in Fiji, especially because of the relative advantages the discourse offers, allowing for a lot more complexity and disruption of dominant order gender and sexuality.[15]

An example of how sexual minority activists in Fiji have been able to use indigenous terms to strategically articulate with or disarticulate from global movements and hegemonic concepts emerged in the late 1990s, while I was teaching at USP. A small number of student activists formed a group called "Drodrolagi," which is Fijian for "rainbow," the international symbol for gay pride. As George (this volume) documents, the group's visibility petered out when the founding cohort of students moved on, but recently it has been revived at USP under the name "Drodrolagi Movement" or "Dromo," and it is currently garnering significant local and international support both on the ground and in cyber-based communities through the use of social networking and Internet media such as Facebook.

I have laid out some of the relevant terms in Fiji here in order to highlight some of the complexities that need to be accounted for when researching and writing about same-sex orientation in Fiji. What terms are being used in existing literature? What terms are intelligible to potential research participants? Might there be a gap between the existing literature and common vernacular usage? As Smorag notes in her survey of gayspeak (2008), questions of language and terminology are fundamental to social and discursive processes of exclusion and inclusion that can render groups marginal, invisible, or visible. As a code or secret language, gayspeak can serve to cloak or make same-sex subculture invisible to the mainstream and visible only to insiders. Do Fiji's sexual minority communities have their own gayspeak, or codes, and insiders' language? This would certainly be a rich area of research that could challenge the heteronormativity evident in the current lexicography of Fiji—as demonstrated by the silences around same-sex sexuality in dictionaries.

Different Armies

In popular Anglophone discourse, sexual orientation is often cast in metaphors of team sports. Someone who comes out as gay, lesbian, bisexual, transgender, or queer might be described as "switching sides" or "playing for the other team, now" (Smorag 2008, 4). A "team" is thus formed by shared sexual orientation. A team considered to be "other" does not conform to what is considered normal in society—it will be different, perhaps even oppositional. Discourses that take male–female sexual partnerships as the norm are described as heteronormative (see Alexeyeff and Besnier, this volume). Gay, lesbian, bisexual, and transgender same-sex relationships are considered to be beyond the bounds of heteronormativity. This is ironic, because the prefix "hetero-" refers to multiplicity and diversity but a heteronormative discourse privileges only one form of sexual orientation. Although at one point in the late nineteenth-century United States the term "heterosexual" was used to also refer to what today we would call "bisexual" (Katz 1995), contemporary understandings of the term frame it as an exclusively male–female sexual partnership. So the prefix "hetero-" in heteronormativity is misleading, because while it could seem to normalize diversity, in fact it is shorthand for "heterosexual normativity." How heteronormative discourses deal with alternatives can vary: at one end of the spectrum, "other teams" may be considered unremarkable and rendered invisible; at the other end of the spectrum, they could be considered a serious threat and thrown into the spotlight of surveillance. To be oriented toward or involved in same-sex intimate partnerships is thus understood as playing for a different team in a heteronormative society.

An army is a large-scale team. Its primary business, war, is a lot like an extreme sport, except with national policy and pride at stake and death as its inevitable consequence. Military studies assume that membership in an armed force is governed by a transparent logic. To play for this "team," namely to serve in this army, one has to be qualified to do so. The primary qualifications for national military service are often framed around full membership in a society (i.e., citizenship) and full capacity to serve (i.e., able-bodiedness). Although there were variations from age to age and society to society, certainly by the twentieth century, once selected for this team, one became a member of one of the most honored "squads" of a society.[16] This is evident both from the extent to which societies that have militaries tend to invest their trust in them and from the degrees of financial and emotional investment those societies make in military fortification and celebration.

Throughout modern history, however, citizenship has in fact rarely been a transparent category. Armies have not always welcomed, and still do not welcome, all citizens of the nation. Observing military recruitment and admission policies is one way of understanding how nations implement a graduated concept of citizenship. When a military restricts service to one sex, one race, one religion, or one sexual orientation, we learn which identities are privileged in that nation. Debates in the United States over the now defunct "Don't ask, don't tell" (DADT) policy were but the latest example of the recurrent battles for equality of citizenship that take place in modern democracies (Belkin 2008).

The case of Fiji is particularly interesting. It is an ostensibly heteronormative society that is in the unusual position of having its citizens eligible to serve in two different armies: Fiji citizens are currently serving in both the FMF and the BA. Fiji Bureau of Statistics figures from 2007 place the total regular force capacity of the FMF at 4,359.[17] As of July 2008, UK Ministry of Defence statistics record the number of Fijians in the BA at 2,170. In Fiji, military service has historically been considered an elevated category of national citizenship, and for indigenous Fijian males it was often viewed as a reliable vehicle for social mobility. In British colonial Fiji, soldiering was the preserve of European and indigenous Fijian men until early in the twentieth century, when recruitment expanded (somewhat reluctantly) to include Indo-Fijians, and in the late 1980s (slightly more enthusiastically) to include women (Teaiwa 2008). The recently observed phenomenon of sexual minorities from Fiji serving in either the BA or FMF thus raises questions about the ways globalization and militarization are engendering sociopolitical, cultural, and economic transformations around the world. But the questions my current research explores are more specifically comparative.

I have been following and analyzing various dimensions of militarization in the Pacific for over two decades. In 2008, I undertook an investigation into the history of Fiji citizens' respective entanglements in the two armed forces. My curiosity was piqued, for example, by the question of what difference it makes if a Fiji citizen decides to enlist in the FMF rather than the BA or vice versa. What does it mean to enact some of the most idealized forms of citizenship and national service for a country of which one is not even a citizen? How does a national armed force deal with the fact that its citizens have the option to serve another country?

Both the FMF and the BA fulfill functions that are valued highly in their respective societies in terms of providing employment and training opportunities for their own citizens. The BA even extends these privileges to those in its personnel who are not UK citizens but who are part of the British Commonwealth of Nations (see Ware 2012). BA recruitment of Fiji citizens for military service since the late 1990s does not appear to have had a direct impact on FMF—that is, FMF personnel have not been leaving in droves to join the BA. Rather, the BA is drawing recruits from the burgeoning pool of high school leavers and young adults who have not been easily absorbed into Fiji's limited job market. Both militaries are engaged in overseas missions, and both have troops serving in what since 2003 has been one of the most important global theaters of conflict in the twenty-first century—Iraq.

The size, technology, and history of professionalism in the BA of course dwarf that of the FMF. The BA traces its origins to the merger of the Scottish and English armies in 1707, whereas the FMF came into being as a result of British colonial rule in Fiji in 1874. The BA had a force capacity of 177,840 on April 1, 2010, while the FMF in 2012 would have had between 4,000 and 5,000 at least in their full-time trained strength, with around 6,000 territorials. The FMF's nine naval patrol boats cannot compare with the thousands of armored vehicles, over two hundred aircraft, and several landing craft and assault boats of the BA.[18]

The rate of pay for BA new entrants is £13, 895, while the basic pay for privates in the FMF is reportedly F$10,194.[19] Thus, BA soldiers earn almost four times more than their FMF counterparts by 2013 exchange rates, but the cost of living in the UK is also significantly higher than in Fiji, so FMF soldiers may in effect have a higher standard of living, or at least more disposable income, than their BA counterparts. A further consideration is that Fiji citizens are for the most part excluded from serving as officers in the BA, whereas Fiji citizenship is explicitly advertised as a criterion for officer recruitment in the FMF.

A notable point of comparison between the two armed forces is their policies toward same-sex partnerships. In the case of the FMF, an informal DADT policy appears to be at work.[20] When I enquired of my military liaison officers about policy documents governing personnel issues in the FMF, I was directed to the Fiji Public Service Commission Guidelines for Public Servants and told that these also applied to servicemen and women. While I could locate no explicit injunctions against same-sex or non-normative gender behavior in them, the Guidelines for Public Servants clearly rely on the Laws of Fiji to define the parameters of legal behavior.[21] In spite of the fact that the Constitutional Amendment Act of 1997 included a preamble that enshrined the principle of freedom from discrimination on the basis of sexuality, the Penal Code of the Laws of Fiji at the time considered "unnatural offences" to be felonies, including "carnal knowledge of any person against the order of nature" and "indecent practices between males" in public or private. The maximum sentences for these offenses were fourteen years and five years respectively, with options for corporal punishment. While Fiji inherited much of its legislation from its former colonial authority, it took over four decades for its penal code to catch up with Britain's 1967 Sexual Offenses Act, which decriminalized consensual sex in private between males over the age of twenty-one. The circumstances under which homosexuality was decriminalized in Fiji in 2010, however, are very particular: rather than resulting from a process of democratic legislative reform, it took place in the context of an unelected and *military* regime (Chand 2010).

To be fair, it also took the BA several decades to align its policies with British legislation, and the institution did not lift its ban on homosexuality until 2000, and then only to comply with a European Community Human Rights ruling (Belkin and Evans 2000). Nonetheless, within the year, it opened the door for same-sex partnerships to be formally recognized by the military and administered by the institution to the same extent as heterosexual ones (Burke 2001). By 2004, British armed services were actively recruiting at gay-pride festivals (Keller 2004), and several branches of the defense forces had joined a "diversity champions" program run by Britain's leading charity for gays, lesbians, and bisexuals—Stonewall—participating in regular workplace equity benchmarking.[22] In the same year, the passage of a Civil Partnership Law in the UK translated into legal recognition of same-sex unions, and for the military this meant that all housing, allowances, and pensions accorded to married service personnel were to be extended to personnel in same-sex partnerships.[23] Today, an association for gay, lesbian, bisexual, and transgender military personnel runs an online networking, support, and information service called "Proud 2 Serve."[24]

The contrast between the radical extralegal reforms of same-sex sexuality legislation undertaken by Fiji's military regime and the resounding official silence about sexual minorities in its military service on the one hand and, on the other, the apparent progressiveness and consistency of Britain's laws and military policy is striking. It is tempting to assume that Britain and the BA would provide safer environments for Fiji soldiers with same-sex orientations. But nationalism can also claim a progressive, liberal identity for itself, exemplified in the form of securing rights for sexual minorities, while still casting "others" as regressive and backward; Puar (2011) and others have called this "homonationalism," reminding us of the dangers of simplistic comparative readings. The simultaneity of increasing protection of sexual minority rights in Israel and the persistent framing of Arab, including Palestinian, cultures as intolerant of gender equality and same-sex orientation that Puar writes about begs further exploration in regard to the ongoing deployments of FMF forces and BA forces with personnel from Fiji to the Sinai and Iraq. Anecdotal evidence indicates that FMF participation in UN peacekeeping operations in the Sinai since 1982 has strengthened the admiration that indigenous Fijians have for Israeli armed forces. But how might FMF personnel think of the state of Israel's reforms around sexual minority rights? Would they see their own country's policy reforms in the area as necessarily or unnecessarily emulating this trend? Would Fiji soldiers in the BA feel comforted by the alignment of British and Israeli policies on sexual minorities? Or would social and cultural pressures toward preserving heteronormativity incline Fiji's service personnel in the BA and in the FMF to identify more with Palestinian and Arab cultures (simultaneously buying into Israeli homonationalist representations of them)? These complex questions clearly demand further research. There is an easy temptation to judge the FMF negatively in comparison to the BA on the issue of formally institutionalizing the protection of sexual minority rights. But it bears recalling here that, although my former student felt comfortable expressing himself as a member of a sexual minority in the BA, another Fiji soldier could be killed by a fellow countryman in circumstances that were at least rumored to have homophobic dimensions.

Hegemonic Christianity's role in reinforcing heteronormativity (Chaney and Patrick 2011; Linneman 2004) makes it a crucial context for understanding homophobia and its production of sexual minority invisibility among Fijians in the military at home and abroad. Halapua (2003) has documented extensively the way in which the Methodist Church has historically exercised a monopoly over clerical and cultural ministry in the Fiji military as well as over its political ideology, especially in the buildup to and the aftermath of the 1987 coups. George (2008) also refers to the collapse of sexual minorities' euphoria about the 1997 constitutional changes when the Methodist Church mobilized homophobic sentiment around the John Scott and Greg Scrivener murders in 2001.[25] In her analysis, the Methodist Church at the time enforced a return to gay invisibility, and she quotes the Women's Action for Change (WAC) nongovernmental organization's Sexual Minorities Project (SMP) describing the Methodist Church in Fiji as "the most serious promoter of homophobia in Fiji" (George 2008, 175–179, this volume). Of course, this characterization is unfair to those members of the Methodist Church in Fiji who resist both ethno-nationalist and homophobic beliefs and practices, although in broad terms the Methodist church officially toes an antihomosexual line.

In the end, 2001 became something of a swansong for a particular group of ethno-nationalist Methodist leaders. The church had faced a severe threat from Pentecostal churches in the previous decade as a result of the growing perception among indigenous Fijians that the Methodist Church's articulation with chiefly and village-based hierarchies was stifling the social mobility and financial well-being of individuals and nuclear family groups (Brison 2007; Barr 1998; Ernst 1994). The popularity of Pentecostal churches and "new religious movements" grew exponentially in the 1990s, and then again after the most severe attack on the Methodist Church's claim to represent indigenous Fijian interests, when FMF's commander, Commodore Frank Bainimarama, effectively designated it an enemy of the state with his coup in 2006 (Tomlinson 2013, 82).

As George aptly recognizes, the military's dismantling of the Methodist Church's authority in the period after 2006 has specific ramifications for sexual minority invisibility in Fiji: "While the military-led government [of Bainimarama] could certainly be accused of encouraging self-censorship within civil society in Fiji at the current moment, and of once again reinforcing the relationship between hegemonic masculinity and militarization, some of the new regime's actions might also be viewed, somewhat ironically, as strengthening the hand of gay activists in Fiji" (George 2008, 180). It is indeed tempting to interpret the actions of Fiji's military regime as socially progressive in this instance, but it would be simplistic. As I laid out in the introduction to this chapter, circumstances in Fiji are prone to change, inconsistency, and contradiction. The focus on the Methodist Church in WAC SMP's analysis neglects the position of its rival Pentecostal churches; for it would seem unrealistic to expect that new religious groups would be more tolerant of sexual minorities than mainstream churches in Fiji. As Ernst (1994, 12, 272) observes, new religious groups in the Pacific Islands tend to import fundamentalist and right-wing agendas almost wholesale from the United States, including opposition to abortion, feminism, labor unionism, and sexual minority rights on one hand and, on the other, advocacy for a strong military. More detailed research on homophobia in Fiji and its diasporic communities, I suspect, would reveal that, while the official conditions afforded soldiers in same-sex partnerships may ostensibly be better in the BA, notions of cultural authenticity and appropriate social behavior are likely to be policed more directly and even brutally in migrant communities abroad than they are among Fijians at home.[26] This is even more likely when, in the absence of other counterbalancing cultural institutions, religious worship and identification become the focus of indigenous social organization for Fiji's military migrant communities.[27]

Research and (In)visibility

So far, I have outlined some of the linguistic, institutional, and cultural conditions that in many ways embed sexual minorities in the FMF and BA. There are certainly contrasting conditions of same-sex invisibility in the FMF and BA. The FMF's version of DADT encourages the invisibility of same-sex orientation, as does the ethnic and cultural dominance of indigenous Fijians within the force—sexual minority identity becomes subsumed under the ethnic identity of indigenous Fijians. Yet in spite of the BA's official recognition of same-sex partnerships, the BA's size and demographics also seem to render sexual minorities from Fiji invisible. (The numerical minority status of Fijians in the BA, however, does not prevent their rugby players from gaining regular visibility in forums such as the BA's monthly *Soldier* magazine.)

The twin problematics of visibility and invisibility both raise particular challenges for research on sexual minorities from Fiji in the FMF and BA. Where a phenomenon is easily visible, the researcher should be willing to probe below the surface of appearances. Many authors in this volume are doing precisely the kind of probing that is needed in their considerations of Polynesian same-sex visibility and the too easy conflation of visibility with acceptability. By its very definition, investigating any form of social invisibility or marginalization requires adopting an epistemological standpoint that will either have to resist or heavily negotiate with empiricist demands for evidence. Given that the precise topic of sexual minority invisibility among Fijians in the BA and FMF has not been previously explored; that there is little to no official data available on the numbers of military service personnel from Fiji with same-sex orientation or in same-sex partnerships in either the FMF or the BA; that ethnographic or analytical literature on same-sex relationships in Fiji is very limited; and that homophobic violence represents a real threat, the researcher's task is a delicate and difficult one.

If one seeks a historical understanding of the topic, access to military archives in Fiji can be problematic, as these are not held in the National Archives repository but at the Queen Elizabeth barracks in Nabua, Suva. The last major scholarly work to be published utilizing sources in the FMF archives was on New Zealand's participation in the British anticommunist campaign in Malaya (Pugsley 2003). The fact that the Malaya campaign is central to the FMF's heroic narrative and that the researcher was based at the prestigious Sandhurst Military Academy in Britain literally opened the archive doors. Although I was given virtually unimpeded access to FMF personnel for interviews during my six months of fieldwork in Fiji in 2008–2009, all my requests for access to the archives and official policy documents were politely ignored.

While historical BA records are held in the public British National Archives at Kew, other factors can affect their accessibility. When visiting Kew in 2008, I was fortunate that files pertaining to the recruitment of Fiji soldiers into the British Army in 1961 had by then been declassified. This allowed me to excavate some of the history and politics surrounding the recruitment of Fiji women in that cohort. The one file available on the 1961 cohort focused on their recruitment and did not capture any of their experiences of training and service. Perhaps other files will be declassified in due course; perhaps no other files were kept on the cohort as a discrete group. Personnel files for each BA soldier exist, but posthumous access to these is restricted, understandably, to immediate family members. Any records on Fiji soldiers recruited into the BA since 1998 would still be classified. British military court-martial records and decisions are also only selectively made available online, so access to information about disciplinary or criminal charges against soldiers is limited. While I would be surprised to find evidence of same-sex orientation in any of the official files of the 1961 Fiji cohort in the BA (and I would probably be more inclined to look for records of homophobic harassment or violence), it is of course advisable not to assume anything.

When I embarked on my research on Fiji women soldiers, the central focus of my inquiry and analysis was on gender—sexuality was not an area of priority for me. It was only after meeting and talking with members of sexual minorities from Fiji in military service that I realized I should have sought ethical approval from my university to investigate a broader base of questions. But every request for an interview on the topic of sexual orientation is potentially a form of "outing"—that is, of exposing individuals' private lives to public scrutiny (Smorag 2008)—and that would be a reprehensible outcome of research. I subsequently sought and received ethical approval from my university to interview service personnel about same-sex partnerships, on the condition that the topic arose organically out of our interviews, and that research participants' anonymity and confidentiality be preserved. I certainly did not want to shine surveillance spotlights on anyone, and neither did I want to have military doors slammed in my face as a result of explicitly asking people to be interviewed about sexual minority issues. Although my initial motivation for broadening my research from women soldiers to same-sex sexual orientation in the military emerged out of a concern for potential and actual victims of homophobic discrimination and violence, I came to realize that such a focus lent itself to sensationalized and superficial readings and reactions. With careful consideration of ethical questions—especially concerning the safety of research participants—bona fide research on sexual minorities in the military can more generally help to increase our understanding of the limits of and possibilities for cultural change within one of the most powerful and influential institutions in modern society.

In my own field visits to BA and FMF sites between 2008 and 2009, there were very few occasions when I might have thought, "Hmm . . . that soldier looks gay or that servicewoman looks like a lesbian." I do remember being quite impressed by the appearance of one Fiji servicewoman, though, who had shaved her hair very close to the scalp, with the result that her attractive facial features and lean physique projected a steely and formidable "GI Jane" aura. I was informed by other servicewomen I interviewed that she identified herself as a lesbian, but I did not have a chance to speak to her, and encountered few others like her in my travels. Certainly there is always the problem of the culturally informed limits of our perception— someone who might easily be assumed to be a "dyke"' in Western society because of her solid build, short hair, and authoritative speaking voice could very easily be a vigorously heterosexual mother of four in a Pacific Island society.[28]

While it is often a matter of pride among members of sexual minority communities to develop and sharpen one's "gay radar" or "gaydar" (Nicholas

2004; Shelp 2002), presuming or predicting a potential research partici- pant's sexuality is fraught with difficulties for researchers. But the flip side of erroneously trusting one's gaydar is to erroneously assume universal het- eronormativity, thereby excluding or marginalizing sexual minorities, as if social blindness were a viable defense. Whenever I did find myself among soldiers I was meeting for the first time who openly asserted a same-sex orientation, I was often surprised, though I was able to exercise enough restraint not to show it.

In my formal research on women soldiers, only two of the nineteen oral histories recorded mentioned same-sex orientation. One of the members of Fiji's pioneer 1961 BA cohort told me that she had encountered lesbians for the first time in her life during basic training. She made the statement casually, commenting that it seemed only natural to her in a context where women had little daily contact with men. Although I was curious to hear more, I did not pursue the matter, as she had been a little anxious during our interview and occasionally asked me to turn off the recorder when she thought our conversation might have been straying into controversial ter- ritory. Even though it seemed as if she had no reservations about bringing up the topic of lesbians, I did not want to press her.

The other interview dealt with same-sex questions in the military at more length, and was with a member of one of the post-1998 cohorts. While the servicewoman I was interviewing did not like to label herself explicitly as either a lesbian or bisexual, she was not inclined to try to mask her sexual orientation. She spoke candidly about her own experiences, recounting how one of her commanding officers had once quietly taken her aside to ask if she was no longer "that way." She took this to mean that he was inquiring about whether she was still pursuing women as sexual partners. She noted with chagrin, however, that the harshest penalty she had ever received in the military came in the form of a demotion in rank when her superiors learned that she had been having an affair with a mar- ried male colleague. In spite of this career setback, she continued to serve with enthusiasm.

Although aspects of her circumstances are unique, this research partici- pant also indicated that there were several officers (all male) and other ranks of personnel (some women) who shared a same-sex orientation. However, any sense of recognition or community among these service personnel did not appear to translate into visible or formal types of organization, commu- nity building, or leveraging of institutional support for sexual minorities. If sexual minorities are invisible in the FMF, it may be because they remain atomized individuals in their institutional setting. If Fiji's sexual minorities are visible in the BA as individuals but invisible as a political group, it may be because they are negotiating between the civil rights guaranteed them by the state and the army and the pressures to conform culturally in their diasporic communities. Sexual minority invisibility in either the FMF or the BA is best understood as a product of a combination of individual choices and survival strategies, and structural, institutional, or cultural conditions.

The field is wide open for researchers, but it is crucial that sensationalist urges be tempered. As McIntosh (n.d.) argues, the most important things to understand about same-sex sexuality or sexual minorities—when heterosexuality is still considered the norm—are not so much sexual, but social. In that vein, my reflections here have identified some areas for further research: gayspeak in Fiji, and the Israeli–Palestine interface for Fijian peacekeeping personnel and its impact on sexual politics, among other topics. In spite of over thirty years of contracted service with the United Nations, not enough is known about either the formal or informal sexual provisioning of Fijian troops while on peacekeeping and other security deployments for the UN. Neither do we know much about the relationship between FMF and BA soldiers and sex workers in Fiji. No significant research appears to have been done on the formal policies, informal attitudes, or social and cultural changes taking place that are related to either heterosexual or same-sex relationships among Fiji's military service personnel. Occasionally, matters of sexual health or reproduction in the military such as HIV and other STDs emerge in the media, or there is coverage in the news of the FMF cooperatively working with women's NGOs to address issues of domestic violence, but same-sex issues remain invisible.

Same Sex, Different Armies: More Work

To understand the conditions of invisibility of sexual minorities from Fiji in the FMF and BA, we have to examine contexts. The first context I explored in this chapter was terminology. Attentiveness to colloquial, formal, and political registers and naming helps us understand how sexual minorities are made visible or invisible in the culture. The second context for understanding invisibility was in relation to the institutions and cultures of the military. In the case of the BA, it would seem that official recognition of same-sex partnership would guarantee visibility. However, because of numeric and minority cultural reasons, Fiji's same-sex-oriented service personnel are nevertheless rendered invisible in the BA. While invisibility presents particular challenges to research, which I discussed in the third section, there may be valid reasons to maintain invisibility, such as preserving the safety and privacy of individuals.

What might be more problematic than invisibility, however, is the silence of activists, intellectuals, and researchers in regard to the processes of militarization among Fiji's minorities. As I have described in an earlier work, there has been a remarkable lack of public debate in Fiji around women serving in the military (Teaiwa 2008). This is surprising given that Fiji has had a robust feminist and women's rights movement since the 1970s and indigenous notions of gender propriety would exclude women from martial service. Fiji's feminist movement has avoided the trajectory of liberal feminism that is perhaps best exemplified by the United States' National Organization of Women's submission of an amicus curiae to the Supreme Court in the 1980s "calling for equality in policies shaping military conscription in the name of equality" (Shigematsu 2009, 418). But if the absence of any debate about women in the military in Fiji is notable, there is also no public discourse at all about sexual minorities in relation to the military. Several possible explanations for such silence and the resulting invisibility of sexual minority soldiers in the contemporary era remain to be investigated. Some of these explanations will be particular to the individual and his or her circumstances, but many are shaped by broader social, political, and cultural structures and institutions. The series of events that first drew my attention to the complexities surrounding sexual minorities in the FMF and the BA involved two young men. One is my former student living his life to the fullest in the BA, the other is a young man whose life was ended too early—not in the warfare or peacekeeping he was trained for—but in an act of interpersonal violence. The issues faced by Fiji's sexual minority soldiers demand careful inquiry and critical reflection. There is so much more work to be done.

Acknowledgments

I would like to thank Kalissa Alexeyeff and Niko Besnier, Maciu Raivoka, Apolonia Tamata, Luisa Tora, Malcolm McKinnon, and Sean Mallon for their advice and constructive feedback as I worked on this chapter. I dedicate this work to my sons, Vaitoa Mallon and Manoa Teaiwa.

Notes

1   The title of my chapter resonates with the title of Herdt's book, *Same Sex, Different Cultures* (1997).

2   USP stands for the University of the South Pacific, a regional university owned by twelve Pacific Island nations. Its main campus is in Suva, Fiji; the law school, in Vila, Vanuatu; the agricultural school, in Alafua, Samoa; and distance education centers are in each of the member island countries.

3   In a survey of what she calls "gayspeak," Smorag notes that the term "camp" emerged out of *Polari*, a lexicon of five hundred words used in gay communities in the 1950s and 1960s in the United States. It originally meant "effeminate" or "outrageous" (2008, 3) and was "recaptured in 1964 by the American writer Susan Sontag who coined two new phrases, high camp (sophisticated, tongue-in-cheek wit, and self-aware) and low camp (showing a lack of sophistication and self-awareness)" (Smorag 2008, 6).

4   Smorag notes that "flamer" is another term used to signify an "effeminate gay man" (2008, 4).

5   In July 2009, India's High Court decriminalized homosexuality with explicit reference to legal precedents in Nepal and Fiji (Khosla 2011). But, in my opinion, the initiative taken in drafting the preamble and much of Fiji's 1997 constitutional amendment was much more about the drafters' aspirations than it was a response to or a reflection of a widespread social movement or universally held beliefs in Fiji. Indeed, the 1997 constitutional amendment preceded the reform of laws criminalizing sodomy. In the late 1990s, when the Fiji Women's Rights Movement spearheaded legal reform around rape and sexual violence, I recall participating in consultations where participants were informed that the laws on sodomy were strategically dropped from the feminist agenda, ironically reproducing the sorts of political prioritizing that often sees women's issues deferred until "after the revolution" (see George, this volume).

6   Tora, Perera, and Koya-Vaka'uta recall that Fiji police granted a permit for church groups to organize a march against sexual minority rights in 1997 (2006, 58).

7   Although the military regime has decreed that all citizens of Fiji may be described as "Fijian," that term has historically been used to signify indigenous or ethnic Fijians rather than any of the other ethnic populations in the country. Whenever I use the term "Fijian," I am referring only to indigenous citizens of Fiji. Whenever I use the term "Fiji" as an adjective rather than a noun, I am signifying a national identity rather than an ethnic one. For example, my research on Fiji women soldiers is not just about Fijian women soldiers.

8   By contrast, the neighboring Pacific Island countries, particularly Tonga and Samoa, have prominent indigenous gender-liminal categories that for some time have attracted scholarly attention on questions of gender and sexuality (e.g., Wallace 2003; Besnier 1997, 2002).

9   "Poofter" is defined in Geraghty, Mugler, and Tent as "'male homosexual,' the use of this word may give offence" (2006, 421). See also http://www .etymonline.com/index.php?term=poof and http://www.peevish.co.uk/slang/p .htm. Confirming the connotations of homosexuality and effeminacy, Adinkrah (2000, 158) also notes that "[w]ithin male peer groups [in Fiji], those who display hesitancy or an unwillingness to participate in peer-approved displays of machismo are ridiculed as weak or are labeled 'poofter.'"

10   *Editors' note:* While poofters in Fiji may be defined as males with a same-sex orientation, within their own communities there may be proscriptions against partnering with those who were similarly defined.

11   My father is from the ethnic minority community of Banabans in Fiji whose first language is Kiribati, but he speaks Fijian fluently as a result of spending eight years in an all-male predominantly indigenous Fijian boarding school and working for over thirty years in agricultural extension and rural development. As I was working on this chapter, I asked him what words he knew that referred to same-sex orientation in Fiji, and he volunteered the term *wādua* and did not recognize the term *qauri*. Further research into the changing currency of same-sex terms in Fiji could be revealing of generational and other sociocultural shifts in attitude and thinking.

12   Interestingly, *pufta* (which is a more phonetically intelligible spelling of "poofter" for speakers of Fiji English) and *qauri* are listed as synonyms in the entry for *vakasalewalewa,* but neither term has its own entry in the dictionary.

13   *Na Ivolavosa Vakaviti* (2005) does not include *vakayalewa* or *vakatagane* in its listings. However, *dauyalewa* and *vakamoceyalewa* are designated in the dictionary as male activities, and *dautagane* and *vakamocetagane* are designated as female activities, that is, there appears to be a heteronormative injunction in the dictionary's glossing of these terms.

14   I thank Maciu Raivoka and Dr. Apolonia Tamata for their illumination of these terms for me. *Vinaka vaka levu sara.*

15   Queer sexuality is not just about feminine men having sex with masculine men, or masculine women having sex with feminine women, but covers more nuances of sexual orientation than I am able to account for in this chapter. Smorag (2008) notes, for example, that heterosexual children of gay parents might also identify as queer.

16   In colloquial parlance, regular BA soldiers are called "squaddies."

17 See Fiji Bureau of Statistics website: http://www.statsfiji.gov.fj/Key%
    20Stats/Employment%20&%20Wages/9.4%20Paid%20employment%
    20by%20occup.pdf (accessed February 15, 2013).
18 See Ministry of Defence: http://www.dasa.mod.uk/applications/newWeb/
    www/index.php?page=48&pubType=1&thiscontent=10&PublishTime=
    09:30:00&date=2010–09–29&disText=2010&from=listing&topDate=
    2010–09–29 (accessed September 15, 2011). In addition, the UK Ministry
    of Defence also has the Royal Air Force and the Royal Navy as part of its
    force capacity.
19 See The Defence Suppliers Directory: http://www.armedforces.co.uk/
    armypayscales.htm and the Fiji Coup 2006 blogsite at http://www
    .fijicoup2006.com/2011/08/army-privates-paid-more-than-usp_19.html#
    .UR36FaW9ZSU (both accessed February 15, 2013).
20 While the FMF is not interested in pursuing its service personnel on questions
    of sexual orientation, there is a concomitant lack of interest among Fiji NGOs
    about the impact of domestic militarization on the sexual health of the wider
    community. The most extensive survey of MSM in relation to HIV and AIDS
    in Fiji, for example, makes no reference at all to the influence of the military
    on sexual practices in the country or on the incidence of HIV and AIDS
    (Bavinton et al. 2011). The significance of the invisibility of the military
    altogether in sexual health and policy research literature on Fiji and the Pacific
    (e.g., PIAF 2010, 2011; UNDP Pacific Centre and UNAIDS 2009) deserves
    to be explored in greater detail.
21 See Fiji Public Service Commission, Legislation and Policies at http://www
    .psc.gov.fj/index.php/legislations-policies/policies (accessed February 15, 2013).
22 See Proud to Serve.Net, the British Armed Forces LGBT e-network website:
    http://www.proud2serve.net/lgbt-organisations/227-workplace-equality
    -index-stonewall-benchmarking (accessed February 15, 2013).
23 See Proud to Serve.Net, the British Armed Forces LGBT e-network website:
    http://www.proud2serve.net/civil-partnerships (accessed February 15, 2013).
24 See Proud to Serve.Net, the British Armed Forces LGBT e-network
    homepage: http://www.proud2serve.net/ (accessed February 15, 2013).
25 The extent to which human rights pertaining to sexuality have been considered
    expendable enough in Fiji to garner broad public support is perhaps best
    demonstrated by the populist move made by Mahendra Chaudry, as the first
    Indo-Fijian prime minister of the country in 1999, proposing to delete the
    antidiscrimination clause as one of his first legislative acts. Unfortunately for
    Chaudry, rather than winning him support from right-wing Christian Fijian
    nationalists, his willingness to tamper with the constitution raised alarms and
    helped to feed fears among indigenous Fijians about his intentions in regard to

their constitutionally protected land rights. Chaudry's term as prime minister was short-lived, for in May 2000 the ethno-nationalists mobilized not only to remove him from office but to hold him and his cabinet hostage for over fifty days.

26   For a discussion of the heteronormative pressures in migrant communities, see, for example, Gairola 2009.

27   For a comparative example from the Nigerian diaspora, see Kuku-Siemons 2011.

28   French primitivist painter Paul Gauguin, whose works have become iconographic of Pacific Islands sexuality, wrote in his memoir *Noa Noa* (1919) of his frustration in not being able to tell Tahitian men from women when viewing them from behind. He recounts an incident where he was admiring the feminine form of a native walking in front of him, only to find when the native turned around that it was a man. By the same token, those natives he took to be men turned out sometimes to be women.

References

Adam, Barry D., Jan Willem Duyvendak, and Andre Krouwel, eds. 1999. *The Global Emergence of Gay and Lesbian Politics: National Imprints of a Worldwide Movement.* Philadelphia: Temple University Press.

Adinkrah, Mensah. 2000. Female Perpetrated Spousal Homicides: The Case of Fiji. *Journal of Criminal Justice* 28: 151–161.

Barr, Kevin. 1998. *Blessed Are the Rich, Praise the Lord: An Examination of New Religious Groups in Fiji Today.* Suva, Fiji: Fiji Council of Churches.

Bavinton, B., N. Singh, D. S. Naiker, M. N. Deo, M. Talala, M. Brown, R. R. Singh, S. Dewan, and S. Navokavokadrau. 2011. Secret Lives, Other Voices: A Community-Based Study Exploring Male-to-Male Sex, Gender Identity and HIV Transmission Risk in Fiji. Suva, Fiji: AIDS Task Force of Fiji.

Belkin, Aaron. 2008. Don't Ask, Don't Tell: Does the Gay Ban Undermine the Military's Reputation? *Armed Forces and Society* 34: 276–291.

Belkin, Aaron, and R. L. Evans. 2000. The Effects of Including Gay and Lesbian Soldiers in the British Armed Forces: Appraising the Evidence. Santa Barbara: Center for the Study of Sexual Minorities in the Military, University of California at Santa Barbara.

Besnier, Niko. 1997. Sluts and Superwomen: The Politics of Gender Liminality in Urban Tonga. *Ethnos* 62: 5–31.

———. 2002. Transgenderism, Locality, and the Miss Galaxy Beauty Pageant in Tonga. *American Ethnologist* 29: 534–566.

Brison, Karen. 1999. Hierarchy in the World of Fijian Children. *Ethnology* 38: 97–119.

———. 2007. The Empire Strikes Back: Pentecostalism in Fiji. *Ethnology* 46: 21–39.

Burke, Jason. 2001. Armed Forces Are Set to Give Spouse Rights to Gay Partners; *The Observer*, August 12; http://www.guardian.co.uk/uk/2001/aug/12/military.jasonburke (accessed February 2012).

Capell, Alfred. 1991. *A New Fijian Dictionary*. Suva, Fiji: Government of Fiji.

Chand, Shalveen. 2010. Same Sex Law Decriminalised. *The Fiji Times* Online, February 26; http://www.fijitimes.com/story.aspx?id=140812 (accessed June 2012).

Chaney, Cassandra, and Le'Brian Patrick. 2011. The Invisibility of LGBT Individuals in Black Mega Churches: Political and Social Implications. *Journal of African American Studies* 15: 199–217.

Ernst, Manfred. 1994. *Winds of Change: Rapidly Growing Religious Groups in the Pacific Islands*. Suva, Fiji: Pacific Conference of Churches.

Gairola, Rahul K. 2009. Capitalist Houses, Queer Homes: National Belonging and Transgressive Erotics in *My Beautiful Laundrette*. *South Asian Popular Culture* 7(1): 37–54.

Gauguin, Paul. 1919. *Noa Noa*. New York: Nicholas Brown.

George, Nicole. 2008. Contending Masculinities and the Limits of Tolerance: Sexual Minorities in Fiji. *The Contemporary Pacific* 20: 163–189.

Geraghty, Paul, France Mugler, and Jan Tent, eds. 2006. *The Macquarie Dictionary of English for the Fiji Islands*. North Ryde, NSW: Macquarie Library.

Goldson, Annie. 2008. *An Island Calling*. Documentary (75 min.), distributed by Occasional Productions.

Halapua, Winston. 2003. *Tradition, Lotu and Militarism in Fiji*. Lautoka, Fiji: Fiji Institute of Applied Sciences.

Herdt, Gilbert. 1997. *Same Sex, Different Culture: Exploring Gay and Lesbian Lives*. Boulder, CO: Westview.

Katz, Jonathan Ned. 1995. *The Invention of Heterosexuality*. New York: Dutton.

Keller, Sinead. 2004. RAF Targets Manchester's Gay Pride Festival in Recruitment Drive. *The Guardian*, August 27; http://www.guardian.co.uk/uk/2004/aug/27/gayrights.military (accessed February 2012).

Khosla, Madhav. 2011. Inclusive Constitutional Comparison: Reflections on India's Sodomy Decision. *American Journal of Comparative Law* 59: 909–934.

Kuku-Siemons, Diepiriye. 2011. Moral Discourse, Homophobia, and the Nigerian Diaspora; http://northampton.academia.edu/DiepiriyeKukuSiemons/Papers/679323/Moral_Discourse_Homophobia_and_the_Nigerian_Diaspora (accessed June 2012).

Laws of Fiji. Chapter 17: Penal Code; http://www.paclii.org/fj/legis/consol_act_OK/pc66/ (accessed February 2012).

Linneman, Thomas J. 2004. Homophobia and Hostility: Christian Conservative Reactions to the Political and Cultural Progress of Lesbians and Gay Men. *Sexuality Research and Social Policy* 1(2): 56–76.

McIntosh, Tracey. 1999. Words and Worlds of Difference: Homosexualities in the Pacific. Social Policy and Sociology Working Paper 3/99. Suva, Fiji: University of the South Pacific.

———. n.d. Homosexuality in the Pacific. Unpublished paper; http://www.vanuatu.usp.ac.fj/sol_adobe_documents/usp%20only/pacific%20general/mcintosh.htm (accessed June 2012).

Nicholas, Cheryl L. 2004. Gaydar: Eye-Gaze as Identity Recognition among Gay Men and Lesbians. *Sexuality and Culture* 8: 60–86.

Pacific Islands AIDS Foundation (PIAF). 2010. Pushing the Boundaries Further: 2010 Progress Report for the United Nations Special Session on HIV/AIDS. Lautoka: Pacific Aids Foundation; http://www.pacificaids.org/images/pdf/PIAF%20UNGASS%20Report%202011.pdf (accessed February 2012).

———. 2011. Experiences and Perspectives of Women Living with HIV in Fiji and Papua New Guinea. Lautoka: Pacific Islands AIDS Foundation; http://www.pacificaids.org/images/pdf/expperscopy2.pdf (accessed February 2012).

Peteru, Andrew. 1997. The Sexuality and STD/HIV Risk Related Sexual Behaviours of Single, Unskilled, Young Adult, Samoan males: A Qualitative Study. MA thesis, Department of Health Social Science, Mahidol University.

———. 2002. Heterosexual Male Issues in the Pacific. Paper presented at the Pacific History Association Conference, Apia, Samoa.

Puar, Jasbir. 2011. Citation and Censorship: The Politics of Talking about the Politics of Sexuality in Israel. *Feminist Legal Studies* 19: 131–142.

Pugsley, Christopher. 2003. *From Emergency to Confrontation: New Zealand Armed Forces in Malaya and Borneo, 1949–1966.* New York: Oxford University Press.

Scott, Owen. 2004. *Deep beyond the Reef.* Auckland: Penguin.

Serelini, Kelera. 2011. Homosexuals are. . . . *Kaila,* June 26, p. 3.

Shelp, Scott G. 2002. Gaydar: Visual Detection of Sexual Orientation among Gay and Straight Men. *Journal of Homosexuality* 44: 1–14.

Shigematsu, Setsu. 2009. Aftermath: Feminism and the Militarization of Women's Lives, A Dialogue with Cynthia Enloe and Eli Paintedcrow. *International Feminist Journal of Politics* 11: 414–428.

Smorag, Pascale. 2008. From Closet Talk to PC Terminology: Gay Speech and the Politics of Visibility. *Transatlantica* 1: 2–17.

Tabana ni Vosa kei na Itovo Vakaviti. 2005. *Na Ivolavosa Vakaviti.* Suva, Fiji: Valenitabaivola ni Matanitu.

Teaiwa, Teresia. 2008. On Women and "Indians": The Politics of Inclusion and Exclusion in Militarized Fiji. In *Security Disarmed: Gender, Race and*

Militarization, ed. Barbara Sutton, Sandra Morgen, and Julie Novkov, pp. 111–135. New Brunswick, NJ: Rutgers University Press.

Tomlinson, Matt. 2013. The Generation of the Now: Denominational Politics in Fijian Christianity. In *Christian Politics in Oceania,* ed. Matt Tomlinson and Debra McDougall, pp. 78–102. New York: Berghahn.

Tora, Luisa, Carlos Perera, and Frances Koya-Vakaʻuta. 2006. Masculinity, Identity, and Fiji's GLBT Community. *Women in Action: Isis Women International* 1: 56–65.

UNAIDS. 2006. HIV and Men Who Have Sex with Men in Asia and the Pacific; http://data.unaids.org/Publications/IRC-pub07/JC901-MSMAsiaPacific _en.pdf (accessed February 2012).

UNDP Pacific Centre and UNAIDS. 2009. Enabling Effective Responses/HIV in Pacific Island Countries: Options for Human Rights-Based Legislative Reform. Suva, Fiji: UNDP Pacific Centre; http://www.undppc.org.fj/ _resources/article/files/LowRes_3011.pdf (accessed February 2012).

Wallace, Lee. 2003. *Sexual Encounters: Pacific Texts, Modern Sexualities.* Ithaca, NY: Cornell University Press.

Ware, Vron. 2012. *Military Migrants: Fighting for YOUR Country.* London: Palgrave Macmillan.

CHAPTER 13

In Sickness and in Health

Evolving Trends in Gay Rights Advocacy in Fiji

Nicole George

The terrain of gender politics in Fiji is complex and variegated. Since the 1960s, women's organizations in this Pacific Island country have been a powerful political force. Although their efforts to promote gender equality have been far from uniform and buffeted by frequent episodes of serious political upheaval, they have had a significant impact on the formalized realm of policy making both in Fiji and, more broadly, across the region. It is against this backdrop, and perhaps thanks to the vibrancy of this terrain, that gay rights advocacy has also emerged as a distinct site of political activity in the past decade. Advocates have been able to expand on the political space that women's rights activists had opened up, challenging sociocultural, political, and economic structures they have viewed as discriminatory. This has made Fiji one of the few sites in the Pacific Islands where the political status of homosexuality is openly debated, where groups promoting gay rights have a visible presence in civil society, and where legislative protection has been offered to those who openly articulate a same-sex sexuality.

Fiji may be somewhat distinctive in this regard, but this does not mean that the political waters navigated by gay rights activists are free of hazard. Gay rights advocacy has also taken place against a backdrop of religious conservatism and ethno-nationalism, which has promoted a distrust and intolerance of those whose sexuality differs from socioculturally proscribed norms (George 2008). These norms tend to deny the prevalence of male homosexual experimentation within Pacific Island societies, which if not generally publicly acknowledged, is at least met with a tacit "boys will be boys" type of tolerance. This rigid denial of homosexuality also ignores the customary acceptance of homosexual ritual or gender liminality in many Pacific societies (see Alexeyeff and Besnier, this volume; also Besnier 1994, 229; Schmidt 2003, 423; Herdt 1981, 1984, 1994, 1997). The military regime currently in power in Fiji has sought to reduce the political influence of the Methodist Church, a vocal opponent of gay rights groups, and in March 2010 passed a decree to decriminalize homosexuality. Even so, homophobia remains a powerful feature of political and religious rhetoric in Fiji. This poses important challenges for those who aim to promote acceptance of same-sex sexuality in social, cultural, and legal terms.

This chapter analyzes the changing directions that gay rights politics in Fiji has taken over the past decade. In particular, it considers the advantages and risks that have accrued from past efforts to promote tolerance of diverse sexual orientations through a human rights framework and from more contemporary advocacy programs that approach homosexuality through the lens of sexual health (also see Stewart, this volume). I show how international aid and development regimes, in combination with local and national factors, have shaped the direction of this political activity in Fiji.

Dennis Altman's (2001) work on the emergence of a global gay identity has set the foundation for debate about the ways in which global economic and political trends have increased the visibility of a transnationally and cross-culturally articulated gay counterculture. The political ramifications of this are becoming increasingly apparent at the international level. The formulation of the Declaration of Montreal in 2006 by the International Conference on Lesbian, Gay, Bisexual and Transgender Human Rights (LGBT) was followed later in the same year by the development of the Yogyakarta Principles, which also aimed to establish human rights recognition of LGBT groups (Waites 2009). A growing momentum around gay rights advocacy has weakened opposition from conservative religious states. This enabled the UN Human Rights Council (HRC) to pass, in July 2011, a resolution entitled "Human Rights, Sexual Orientation and Gender Identity," albeit with a slim margin of HRC member-state acceptance and a number of abstentions (Zebly 2011). Thus, while it may be premature to celebrate the emergence of a new norm of same-sex tolerance in international politics, nonetheless such developments have been hailed as evidence of an intensified global struggle led by LGBT movements and increasingly effective deployment of international human rights law in the "sexuality arena" (Kollman and Waites 2009, 1; Stychin 2004).

Yet questions have also been asked about how this global activity artic-
ulates with, and potentially challenges, preexisting "vernacular" homosexual
identities or practices in localized settings (Puri 2008, 71). While these
types of political gains are often challenged by conservative political, cultural, and religious actors they may also be rejected by the very people they
aim to represent. This indicates a need for detailed and localized political
analysis of the advantages and disadvantages of gay activists' efforts to rein-
terpret in local settings the global discourse around same-sex sexuality and
rights (Massad 2002; Puri 2008). In many sociocultural contexts, same-
sex practices may not be lived as same-sex identities (see, e.g., Seckinelgin
2009, 106). Advocacy that uses the LGBT discourse as a kind of "catchall"
framework may therefore be alienating for individuals who do not think
of their sexuality in these "globalized" terms. These labels may be rejected
because they stamp a fixity on sexualities that are expressed in a more mutable fashion. They may also be rejected because they fit poorly with localized
cultural articulations of same-sex sexuality that have their roots in tradition
but also have shifted with time.[1]

These questions are pertinent to an analysis of advocacy aiming to promote acceptance of same-sex sexuality in the Pacific Islands. The activity discussed in the following pages tends, in large part, to emulate global
advocacy frameworks. Gay rights advocates in Fiji usually are urban-based,
hold liberal attitudes, and, until recently, were drawn principally from the
country's indigenous population.[2] These activists are heavily influenced by
global developments in the advocacy realm. They tend to be well networked
internationally, recognized by international donor agencies, and invited
regularly to attend events staged by networks such as the International
Lesbian and Gay Association (ILGA). This means that, like many other
activists around the globe, they tend to talk about same-sex sexuality as
a deliberate expression of identity. But this advocacy tends often to leave
aside more complex discussions of same-sex behavior. This behavior may
be random, opportunistic, or transactional, and involve individuals who
do not identify as gay, lesbian, or bisexual. It also leaves aside the issue of
localized forms of gender liminality and the status of populations such as
the Samoan *fa'afafine* or the Tongan *leitī* that do not necessarily identify
with the globalized "transgender" tag. These groupings find themselves in
increasingly vulnerable positions within Pacific Island societies as globalizing forces break down communal traditions that previously provided them
with security (Schmidt 2003, 420–421).

It is therefore important to note that, while gay rights activists in Fiji often formulate their political claims in ways that aim to provide further local and global impetus to the struggle against same-sex discrimination, their emulation of global advocacy vocabulary has local limitations. The LGBT framework may marginalize or exclude Pacific Islanders who engage in same-sex practices but do not articulate a LGBT identity as an "individually embodied sexuality" (Schmidt 2003, 421). Seckinelgin describes this scenario as a "double movement" in gay rights politics, which "opens up spaces" for resistance against homophobia and sexuality-based discrimination but also "closes down spaces" that might allow for the articulation of "localized subjectivities" (2009, 106).

In this chapter, I demonstrate how another aspect of this "double movement," or simultaneous opening and closing of political space, is relevant to the debate around same-sex sexuality in Fiji. My discussion shows that this scenario is also evident when we examine the enabling and constraining consequences of advocacy that emphasizes gay rights as human rights and, alternatively, advocacy that focuses on gay populations and sexual health. In Fiji, gay advocates' increasing emphasis on sexual health and vulnerability to disease has displaced earlier advocacy strategies, which were predominantly focused on claims for social and political acceptance and defended on human rights grounds.

At one level, this is an understandable local response to current military rule and the authoritarian political climate in Fiji, which currently makes the promotion of human rights claims difficult. Moreover, in a regional context where fears about HIV/AIDS transmission rates are increasing, development programs are increasingly prioritizing public health programs that focus on sexual health. Focusing on this issue provides gay activists with international authorization to open up local political space for a discussion of same-sex sexuality in a way that avoids the contention that currently dogs debate on human rights. At another level, however, this medicalized advocacy framework also meshes in an unfortunate fashion with conservative religious rhetoric in the Pacific Islands, which has often pathologized homosexuality as a blight on society (George 2008, 166). As such it can be seen as potentially closing down the space for any discussion of tolerance and understanding of same-sex sexualities that might venture into politicized territory. This type of advocacy may also close down the political space available to lesbian women who, in other settings, have complained that advocacy strategies focused predominantly on the sexual health of gay men ignore the need for a broader politics of solidarity that recognizes the place of women within Fiji's gay movement. These issues are dealt with in detail in the final sections of this chapter.

Rights, Risk, and Changing Attitudes

I first started researching advocacy around questions of homosexuality in Fiji as an unexpected sideline to my broader research into the history of women's organizations. My interest in gay rights emerged as a result of my volunteer work in 2002 with a small, diverse, and welcoming Suva-based nongovernmental organization known as Women's Action for Change, or WAC. WAC's offices were situated high on Waimanu Road in Suva, overlooking the city's working harbor and its dramatic surrounding topography. Although this location seemed to allow the office to float above the intensity of downtown Suva while at the same time maintaining close proximity to it, the organization also had its own hectic energy, largely generated by the diversity of the people who constantly moved through its always open door.

WAC had operated as an organization committed to the advancement of women's rights for over ten years. Yet by 2002 it had broadened this platform in a number of innovative, even unconventional, ways. When I became involved, it was operating as an umbrella organization for a number of projects, which included the coordination of a child-care center for women-headed households, a community-theater group promoting human rights values, an emerging project providing welfare and counseling support for young single mothers, and a prisoner rehabilitation scheme. WAC's efforts to work with marginalized groups demonstrated an inclusive approach to gender advocacy, underpinned by the idea that, to improve women's lives, one needs to work with women *and* men. In addition, the organization's approach to gender equality was attentive to power dynamics among men. Although not described in these terms, this suggested a keen sensitivity to the ways in which "hegemonic masculinities" (Connell 2005) disempower vulnerable groups of men as well as women. For these reasons, WAC sought to develop projects assisting the needs of ex-prisoners and of male homosexuals, and in certain instances even brought these groups together so that they might learn from one another (WAC 2001).[3]

The "Sexual Minorities Project" (WAC/SM) formed an important component of WAC. Indeed, it set WAC apart from other women's groups operating at that time in Fiji as the only group that openly addressed the issue of homosexuality in public debate.[4] WAC/SM aimed to promote gay and lesbian rights, increase the self-esteem of the gay and lesbian, bisexual, and transgender people, and provide counseling and support. The project also aimed to develop a sense of community among Fiji's diverse lesbian, bisexual, gay and transgender populations (WAC 2000). WAC/SM was founded in 1998 at the request of a lesbian couple who had been dismissed from their employment because of their sexual orientation. They had approached WAC because of the organization's commitment to the development of a society free from prejudice on the basis of race, gender, and sexuality. This vision had appealed to the two women, who were looking for civil society assistance as they set about challenging the discriminatory treatment to which they had been subjected. But though the sexual minorities project was started in response to a case of workplace discrimination, before long it became a site that drew homosexual women and men together in what was generally articulated as a common struggle for political and social recognition (Tora 2006). As I too became interested in this struggle, I encountered a slice of Suva society and became part of conversations that would have perhaps been closed to me had I chosen to work with another women's development organization.

The Sexual Minorities project was formed at an interesting moment in Fiji's eventful postcolonial political history. Nineteen ninety-eight was the year in which political leaders promulgated a new constitution that enshrined, among other human rights principles, respect for sexual diversity and outlawed discrimination on the grounds of sexual orientation. This constitutional provision was hotly debated in the country's media and among conservative religious leaders and elected parliamentarians. As the controversy strengthened in 1999–2000, Fiji's newly elected Labour government announced its intention to remove the contentious provision (Chandra 2000; George 2008; Tarte 2001).

This decision provoked members of WAC's Sexual Minority project to stage public demonstrations in support of the provision. They articulated their political claims by emphasizing their human right to receive the same social and political consideration as other citizens of Fiji. They also contended that the proposed change to the constitution contradicted efforts that had been made in 2000 by the national tourism board to market Fiji internationally as a gay-friendly destination (*Daily Post*, April 11, 2000).

A civilian coup in 2000 overturned the Indo-Fijian–headed coalition government and quieted civil society debate on this issue. The coup was followed by significant violence and lawlessness. As images of hypermasculine aggression dominated the coverage of the rebel insurgency in both local and international media, gay rights activists sought to reduce their visibility. They feared that they might also become the targets of violence that had seriously threatened the country's Indo-Fijian population but that also seemed to have an alarmingly indiscriminate quality (Emde 2005; George 2008, 173; Kelly and Kaplan 2001, 186; Robertson and Sutherland 2001). The unrelated gruesome murder of high-profile Red Cross worker John Scott and his partner Greg Scrivener in 2001, and the media interest in the homophobic statements that Suva's then police commissioner, Isikia Narube, issued about this affair (Scott 2004, 148), further aggravated feelings of insecurity in the gay rights movement. Those at the forefront of the movement became reluctant to put themselves into media spotlight (Sipeli, cited in *The Daily Post,* July 5, 2001).

Toward the end of 2002, gay activists' feelings of vulnerability began to abate (George 2008). The vilification of homosexuality continued to be a constant feature of mainline church rhetoric, but developments in the realm of institutional politics seemed to aid the activist agenda. Despite its efforts, the post-coup regime was unable to win judicial support for the military's suspension of the 1998 Constitution, which had occurred as part of efforts to reestablish state authority in the uncertain weeks that had followed the 2000 insurgency. A High Court ruling in March 2001 upheld the 1998 Constitution in its entirety; this included the provision that outlawed discrimination on the basis of same-sex sexuality. At the same time, regional events such as the 2002 Sydney Gay Games, which a dozen local activists attended, attracted some local media coverage. This event provided the gay rights movement in Fiji with an internationally endorsed lobbying platform and legitimated their public advocacy agenda. By 2005 the Sexual Minorities Project representatives were once again making themselves heard regularly in the local and international media, challenging conservative elements of Fiji's society (Radio Australia, November 8, 2005; Women's Action for Change: Sexual Minorities Project 2005).

Again, these political claims were framed chiefly in human rights terms, with advocates condemning the Methodist Church in particular for its ongoing attacks on the gay and lesbian community and its calls for antigay marches (Nagalu 2005). This advocacy insisted that the human rights of Fiji's gay and lesbian population be protected, and recalled the fact that this protection was enshrined in the democratic values of the 1998

Constitution. The following excerpt, drawn from a WAC/SM press statement issued in July 2005, indicates how rights for gay people and ideas about democracy were linked:

> At the heart of every democracy, that so many have fought and worked for here in Fiji, is a genuine respect for the rights of ALL. At the heart of democracy is equality before the law. If we attack any minorities on religious principles, we are getting dangerously close to fundamentalist statehood, and this has implications for all of us in Fiji who believe in democracy, human rights and rule of law. The measure of a government is in the way that it tries to address the rights of all. The measure of the worth and greatness of a country is how it treats diversity. We strongly affirm . . . religious freedom . . . but with such rights come great responsibilities and that means that all of us must see ourselves as the protectors of the human rights of people in Fiji. (WAC 2005a)

At this time, WAC also circulated a second statement on the issue of gay rights, this one authored by the New Zealand AIDS Foundation. This statement was strongly critical of the Fiji Methodist Church's call to return to colonial-era statutes criminalizing homosexuality. It asserted that this was "completely contrary to good public health practice" and risked driving "Fijian gay men deep underground where they would be almost impossible to reach with HIV education and prevention programs and resources such as condoms and lube" (WAC 2005b). This statement was noteworthy both for the way it framed the links between political recognition and health risk and the emphasis it placed on human rights protection as a necessary precursor to sexual health. The New Zealand AIDS Foundation argued that the sexual health of Fiji's gay community would be far more difficult to protect in a political environment where public vilification and stigmatization of this population were acceptable. It argued that an "extension of human rights legislation which would outlaw discrimination on the grounds of sexual orientation or the presence of disease" would ultimately be successful in helping to contain the HIV/AIDS epidemic among gay men (WAC 2005b). WAC's circulation of both these press statements clearly indicated a faith in the relevance of human rights to Fiji and a belief that the political fortunes and the sexual health of Fiji's gay population could be positively safeguarded only if these rights were protected.

WAC/SM also used more creative means to promote the idea that better recognition of the rights of Fiji's homosexual community would help minimize this community's exposure to risk. Since early 2002, WAC's community theater group had been writing and staging a play that portrayed the stigmatization, ostracism, and in some cases violence to which gays and lesbians who are "out" to their family or village are subjected. Drawing from the experiences of people associated with the partner SM project, the performances depicted young gays and lesbians feeling they had to leave their village homes and head for the country's bigger cities where they could lead more anonymous lives. But, as the play also demonstrated, such escape could be a double-edged sword, as it also exposed young men and women to sexual violence and possible involvement in transactional sex.[5] Fleeing from violence in the familiar setting to a realm of violence in an unfamiliar one could compound rather than alleviate vulnerability and marginalization (WAC 2002). The play thus presented an important counternarrative to the extreme political rhetoric of Methodist Church leaders, exposing the heavy personal costs that prejudice and intolerance exacted from gay people. Whether developed within the creative structures that WAC Theater favored or articulated as a set of formal political claims, WAC/SM's public advocacy seems to have been informed by the idea that more open debate on the question of same-sex sexualities was needed. The aim seems to have been to create respect for the human rights of gay men and women and to expose the physical and sexual health risks that this population would face if these rights were ignored.

The logic of human rights was entirely in keeping with the way in which the broader terrain of gender politics in Fiji was evolving at the time. As Fiji was recovering from its third coup since 1987, women activists were devoting a great deal of energy to developing advocacy strategies that linked gender equality, respect for democracy, and human rights. The Fiji Women's Crisis Centre (FWCC) was a vocal proponent of the idea that women's rights were human rights and that social acceptance of violence against women was a violation of their human rights. This idea had taken hold in international policy-making circles since the early 1990s but was given significant impetus during the 1995 United Nations Fourth World Conference on Women held in Beijing (Brown Thompson 2002; Connors 1996; Joachim 1999, 2003; Otto 1996). While the conference had endorsed women's right to live their lives free of violence as a legitimate human rights concern, the Beijing Platform for Action also noted the human rights violations experienced by women as a result of efforts to police their reproduction and sexuality, and due to their restricted access to health infrastructure (Jaquette 2003; Keck and Sikkink 1998; Pietilä and Vickers 1996; West 1999).

When FWCC representatives articulated the "women's rights as human rights" message in Fiji, they often adapted it to local sociocultural and religious values. Indeed, they often had to do so to gain the support of indigenous Fijian cultural figures or religious leaders. They were also careful to frame their advocacy in ways that did not antagonize the post-coup political elite, which at that time was highly protective of indigenous cultural values and suspicious of such "universalizing" discourses.

This rejection of "universalism" had a well-established political pedigree in Fiji and was strongly linked to antidemocratic rhetoric. The allegation that democracy in Fiji was a "foreign flower unsuited to Fiji's soil" was first voiced by indigenous Fijian nationalists in 1987 as they sought to justify their overthrow of a democratically elected government, which they claimed was dominated by nonethnic (predominantly Indian) Fijians (Tabakaucoro 1987). The doctrine of indigenous paramountcy was enshrined in Fiji under British colonial rule in order to safeguard Fijian land and culture, and to coerce Fijian acceptance of an Indian population descended from indentured workers imported to work on the colonial sugar plantations and, later, of free settlers (Denoon 1997; Firth 1997). In the post-independence context, because the Fiji Indian population had grown to outnumber Fiji's indigenous citizens, the doctrine of indigenous paramountcy was again drawn upon to legitimate the antidemocratic ambitions of an emergent Fijian nationalist movement known as the Taukei Movement (Kelly and Kaplan 2001). As Fiji's political environment became convulsed by the nationalist-inspired coups of 1987 and 2000, a creeping "ethnicization of the state" ensued (Naidu 2009, 238). In this context, activists aiming to promote local acceptance of human rights or democratic values were often accused of importing foreign ideas ill-suited to the local sociocultural context.[6]

To avoid this reaction, women's groups had developed a range of "translation" strategies (Merry 2006), which aimed to show local populations that human rights discourses were compatible with Pacific Island cultures. These acts of translation included disputing the accepted secondary status of women in Pacific churches and cultures, reminding Pacific peoples that decision making involving women and matrilineal land ownership were evident in their cultures, and that even Fiji's indigenous customs included traditional practices that privileged the position of women (Daurewa 2009).[7] At the same time, women activists also argued that Fiji had committed itself to upholding the principle of women's rights as human rights at the United Nations and was under an obligation to abide by this commitment in national policy making (Shamima Ali, personal communication, April 2002). Despite the potential for hostile reactions, women activists remained convinced that the discourse of human rights provided an important avenue for advocacy that aimed to improve the physical security of women and limit their exposure to violence.

In addition, women activists yoked their human rights advocacy to concerns about the prospects of democracy in Fiji (despite its disputed status) and the survival of the country's 1998 democratic constitution. The Fiji Women's Rights Movement, another important organization, was involved in a range of activities that sought to protect the constitution. Controversially, this included contributing preparatory legal work to a case appearing in Fiji's High Court in June 2000 that ultimately declared the military's abrogation of the constitution illegal (George 2009; Lal 2003). In addition, the FWRM conducted a "Democracy is for Fiji" campaign that challenged Taukei nationalist antidemocracy rhetoric. The posters and pamphlets used in this campaign were translated into English, Hindi, and Fijian, and featured a frangipani flower, an imported species to Fiji but one that has become so "nativized" that it features as a symbol of Pacific Islands authenticity and is often used to promote local cosmetic products such as those manufactured by the globally successful brand "Pure Fiji." This was a clever strategy, aimed to counter nationalist characterizations of democracy as a "foreign flower." FWRM argued that "democracy is a precondition for the attainment of women's rights" (FWRM 2001) and justified a public course of action that pushed "aggressively . . . for [Fiji's] return to constitutional rule" (FWRM 2001; George 2012, 151).

Gay rights advocacy that invoked human rights ideals and emphasized the importance of democracy for the protection of these rights can therefore be seen as further "opening up" the political space that high-profile women's groups had already created when they linked these issues to the promotion of women's rights. Of course, this was not a discourse that characterized the women's movement as a whole in Fiji, in that more conservative women's groups, and particularly those with strong links to the indigenous community, tended to view this type of political agenda with a level of circumspection. Nonetheless, references to human rights had become an almost routine feature of advocacy agendas promoted by the more liberal and high-profile women's groups at this time, and this allowed gay rights groups to exploit similar territory.

But this strategy was also made possible by trends occurring at the global level. At this time, the human rights framework was increasingly important within global gay rights networks as a productive way to challenge discrimination. Implicit in this type of advocacy are two interlinked strategies aimed at "opening up" mainstream deliberation on gender human rights. The first seeks to expand the boundaries of society in ways that will promote cosmopolitan rights claims over communalist rights claims, the latter tending to oppose recognition of sexual identity and gender in order to ensure that "cultural authenticity" and "specificity" are maintained. The second strategy seeks to open up "the wider potential of human rights" to include a more specific focus on same-sex sexuality—a consideration that until only recently has lain outside the ambit of human rights debate (Stychin 2004, 957–966). Each of these aspects of human rights advocacy was relevant to the situation in Fiji.

On the one hand, gay activists were challenging nationalist leaders' defense of indigenous Fijian paramountcy, which frequently included a demonization of alleged "foreign influences," a tag that was applied to political principles like democracy and multiculturalism as well as to specific groups of people—Indo-Fijians and the "out" gay community. On the other hand, gay activists were also seeking to break new ground for the deliberation of human rights principles in Fiji. Their strategy here was to expand on the efforts made by local women's groups to promote gender discrimination as a human rights issue by arguing that discrimination on the basis of sexual orientation also violates human rights principles.

By the end of 2006, however, these strategies were to lose some of their appeal as Fiji experienced new political upheaval, and the local space for the public articulation of a political agenda framed in human rights terms was considerably reduced. These new developments also had important implications for the advocacy strategies devised by the gay rights movement in later periods.

Risk and Rights Uncoupled: Changing Behavior

Two thousand and six was an eventful year for the members of WAC/SM. Up until this point, the project had operated in an ad hoc manner, engaging in public advocacy where it felt it was needed, promoting the development of the LGBT community, and providing a range of counseling services when called upon to do so. Funding constraints explain this situation: compared to organizations that focused on more conventional gender issues, WAC/SM had secured only a small amount of funding, and it remained a fledgling organization. By 2006, this situation had started to change. The project began to strengthen its profile independently of WAC, and Carlos Perera, its coordinator, frequently received national and international media exposure. Such was the growing status of the organization and its profile as a body committed to human rights ideals that the UNDP-sponsored Regional Rights Resource Team awarded it a regional prize for its advocacy.

On the back of this success, Perera and his fellow activists chose to take the organization in a new direction and end, albeit amicably, its original association with WAC. A new organization, Equal Ground Pasifik (EGP), was launched. For Perera, the name change was significant. "Sexual minorities" could be read as "derogatory," he argued, and could perpetuate the stigmatization of gays and lesbians by marking them as different and somehow lesser (Vunileba 2006). Renaming the project "Equal Ground" encapsulated the idea that they were at the "same level as everybody else" (ibid.). But the move to separate from WAC was also motivated by the fact that the group was beginning to attract significant international attention from donors in its own right. While linked to WAC the status of the gay and lesbian group had been uncertain. As an independent body, it was more visible to potential donors and able to strengthen its relationship to funders. At this time, EGP also moved from the WAC offices on Waimanu Road to new premises it shared with the Fiji Aids Task Force in central Suva. The physical proximity of the two organizations reflected an increasing philosophical proximity, as EGP's advocacy work became more focused on questions of sexual health and HIV/AIDS prevention.

When they were part of the WAC collective, SM members had certainly paid close attention to sexual health and risk, as its circulation of the New Zealand AIDS Foundation press statement in 2005 demonstrates. It had received funding from regional partner organizations such as Sexual Health and Family Planning Australia (SH&FPA) to run sexual health programs for gay men in Fiji and had devised its own peer education program entitled SMART Choices (AusAID 2008). Nonetheless, from 2006 onward, EGP began to form independent relations with local NGOs, aid providers, and regional partner organizations. This appears to have encouraged the group to become more involved in sexual health advocacy and to move away, to some degree, from its earlier human rights–focused activities.

At this time, EGP members characterized their work as partnering the AIDS Task Force in Fiji. They justified their shifting focus on sexual health by stating that homosexual men and male sex workers had experienced "victimization and verbal abuse" when they tried to access health care services (Bondhyopadhyay 2007). As a result, they began to prioritize liaisons with government departments and civil society organizations in order to facilitate access to health care. They also argued that EGP's programs were better designed to cater to the interests of gay men than other health care programs in the country, "none [of which had] efficiently addressed sexual health issues of men who have sex with men" or "dared talk about anal sex, oral sex, masturbation [or] HIV/AIDS in the GLBT perspective" (Bondhyopadhyay 2007, 17).

Fiji's public service, as well as donors and regional partner organizations, were increasingly enthusiastic about the role that EGP members could play in preventive sexual health campaigns targeting gay groups. In 2006, EGP began working in collaboration with the Ministry of Health and the Secretariat of the Pacific Community (SPC), a regional intergovernmental organization with a dedicated public health stream that was addressing HIV/AIDS and STI transmission in Pacific countries. EGP was commissioned by these partners to deliver a series of workshops focused on changing sexual behavior and reducing exposure to infection. The SH&FPA also engaged EGP to continue its SMART choices education program; and the Aids Task Force found its association with EGP beneficial too, as both organizations developed their collective capacity to promote sexual health among the broader population. In a 2008 report commissioned by AusAID, Aids Task Force representatives stated that EGP had built "trust among the GLBT community to attend and use the services of the [Task Force sexual health] clinic" (AusAID 2008). EGP's developing expertise on sexual health for the community was also highly valued by the emerging Pacific Sexual Diversity Network, a regional body that looked to develop relationships with representative organizations in Pacific Island countries whose work was focused on HIV/AIDS and STI prevention (UN AIDS Pacific Region 2009).

There is no doubt that this work was vital to sexual health education in the broader community. As many observers noted, it occurred in difficult, indeed often hostile circumstances, as the gay community remained the target of prejudice and harassment from the police and the military as well as from Fiji's Christian churches (Peni Moore, cited in AusAID 2008; Bondhyopadhyay 2007). Yet this increased focus on sexual health was also encouraged by changing political circumstances. The focus on sexual health risk seemed to depoliticize the status of same-sex sexuality, almost at the expense of a focus on human rights. This shift becomes more understandable, however, if we consider that by late 2006 Fiji was once again experiencing political turmoil as its citizens dealt with the fallout from another military coup and human rights activists became the targets of heavy-handed intimidation by the new regime.

Military leader Voreqe (Frank) Bainimarama justified his political takeover as an attempt to rid Fiji's politics of nationalism and corruption. At the time of the takeover, he also claimed he would keep Fiji's 1998 constitution intact. In practice, however, his regime's efforts to stabilize its hold on the country made a mockery of the constitution and its provisions in the area of democracy and human rights. Public opposition was quickly silenced, national media outlets were monitored, and the transmission of foreign news sources such as Radio Australia was locally blocked. Activists critical of the regime were detained, physically intimidated, and deprived of their rights to travel. Foreign reporters were deported, and scholars critical of the regime were accused of inciting resistance. There were even attempts to shut down the private blogs that had mushroomed after the coup in an attempt to provide alternative sites of critical political commentary (George 2008).

The military's intervention also seemed to reduce the political authority of the Methodist Church, which had exercised significant influence over the ethno-nationalist political elite during earlier periods. In February 2007, Methodist Church leaders had voiced strong criticism of the military intervention and released a report accusing the military of treason (Radio New Zealand International, February 6, 2007).[8] For this, they were treated like all others who had voiced criticism of the regime and were taken into the barracks for questioning, a move that signified in no uncertain terms that the new regime no longer privileged Methodist Church authority in Fiji's political affairs.[9]

However, the Methodist Church's reduced influence did not necessarily benefit gay rights activists. The military's oppressive efforts to silence its critics were strong reminders to all activist groups that the new regime was authoritarian and intolerant of criticism. This view was further reinforced in April 2009 when it finally abrogated the 1998 constitution, a move that allowed it to tighten its control over the country and hold off any challenge to its legality (Fraenkel 2009). This situation presented significant challenges to Fiji's vibrant activist community. For the best part of a decade they had drawn heavily on the discourse of rights to challenge state decision making in areas ranging from policy on gender equality to disputes over fair pay. Such strategies were well rehearsed and internationally validated (as was certainly the case for women activists operating in Fiji). Yet, in the post-coup era, and with the constitution in tatters, the political weight of this kind of activism was no longer certain and could potentially imperil activists.

Fiji's gay rights activists were of course equally in danger. Like many other members of civil society groups, those associated with EGP were now far less inclined to contest discriminatory treatment in ways that emphasized human rights. Instead, they invoked a discourse of risk without the partnering notion of rights that had formerly been an important advocacy tool. Even with the general taboo surrounding public discussion of questions related to sexual health in Fiji and the difficulties of raising issues such as HIV/AIDS transmission in the public domain, this new direction of advocacy was viewed in the post-coup context as a more prudent course of action, less likely to elicit a hostile reaction from the government. Within a highly constrained and regulated political environment, gay activists' focus on sexual health can therefore be seen as a successful strategy that opened up at least some political space for public debate on same-sex sexuality.

However, local factors alone do not wholly explain this changed advocacy strategy; a combination of transnational factors also prompted this shift. As I have already discussed, EGP had received significant levels of funding from external NGOs and national and regional institutions to develop sexual health programs. From 2001, HIV/AIDS prevention in the Pacific Islands became a high-priority area for development practitioners and aid providers, as international observers feared that the disease was on the verge of becoming a regional pandemic or, in "AIDS industry" parlance (Altman 1998), an "African-style" pandemic.[10] Indeed, it was in this period that the United Nations established a regional branch of UNAIDS to tackle the expected health problem and provide recommendations to the governments of the region. This international focus meant even more money flowing into the region for HIV/AIDS-related public health programs. This further encouraged groups such as EGP to make this issue a core theme of their public advocacy program.

A report prepared in 2009 by UNAIDS Pacific demonstrated the scale and impact of increased HIV/AIDS-related funding in this period. Between 2001 and 2007, external donors increased their funding five-fold; and in 2008 alone, over US$77 million was made available for HIV/AIDS-related work (UNAIDS Pacific Region 2009, 4). AusAID also increased aid dramatically, spending over A$60 million between 2002 and 2007 on HIV-related activities in PNG alone (Hammar 2007, 80). The Secretariat of the Pacific Community played a significant role in coordinating and managing the regional response to HIV/AIDS, becoming the principal recipient of funds distributed by the WHO's Global Fund for AIDS, Tuberculosis and Malaria, managing the Asian Development Bank's regional AIDS Program, and acting as regional secretariat for a policy program known as the Pacific Islands Regional Country Coordinating Mechanism. These expanding responsibilities explain why Secretariat staff working on STIs and HIV/AIDS also increased from two to twenty-six during this period (UNAIDS Pacific Region 2009, 61).

This new focus on the pandemic, however, was almost wholly externally driven. Ninety-five percent of HIV-related funding in the region flowed from outside (Hammar 2007, 81; UNAIDS Pacific Region 2009, 61). Pacific Islands states, with under-resourced bureaucracies and distracted by the "many and competing health and development issues facing the region" (UNAIDS Pacific Region, 2009, v), were in no position to match the enormous amount of international resources now being put into HIV/AIDS prevention. The impact of this externally driven response has been subject to criticism, both for the ways in which it has shaped understandings of the epidemic and for the policy responses to the challenge (Hammar 2007, 2008). As I will demonstrate in the final section of this chapter, the dramatic increase in AIDS-related funding also had an important impact on the evolution of the gay rights politics in Fiji.

Emulating "Industry" Frameworks of Risk

UNAIDS Pacific Region noted that an inordinate reliance on external funding threatened to undermine the "national- and community-level engagement" necessary for an "effective" response to the pandemic (2009, 4). It recommended that civil society groups increase their role in the delivery of these externally funded programs, stipulating that "community-based programs are best delivered by communities themselves" (2009, 6, 66). It emphasized the important role that civil society and gay groups could play through their peer networks in reaching out to "underground" gay, bisexual, and transgender communities (2009, 40).

The idea that closer engagement with civil society organizations would enhance the effectiveness of aid industry responses to HIV/AIDS in the Pacific found a more general analogue in discourses about good governance and development in the region. The Australian government, the region's largest provider of bilateral aid (von Strokirch 2003), had incorporated these principles into its development policy programs since 1997. That year, the Australian Minister for Foreign Affairs had argued that foreign aid should support NGOs aiming to increase local participation in governance (Larmour 1998, 1). By 2000, AusAID's policy on good governance emphasized the importance of a "strong and pluralistic civil society" supporting the values of "freedom of expression and association" (AusAID 2000, 7, 8). In line with this focus, AusAID's Pacific Regional Strategy, released in 2002, stated a commitment to strengthening local civil society capacity and an increased role for local organizations in community and humanitarian programs (AusAID 2002). Donors' efforts to develop strong working relationships with community-based organizations that might partner their efforts to combat HIV/AIDS can therefore be viewed as replicating policy directions in other development areas. This certainly helps explain increasing donor interest in the activities of the EGP.

This global shift also helps explains EGP's own local shift. On the one hand, reorienting the face of gay advocacy in Fiji away from a human rights focus allowed EGP to avoid intimidating attention from the military regime. On the other hand, this focus on sexual health dovetailed neatly with ambitions of international actors such as the World Health Organization and AusAID, which had large pools of funding available to local organizations. Yet increased access to funds was not enough to ensure EGP's long-term sustainability. Ultimately, donor enthusiasm for the organization's sexual health advocacy was not matched by a realistic understanding of the constraints that EGP staff faced in terms of their capacity both to manage the growing administrative demands that new funding relationships placed on the organization and to deliver sexual health programs (Noelene Naboulivou and Peni Moore, personal communication, February 2009). By early 2009, the ambitious agendas that external donors and EGP personnel had developed had all but vanished. EGP's ultimate failure to absorb and account for the funds that were flowing into the organization too heavily and too fast was a poignant reminder of the challenges posed by overin-flated aid regimes that, with the best of intentions, demand too much of local recipients.[11]

In early 2009, a new representative group for the gay community was formed in Fiji, named Men's Empowerment Network (MEN). One of the group's founding members, Atunaisa Dokonivalu, was a public health worker who had worked on sexual health campaigns with Marie Stopes International and Fiji's Ministry of Public Health.[12] Dokonivalu and oth-ers maintained a strong advocacy focus on sexual health promotion, build-ing on the work that had already been done by EGP. While this work was encouraged by international donors, it also seemed increasingly focused on the needs of gay men, a target population which MEN defined using the category "men who have sex with men" or MSM.

This term had gained international currency in the early 1980s as part of public health sexual behavior "surveillance" related to the intensification of global efforts to confront the epidemic. The original category, "men who have sex with men but do not identify as gay," later shortened to MSM, aimed to focus on sexual behavior rather than on sexual identity and was used to identify populations viewed as having an elevated risk of exposure to HIV/AIDS (Boellstorff 2011, 291, 294; Hammar 2008, 78; Seckinelgin 2009, 114). Increasingly, gay groups have used this term to describe their own subject position, but it has also been denounced as having a depoliti-cizing and medicalizing effect (Boellstorff 2011, 291). The allegation here is that the term "MSM" categorizes activity rather than defending "the right to be from a different sexuality" (Seckinelgin 2009, 114).

The term is also problematic from the point of view of lesbians, who have argued that the current global focus on HIV/AIDS related programs for gay men has drawn attention away from global debate on female same-sex sexuality. Lesbians who are unable to link their advocacy agenda with the global public heath focus complain increasingly of feeling "isolated and ignored" (Seckinelgin 2009, 115). This helps explain why, in Fiji, the "equal ground" that had provided gay men and lesbians a mutual space for advo-cacy in the previous ten years appeared by 2009 to have given way to a far more male-oriented advocacy focus. While the globalization of an MSM advocacy framework can be viewed as opening up political space for some local debate on same-sex sexuality, it is hardly inclusive. By the very choice of its acronym, MEN, the new advocacy group seemed to close down the possibility of a broader politics of solidarity between gay men and lesbians.

As a result, the visibility of gay women in Fiji was greatly reduced in comparison with previous decades, when the focus on advocacy had been more squarely focused on human rights and more closely linked with the political agendas promoted by Women's Action for Change.

As key spokesperson for MEN Fiji, Dokonivalu seemed unperturbed by the restricted focus of his organization and unaware that gay rights advocacy in Fiji partly owed its origins to the activities of women. He claimed that he was comfortable defining gay men as "MSMs" because the term avoided the more derogatory "sexual minorities" label that had been used in the past. But he also conceded that many in the local context saw this term "as a joke" (personal communication, October 2009), and that the explicit reference to sexuality was often greeted with a kind of sniggering humor.

On the other hand, the new organization found favor with international donors, who seemed to have confidence in its future prospects. Dokonivalu was conscious of the factors that had led to EGP's demise and pleaded with donor organizations to wait until MEN had become more established and managed to get "some runs on the board." The concern was that the organization would be asked to "run before it could walk" and thus might "fall over and ruin things" (personal communication, October 2009). This said, the new group received funding to conduct research on sexual behaviour among Fiji's gay men and hired a local demographic researcher with expertise in youth and sexuality. When I asked Dokonivalu about MEN's intention to take up a more politicized gay rights agenda, he responded that, while important, these types of issues "would have to wait," as the "time was not right" (personal communication, October 2009).

At the time, a religious group describing itself as the New Methodists was attracting considerable media attention for its homophobic pronouncements. The group's leader, pastor Atu Vulaono, had issued statements condemning homosexuals as being beyond "the kingdom of God" and defying "God's will" (Simpson 2009, 19). The group's conservative moral code also opposed the consumption of alcohol and kava. As the brother of the police commissioner, Vulaono had links to the military government and for a short while seemed to enjoy political favor when he was asked to lead a revival crusade in the police force. In this role, he sought to assist the force's fight against crime through evangelical preaching that insisted that "turning to Christ was the way to deal with crime" (McGeogh 2009). Although Dokonivalu dismissed pastor Vulaono as an "uneducated man" and a temporary threat, the rise of the New Methodists signaled once again that the political space available to gay activists in Fiji could be dually constrained. On the one hand, this space was shaped by authoritarian political actors who were uneasy with political action framed in the language of rights. On the other, the space was under attack from religious leaders who condemned behavior that they believed violated their interpretation of morality, a position that also elicited a degree of state support.

However, representatives of the gay community—albeit unwittingly—were perhaps contributing to this climate of intolerance through their focus on sexual health, which occasionally was given national media coverage in ways that helped reinforce its visibility in the public consciousness. The equation of homosexuality with risk suggested that there was an inevitable relationship between the two. No one could fault the underlying intention, but the constant invocation of disease seemed to replicate the negative imagery that religious leaders in Fiji were using to condemn those who articulated their homosexuality publicly.

Rather than providing a framework for tolerance and understanding, then, efforts to promote the sexual health message leaked into the public media and coincided with extremist religious rhetoric that condemned male homosexuality as immoral and pathological. As Lawrence Hammar argues in the PNG context, the language of risk is one that "meshes easily with the language of sin and retribution" (2008, 76). Without an accompanying emphasis on rights, risk advocacy provided ammunition for parochial voices in Fiji's civil society that had earlier demonized homosexuality as alien to Pacific societies.

Similar observations have been offered by Hakan Seckinelgin, who expresses concern about the broader ramifications of the MSM advocacy framework and its tendency to emphasize risk, disease, and pathology (2009, 115). He draws comparisons between mid-twentieth-century discourses that constructed homosexuality as a medical condition to be "cured" and the current MSM advocacy framework, which also emphasizes a medicalized perspective and gay men's vulnerability to STDs. Both perspectives seem to be inextricably bound to the idea that expressions of same-sex sexuality have an inevitable link to malady and are thus pathological.

Emphasizing MSMs' vulnerability to the "signal pandemic of the global here and now" (Comaroff 2007, 198) does little to encourage tolerance or acceptance. AIDS sufferers around the globe have been categorized in ways that emphasize "perversion and shame" (Comaroff 2007, 202). Gay people have been vilified for their alleged role in the transmission of this disease despite overwhelming evidence that the pandemic has much broader prevalence in heterosexual populations (Comaroff 2007, 202; Rao Gupta 2004). While some may wonder why it is that gay activists themselves have shown such willingness to identify with the MSM framework, the previous discussion has shown that in contexts like Fiji, activists can derive global prestige and also open up at least some degree of local space for recognition when they focus on sexual health vulnerabilities. But it also seems counterintuitive that this type of advocacy, so predominantly focused on sexual health risk, could ever expand the political space for meaningful public debate on tolerance of same-sex sexualities in Pacific societies. While it remains uncoupled from more general questions about gender, sexuality, and human rights, risk advocacy seems at best devoid of political potential. At worst, it may in fact further open up the political space that allows conservative agents to stigmatize and demonize gays.

Rights behind the Scenes: Some Hopeful Conclusions

Continued local political instability and international development priorities have, together, shaped the political space available to Fiji's gay activists and encouraged an altered advocacy focus that emphasizes risk over rights. This does not mean that gay activists have completely abandoned more politicized forms of advocacy. In late 2010, the Laucala Bay campus of the University of the South Pacific in Suva was animated by a new push to make gay rights resonate at the level of student politics and beyond. At this time, a lesbian, gay, bisexual, and transgender support group called Drodrolagi (the Fijian word for "rainbow") was formed on campus. The group, under Kris Prasad's coordination, aimed to develop a support network for Fiji's gay community and build upon the work of a group of the same name that had existed at USP some ten years earlier (Kris Prasad, personal communication, May 2011; Bale 2010). This new group aimed to repoliticize the gay rights agenda to challenge the sexual health advocacy route adopted by MEN and EGP. Prasad spoke of the need to reopen political debates on homosexuality in Fiji to ensure that gay people could not be "bullied back into the closet."

This meant that Drodrolagi promoted a defiant political agenda in addition to its more practical ambitions such as the creation of a safe campus environment for gay students and the promotion of the "safe sex" message (Bale 2010). The organization sought to promote increased understanding and to challenge the limited scenario whereby "tolerance of homosexuality" was achieved only when it was articulated as "trivia" or "spectacle," such as transgender beauty pageants (Kris Prasad, personal communication, May 2011). The group was attentive to questions of privilege and had made an effort to extend its membership beyond a university cohort to also reach out to other gay and transgender groups in a more marginal situation such as Suva's transgender sex-worker population.

An important first step in this direction was achieved in May 2011. On the International Day against Homophobia (IDAHO), Drodrolagi staged its first public forum at USP, which featured gay activist speakers and drew a crowd of about a hundred and fifty supporters from within the university and beyond. Importantly, many members of the broader advocacy community also attended. This was a strong show of support for the future of a repoliticized approach (Ashwin Raj, personal communication, May 2011).

Since 2006, other initiatives have also been taken "behind the scenes," indicating that the political objectives of earlier periods had not been altogether abandoned but were being pursued in different ways. This was evident in 2007, for example, when it came to EGP members' attention that the military had been verbally abusing, harassing, and detaining gay men. In addition to documenting this violence, EGP also sought to initiate a dialogue with members of Fiji's military and police to discuss the safety of the gay community.

Whereas Suva's gay rights activists once would have issued strong public statements criticizing this state of affairs, they now opted to raise their concerns less publicly, but also more directly, with the authorities concerned. EGP was not alone in adopting this strategy. Activists in a variety of organizations had begun to appreciate the importance of developing personal connections with the regime and opening up channels for private dialogue. On the surface, this suggests the emergence of a much more sedate advocacy environment than had been evident prior to the military takeover. This did not mean, however, that activists' political or social agendas had been snuffed out altogether, simply that change was pursued through alternative and less public pathways.

The success of this more veiled advocacy was made startlingly evident in March 2010, when the military government issued a decree decriminalizing homosexuality, thereby overturning a colonial-era sodomy statute that the police had used to charge gays even after the promulgation of the 1998 constitution (George 2008). By 2010, the military regime was no longer bound by the 1998 constitutional framework. It was, however, listening closely to the private advice of certain activists with whom it had established relationships of trust. And it was through these channels that human rights principles, and indeed the gay rights agenda, was apparently kept alive in Fiji's decision-making processes.

When this decree was made public, there was a predictable outcry from conservative elements, particularly the mainline churches.[13] Yet the fact that Fiji's gay population now enjoyed greater protection under the new decree also indicated that the effort to uncouple rights and risk had not been fatal to the movement. Clearly, this victory indicated that, "behind the scenes," members of the military regime were willing to be swayed by liberal rights-based arguments.

Even so, in its more public incarnation, gay advocacy has been dominated by sexual health concerns and its attendant focus on risk. At the same time, the authoritarian exercise of power through "government by decree" as it exists in Fiji has resulted in widespread and systematic violation of rights to critical free speech, as well as instances of political detention and intimidation, particularly of activists working on questions of gender equality (George 2013). In combination with the broader health-focused turn in gay advocacy, this suggests a significant narrowing of the political space available to those aiming to contest discrimination on the basis of sexual orientation. When we understand that this type of advocacy had been a significant feature of earlier campaigns around discrimination and sexuality in the 1990s, it becomes clear that, for the gay population in Fiji, the passing of time has brought little progress to celebrate.

Notes

1   On this point, Seckinelgin's (2009, 104) examination of how Indian *hijra*s are aiming to expand understandings of transgender identity is instructive. He shows how this population argues for a greater awareness of cultural understandings of sexuality as well as behavioral understandings.
2   Later sections of this chapter will show that Indo-Fijian gay rights activists have recently begun to play a stronger role in the movement.
3   I had first been exposed to this kind of initiative when I accompanied WAC to a workshop they conducted jointly with ex-prisoners and self-identifying homosexual men in Nadi in October 2002. The workshop was part of a broader program that aimed to increase the entrepreneurial skills of attendees so that they might be empowered to access micro-finance funds and start their

own businesses. In the first two days of the workshop, WAC ran confidence-building and group work sessions. WAC Coordinator Peni Moore conceded that, although the groups were unlikely allies, each existed at the margins of society in their own way and could learn from each other about the common challenges they faced in pursuing their ambitions for the future.

4   Members of women's groups such as the Fiji Women's Crisis Centre or the Fiji Women's Rights Movement enjoyed a high public profile at that time, but while they did not discriminate against homosexual women in any way, they also avoided raising questions about the status of homosexual women in the public domain for fear of becoming embroiled in controversies that would jeopardize their more mainstream political objectives, such as raising awareness about violence in the home or improving the legal and political standing of Fiji's women (personal communication, women activists 2002).

5   The *Turning the Tide* report (UNAIDS Pacific Region 2009) featured a personal narrative, first appearing in the *Fiji Times* on November 16, 2008, of a young openly gay man who had been exposed to violence in his home village, escaped to town, and turned to sex work to survive. His story reflected many of the themes explored in WAC's play.

6   Somewhat ironically, this political elite was not averse to invoking a discourse of indigenous rights when discussing how and why indigenous paramountcy should be protected in Fiji and often sought to defend its ethno-nationalist agenda in these terms.

7   As Sally Engle Merry has rightly shown (2006, 41), efforts to demonstrate a resonance between a globalized human rights discourse and local values can in many ways be viewed as weakening the transformative potential of gender advocacy, as concessions are made to local systems of customary or religious belief that may be discriminatory. This fear was often expressed to me personally by women activists in Fiji. Although they felt it was important to demonstrate the local resonance of their human rights claims, they also feared that this type of strategy conceded too much territory to Fiji's conservative nationalist political interests, and most particularly to the powerful Taukei Movement.

8   There was some contention within the church about who had authored the report and how it had been cleared for public release. Some senior church officials sought to distance themselves from the document when it became clear the military would respond harshly to this public criticism. See "Methodist Church Retracts Coup Criticism," Radio New Zealand International, February 6, 2007, located at Pacific Islands Report electronic media archive http://archives.pireport.org/archive/2007/february/02–07-fj01.htm.

9   For a recent report on military surveillance and restriction of Methodist Church activity, see "Overseas Church Responds to Crackdown on Fiji Methodists," Radio Australia, September 1, 2011, located at http://www

.radioaustralia.net.au/international/radio/onairhighlights/overseas-church
-respond-to-crackdown-on-fiji-methodists.

10   In the context of health and governance, observers of Pacific Island affairs tend
to draw comparisons with Africa in ways that negatively and problematically
stereotype both regions and promote the idea of impending crisis (Chappell
2005; Hammar 2007; Reilly 2000).

11   The Turning the Tide report states that, between 2003 and 2005, only 63% of
the available Global Fund Grant for HIV/AIDS-related projects in the region
was allocated and that even less of this money was actually utilized (UNAIDS
Pacific Region 2009, 68).

12   Marie Stopes International is a nongovernmental organization that offers
sexual and reproductive health programs around the globe. It has been working
in Fiji since 2004; http://www.mariestopes.org/Where_we_work/Countries/
Fiji_%C2%AC_Pacific.aspx.

13   See, for example, "Opposition to Fiji Decree Decriminalising Homosexuality,"
ABC Radio Australia, March 3, 2010, located at www.radioaustralia.net.au/
pacbeat/stories/201003/s2834881.htm.

References

Altman, Dennis. 1998. Globalization and the AIDS Industry. *Contemporary Politics*
4: 233–245.

———. 2001. *Global Sex*. Chicago: University of Chicago Press.

AusAID (Australian Agency for International Development). 2000. *Good Governance: Guiding Principles for Implementation*. Canberra: Commonwealth of
Australia.

———. 2002. *AusAID Pacific Regional Strategy 2002–2006*. Canberra: Commonwealth
of Australia.

———. 2008. *ANCP Pacific Cluster Evaluation Report*. Canberra: AusAID; http:
//www.ausaid.gov.au/Publications/Documents/ANCP_pacific.pdf   (accessed
May 12, 2010).

Bale, Tavai. 2010. Gay Students Bank Together. *Fiji Times*, September 29; http://
www.fijitimes.com/print.aspx?id=157058 (accessed July 15, 2011).

Besnier, Niko. 1994. Polynesian Gender Liminality through Time and Space. In
Third Sex, Third Gender: Beyond Sexual Dimorphism in Culture and History, ed.
Gilbert Herdt, pp. 285–328. New York: Zone.

Boellstorff, Tom. 2011. But Do Not Identify as Gay: A Proleptic Genealogy of the
MSM Category. *Cultural Anthropology* 26: 287–312.

Bondhyopadhyay, Aditya. 2007. *A Report on MSM in the Pacific Region: Information
Collected during the 1st Pacific MSM Network Meeting, Apia, Samoa, August 28–31*;
http://www.nfi.net/downloads/APCOM/Pacific%20MSM_APCOM_Aug07
.pdf (accessed May 2010).

Brown Thompson, Karen. 2002. Women's Rights Are Human Rights. In *Restructuring World Politics: Transnational Social Movements, Networks and Norms,* ed. Sanjeev Khagram et al., pp. 96–122. Minneapolis: University of Minnesota Press.

Chandra, Shobna. 2000. Same Sex Marriages Are Out in Fiji. *Fiji Times,* February 22; http://archives.pireport.org/archive/2000/february/02-23-05.htm (accessed August 12, 2012).

Chappell, David. 2005. "Africanization" in the Pacific: Blaming Others for Disorder in the Periphery? *Comparative Studies in Society and History* 47: 286–317.

Comaroff, Jean. 2007. Beyond Bare Life: AIDS, (Bio)Politics and the Neoliberal Order. *Public Culture* 19: 197–219.

Connell, R. W. 2005. *Masculinities.* 2nd ed. Sydney: Allen & Unwin.

Connors, J. 1996. NGOs and the Human Rights of Women at the United Nations. In *The Conscience of the World: The Influence of Non-Governmental Organisations in the UN System,* ed. Peter Willetts, pp. 147–180. London: C. Hurst.

Daily Post. 2000. Gays Warn Fiji PM Chaudhry over Constitution Change. April 11; http://archives.pireport.org/archive/2000/april/04-12-15.htm (accessed August 12, 2012).

———. 2001. Fiji Gays Live in Fear. July 5; http://archives.pireport.org/archive/2001/july/07-06-02.htm (accessed August 12, 2012).

Daurewa, Alisi. 2009. The Power of Fiji's Women. *Fiji Times,* May 1; http://archives.pireport.org.archive/2009/may/05–01-ft.htm (accessed August 15, 2012).

Denoon, Donald. 1997. New Economic Orders: Land, Labour and Dependency. In *The Cambridge History of the Pacific Islanders,* ed. Donald Denoon et al., pp. 218–252. Cambridge: Cambridge University Press.

Emde, Sina. 2005. Feared Rumours and Rumours of Fear: The Politicisation of Ethnicity during the Fiji Coup in May 2000. *Oceania* 75: 387–402.

Fiji Women's Rights Movement. 2001. *Balance: Newsletter of the Fiji Women's Rights Movement July–September.* Suva, Fiji: Fiji Women's Rights Movement.

Firth, Stewart. 1997. Colonial Administration and the Invention of the Native. In *The Cambridge History of the Pacific Islanders,* ed. Donald Denoon et al., pp. 253–288. Cambridge: Cambridge University Press.

Fraenkel, John. 2009. Silence after Abrogation of Fiji's 1997 Constitution. *East Asia Forum* April 28; http://www.eastasiaforum.org/2009/04/28/silence-after-abrogation-of-fijis-2007-constitution/#more-3941 (accessed June 2010).

George, Nicole. 2008. Contending Masculinities and the Limits of Tolerance: Sexual Minorities in Fiji. *The Contemporary Pacific* 20: 163–189.

———. 2009. Women's Organising in Fiji: Shifting Terrains of Transnational Engagement. In *Gender and Global Politics in the Asia-Pacific,* ed. Bina D'Costa and Katrina Lee Koo, pp. 175–193. New York: Palgrave-Macmillan.

———. 2012. *Situating Women: Gender Politics and Circumstance.* Canberra: ANU E press.

———. 2013. Lost in Translation: Gender Violence, Human Rights, and Women's Capabilities in Fiji. Under review.

Hammar, Lawrence. 2007. Epilogue: Homegrown in PNG—Rural Responses to HIV and AIDS. *Oceania* 77: 72–94.

———. 2008. Fear and Loathing in Papua New Guinea. In *Making Sense of AIDS: Culture, Sexuality, and Power in Melanesia*, ed. Richard Eves and Leslie Butt, pp. 60–79. Honolulu: University of Hawai'i Press.

Herdt, Gilbert. 1981. *Guardians of the Flutes: Idioms of Masculinity*. New York: McGraw-Hill.

———. 1984. Ritualized Homosexual Behavior in Male Cults of Melanesia, 1862–1983: An Introduction. In *Ritualized Homosexuality in Melanesia*, ed. Gilbert Herdt, pp. 1–18. Berkeley: University of California Press.

———. 1994. Introduction: Third Sexes and Third Genders. In *Third Sex, Third Gender: Beyond Sexual Dimorphism in Culture and History*, ed. Gilbert Herdt, pp. 21–81. New York: Zone.

———. 1997. *Same Sex, Different Culture*. Boulder, CO: Westview Press.

Jaquette, Jane. 2003. Feminism and the Challenges of the "Post-Cold War" World. *International Journal of Feminist Politics* 5: 331–354.

Joachim, Jutta. 1999. Shaping the Human Rights Agenda: The Case of Violence against Women. In *Gender Politics in Global Governance*, ed. Elisabeth Prügl and Mary K. Meyer, pp. 142–160. Lanham, MD: Rowman & Littlefield.

———. 2003. Framing Issues, Seizing Opportunities: The UN, NGOs and Women's Rights. *International Studies Quarterly* 47(2): 247–274.

Keck, Kathryn, and Margaret Sikkink. 1998. *Activists beyond Borders*. Ithaca, NY: Cornell University Press.

Kelly, John, and Martha Kaplan. 2001. *Represented Communities: Fiji and World Decolonization*. Chicago: University of Chicago Press.

Kollman, Kelly, and Matthew Waites. 2009. The Global Politics of Lesbian, Gay, Bisexual and Transgender Human Rights: An Introduction. *Contemporary Politics* 15: 1–17.

Lal, Brij. 2003. Fiji's Constitutional Conundrum. *The Round Table* 372: 671–685.

Larmour, Peter. 1998. Introduction. In *Governance and Reform in the South Pacific*, ed. Peter Larmour, pp. 1–20. Canberra: National Centre for Development Studies.

Massad, Joseph. 2002. Re-Orienting Desire: The Gay International and the Arab World. *Public Culture* 14: 361–385.

McGeough, Paul. 2009. An Unholy Alliance of Church and State. *Sydney Morning Herald*, November 29; http://www.smh.com.au/world/an-unholy-alliance-of-church-and-state-20091128-jxwu.html (accessed June 2010).

Merry, Sally Engle. 2006. Transnational Human Rights and Local Activism: Mapping the Middle. *American Anthropologist* 108: 38–51.

Nagalu, Maika. 2005. Fiji Methodists Plan March against Gays. *Fiji Sun,* June 23; http://archives.pireport.org/archive/2005/june/06-24-09.htm (accessed June 2010).

Naidu, Vijay. 2009. Headed for the Scrap-Heap of History? The Consequences of the Coup for the Fiji Labour Movement. In *The 2006 Military Takeover in Fiji: A Coup to End all Coups,* ed. Jon Fraenkel, Stewart Firth, and Brij V. Lal, pp. 237–251. Canberra: ANU E Press.

Otto, Di. 1996. Non-Governmental Organisations in the United Nations System: The Emerging Role of International Civil Society. *Human Rights Quarterly* 18: 107–141.

Pietilä, Hilkka, and Jeanne Vickers. 1996. *Making Women Matter: The Role of the United Nations.* London: Zed.

Puri, Jyoti. 2008. Gay Sexualities and Complicities: Rethinking the Global Gay. In *Gender and Globalization in Asia and the Pacific,* ed. Kathy Ferguson and Monique Mironesco, pp. 59–78. Honolulu: University of Hawai'i Press.

Radio Australia. 2005. *Fiji: Methodists Postpone Anti-gay March.* November 8; http://www.radioaustralia.net.au/international/radio/onairhighlights/methodists-postpone-antigay-march (accessed June 28, 2010).

Rao Gupta, Geeta. 2004. Globalization, Women and the HIV/AIDS Epidemic. *Peace Review* 16: 79–83.

Reilly, Benjamin. 2000. The Africanisation of the South Pacific. *Australian Journal of International Affairs* 54: 261–268.

Robertson, Robbie, and William Sutherland. 2001. *Government by the Gun: The Unfinished Business of Fiji's 2000 Coup.* Annandale, NSW: Pluto Press.

Schmidt, Joanna. 2003. Paradise Lost? Social Change and *Fa'afafine* in Samoa. *Current Sociology* 51: 417–432.

Scott, Owen. 2004. *Deep beyond the Reef: A True Story of Madness and Murder in the South Pacific.* Albany, New Zealand: Penguin.

Seckinelgin, Hakan. 2009. Global Activism and Sexualities in the Time of HIV/AIDS. *Contemporary Politics* 15: 103–118.

Simpson, Stanley. 2009. The Rise of the New Methodists. *Mai Life* (August), 18–22.

Stychin, Carl F. 2004. Same-Sex Sexualities and the Globalization of Human Rights Discourse. *McGill Law Journal* 49: 951–968.

Tabakaucoro, Adi Finau. 1987. Foreign Flower, Letters to the Editor. *Fiji Times,* May 22. Reproduced in Arlene Griffen, ed. 1997. *With Heart and Nerve and Sinew: Post-coup Writing from Fiji,* insert between pp. 228–229. Suva, Fiji: Christmas Club.

Tarte, Sandra. 2001. Melanesia in Review: Issues and Events: Fiji. *The Contemporary Pacific* 13: 529–541.

Tora, Luisa. 2006. Masculinity, Gender Identity and Fiji's LGBT Community;

http://www.isiswomen.org/index.php?option=com_content&view=article &id=269%3Amasculinity-gender-identityand-fijis-glbt-community&catid =66%3Aqueering-social-movements&Itemid=28 (accessed June 27, 2010).

UNAIDS Pacific Region. 2009. Turning the Tide: An OPEN Strategy for a Response to AIDS in the Pacific, Suva, Fiji: UNAIDS Pacific Region. http:// www.unaids.org/en/media/unaids/contentassets/dataimport/pub/report/ 2009/20091202_pacificcommission_en.pdf (accessed August 2011).

Von Strokirch, Karen. 2003. The Region in Review: International Issues and Events. *The Contemporary Pacific* 16: 370–381.

Vunileba, Amelia. 2006. Award Brings Joy to Carlos. *Fiji Times,* February 22, p. 5.

Waites, Matthew. 2009. Critique of "Sexual Orientation" and "Gender Identity" in Human Rights Discourse: Global Queer Politics beyond the Yogyakarta Principles. *Contemporary Politics* 15: 137–156.

West, Lois. 1999. The United Nations Women's Conferences and Feminist Politics. In *Gender Politics in Global Governance,* ed. Mary K. Meyer and Elisabeth Prügl, pp. 177–193. Lanham, MD: Rowman & Littlefield.

Women's Action for Change. 2000. *WAC Annual Report 2000.* Suva, Fiji: Women's Action for Change.

———. 2001. *WAC Annual Report 2001.* Suva, Fiji: Women's Action for Change.

———. 2002. *Just Like Any Man.* Play performed in schools in Suva and surrounding provinces in November/December.

———. 2005a. WAC Press Release, July 7. Posted to Pacific Women Information Network Internet Discussion List.

———. 2005b. WAC Press Release, September 2. Posted to Pacific Women Information Network Internet Discussion List.

Women's Action for Change: Sexual Minorities Project. 2005. Public statement, August 31. Posted to Pacific Women Information Network Internet Discussion List.

Zebly, Julia. 2011. UN Rights Council Passes First Gay Rights Resolution. *Jurist;* http://jurist.org/paperchase/2011/06/un-rights-council-passes-first-gay -rights-resolution.php (accessed August 2011).

CHAPTER 14

On the Edge of Understanding

Non-Heteronormative Sexuality in Papua New Guinea

Christine Stewart

Timothy and I are perched on the edge of a *hauswin,* a roofed, open-sided platform in the gardens of the Poro Sapot Project, an initiative of the international NGO Save the Children. The project is the only one of its kind in Papua New Guinea (PNG) to focus explicitly and specifically on what in the world of international organizations are termed "sex workers" and "MSM," or "men who have sex with men." It works through a system of outreach volunteers to provide HIV awareness, clinic facilities, and paralegal assistance for these sexual minorities. The *hauswin* serves as a drop-in center for the MSMs; the drop-in center for the other group, the female sex sellers (known by the internationally accepted acronym "FSW," or female sex workers) is hidden behind the main office building. There is shade and privacy here in the leafy tropical garden behind the high tin fence typical of residences and offices in Port Moresby, the capital of PNG, where personal security is always at a premium. Security is even more of a problem for this project, dealing as it does with two of PNG's most stigmatized groups, regarded as criminals by the laws of the state.

Timothy is a Papua New Guinea national in his thirties of "mixed" ethnic origins, like so many in Port Moresby today. He stays with a group of friends because he doesn't feel comfortable living with his family, although he sometimes goes to visit them. He earns his living by trawling higher-class hotel bars and clubs to sell sex, and lately has become a Poro Sapot Project outreach volunteer. He has recently returned from attending an international HIV conference as one of PNG's MSM representatives and is still struggling to understand all that he learned there:

> Sometimes we have tags on. I have a special kind of a tag; it's a permanent tag on me, meaning that I'm a *gay*, *gay* meaning that I have sex with men. Some *gays* may be a bisexual, they are playing both ways, or some sex can be insertive-receptive, they can give and they can take, but they come under one tag. When you open it, there are lots of colors coming up. Sometimes it's very hard to identify a straight man but he's a *gay* . . . it's a gender problem! We know where we are going to, we know how we are playing. But sometimes I confuse myself, I sometimes sit down and think, what am I?

Timothy is well aware of sexual needs, desires, and activities. But he is confused, not only about how to categorize his gender and sexual identity, but also about the need to categorize it at all.

Compared to many other Pacific Island societies, there is little scholarship on modern non-heteronormativities in PNG. Nor are there any conspicuously visible and identifiable groups of non-heteronormative people in mainstream PNG life, as there are farther east in the region (see Dolgoy, Kuwahara, Tcherkézoff, Presterudstuen, Good, this volume; also Morin 2008 for Papua, the Indonesian-ruled western half of the island of New Guinea). There is far less sense of shared identity than in other parts of the Pacific, and far more concealment of non-heteronormative character traits, due in part to the fact that such people attract a high level of stigma, discrimination, harassment, and violence. Sexual activity between two males is criminalized and may incur a prison sentence.

This chapter draws on PhD fieldwork focused mainly in Port Moresby in the mid- to late 2000s, work intended to gather evidence that could assist in moves at the time to reform the laws about consensual sex by describing the lived experiences of non-heteronormative people in contemporary PNG. In contrast to Greg Dvorak's (this volume) expressed misgivings about revealing issues of Marshallese sexuality, I undertook my research with the intention of eliciting untold stories in order to assist in the best way I knew: by providing evidence-based research for purposes of law reform. In contrast again to the easy-going and accepting attitude of Dvorak's Marshallese friends, I learned that attitudes and practices in

Papua New Guinea oblige non-heteronormative people to live in fear. "Nobody's going to be stupid enough to say 'I'm an active homosexual,' they'll be [thrown] in jail, they've got that hanging over them," said one sympathetic expatriate in despair.

HIV has been present in PNG for some twenty-five years, unlike in other Pacific countries that are only now beginning to grapple with the realities of the epidemic, and has thrown a spotlight on sexual behaviors. Early interventions were premised on alien concepts of individual autonomy and free choice, resulting in behavioral surveillance and research that focused on quantifying sexual encounters, HIV awareness indicators, and condom use. I wanted to broaden the field of inquiry to include people's lived experience of non-heteronormativity in relation to the wider community, and indeed my work (Stewart 2011) has uncovered a wealth of historical and ethnographic information that hitherto had remained uncollated and undocumented.

I started many of my interviews by stressing that my interests lay in understanding how my respondents described themselves, their processes of developing self-understanding, how they fit into the general society, and the worst experiences of discrimination they had encountered. The findings presented in this chapter are aimed at assisting the development of a more sophisticated and truly comparative analysis of non-heteronormative gender and sexuality in the Pacific.

Putting Names to Tags

Developing this analysis is not, however, a straightforward task. In PNG, two factors complicate it: the cultural diversity of the country, and the absence of any clearly identifiable category equivalent to the *fa'afāfine*, the *leitī*, and the *'akava'ine* of Polynesia. PNG is a country of proverbially extreme diversity—in languages (over eight hundred), ethnicities, cultural values, social structures, histories of colonial contact, speed and form of Christian conversion, unequal educational and economic opportunities, and exposure to the influences of modernity (Garap 2000, 162; Zimmer-Tamakoshi 1998, 1–2). The terrain is rugged, and the nation's capital has very few roads connecting it to rural communities, the bulk of which are accessible only on foot, by air, and, in the case of coastal and island communities, by coastal shipping and canoes. Over the last century, the capital has grown from a colonial administrative outpost to an overcrowded metropolis of highly mobile migrants from all parts of the country. The early migratory influxes of the 1950s and 1960s have now produced second and third generations of urban inhabitants who dwell in anything from high-rise luxury to settlement squalor, while maintaining varying degrees of connection to their rural origins.

PNG's cultural diversity is reflected in the range of non-heteronormative people and practices I found in my fieldwork. My respondents were mainly Papua New Guinean nationals, aged anywhere from their early twenties to sixties, originating from all over the country and a plethora of different cultural settings. Some were of "mixed" ethnicity, meaning that their parents came from different ethnic groups within the country. Some grew up in town; others came straight from the village to the city. Some scraped a living selling imported Chinese trade goods, cigarettes, betel nut, lollies, and ice blocks, and topped up their meager earnings by selling sex; others with higher levels of education found work in fast-food outlets, hotels, bars, and restaurants; yet others were tertiary-educated professionals. Some had been cast out of home as teenagers; others still lived in the parental home in situations of varying degrees of acceptance by parents and siblings; yet others found solidarity by sharing with others and forming surrogate families. One or two were married and lived with their wives and children. Some were in long-term relationships, but most were not; some had sex only with other males, some were bisexual; some had both receptive and insertive sex; many sold sex to both males and females (for quantitative details, see Kelly et al. 2011). I also talked with several homosexual expatriates who had come to work in various capacities in the country, in government, business, or NGOs, often for considerable periods of time.

The absence of clearly defined categories of non-heteronormativity in PNG also has profound consequences for understanding the formation of sexual identities. Most of my respondents came to awareness of their sexuality in isolation from others ("I thought I was the only one in the world," one confessed to me), and they had few, if any, public role models or behavioral formats that could serve as reference points. The effect of this diversity and the absence of existing forms of categorization are reflected in the terminological confusion Timothy expressed. He could not put a name to the "tag," let alone the different "colors" under the tag. The internationally recognized terminology "men who have sex with men" (UNAIDS 2011) and its acronym MSM describe behavior, not identity, even though they are becoming accepted in many countries and cultures as an identity appellation (Boellstorff 2011). The term "encompasses a range of identities, networks, behaviors and collectivities, and includes sexual behaviors of those who do not self-identify as practicing sex between males at all" (the definition used at the "Risks and Responsibilities Male Sexual Health and HIV in Asia and the Pacific" International Consultation, New Delhi, India, September 23–26, 2006, and set out in *Pukaar* 56 [January 2007]: 15). It has been imported into PNG as part of HIV-prevention discourse and is most commonly used in NGO settings (Hershey 2008). But it has encountered a measure of disfavor, even where ascribed to behavior rather than identity. Various writers have noted the limitations inherent in the term in cultures where sexual practices may include sex with both men and women, whether commercial or otherwise (Kelly et al. 2011; Maibani-Michie and Yeka 2005; Reid 2010; and see Jenkins 2006 and Pisani 2008, 50–51 for the impossibilities of putting sexual behavior "into boxes"). The terms "MSM" and "homosexual," derived from the global lexicon, are not popular with most non-heteronormative men in PNG, where they are almost universally rejected unless they are being deployed for purposes of job seeking, grant funding, or currying favor with aid workers.

Asking my respondents how they would describe themselves proved to be a good opening gambit in interviews, eliciting many different responses and occasional lengthy discussions. The same terms were even used in very different ways, demonstrating how "on the edge" is the experience of being non-heteronormative in PNG. Many who prefer to conceal their gender identity in public described themselves to me as *gay*. Those who identify as what I will term "transgender"—that is, as "male-bodied, femininity-performing, men-desiring subjects" (Elliston, this volume)—are constantly inventing a whole complex system of terms for themselves. The term *flower* was sometimes used, and the difference between *closed flowers* (those not obviously effeminate) and *open flowers* (those who are obviously effeminate in certain contexts) was carefully explained to me. Some individuals suggested that "*gay* means all of us," although there was some confusion over whether a *closed flower* was the same as a *gay*. A popular local term for transgender or *open flowers* at one time during my fieldwork was *palopa,* a neologism derived from "Jennifer Lopez." *Sister-girl,* a term that I surmise has been borrowed from across the Torres Strait, was initially used for *open flowers* and has recently begun to displace *palopa*. Others rejected categorization altogether. Colin, an NGO outreach worker in his thirties, doesn't like to call himself anything at all, saying he just likes "going out" with "other men" (presumably men who desire him) rather than with women.

Most non-heteronormative Papua New Guineans are not interested in public displays of their sexuality. They are far more concerned with concealing their gender identities and sexual practices from the outside world and operating within their closed social circles. They are accustomed to hiding and dissembling. They are generally spatially dispersed and adjust their behavior to the needs of each situation in which they find themselves, as Timothy explained: "If a street man [a stranger in the street] come and talk to me, I can't admit to him what I am, I cannot tell him what I face, with my family, or with the public, with the community that I live in. It is something that is confined in me, unless I find somebody who's got the same understanding as me, then I can tell what I am."

In this chapter, I use the italicized terms *"gay"* to refer to non-heteronormative males and *"palopa"* when describing those who display openly effeminate behavior. *Gay* is not simply a Western gay with a foreign accent: it is a subject position with its own dynamics, albeit a recently adopted term (Boellstorff 2003, 22). In PNG, terms such as *"she," "girl,"* and *"sister"* are often used by *gays* and *palopas* to refer to each other, and many, borrowing from practice overseas, have assumed female nicknames, which they use among themselves in e-mails, text messages, and phone calls. But here I will stay with the pronoun "he" in deference to my respondents' attempts to maintain in public an appearance of heteronormative masculinity. In this regard, it should also be noted that most PNG languages, whether Austronesian or Papuan, do not have distinct masculine and feminine pronouns.

Culture and Change

Just as "homosexual" behavior is most likely to occur everywhere (e.g., Jenkins 2004; Murray 1992; Wilets 1994–1995, 5), it also appears to be widespread throughout PNG (NSSRT and Jenkins 1994, 98–101). Analyzing newspaper reports and judicial casebooks covering the years from 1948 to 1953, historian Robert Aldrich (2003, 246, 258) found abundant evidence from all over the country of

a range of homosexual arrangements and behaviors . . . sex conceded after intimidation and sex given for money, sex between New Guineans and between Europeans and New Guineans, as well as between Europeans, sex on the beach, in a car and in a house, sex that may have been "situational" among laborers without women companions, but also sex that fell into a regular pattern of cruising to find partners and continuing links between homosexuals, sex between men conscious of their homosexual desires or considered repeat offenders by the authorities and between men who said homosexuality was their "fashion." And away from European eyes flourished homosexual practices as part of initiation rites. Colonial law banned homosexual acts, while administrators and clerics worried about vice and tried to combat "native savagery" and European immorality, but, in the tropical shadows, "sodomy" flourished.

This cultural and sexual diversity means that it is well-nigh impossible to make any generalizations about sexual practices in PNG. In the huge body of ethnographic literature, one finds scattered descriptions of a range of gender relations and gendered cultural practices (e.g., Hogbin 1946, 1963; Goodale 1980; Knauft 1986, 1999; Lutkehaus and Roscoe 1995; Wardlow 2006). Some ethnographies (Herdt 1984, 1987, 1992; Knauft 1987) discuss what was originally termed "ritualized homosexuality," although these practices (the "initiation rites" to which Aldrich refers above) are less about erotic desire than male initiation rituals designed to ensure that an innate male essence, tenuous in childhood, is enhanced through the uptake, orally or anally, of adult male semen and thereby "grown" into adult masculinity (Elliston 1995; see also NSRRT and Jenkins 1994, 99–101; Knauft 1993).

Gilbert Herdt's later work (1997) challenged the Western ideology of a fixed sexual orientation, showing that cultural changes have altered sexual practices and perceptions. These changes have been largely brought about by the social norms that underpinned the introduced legal system and those of the Christian mission endeavor and have led to an almost total disavowal of such traditional sexual practices as "ritual homosexuality" (see also Knauft 2003). By a process similar to that noted by Tom Boellstorff for Indonesian *gays* (2003) and Peter Jackson for Thai *kathoey* (1997, 2000), PNG *gays* base their newfound identities on those they have drawn from global modernity and have given a local inflection. Categories of sexual identity and practice have often been altered in recent decades in the wake of advancing global trends, sometimes obliterating previous forms. In PNG, the Gebusi of Western Province, for example, have reconfigured their sexual practices so that, in a single generation, they completely abandoned openly proclaimed male homoeroticism in favor of "modern" heteronormativity (Knauft 2003; see also Herdt 2012 for changes in Sambia sexual culture).

Gay Today

The rupture of modernity was evident in many of my respondents' recollections of childhood isolation. An airline worker in his thirties, who had moved away from his home village in an island province because of persecution for his girlish behavior, had thought he was "the only one in the world" until he came to Port Moresby and found others like himself. Others felt compelled to conceal an interest in women's clothing and girls' sports as they were growing up—from their families, their classmates, their friends. In contrast, in various parts of the country, other individuals spoke of family acceptance of their effeminacy. One young respondent of mixed coastal and Highlands parentage told me of his Highlands aunties' amused indulgence of his childhood predilection for putting flowers in his hair and dancing "hula-style"; another from a coastal area recalled how his mother had so wanted a girl child after several sons that she insisted for many years on dressing him in a grass skirt. Some recollected how they were obliged by their mothers to fetch firewood and water, mind the babies, wash the dishes, and perform other "girls' tasks."

However, unlike in other parts of the Pacific, my respondents did not refer to labor practices as a primary sign of gender identification. Rather, their first indication was usually an awareness of a preference for socializing and playing sports with girls while failing to feel any erotic interest in them. Occasionally, an early homoerotic experience was recalled. Sometimes these first sexual experiences were pleasant, sometimes not; and sometimes they took place during childhood. Victor, a tertiary-educated human rights activist from a provincial village in the Islands region, at age ten was bribed by a local man to perform oral sex in the bushes. Oscar, from the Gulf province in the Southern region, met his "white man" boyfriend in a Port Moresby nightclub at age thirteen and established a loving long-term relationship, which only ended when the expatriate's work contract expired and he had to leave the country. "We cried and cried," Oscar confessed.

Moving to town and the chance discovery of "sisters" and networks helped to establish and legitimize identity. Port Moresby is not so large that like-minded people cannot be located—there they find others and form asexual friendships and pseudo-families. Overall, though, it is dangerous to be openly effeminate anywhere in PNG. There are good reasons for remaining secretive and engaging in concealing tactics. Stigmatization and shaming treatments occur frequently. Timothy for example, is afraid to speak up in public, fearing that his girlish voice may betray him and elicit insults: "They can tell you right in front of you: you're a receiver from the anals, you're a sucker. I don't open my mouth; once I open my mouth, that's the time when you are worse. You try and open your mouth, then you'll be in the shark's mouth [in trouble]." One of Timothy's colleagues, who also sells sex, added: "In PNG, it's a very shameful act that we are going through. In our society, men, they do practice it. They like sleeping with men but they don't want it to be known or being publicized. We are very creative and flexible, better than the ladies, even the wife too. Many of our clients will say: you are better than my wife."

Coping strategies must be developed. "Passing" is common. A young *palopa* in group discussion explained: "Change your way of walking and talking. What we do, we try to train ourselves to carry ourselves in public. We have calling codes, hallo, *koti,* things like that. We do sign languages, things like that. If 'she' says yes, if you feel that it is okay, you can 'break your wrist' [make a limp-wrist gesture of effeminacy]. If it feels okay."

In particular, the shame visited on families makes any admission regarding sexuality highly problematic. Mothers and sisters are usually more accepting than fathers and brothers, though this is not always the case. A young man in his twenties from a village near Port Moresby described how he could not come out to his mother, preferring instead to tell a close female cousin. Another, from a different region, told of his brother's acceptance; yet another, again from another part of the country, of furious rejection by his sisters. Teenagers have been thrown out of their homes. Those who stay and maintain the pretence of being heterosexual are frequently pressured into marriage—sometimes these relationships are successful, but more often they are not.

Many *gays* face problems in employment or study. Henry, from the Momase region of the mainland north coast, related how he was seduced for the first time at university. Then his seducer beat him, proceeded to blackmail him, and induced other students to abuse him. Appeals to the student director and student counselor only provoked further harassment, and in the end Henry dropped out of university altogether. In the workplace, many *gays* feel they are constantly under threat of dismissal, often on some minor pretext when it is really their sexuality that is the issue. Or their promotion is blocked. A high-ranking public servant from Central Province, now in his fifties, is sure he was prevented from attaining department-head status on these grounds. Hospital and clinic staff are notorious for their discrimination against sexual minorities, for their propensity to preach and blame, for their negative conceptualizations of non-heteronormativity, and for an inability or unwillingness to observe principles of patient confidentiality.

Blackmail of non-heteronormative individuals is common, either as an opportunistic attempt to make a fast buck or as part of an organized gang enterprise. Blackmailers threaten exposure to police or family, or simply resort to violence. Moneyed professionals are the targets—both nationals who appear to be well-off and expatriates, who are always assumed to be rich. They suffer intimidation, with police (either genuine or masquerading) involved to apply pressure, as well as housebreaking and violence, even abduction and kidnapping. To avoid blackmail, many professional national *gays* dress down outside the workplace and pretend to be poor and uneducated in public during leisure hours. Expatriate *gays* use their influence and connections, tough it out, or leave the country.

Furthermore, for *gays,* the exposure of their sexual identity can elicit more than shame and discrimination. Being obviously non-heteronormative in PNG can be dangerous. For example, a group of *palopas* related to me the story of a shopping expedition for drag show outfits in Port Moresby. They pulled their caps down low to conceal their plucked eyebrows, wore loose mannish clothing so they would not be recognized—all except for one, who insisted on wearing hair extensions and acting in an effeminate way. Sure enough, they were spotted in a mall by some "street kids" and a wild and desperate chase began, up and down stairs and elevators, through the underground car park, until they all managed to bundle into a cab and escape.

These *palopas* were lucky. Violence, brutal gang rape, even murder are not unknown, and the police are often implicated as perpetrators of the violence. One respondent even declared that he would never again associate with any of the disciplined forces after he was picked up in a bar by a policeman and then gang-raped nearly to death in the police barracks. One of the most horrific stories I heard came from Victor, a *gay* activist involved in awareness and intervention programs relating to drugs and alcohol, gender, human rights, child abuse, and HIV (Stewart 2010). Although he tried to conceal his *gay* identity, he could not escape media attention and suffered a torrent of abuse from strangers. Following a punitive gang rape (he was ambushed at his front gate one night), he fled the country. He felt he had no other choice. He did not trust the police to help him or hospital and clinic staff to maintain confidentiality, and the shame he had brought on his family was more than he could bear. Even if he had overcome his fears, even if arrests had been made, he would have been in great danger from the friends and relatives of the youths who raped him. The PNG payback system would ensure that, in retaliation for the arrests, he would be harmed once again.

Given these high levels of stigma, discrimination, and abuse, safe spaces for non-heteronormative men are highly valued. Port Moresby, and possibly other major towns in PNG, provide space and opportunity for them to find like-minded individuals, to locate safe living spaces, and to take steps toward creating surrogate families. The village of Hanuabada on the edge of Port Moresby's downtown harbor is one such safe space. The township was established adjacent to the original village and quickly absorbed the villagers—first as domestic servants, then in other forms of employment, including the provision of paid sex by both males and females, initially to colonists and later to all the city's inhabitants. Hanuabada has developed a reputation as the place to go to "hunt" for sex, a feature much deplored by its village leaders (Oram 1976; Wolfers 1975). Today, Hanuabada is one of the very few places in or around Port Moresby where *gays* from all parts of the country can find refuge and openly be "themselves," wearing miniskirts, blouses, hair extensions, earrings, and makeup, manifesting all the appurtenances of the glamour of queer modernity (compare Dolgoy, this volume). Following customary trends common throughout PNG, outsiders received into this village are anchored by "associative kinship" family structures (compare Ikeda, this volume). A childless couple may take in some half-dozen *flowers* who do the housework and contribute to household expenses by selling sex. Thursdays, Fridays, and Saturdays, when clients arrive from town flush with cash from their pay packets, are good nights for business. Selling sex is a normalized way to earn a living in today's PNG (Kelly et al. 2011).

Although there are no specifically "gay" bars in PNG, certain bars do cater to non-heteronormative clientele. Although caution must be exercised, as it must all over town in public spaces, some bars and nightclubs are considered to be good pick-up places, where one can sit quietly with a glass of iced water, waiting for an approach to be made. A few clubs, most of which are Asian-owned, provide venues for the increasingly popular drag shows. These shows emerged from an initiative started in the late 1990s by Moses Tau, a *gay* pop singer and rights activist from a Motuan village near Port Moresby. Moses has become hugely popular for his "Pacific-style" songs and the accompanying video clips where he dresses in island-style "drag" costumes he has designed. As with all locally produced PNG music, these are frequently played on radio and TV throughout the country and distributed on DVD (Tau 1999, 2005; and for further description, see Stewart 2011).

Aged in his thirties at the time, Moses braved vociferous condemnation by many, particularly his own local council elders, to make a high-profile appearance as the "Pacific Queen" in the Sydney Mardi Gras parade of 2001, after which he returned to start up Port Moresby's drag competitions. Word spread rapidly, "sisters" brought "sisters," and for many they became a revelatory and exhilarating experience. Clubs that once catered only to male–female sexual networking now dedicate specific nights for the drag shows. Attendees include many *gay* spectators as well as the usual club membership, both heterosexual and not. Contestants compete in complex programs of "categories" (traditional, sport, casual, dance, evening wear, and so on) with heats, semifinals, and finals. As with drag shows elsewhere in the Pacific (Besnier 2002, 535), competitors are predominantly lower-class, poor, and young, although this is not always so—even tertiary-educated *gays* are known to have competed. Performance is borrowed directly from Western beauty contests and involves dance routines, both Western disco-style and "traditional," and lip-synching to popular Western songs. All contestants, win or lose, receive at least a small payment for participating in each heat, and winners receive significant cash prizes.

Good security at these events is essential. Gangs of youths and even carloads of police officers lie in wait for departing *gays,* so managements provide transport home for contestants. Spectators too must be very careful, but this goes for any nighttime activity in the city. Security issues notwithstanding, drag shows are definitely good for business and good for the contestants as well, providing at least some measure of remuneration. They have become a critical factor, in Port Moresby at least, for assisting in much needed confidence building for non-heteronormative individuals, providing a space for self-expression and a means for the indigent to earn a little cash.

Not all *gays* participate, though. The imprecise boundaries of PNG non-heteronormative categorization become strikingly evident at these events. Some who described themselves as *gay* claimed to be unable to participate (except as judges or spectators) because, I was told, "our bodies are not right," while others who to my eye appeared similarly "not right" told proudly of their prize-winning competition performances.

Islands of Difference

Medical anthropologist Carol Jenkins makes the point that, although many cultures have not been openly hostile or abusive toward people of non-mainstream sexuality and gendering, "the sum impact of Western values on indigenous homosexualities has been negative" (Jenkins 2004, 11). She joins James Wilets (1994–1995, 5–6) in attributing this to the effects of Western colonialism and the negative attitude to sexuality of Judeo-Christian and Islamic religions. In PNG, colonialism introduced the Anglo-Australian common-law system, along with its criminalization of male–male sexual practices, and the Christianity of many denominations has taken firm hold nationwide over more than a century. Both these dynamics, however, are present to some degree in other Pacific nations (Farran, this volume), begging the question as to why the effects of discrimination seem to be more extreme in PNG.

Sex between adult males is criminalized in PNG's English-derived common-law system through two main offenses, one of committing or permitting "an act of gross indecency with another male person" (Section 212 of the *Criminal Code:* "Indecent Practices between Males") and another of anal penetration, irrespective of the gender of the recipient (Section 210 of the *Criminal Code:* "Unnatural Offences"). The latter offense was originally worded "carnal knowledge of any person against the order of nature," but in 2002 this archaic terminology was replaced by the wording "sexually penetrates any person against the order of nature." The courts have always interpreted this offense as referring to anal penetration, and it is commonly known as the "sodomy offence." It is considerably more serious than the former offense and carries a maximum penalty of fourteen years' of imprisonment. Consent is immaterial, and actual coercion or real fear must be proven to mount a successful defense. A long string of cases from all over the country dealing with male rape and sex with boys of all ages has dominated PNG's legal scene from early colonial times, to the point where the term "sodomy" is applied pejoratively to any form of sex between males, irrespective of age and questions of consent or force (some of these cases are discussed in detail in Stewart 2008; see also Aldrich 2003). This situation has had the unfortunate effect of encouraging community antipathy, which in turn makes reform initiatives increasingly difficult.

There may be differences between jurisdictions in the Pacific Islands in the extent and magnitude of implementation of these laws, but what is evident is that homosexuality laws in PNG have always been strongly enforced. As Aldrich noted, the colonial administration disapproved strongly of homosexual "vice" from the earliest days of contact and prosecuted cases vigorously. The *British New Guinea Annual Report* of 1888, for example, contains a reference from government officer Hugh Milman regarding the village of Mowat or Mowatta, on the coast of what was then the remote Western District, to the effect that a newly appointed "chief" had been urged to "put down the hideous practice of sodomy" almost openly included in initiation ceremonies (Queensland Government 1889, 16–17; see also Beardmore 1890, 464). Gradually, the development of the colonial economy promoted the mass migration of people from villages to distant areas as recruits for plantations, mines, and portage work. A large and constantly changing contingent of young and mainly unmarried village men a long way from home, was housed together in barracks called "labor lines," while women remained in the village. Their men were returned to them after a fixed period of indenture in order to provide the next generation of laborers and to ensure some measure of social continuity (Murray 1925, 112–113; Rowley 1966, 103–104, 109). One study noted the high incidence of sodomy "when large numbers of natives are herded together on plantations and so on away from their women and the normal outlet for their sexual energies" and access to local village women severely restricted by the villagers themselves, but considered it a "nontraditional" product of an abnormal lifestyle (Todd 1934–1935; see also Roberts 1928; Reed 1943, 220–221; Hogbin 1951, 190–191, 1963, 97–98; Worsley 1970; Hiery 1997). Under the Australian administration throughout the colonial period, cases were prosecuted vigorously and penalties were harsh (Aldrich 2003, 247–257; Stewart 2008).

After independence in 1975, several successful initiatives aimed at the reform of the criminal law were introduced—for example, the abolition of the Native Regulations and the replacement of the police offenses ordinances with a new *Summary Offences Act*. But there was no reform to the sodomy laws. Court records for the 1990s include between two and six cases per year for acts of "sodomy," but do not indicate whether they involved consensual sex, forced sex, or sex with minors. In 1996, a clear case of consensual sex in private between male adults resulted in a prison sentence of two years for the national involved, while his expatriate partner fled the country (Stewart 2011). Although details of the offense of "sodomy" are not well understood in *gay* circles in Port Moresby (even a *gay* law graduate I talked with failed to grasp some of the finer points), it is well-known that a crime is involved and that all *gays* are in danger of being charged with committing these offenses. The fact of criminalization also means that unscrupulous people are aware that they can use the threat of police involvement or prosecution to extort money.

Christianity arrived in the Pacific Islands as part of the colonization process, often before the establishment of formal colonial administration. No single church predominates in PNG. Rather, early missionization in various parts of the country saw Catholicism and various Protestant denominations alienate land and convert people. Colonial attempts to demarcate separate spheres of influence for different churches and restrict the entry of new missionaries were undone at independence by constitutional guarantees of freedom of religion and freedom of movement throughout the country for all citizens. In keeping with global trends, recent times have seen a significant spread of charismatic and fundamentalist forms of Christianity, while sects of the mainline churches have evinced strong evangelical tendencies (Gibbs 2002, 16; Jorgensen 2005, 445). A large part of their ideology consists of a fundamentalist insistence on the sinfulness of "deviant" sexual behavior such as prostitution and "sodomy." This has greatly hampered decriminalization initiatives. PNG's only female politician in the 2007–2012 National Parliament, Dame Carol Kidu, Minister for Community Development and champion of the movement for the decriminalization of sex work and sodomy, was roundly castigated in the press in 2010 for her efforts, which were said to be "morally wrong" and "against Christianity." She was told that she should "say sorry to God and the people of PNG over her moves" (various articles in *The National* and *Post-Courier* daily newspapers, November 8–10, 2010).

Worlds of Difference

Why do social perceptions and practices in PNG differ so markedly from those in the other Pacific Island countries documented in this volume? There are several reasons. First, the implementation of criminal law and the promulgation of Christian fundamentalist opposition to non-heteronormative sex are more vigorous in PNG than in other countries of the region. While laws about sex between men are similar throughout the English-speaking Pacific, levels of observance may vary. In some parts of the Pacific, due to the incorporation of these laws into formal legal systems, "sexual and gender diversity are . . . now viewed as antithetical to traditional Pacific cultural practices" (Human Rights Watch 2008; Pacific Sexual Diversity Network and AIDS Council of New South Wales 2009). PNG has a colonial and post-independence history of prosecuting acts of non-heteronormative sex, with little regard for the circumstances. An argument often advanced is that proscriptive laws when not enforced have no effect and are therefore not harmful. But research has shown that, in fact, decriminalization does bring about some measure of improvement in social attitudes, even where the laws have rarely been enforced (Farran, this volume; Goodman 2001). However, mere legal tolerance does not equate with social acceptance (Weeks 1989). The most that can be said for the apparent differences among Pacific Island countries in the level of tolerance of a criminal sexual act is that the presence of an offense on the statute book may color social attitudes, but this does not go far enough in explaining differences between countries in the attitudes of their people toward that offense. Indeed, even in comparatively tolerant Pacific countries, the criminal laws are viewed as a threat to progress toward reducing discrimination (Tonga Leitis' Association 2010).

The same issues may be argued in relation to Pacific Christianities. As the Pacific Sexual Diversity Network and AIDS Council of New South Wales (2009) point out: "Criminal laws around sexual behaviour and gender identity and expression were not the only colonial imports which have had a significant impact on the lives of MSM and transgenders in the Pacific. Religious doctrine and beliefs around sexuality and gender have also played, and continue to play, a central role in shaping the experiences of MSM and transgenders." The growth of fundamentalist Christianities is leading to increasing stigma being attached to non-heteronormative people throughout the Pacific. Biblical teachings, for example, may be invoked to condemn them (ABC Radio Pacific Beat 2005). In a number of denominations, ideologies in the name of Christianity have spread through the region, adapting, naturalizing, and melding with the spirituality of local cultures.

A second significant difference between PNG and other Pacific Island societies lies in the fact that PNG is a collection of vastly diverse communities thrown together by geography and the politics of distant metropoles rather than by any strong internal sense of traditional community. By contrast to other Pacific Island countries, which have only a few if any different culture groups and languages, Papua New Guinea has over eight hundred (if one assumes a language to correspond to a cultural grouping, which it often does). There is far less internal social cohesion, little sense of a united national identity, and a high level of interethnic suspicion and hostility. PNG's "culture of violence" is related to this cultural fragmentation—communities are not so much disrupted as protected if violence is directed against "foreigners" who may live no farther away than the next valley. The role of the administration in the early days of colonialism was one of "pacification" of the frontier, often by violent means. The patrolling *kiap,* as district and patrol officers were called, was accompanied and aided in his endeavors by an armed native constabulary, who were often selected for their warrior-like qualities traditional in their communities of origin. Police on patrol, and even on the government station, were required to repel attacks and enforce the colonial presence, and to do this they were entitled to use armed force, often against people with whom they had no prior relationship and whom they regarded as alien—although according to the colonists they were all "Melanesian" (Dinnen 1998, 260; Gammage 1996, 162, 168–169; Jinks, Biskup, and Nelson 1973, 61–64; Nelson 1982, 52–56).

This quasi-militaristic tradition has left its legacy in the retributive and violent nature of policing today. Police readily enact punitive violence on any person whom they perceive as threatening standards of PNG masculinities, which stress physical strength and a propensity for violence (Macintyre 2008). Their own sense of impunity is heightened by the knowledge that those whom they are persecuting are in some way "criminals," even if the niceties of the crime are not well understood. And community members, particularly males who feel the need to protect their own masculinity and that of their kinsmen (Jenkins 1996, 199–200), willingly join in this project of social cleansing, its object being to rid the community of those who are both criminal and deviant.

A third difference resides in the varying constructions by European colonizers of islanders as sexualized beings, which viewed Polynesians and Micronesians positively and Melanesians negatively, as primitive and barbaric (see Alexeyeff and Besnier, this volume). Regardless of whether these romanticized constructions privileged heteronormativity, to the eye so inclined the Melanesian male embodied primitive savagery and a propensity to engage in bestial acts that included homoerotic practices (Aldrich 2003, 246–247, 272).

A final difference, but a highly significant one, is HIV. Other Pacific Island countries are only now beginning to confront the reality of the epidemic, and are able to do so with the benefit of management practices that include drug therapy and a vastly improved store of wisdom in management and prevention techniques. PNG, where HIV was first detected in the Pacific Islands in 1987, now has the region's largest epidemic, with heterosexual sex being the dominant mode of transmission. This contrasts with smaller Pacific Island countries, where transmission mainly occurs through unprotected sex between men (UNAIDS 2010). Efforts toward managing HIV have been supported in these smaller countries by AIDS organizations based in the regional metropoles, principally Australia and New Zealand, which have themselves been assisted in epidemic management by gay organizations (Ballard 1998; see also George, this volume). In the smaller Pacific Island countries, these efforts emphasize the need to end discrimination and promote equality of non-heteronormative people. In PNG, in contrast, the country has been flooded with management interventions, some of which have been quite deleterious. Awareness and behavioral change campaigns are dominated by a focus on heteronormative sexual practices, such as the maintenance of marital fidelity. Until recently, there have been virtually no programs for non-heteronormative men, or indeed any men at all (Hershey 2008; Law 2008).

The earlier arrival of the epidemic in PNG meant that some of the worst features of early epidemic management rapidly became evident. Drugs to manage the virus had not yet been invented and certainly were not yet available in the developing world, so the prospect of certain death fueled levels of fear, stigma, and blame. Early behavior-change campaigns included the inappropriate and ineffective "ABC" (Abstain, Be faithful, use a Condom); and the identifying and targeting of "high-risk groups," a concept that was later altered to "high-risk settings" and then to "key populations at higher risk" (UNAIDS 2011)—none of which succeeded in avoiding the stigmatizing concept of "risk," usually interpreted by those who heard it as risk *to* themselves. AIDS was a death sentence: those "risky" people were to be avoided, locked up, and even killed. The dynamics of HIV stigma in PNG are driven by a dichotomy between the "general population," consisting primarily of heterosexual males and their families, and "risk groups" of varying degrees of infectiousness (Waldby, Kippax, and Crawford 1993). Foremost among these are loose women, followed by sexually deviant males, if they are considered at all.

Understanding

While forming a broad backdrop for an understanding of non-heteronormative men in PNG, these issues do little to illuminate the lived experience of *gay* individuals. No wonder Timothy is confused. He is not alone in this: "What I feel, my gay friends feel the same . . . how I go through life, they also go through the same thing. Sometimes we come to a very hard shape, where we cannot see the light. The government is saying that's the boundary; the religious are saying that's against the law in the Bible; the people are saying that's the discrimination rule; the legislators, they ignore human rights. At the moment, I'm like in prison. I can't walk out of my gate."

Perhaps, one day, decriminalization initiatives will bear fruit, and Timothy will be able to walk out of the gate of his prison, a prison constructed by the law, religion, government policy, and societal norms. One day, he may be able to claim sexual citizenship and the freedom, recognition, and understanding that this would entail: "I want to be recognized for who I am. I want to be respected as what I am. I want to have freedom of speech. I want freedom to act. I want freedom of movement. I will never become a real man, and I will never get married to a lady, because what is inside me is inside me. I'm looking forward to marrying to a man that can look after me, that can understand my situation, that can understand me as who I am."

Acknowledgments

This work was carried out as part of my research for my PhD thesis (2011). I acknowledge the support of the Australian National University and the Australian Government through the funding of the Australian Research Grant *Oceanic Encounters,* and I thank Niko Besnier, Kalissa Alexeyeff, and Margaret Jolly for giving me every encouragement to undertake this project.

References

ABC Radio Pacific Beat. 2005. *Fiji: Methodists Want Sodomy Laws Enforced.* Australia.

Aldrich, Robert. 2003. *Colonialism and Homosexuality*. London: Routledge.

Ballard, John. 1998. The Constitution of AIDS in Australia: Taking Government at a Distance Seriously. In *Governing Australia: Studies in Contemporary Rationalities of Government*, ed. Mitchell Dean and Barry Hindess, pp. 125–138. Melbourne: Cambridge University Press.

Beardmore, Edward. 1890. The Natives of Mowat, Daudai, New Guinea. *Journal of the Anthropological Institute of Great Britain and Ireland* 19: 459–466.

Besnier, Niko. 2002. Transgenderism, Locality, and the Miss Galaxy Beauty Pageant in Tonga. *American Ethnologist* 29: 534–566.

Boellstorff, Tom. 2003. I Knew It Was Me: Mass Media, "Globalization," and Lesbian and Gay Indonesia. In *Mobile Cultures: New Media in Queer Asia*, ed. Chris Berry, Fran Martin, and Audrey Yue, pp. 21–51. Durham, NC: Duke University Press.

———. 2011. But Do Not Identify as Gay: A Proleptic Genealogy of the MSM Category. *Cultural Anthropology* 26: 287–312.

Dinnen, Sinclair. 1998. Criminal Justice Reform in Papua New Guinea. In *Governance and Reform in the South Pacific*, ed. Peter Larmour, pp. 253–272. Canberra: National Centre for Development Studies, Australian National University.

Elliston, Deborah A. 1995. Erotic Anthropology: "Ritualized Homosexuality" in Melanesia and Beyond. *American Ethnologist* 22: 848–867.

Gammage, Bill. 1996. Police and Power in the Pre-War Papua New Guinea Highlands. *Journal of Pacific History* 31: 162–177.

Garap, Sarah. 2000. Struggles of Women and Girls: Simbu Province, Papua New Guinea. In *Reflections on Violence in Melanesia*, ed. Sinclair Dinnen and Alison Ley, pp. 159–171. Leichhardt, NSW: Hawkins Press.

Gibbs, Philip. 2002. Religion and Religious Institutions as Defining Factors in Papua New Guinea Politics. *Development Bulletin* 59 (October): 15–18.

Goodale, Jane C. 1980. Gender, Sexuality and Marriage: A Kaulong Model of Nature and Culture. In *Nature, Culture and Gender*, ed. Carol P. MacCormack and Marilyn Strathern, pp. 119–173. Cambridge: Cambridge University Press.

Goodman, Ryan. 2001. Beyond the Enforcement Principle: Sodomy Laws, Social Norms, and Social Panoptics. *California Law Review* 89: 643–740.

Herdt, Gilbert. 1984. *Ritualized Homosexuality in Melanesia*. Berkeley: University of California Press.

———. 1987. *The Sambia: Ritual and Gender in New Guinea*. Fort Worth, TX: Holt, Rinehart, & Winston.

———. 1992. Semen Depletion and the Sense of Maleness. In *Oceanic Homosexualities*, ed. Stephen O. Murray, pp. 33–68. New York: Garland.

———. 1997. *Same Sex, Different Cultures: Gays and Lesbians across Cultures*. Boulder, CO: Westview Press.

————. 2012. Intimate Consumption and Sexual Stigma: Embodiment, HIV Rights, and Cultural Transformation across Time among the Sambia of Papua New Guinea. Paper presented at the annual meeting of the American Anthropological Association, San Francisco, California.

Hershey, Christopher. 2008. Reflections on Poro Sapot: One Model of Care for Men's Sexual and Reproductive Health (paper). In *PNG Association for Public Health Videoconference: Men's Sexual and Reproductive Health in PNG.* Port Moresby: National Department of Health, PNG Association of Public Health and Global Development Learning Network (World Bank).

Hiery, Herman. 1997. Germans, Pacific Islanders and Sexuality: German Impact and Indigenous Influence in Melanesia and Micronesia. In *European Impact and Pacific Influence: British and German Colonial Policy in the Pacific Islands and the Indigenous Response,* ed. Herman J. Hiery and John M. MacKenzie, pp. 299–323. London: I. B. Tauris.

Hogbin, H. Ian. 1946. Puberty to Marriage: A Study of the Sexual Life of the Natives of Wogeo, New Guinea. *Oceania* 16: 185–209.

————. 1951. *Transformation Scene: The Changing Culture of a New Guinea Village.* London: Routledge & Kegan Paul.

————. 1963. *Kinship and Marriage in a New Guinea Village.* London: University of London Press.

Human Rights Watch. 2008. *This Alien Legacy: The Origins of "Sodomy" Laws in British Colonialism.* New York: Human Rights Watch.

Jackson, Peter. 1997. *Kathoey>*<Gay><Man: The Historical Emergence of Gay Male Identity in Thailand. In *Sites of Desire, Economies of Pleasure: Sexualities in Asia and the Pacific,* ed. Lenore Manderson and Margaret Jolly, pp. 166–190. Chicago: University of Chicago Press.

————. 2000. An Explosion of Thai Identities: Global Queering and Re-Imagining Queer Theory. *Culture, Health and Sexuality* 2: 405–424.

Jenkins, Carol. 1996. The Homosexual Context of Heterosexual Practice in Papua New Guinea. In *Bisexualities and AIDS,* ed. Peter Aggleton, pp. 191–206. London: Taylor & Francis.

————. 2004. Male Sexuality, Diversity and Culture: Implications for HIV Prevention and Care. Geneva: UNAIDS.

————. 2006. Male Sexuality and HIV: The Case of Male-to-Male Sex. Paper presented at the Risks and Responsibilities: Male Sexual Health and HIV in Asia and the Pacific International Consultation, New Delhi, September 23–26.

Jinks, Brian, Peter Biskup, and Hank Nelson, eds. 1973. *Readings in New Guinea History.* Sydney: Angus & Robertson.

Jorgensen, Dan. 2005. Third Wave Evangelism and the Politics of the Global in Papua New Guinea: Spiritual Warfare. *Oceania* 75: 444–461.

Kelly, Angela, Martha Kupul, Wing Young Nicola Man, Somu Nosi, Namarola
    Lote, Patrick Rawstorne, Grace Halim, Claire Ryan, and Heather Worth.
    2011. *Askim na Save (Ask and Understand): People who Sell and/or Exchange Sex
    in Port Moresby*. Sydney: Papua New Guinea Institute of Medical Research
    and the University of New South Wales.
Knauft, Bruce M. 1986. Text and Social Practice: Narrative "Longing" and
    Bisexuality among the Gebusi of New Guinea. *Ethos* 14: 252–281.
——. 1987. Homosexuality in Melanesia. *Journal of Psychoanalytic Anthropology*
    10: 155–191.
——. 1993. *South Coast New Guinea Cultures: History, Comparison, Dialectic*.
    Cambridge: Cambridge University Press.
——. 1999. *From Primitive to Postcolonial in Melanesia and Anthropology*. Ann
    Arbor: University of Michigan Press.
——. 2003. Whatever Happened to Ritualized Homosexuality? Modern Sexual
    Subjects in Melanesia and Elsewhere. *Annual Review of Sex Research* 14:
    137–159.
Law, Greg. 2008. Men's Sexual and Reproductive Health: The PNG Scenario
    (paper). In *PNG Association for Public Health Videoconference: Men's Sexual
    and Reproductive Health in PNG*. Port Moresby: PNG National Department
    of Health, PNG Association of Public Health and Global Development
    Learning Network (World Bank).
Lutkehaus, Nancy, and Paul B. Roscoe, eds. 1995. *Gender Rituals: Female Initiation
    in Melanesia*. New York: Routledge.
Macintyre, Martha. 2008. Police and Thieves, Gunmen and Drunks: Problems with
    Men and Problems with Society in Papua New Guinea. *The Australian Journal
    of Anthropology* 19: 179–193.
Maibani-Michie, Geraldine, and William Yeka. 2005. *Baseline Research for Poro
    Sapot Project: A Program for Prevention of HIV/AIDS among MSM in Port
    Moresby and FSW in Goroka and Port Moresby Papua New Guinea (PNG)*.
    Goroka, PNG: Papua New Guinea Institute of Medical Research.
Morin, Jack. 2008. "It's Mutual Attraction": Transvestites and the Risk of HIV
    Transmission in Urban Papua. In *Making Sense of AIDS: Culture, Sexuality, and
    Power in Melanesia*, ed. Leslie Butt and Richard Eves, pp. 41–59. Honolulu:
    University of Hawai'i Press.
Murray, Sir Hubert. 1925. *Papua of Today, or an Australian Colony in the Making*.
    London: P. S. King & Son.
Murray, Stephen O., ed. 1992. *Oceanic Homosexualities*. New York: Garland.
National Sex and Reproduction Research Team (NSSRT) and Carol Jenkins. 1994.
    *National Study of Sexual and Reproductive Knowledge and Behaviour in Papua
    New Guinea*. Goroka, PNG: Papua New Guinea Institute of Medical Research.

Nelson, Hank. 1982. *Taim Bilong Masta: The Australian Involvement with Papua New Guinea.* Sydney: Australian Broadcasting Commission.

Oram, Nigel. 1976. *Colonial Town to Melanesian City: Port Moresby 1884–1974.* Canberra: Australian National University Press.

Queensland Government. 1889. *British New Guinea: Report for the Year 1888.* Brisbane: Queensland Government.

Pacific Sexual Diversity Network (PSDN) and AIDS Council of New South Wales (ACON). 2009. *HIV/AIDS, Men Who Have Sex with Men and Transgender People in the Pacific: Recommendations for an Improved Response;* http://www .acon.org.au/sites/default/files/PSDN-Advocacy-Report-2009-online.pdf (accessed April 2011).

Pisani, Elizabeth. 2008. *The Wisdom of Whores.* London: Granta.

Reed, Stephen Winsor. 1943. *The Making of Modern New Guinea with Special Reference to Culture Contact in the Mandated Territory.* Philadelphia: The American Philosophical Society.

Reid, Elizabeth. 2010. Putting Values into Practice in PNG: The Poro Sapot Project and Aid Effectiveness. *Pacificurrents* 1.2 and 2.1; http://intersections.anu.edu .au/pacificurrents/reid.htm (accessed August 2010).

Roberts, Stephen H. 1928. Racial and Labour Problems. In *The Australian Mandate for New Guinea: Record of Round Table Discussion,* ed. F. W. Eggleston, pp. 74–84. Melbourne: Macmillan.

Rowley, Charles. 1966. *The New Guinea Villager: The Impact of Colonial Rule on Primitive Society and Economy.* New York: Praeger.

Stewart, Christine. 2008. Men Behaving Badly: Sodomy Cases in the Colonial Courts of Papua New Guinea. *Journal of Pacific History* 43: 77–93.

———. 2010. The Tale of an Activist. *HIV Australia* 8(2): 42.

———. 2011. *Pamuk na Poofta:* Criminalising Consensual Sex in Papua New Guinea. PhD thesis, College of Asia Pacific, Australian National University.

Tau, Moses. 1999. *Aito Paka Paka.* Boroko, PNG: CHM Supersound Studios.

———. 2005. *The Best of Moses Tau: Beats and Dances.* Boroko, PNG: CHM Supersound Studios.

Todd, J. A. 1934–1935. Native Offences and European Law in South-West New Britain. *Oceania* 5: 437–460.

Tonga Leitis' Association. 2010. *Strategic Plan 2010–2015;* http://www.nzaf.org .nz/images/uploads/image/tla_strategic_plan_2010-2015.pdf (accessed June 2013).

UNAIDS. 2010. *Global Report 2010 Fact Sheet: Oceania.* Geneva: UNAIDS.

———. 2011. *UNAIDS Terminology Guidelines (January 2011).* Geneva: UNAIDS; http://data.unaids.org/pub/Manual/2008/jc1336_unaids_terminology_ guide_en.pdf (accessed June 2011).

Waldby, Catherine, Susan Kippax, and June Crawford. 1993. *Cordon Sanitaire: "Clean" and "Unclean" Women in the AIDS Discourse of Young Heterosexual Men*. In *AIDS: Facing the Second Decade,* ed. Peter Aggleton, Peter Davies, and Graham Hart, pp. 29–39. London: Falmer Press.

Wardlow, Holly. 2006. *Wayward Women: Sexuality and Agency in a New Guinea Society*. Berkeley: University of California Press.

Weeks, Jeffrey. 1989. Sexual Politics. *New Internationalist* 201; http://newint.org/features/1989/11/05/politics/ (accessed February 2013).

Wilets, James D. 1994–1995. International Human Rights Law and Sexual Orientation. *Hastings International and Comparative Law Review* 18: 1–120.

Wolfers, Edward P. 1975. *Race Relations and Colonial Rule in Papua New Guinea*. Sydney: Australia and New Zealand Book Company.

Worsley, Peter. 1970. *The Trumpet Shall Sound: A Study of "Cargo" Cults in Melanesia*. 2nd ed. London: Paladin.

Zimmer-Tamakoshi, Laura, ed. 1998. *Modern Papua New Guinea*. Kirksville, MO: Thomas Jefferson University Press.

CHAPTER 15

Outwith the Law in Samoa and Tonga

Sue Farran

In Scotland, the term "outwith" is used to locate something or someone beyond the scope of a specific context or category. It is therefore an exclusionary term, but its boundaries may change depending on the context. I use the word in this chapter to engage with the focus of this book from a legal perspective. Globally transgender people have been "outwith" the law, but gradually, as the law's boundaries have changed, some have been brought within the law and their transgender status given legal recognition. In Samoa and Tonga, transgender Pacific Islanders remain beyond or "outwith" the law in a number of respects and yet also within it when the boundaries shift, especially when the locality in which the law applies and the cultural mores that inform the law are taken into account. Reflecting on the legal environment in which *fa'afāfine* and *fakaleitī* are situated, this chapter examines certain domestic laws in Samoa and Tonga, comparative legal developments elsewhere, and the international and national arena of human rights. Noting shifts in the boundaries of inclusiveness versus exclusiveness of the laws of other countries, it considers whether legal changes experienced elsewhere could be introduced into these Pacific Island countries and the possible challenges and consequences of such an action.

Transgender people do not form a homogeneous group in either of the two countries under consideration or more broadly in the Pacific region (Besnier 1997, 1994). While Tonga and Samoa are distinct in many ways, the two countries share certain relevant characteristics. Both came under the influence of English law—Tonga as a protected state and Samoa as a colony. Both countries also share a legacy of introduced English common law and have written constitutions that enumerate various fundamental rights. In the nineteenth century, both countries fell under the influence of Christian missionary efforts, and Christianity subsequently became completely integrated into the daily lives of Tongans and Samoans. Indeed, the constitutions of both countries refer to God and to Christian principles, and the majority of the population in Tonga and Samoa continue to be practicing or baptized Christians.[1] Both are Polynesian countries with close historical, ethnic, and linguistic links, and both have stratified social structures—although Tonga, with its monarchy, nobles, and commoners, may be said to be more hierarchical than Samoa. As in other parts of the Pacific, society in both countries is also characterized by familial and gendered inequalities, strong patriarchal structures, and adherence to value systems that are claimed to represent tradition and are central to the identity of the islanders.

At the same time, many Samoans and Tongans have lived outside the islands since the 1960s, constituting a considerable proportion of the Pacific diaspora in New Zealand, Australia, the United States of America, and elsewhere. Diasporic Samoans and Tongans maintain links with those back in the islands in many different ways, so that island-based Samoans and Tongans do not lead isolated lives but are part of a wider global community. The ebb and flow of people, remittances, news, views, values, and attitudes contrasts sharply with the static nature of the laws that prevail and the very limited legal reform that has taken place since independence. Like many other Pacific Island countries, Samoa and Tonga are therefore characterized by both tradition and change, conservatism and a desire for reform, and communalism and individualism—opposites that attract shifting support and give rise to real or perceived tensions depending on the context and agenda, and that may also prompt calls for legal reform.

In a number of legal systems in the Pacific Island region and elsewhere, the legal status of transgender and other non-heteronormative people has been one area where legal change has occurred in recent years (see George, this volume, on Fiji). It may be thought that similar reforms could be possible in Tonga and Samoa because of the strong colonial and postcolonial links with legal systems from elsewhere—for example, the courts, the role of judges and lawyers, and the laws that apply. Even though Samoa and Tonga are sovereign states, postindependence laws passed by national parliaments tend to reflect dominant colonial or postcolonial legal cultures. Consequently, many of the laws that apply are influenced by introduced value systems and are not necessarily rooted in the customary aspects of contemporary Samoan or Tongan cultures. These dynamics operate in a more general context in which "culture" and "tradition" are equally the products of historical continuity and colonial and postcolonial innovation.

Although the danger of replicating neocolonialism through law reform is mitigated by the fact that, for many Samoans and Tongans, daily life is regulated by customary practices and non-state intervention, the formal legal framework cannot be ignored, given its pervasive nature and its post-colonial integration into Samoan and Tongan perceptions of law. In partic-ular, for the purposes of this chapter, the law attributes to individuals legal status determined by characteristics such as age, gender, and marital status. For example, terms like "wife," "husband," "parent," and "child" all place individuals in legal categories and can have significant legal consequences. Where an individual does not neatly "fit" a recognized legal category, then one consequence may be that they are "outwith" the law—in the Scottish sense of the term—or legally "exiled" (Edwards 1996, 11). For this reason, persons such as *fa'afāfine* or *fakaleitī* present a legal conundrum. Where similar conundrums in respect of those formerly "outwith" have been expe-rienced in other legal systems, in recent years their legal status has improved, partly through innovative judicial reasoning in cases brought before the courts and partly by legislation passed by national legislative assemblies.

For example, in the larger countries of the Pacific Rim, including Australia and New Zealand, as well as in the United Kingdom, a wide range of legal reforms have been implemented to bring homosexuals, trans-sexuals, and same-sex couples within the law.[2] These developments have included a shift in the way the law defines "male" and "female" or "man" and "woman" for the purposes of marriage and a move away from an emphasis on sexual functionality toward an emphasis on gender and sexual orienta-tion, from physiological definitions of sex to considerations of psychologi-cal factors as well as a recognition of changes in social attitudes. Changing perceptions of marriage have brought into question what it means to be male or female while still retaining the basic principle that marriage is a heterosexual union, although even this is now being challenged in some countries, including the United Kingdom. The notion that family rights and obligations apply only to formally married partners of the opposite sex has also been challenged and amended laws reflect this, while the emergence of new reproductive technologies (NRTs) have prompted most industrialized countries to accept that the definition of "family" is rapidly changing and, with it, the rights relating to and arising from family membership. Although still relatively few countries embrace the idea of same-sex marriage, claims to family or relationship rights are increasingly being legally acknowledged regardless of the gender or sex of the parties. Where possible, the law has been rendered gender-neutral to facilitate changes in the legal regulation of pension entitlements, work benefits, succession to tenancies, and property rights, and criminal law has been rephrased so as to enlarge its scope. For example, rape—traditionally a male-on-female crime involving penetration of the vagina by a penis—has been redefined to include penetration by other objects and of other orifices, thereby encompassing the surgically constructed vaginas of transsexuals, prosthetic penises, and consideration of homosexual rape.

A feature of many of these dynamics has been that change has taken place in the public sphere, for example the provision of welfare benefits, housing, and criminal law. In the Pacific region, the state provides few such benefits, if any. The family remains central to the functioning of society and largely immune from state intervention. Thus, undermining or changing aspects of status within family law may have much stronger repercussions in Pacific Island societies than in societies of the global north, where the individual is less dependent on the family for status, support, and resources. However, lack of intervention leaves the rights and obligations of *fa'afafine* or *fakaleitī* to be determined almost entirely "outwith" the formal law.

A consideration underlying state action is international law and the global discourse of rights. For example, advocacy of universal rights inspired by the United Nations' Convention for the Elimination of All Discrimination against Women 1981 (CEDAW), which highlights and seeks to eradicate inequalities toward women regardless of cultural context, has brought gender politics into the public domain, even in the Pacific region, not least because international treaty obligations are monitored and (to a lesser extent) enforced by international agencies that assess the compliance of national legal systems according to global standards.

Elsewhere, women's rights advocacy has often been the precursor of wider debate on gendered discrimination and the platform for law reform. In the Pacific region, CEDAW-compliant law reform has been slow and, unlike changes being experienced elsewhere, the laws in Pacific Island countries, with very few exceptions, have not been reformed to address wider issues of gender discrimination or to bring transgender people within the law (Farran 2009). The question is whether the process and form of changes that have taken place elsewhere offer any useful lessons for Pacific Island countries. In order to make this assessment, I will first consider the legal framework of Tonga and Samoa and contextualize them in the human rights regimes that apply. Second, I will turn to particular laws that are framed in such a way as to disadvantage *fa'afāfine* and *fakaleitī*. Third, I will examine some of the drivers for change that have succeeded elsewhere and ask whether these developments could be implemented in the Pacific context and what obstacles may stand in the way.

The Legal Environment

In order to understand the current legal status of *fa'afāfine* and *fakaleitī*, one needs to understand the legal environment in Tonga and Samoa. Common law was introduced into the Pacific by colonial administrators (Corrin 1997), either directly from Britain or indirectly via other colonies, notably Australia or New Zealand, where English common law was also in effect, and this legal influence has persisted (Farran 2010, 20).

While the plurality of laws in Samoa and Tonga is less complicated than in other Pacific Island countries, different laws nevertheless coexist, some formal and others informal. This situation is largely due to the countries' historical legacies. Samoa was ruled by Germany from 1900 to 1914, then by Britain under a mandate from the League of Nations until 1919, when it came under the colonial rule of New Zealand. At independence in 1962, the Samoa Act 1921 set out what laws were to apply, some of which dated back to 1840. Although almost all introduced legislation was abolished under the Repeal of Statutes Act and replaced by national laws in 1972, under the Samoa Act 1921 (Section 349) and the Constitution (Articles 111 and 114), judicially developed principles of English law remain applicable, unless a Samoan court finds that such principles are inconsistent with the constitution or Samoan laws, or inappropriate to the circumstances of the country. In practice, judges in Samoa continue to refer to the decisions of English courts and courts of other common-law systems.

While Tonga was never formally colonized, it did not escape the influence of English law. It was united into a Polynesian kingdom in 1845 and became a constitutional monarchy in 1875 with a written constitution. In 1900 it became a British protected state and gained independence in 1970. As a protected state, it came under the 1893 British Pacific Order in Council, one consequence of which was the introduction of English law. Under the Civil Law Act 1966, it remained possible, when considering noncriminal cases, for Tongan courts to have recourse to English legislation and the general principles of English law developed through English courts. This only changed in 2003, when the Civil Law (Amendment) Act was passed, and Tongan judges may no longer refer to English legislation, although they still can have recourse to principles of law developed in the English courts by English judges.

In many parts of the Pacific, apart from written laws introduced prior to independence and the nonstatutory legal principles introduced via the case law of the colonial administrators, the role of customary law, custom, or traditional values has been either retained or even enhanced since independence. In Samoa, the constitution states that law includes "any custom or usage which has acquired the force of law in Samoa, or any part thereof, under the provisions of any Act or under a judgment of a court of competent jurisdiction" (Article 111 [1]). Although the application of customary law is largely limited to land and titles, the customary regulation of daily life is endorsed through the Village Fono Act 1990, which gives village councils (*fono*) considerable power to control and regulate the lives of Samoans, including the right to punish misconduct. But the exercise of this power has from time to time brought customary practices into conflict with constitutional law, especially in the area of fundamental rights. Part of the problem is that, although the act states that the *fono* in exercising its power or authority "shall exercise the same in accordance with the custom and usages of that village" (section 2), no further definition of "customs and usages" is provided and there have been considerable debates over what this actually permits the *fono* to do, especially as interpretations of "customs and usages" are malleable in the hands of those exercising the power of the *fono*.

While there is no specific reference to customary law in Tonga's legal system, the "circumstances of the Kingdom" section of the Civil Law Act (section 4) limits the application of English law and can be taken to refer to the social and traditional context in which the law operates. But the Supreme Court in Tonga has held that cultural considerations play no part in interpreting the law, especially if they would result in a diminution of fundamental rights. For example, in *Taione v. Kingdom of Tonga* [2004] TOSC 47, in which the defendants sued the government for curtailing freedom of the press, the court's lengthy judgment commented on the deliberate omission of reference to Tongan customs from the Constitution and the Interpretation Act.

Formally, therefore, the courts in Tonga reject considerations of culture and custom in applying the law (see, however, Philips 2004). Whether or not customary practices and values are sanctioned as a formal source of law they may still be influential in regulating the personal lives of Pacific Islanders and in informing the normative framework for the application of laws.

A final source of law relevant to Pacific Island countries is international law, which becomes integrated into the legal system by way of either customary international law or treaties and conventions to which sovereign states are parties. In the Pacific, a variety of international treaty obligations were inherited from the colonial past. Independent governments adopted many of the pre-independence treaties and incurred new obligations by signing or ratifying additional treaties. Treaties do not become enforceable in national law until incorporated by acts of national parliaments. While these sources of law embed the Pacific Islands in a global legal community and may provide a platform for reform advocacy, they are also viewed with skepticism by some as being "foreign," "imperialist," or simply of limited relevance to Pacific Islanders. These positions concern in particular, international principles relevant to human rights and nondiscrimination.

Human Rights

Failure to incorporate international human rights law into domestic law, however, does not mean that Pacific Islanders lack formal recognition of fundamental rights. Significantly, the constitutions of Samoa and Tonga include bills of rights, which are statements of fundamental rights and freedoms that the state guarantees to individual citizens. For the most part, these bills were drawn up with little reference to the local context or indigenous values.[3] This approach to human rights shaped by liberal post-Enlightenment philosophies has been criticized in the Pacific region on the grounds that it is not compatible with Pacific values (e.g., Angelo 1992; Thaman 1998). These criticisms are particularly pertinent to the advocacy of a universal approach to human rights—for example, as found in CEDAW, which focuses on the individual rather than the group or the community and thus ignores other cultural, philosophical, or normative environments (Civic 1995–1996; Cobbah 1987; Hom 1996–1997). In the postcolonial world, including Pacific Island states, this last point may be taken a step further: not only are universal human rights a Western concept, but they also represent the thinking of former colonial powers and should be rejected for political and ideological reasons.

There is of course a spectrum of positions between radical universalism and radical relativism, and it may be possible to accommodate elements of both. For example, relativists may hold that "rights (and other social practices, values, and moral rules) are culturally determined, but the universality of human nature and rights serves as a check on the potential excesses of relativism" (Donnolly 1984, 400). It may also be the case that local actors negotiate the space between the universal and the relative by strategically building bridges between the two (Merry 2006; New Zealand Law Commission 2006). The localization or "vernacularization" of human rights in the Pacific region has been dealt with elsewhere (Hilsdon et al. 2000), but becomes especially relevant where tradition, Christianity, and discourses of rights are conflated, as is the case in Samoa and Tonga, and creates particular challenges for addressing inequalities experienced by specific minority groups.

It is against this legal environment that legal questions concerning *fa'afāfine* and *fakaleitī* should be considered. At the same time, it is important to recognize that not all conduct or daily transactions attract legal consequences and many aspects of people's lives take place without any state intervention. Where the law does intervene, however, the outcomes may be positive (e.g., the protection of those who have been wronged) or negative (e.g., the punishment of criminals). But if a person is not recognized as being a potential victim of ill-treatment or harm or claims to have rights that are not recognized in law, he or she may have no legal recourse for redress—and in this way be "outwith" the law. While, in democratic states—in the Pacific and elsewhere—the laws in theory reflect the values and wishes of the people they serve, in practice they reflect the interests of those in power, often the heirs of colonial domination. Problems also arise where the law-making process is not entirely democratic, as may be argued of both Samoa and Tonga, or where advocacy for legal change (e.g., by lobbying groups, the press, victims of rights' violations) is suppressed or criminalized. In the Pacific region, a number of these features may be encountered and can have a significant impact on the legal environment in which transgendered people find themselves.

Gender and the Law

Legal status, whereby a person acquires upheld and enforceable rights, powers, duties, and obligations, is a legal construction. The laws that inform this process may be shaped by customs, legislation passed by various law-making bodies such as parliament, or decisions of judges or adjudicators determining individual cases that may have repercussions beyond the case being considered. Not all characteristics of individuals have legal consequences, and those to which the law attaches significance can change over time. For example, to be born with a disability today may be of legal significance because it may entitle a person to welfare or social security benefits. These provisions, however, are relatively recent innovations and, prior to their emergence, to be born with a disability was merely a misfortune— which in some societies could even justify being banished or put to death.

One of the most basic human characteristics to which the law has long attached significance is whether a person is born male or female (Edwards 1996). For most people, this characteristic is not a legal matter but a matter of physiology. After a cursory glance at his or her external genitalia, a newborn is declared to be a boy or a girl. The fact is recorded and remains significant for the rest of the person's life—for example, in reference to laws that operate differently on the grounds of sex, for purposes of taxation, social benefits, contractual capacity, and property rights. Sex may determine whether a person can commit or be the victim of certain crimes, such as rape, infanticide, or sodomy. Similarly, it determines the role that an individual can assume within family law: wife or husband, mother or father, and brother or sister. There are also, of course, a number of gender roles within families that do not attract legal consequences but that may be shaped by customs or traditional practices, and that in turn may have some bearing on other legal determinations. For example, in many (but not all) social and historical contexts and for some social groups, the roles of homemaking and child care were the preserve of women and the roles of provider, decision maker, and financial manager that of men. These norms could influence (and often still do) a court in disputes about child custody or the assessment of spousal dependence. While civil education and the laws and their operation through court decisions may change them, these stereotypes tend to persist. This framing of legal rights and obligations on the basis of sex or on assumptions about gender roles presents a dilemma for those who, while of one sex, adopt aspects of the conduct, lifestyle, or demeanor of another gender. Thus transgender individuals may be "outwith" the law, either because they do not fit neatly into a sexual category (man vs. woman, girl vs. boy), or because their gender identification does not bring them within the benefits of the law when these benefits are afforded on the basis of sex and gender (such as parental allowance for child care). In many countries, these dilemmas have been solved through law reform that brings transgender individuals within the law, either through the adoption of gender-neutral language or by making specific provision for those who fall within a legally defined (and therefore imperfect) transgender group.

In Tonga and Samoa, there is limited scope to bring transgender people within the law. The starting point in considering the legal position of transgender people are the constitutions. The 1960 Samoan Constitution specifies, among the fundamental rights, that "All persons are equal before the law and entitled to equal protection under the law" (Article 15[1]), prohibits discrimination on the grounds of "descent, sex, language, religion, political or other opinion, social origin, place of birth, family status, or any of them" (Article 15[2]), but does not prohibit discrimination on the grounds of sexual orientation or gender identification. Given its vintage, this exclusion is not particularly surprising, and in fact Samoa was arguably ahead of its time in prohibiting discrimination on the basis of whether a person was male or female.

The 1875 Constitution of the Kingdom of Tonga also contains a declaration of rights and provides that it applies to all persons regardless of class (Article 4, Part I) but, not surprisingly, fails to provide for protection against discrimination on the grounds of sex or sexual orientation. In interpreting and applying the law stated in the constitution, the Tongan court has held that a literal or rigid interpretation that focuses only on the words used should be avoided in considering fundamental rights law.

In light of this, although in neither Tonga nor Samoa does the law make discrimination on the grounds of sexual orientation or gender identification illegal, there is scope for proactive judges to bring *fa'afāfine* and *fakaleitī* within the law, were they so minded. Changes at this level—on constitutional interpretation—could then have an impact on specific domestic laws that currently have an adverse effect on transgender people in Samoa and Tonga. This is illustrated by considering aspects of family law and criminal law in these countries.

Family Law

Family law is one of the areas where persisting colonial and postcolonial influences are evident. For example, Tonga has no national legislation governing marriages, only the registration of marriages, so it seems likely that, under the Civil Law Act 1966, the English law of marriage applies (despite the Civil Law [Amendment] Act 2003). The English law of marriage introduced into the region was firmly heterosexual, as defined by the leading English case on marriage, *Hyde v. Hyde and Woodmanse* (1866) LR 1 P & D 130, 133. Although this was a case concerning the validity of a polygamous marriage, the statement by the judge that "marriage . . . may be defined as 'the voluntary union for life of one man and one woman, to the exclusion of all others'" has subsequently been taken by the courts as being the foundation for marriage in the common law and referred to with approval in subsequent cases in which transgender issues have been raised. Although the English Marriage Act itself makes no reference to the sex or gender of either party, the Nullity of Marriage Act 1971 (Section 1 [c]), provides that a marriage is void unless the parties are respectively "male and female." In Samoa, the Marriage Ordinance 1961 does not stipulate that the parties must be male and female, and in neither Samoa nor Tonga does the law state that a marriage is void if the sex of the parties does not conform to a prescribed pattern.[4] However, the combined influence of foreign law, Christian principles, and reference to English case law has led to a presumption that a valid marriage is monogamous and between two parties of the opposite sex.

This legal assumption in the laws of both countries that marriage is a heterosexual union is strongly linked to the association of marriage with legitimate procreation that underlies English law and the laws derived from it. Although parties to a marriage are not required to establish either their sexuality or their reproductive capacity, failure to consummate a marriage may be a ground for annulment in Samoa and a ground for divorce in Tonga. The understanding that marriage is for procreation also finds support in Pacific Island cultures, in which marriage is perceived as an alliance between kinship groups that ensures social and biological reproduction and contributes to social stability. While many traditional practices regarding marriage (e.g., polygyny among the high-ranking) have disappeared, marriage remains a fundamental and socially valued institution, especially where the disapproval of extramarital sex for women and born-out-of-wedlock children is supported by religious institutions (Park and Morris 2004).

This is not to suggest that all Pacific Islanders share these views or are immune to changes taking place elsewhere both in the law and in social attitudes. For example, in some common-law systems, as in Australia and New Zealand, the absence of consummation is not a ground for either divorce or annulment, and in no common-law jurisdiction is successful reproduction a requirement of marriage. The Pacific diaspora may therefore have been exposed to very different views and practices from those still living in Tonga or Samoa. Within the island countries, however, there are a number of legal obstacles in existing laws to *fa'afāfine* or *fakaleitī* wishing to live openly in an intimate relationship with a person of their choice or to have their own families (Farran 2004). First, they cannot marry if they wish to (Besnier 2004, 313), and so any legal benefits deriving from marriage are not available to them. Second, they may not be legally regarded as a family unit, even if they adopt children in custom. Third, any sexual relationship they may have with their chosen partner may be criminalized.

The extent to which this potential exclusion from family law adversely impacts *fa'afāfine* or *fakaleitī* is unknown. While many feel that their status within the existing social structure entails considerable personal investment and rewards (Besnier 2004, 314–315), offered the possibility, some might choose an alternative lifestyle (as indeed some do when they move elsewhere), even if the pursuit of such individualistic projects violates cultural conventions of group membership and family affiliation. Indeed, even if *fa'afāfine* and *fakaleitī* are content with their integration into customary Tongan or Samoa family structures and there is no great urge to challenge or change family law, the expression of personal sexual desires may evoke not only general condemnation in societies that disapprove of any public manifestations of sexuality (see Tcherkézoff, this volume) but also criminal sanctions.

Criminal Law

Especially in those countries where changes to the law have not been implemented to reflect greater gender equality, criminal law tends not to be gender-neutral, so in many areas of criminal law it is important to ascertain if the perpetrator or the victim is male or female. This is particularly so in the case of sexual assault. Rape, for example, is defined in Samoa as "the act of a male person having sexual intercourse with a woman or girl" (Section 47 Crimes Ordinance). Similarly, in Tonga, only a female can be a victim of rape, although the law does not specify the sex of the perpetrator (Section 118 Criminal Offences).

Specific criminal laws can also operate in a discriminatory fashion by criminalizing conduct that is potentially victimless, and that may affect transgender groups in particular. An example can be found in Samoa in the Crimes Ordinance 1962. Section 58D of this law criminalizes "indecent assaults" and "indecent acts" committed by or permitted by one male on another male, regardless of consent. This section, which appears to have been adopted directly from section 141 of New Zealand's Crimes Act 1961, effectively criminalizes any physical contact of a sexual nature between male-bodied people.

Section 58N of the same law makes it an offense for a male person to have "on or about his person any article intended by him to represent that he is a female or in any other way is impersonating or representing himself to be a female." The offense must be committed in a public place and with the intent to deceive any other person as to his "true sex." There is no equivalent section to be found in the New Zealand Crimes Act 1961, which suggests that this offense may have been specifically created for Samoa (Farran and Su'a 2005).

Although this section is located in provisions of the criminal law addressing prostitution, it can arguably apply to any *fa'afafine* who may be wearing female clothing other than in the privacy of his own home and opens up the question of when an "article" can be deemed to be "female." As many *fa'afafine* engage in some form of cross-dressing at work, at home, or on social occasions (including sometimes attending church), they theoretically run the risk of being arrested under suspicion of having committed this offense, particularly since it is not clear whether the impersonation of a "female" means impersonating a specific person of the female sex or of the female gender. In addition, the section does not specify whether the test is objective or subjective: Must it be shown that the accused intended to mislead, or is it sufficient to demonstrate that the complainant was misled or that "the reasonable person" would have been misled? Most Samoans would recognize a *fa'afafine* as just that rather than as a man who seeks to pass as a woman, so it may be the case that this provision was historically intended to protect unwary foreigners. If the offense is related to soliciting, then a general provision against prostitution would suffice.

In Tonga, the Criminal Offences Act (Cap 18) makes it an offense under section 80(6) to keep, manage, act, or assist in the keeping or management of a brothel, including premises where "lewd homosexual practices" take place. It is not clear whether the act refers to all homosexual practices or only those considered to be lewd. In addition, section 81(5), which was added in 1978, makes it an offense for any male person who is soliciting for an immoral purpose to impersonate or represent himself as a female with the intention of deceiving any other person as to his true sex. The scope of this provision is slightly narrower than in Samoa, as it is limited to soliciting. However, homosexual acts, whether consensual or not, are criminalized in sections 136–140 under the provisions for sodomy, bestiality, indecent assault, and attempted sodomy. While sodomy requires penetration, indecent assault on a man (added by Act 9 of 1987) does not and could include other sexual acts committed by a male offender against a male victim.

I have not come across any publicly available reported cases of prosecutions under these cross-dressing provisions of the Criminal Offences Act (Cap 18) of Tonga or the Crimes Ordinance 1962 of Samoa, and anecdotal evidence indicates that the laws are not enforced (see also United States Department of State 2012), although other laws reflecting society's disapproval of certain behaviors that are often stereotypically associated with *fa'afāfine* and *fakaleitī* are enforced, such as swearing, causing a nuisance, or being intoxicated in a public place.[5] It might therefore be asked: Why are these offenses retained on the statute books? It could simply be due to lack of legislative engagement; because of the controversial nature of introducing reform in parliament (see Stewart, this volume, about Papua New Guinea, and below regarding Samoa); or because their retention represents a bulwark against the perceived or imagined increase in sexual promiscuity.

It is similarly difficult to ascertain if there are police prosecutions of adult homosexual conduct (there are reported prosecutions of sodomy with boys under the age of sixteen). Nevertheless, the continuing criminalization of homosexual sex may both inform mainstream perceptions of homosexuality and be informed by the broader public inhibition of expressions of sex and sexual orientation, which in turn may be influenced by Christian fundamentalism. Whatever the reasons, the retention of gender-explicit terminology in the criminal law means that transgender Pacific Islanders may remain "outwith" the law both as offenders and as victims.

Legal Transplants and Transgender Issues in Samoa and Tonga

In legal systems that create a more favorable legal environment for transgender people, these changes have been accompanied by a number of altered perceptions. For example, judicial attitudes toward marriage have been marked by a shift away from marriage as a means to legitimate procreation to marriage as a relationship of companionship and mutual support. Views of how individuals should be categorized or classified have also changed, and there is growing awareness—long recognized as problematic in Samoa and Tonga—that the binary distinction between male and female is simplistic. Linked to this (but not limited to it) is increasing juridical attention to individual rights, including respect for and tolerance of differences on a range of grounds, including sexual orientation and gender identification. Many of these developments have been driven by identity politics, gender-based rights movements, and advances in medical sciences, including a better understanding of gender orientation, technical advances in surgical sex reassignment, and NRTs. In decisions concerning transgender claimants, the courts have also played an important role, as have lobbying groups using the media and parliamentary processes to advocate for changes to the laws.

In considering the extent to which legal developments from elsewhere may be relevant to *fa'afāfine* or *fakaleitī*, the first question is whether the approaches adopted in different contexts will "fit" the specific environments of Pacific Island countries. In part, this is a question about legal transplants: Can legal ideas, institutions, and rules be successfully transplanted from one legal system to another? In part, it is also a matter of agency: Who is to determine the ideas, institutions, and rules to be transplanted, and who is to perform this operation? Samoa and Tonga are no strangers to legal and other transplants. Indeed, there are two transplanted elements that contribute to the challenge of bringing *fa'afāfine* and *fakaleitī* within the law: the present framework of the introduced common law and the strongly held Christian principles that shape the value system of many people in Tonga and Samoa, including *fa'afāfine* and *fakaleitī* and that are integral to claims of tradition and custom.

Localized Christian principles today regulate sexual behavior and moralities in general and homosexuality in particular. Although there may be considerable ambivalence about heterosexual (male) promiscuity (James 1994; Shore 1982, 196), antagonism toward same-sex (male and female) intimate relationships is unconcealed in parts of the Pacific region (Alexeyeff and Besnier, this volume; McIntosh 1999; Jowitt 2005; George 2008; Stewart, this volume), and advocacy for the liberalization of rights may attract social disapproval, if not legal sanction. While there is much greater awareness of non-heteronormative identities and practices due to access to global media, the mobility of Pacific Islanders, and exchanges with the Tongan and Samoan diaspora, Pacific Island societies are essentially conservative, and although there is an increasing engagement with human rights advocacy, there is the danger that once this turns to transgender or gay rights there will be a backlash.[6] While the form of intolerance may differ, especially between those living in the islands and those living in the diaspora, one of the issues to be taken into account when advocating legal change is whether what has happened elsewhere is likely to succeed if transplanted to a different environment.

In Samoa and Tonga, it is not only the religious nature of society that is an important aspect of this environment, but also the role of the family and the status of families and individuals within the family. *Fa'afāfine* and *fakaleitī* are members of families, kinship groups, and social groups just as others are. They are consequently bound by established codes of conduct and expected to conform with the *fa'a-Sāmoa* or the *anga faka-Tonga;* so, for example, they are often valuable members of the church, singing in choirs and participating in fund-raising, acting as deacons, Sunday school teachers, and church youth leaders, participating in many church activities—some of which may capitalize on their feminine attributes. They may also play significant roles in their families and certainly have obligations arising as a result of membership in the group. It is through these observances that *fa'afāfine* and *fakaleitī* are integrated into their communities. Although some may be rejected by their families and become victims of abuse and exploitation—which in turn may be due as much to class, poverty, lack of education, and other factors as it is to gender—many *fa'afāfine* and *fakaleitī* have a considerable investment in the status quo, which advocacy for change might damage. Indeed, most identify themselves within the context of traditional social structures, practices, and organization, rather than their individual sexual orientation or gender identification. In many respects their *fa'afāfine*-ness or *fakaleitī*-ness is possible because it is accommodated within the accepted family, church, and society organization. Provided the individual *fa'afāfine* or *fakaleitī* observes the correct mores, such as church attendance, respect, sobriety, and generosity, which are directed at maintaining social harmony and equilibrium, then they are generally tolerated.

To effect legal reform, therefore, may be to jeopardize those very elements of society that give it stability. So, for example, the advocacy of legal reform on the grounds of considerations of fundamental rights, principles of equality, and nondiscrimination immediately encounters obstacles in Tonga and Samoa because the societies are essentially non-egalitarian. This is illustrated by the facts that, in Samoa, only *matai* can stand for election to the national parliament, and since few women hold *matai* titles, women are grossly underrepresented in national politics; and in Tonga, despite recent reform, society continues to be a hierarchy headed by the monarch and supported by an elite class of nobles. There is also opposition to the implementation of equal rights (including opposition from women) on the grounds that it would destabilize family and social structures and undermine the values that underpin them. The point is significant insofar as, in other countries, mobilization for gender equality for women has invariably preceded mobilization for equality for other groups.

In this environment, any lobbying for equal rights on the grounds of sexual orientation or gender (as opposed to discrimination on the grounds of sex) is likely to be opposed, especially if it is seen as being driven by external agencies. These challenges are potentially exacerbated if they become associated with a Western LGBT political action. Although LGBT associations have been successful elsewhere in arguing for legal change, the present criminalization of even consensual homosexual acts in Samoa and Tonga suggests that these associations could do more harm than good by alienating the existing tolerance manifest, for example, in qualified support for transgender pageants (Besnier 2002, 2004) and aligning *fa'afāfine* and *fakaleitī* with Western-inspired social deviance. Indeed, suggesting that LGBT categories are unproblematically and universally defined across societies and countries (and with them the nature of the violence to which they are exposed) can be counterproductive (as Massad [2002, 2007] has argued particularly provocatively).

Fa'afāfine and *fakaleitī* may themselves be ambivalent about identifying with LGBT lobby groups. For example, many do not identify as "gay" (although these dynamics are changing). There are also considerable divergences between the views and practices of those in urban and rural areas, or between Samoans and Tongans and islanders living in Auckland, Sydney, and Los Angeles. Indeed, individuals may move between differently identified groups depending on personal circumstances. Moreover, to focus on any one aspect of the complex makeup of *fa'afāfine* and *fakaleitī* can detract from their multifaceted character (as most contributors to this volume document; see also Matzner 2001 and Schmidt 2003). While alignment with group identities that are familiar outside the region, such as homosexuals or transsexuals, can lead some individuals to break away from Pacific Island nomenclatures and seek alternatives that better capture their personal experiences or desired identities, others may wish to strengthen what they see as distinguishing them from what might otherwise be perceived as a homogeneous group. For example, one identity favored in Samoa is expressed by the coined term *"mala,"* which emphasizes the combination of male and female skills and attributes valued by *fa'afāfine* and directs attention away from presumed or preferred sexual orientation (see Alexeyeff and Besnier, this volume, for a discussion of the power and limitations of terms).

Getting the emphasis right in terms of chosen rather than imposed identifying labels is important, because even if some *fa'afāfine* or *fakaleitī* may more or less openly engage in homosexual acts, many argue that this sexual dimension is not the defining feature of their identity. More important is their role in the structure of the family or society and their observance of traditional gendered behavioral norms. Others argue that the sexuality of *fa'afāfine* or *fakaleitī* is not important compared to being feminine in terms of manner and personality within their specific cultural and social context and values. Arguably, therefore, it might be inappropriate to include *fa'afāfine* and *fakaleitī* within the broader umbrella of "LGBT identities" that increasingly finds support elsewhere, and in fact could potentially seriously damage their current acceptance within Pacific Island society by associating them with groups, such as "bisexuals" and "lesbians," that are barely on the horizon of local discourse.

Alternately, *fa'afāfine* and *fakaleitī* may wish to align with only part of the LGBT identity politics, thereby seeking change on an incremental basis. So, for example, legal reforms to the status of "transexuals" may theoretically prove preferable to that of "gays." The question is whether aligning legal reform demands with those made elsewhere by transexuals would lead to a transplantable legal development. *Fa'afāfine* and *fakaleitī* may share some characteristics with transexuals in Western societies, but not all. For example, elsewhere legal reform concerning transexuals has been predicated on the recognition of transexualism as a medical condition (such as "gender dysphoria") and has focused primarily on the right of persons so affected to change their ascribed legal status and to access medical technologies such as hormone therapy and sex-reassignment surgery (Currah, Juang, and Minter 2006; Meyerowitz 2002; Valentine 2007). The problem is that these concerns are completely different from those of *fa'afāfine* and *fakaleitī*, whose ontological basis diverges radically from that of transexuals in the West (Alexeyeff and Besnier, this volume), despite the fact that a few have undergone medical interventions in the diaspora.

Can "outwith" the Law Be Brought "within" the Law?

In this chapter, I have addressed the legal status of transgender Pacific Islanders, considering examples of domestic laws that may affect them adversely and the wider but changing legal environment beyond Tonga and Samoa. I have considered the challenges of bringing within the law those who are now "outwith" the law, especially when legal status in introduced laws has so often been traditionally associated with being biologically male or female. Because *fa'afāfine* and *fakaleitī* do not fit neatly into Western categories of man, woman, male, female, heterosexual, homosexual, or transsexual, and because the law is deeply invested in universal categories that are ultimately Western, they remain largely ignored by the law or are beyond its scope. Yet the law has enormous power. Consequently, Pacific Island transgender are denied many of the protections and rights that others enjoy. It is equally clear that claiming some form of unique legal status will not necessarily improve their lives and could well isolate them within their own societies, as well as exclude them from transnational groups with whom they may share some, but not all, characteristics and concerns.

While all individuals in Tonga and Samoa are entitled to protection under the law and a range of fundamental rights is enshrined in the constitutions of these countries, legal equality on the grounds of sex, sexual orientation, and gender identification is not yet a reality for many. One step that could be considered would be to reform the existing law on discrimination in order to extend its scope. This strategy, however, would not necessarily be a panacea. Although antidiscrimination measures have been the starting point for developments elsewhere, they still tend to rely on shoehorning individuals or groups into recognized boxes and may still not include gender-liminal groups or those who are not straightforwardly male or female. For example, "prohibitions of discrimination on the ground of 'sex' have been interpreted so as not to include transsexuals" (Hunter 2003, 389), and there is the problem of where those who are intersex are to be located. If *fa'afāfine* or *fakaleitī* were to be brought within antidiscrimination measures in a bill of rights, care would have to be exerted over the terms to be included. Would the most commonly used terms in legal language (e.g., "sex," "gender," "gender orientation," "transgender") be sufficiently inclusive? Alternatively, would inclusiveness obliterate any distinctiveness that some *fa'afāfine* or *fakaleitī* might wish to preserve? The process of even mooting legal change could provoke negative reactions to *fa'afāfine*

and *fakaleitī*, with lobbyists being depicted as intent on sabotaging traditional social structures and cohesion. Even if successful, any change may
have adverse consequences for those whom the law reform was intended to
assist because existing family and social structures offer support and inclusiveness to many transgender Pacific Islanders, who have a vested interest in their continuance. Therefore, any proposals for change have to be
considered against this background and in consideration of the possible
consequences of unsuccessful legal transplants.

As with many rights-based issues, it is probable that eventually the
concerns of *fa'afāfine* and *fakaleitī* will increasingly be articulated, perhaps
initially from the diaspora or from within Samoa and Tonga. Indeed, there
are agencies for change already in place. In 2010, for example, following
an identification of issues report in 2009 and stakeholder consultation,
the Samoa Law Reform Commission produced a report on the Crimes
Ordinance 1961 (Samoa Law Reform Commission 2010). The responses
of the Samoa Fa'afafine Association were taken into account, and recommendations were made that the offense of sodomy and related offenses
currently in sections 58G, D, and E of the Ordinance should be repealed,
as should section 58N (impersonating a female). However, these recommendations have not yet become law (although training on a new Crimes
Bill took place in September 2012), and the proposals triggered a vehement
backlash from church leaders (Murphy 2013) and revealed dissent within
the *fa'afāfine* community itself.[7] This serves as a reminder that transgender
Pacific Islanders are not a homogeneous group: there are those who oppose
change, including those currently adversely affected by the status quo.
For example, advocacy for same-sex marriage in New Zealand has been
firmly rebuffed in Samoa by the president of the Fa'afafine Association
(PacificEyeWitness 2012). In Tonga, resistance to even moderate change
conflates the removal of discrimination against women with advocacy of
same-sex unions and abortion, as evidenced by the views of male and female
candidates standing in the 2010 elections (Matangi Tonga 2010) and the
views of representatives of the Methodist Church in Tonga (Murphy 2013).

Before appropriate transplants can be considered or reforms proposed,
more needs to be done to ascertain what it is, in the field of law reform, that
fa'afāfine or *fakaleitī* want. There is, for example, insufficient data concerning the circumstances under which many transgender emigrate because of
actual or feared persecution or discrimination at home, how many seek
gender-reassignment surgery abroad, or how many enter into same-sex

marriages or legally recognized civil partnerships in countries where these are permitted. Unless it is to be imposed by decree (as in Fiji), successful legal change needs to come about by consensus of many viewpoints. If transgender Pacific Islanders wish to be agents of legal change in their own countries and to resist introduced legal transplants, it is important that more work of the kind presented in the chapters of this book is undertaken in order to establish what factual circumstances and needs the present laws must respond to and what models, if any, transgender Pacific Islanders wish to adopt to bring them more securely within the law.

Acknowledgments

I would like to thank Alex Su'a (Samoa) and Sela Moa (Tonga) for their replies to various enquiries and the helpful comments of anonymous reviewers of an embryonic version of this chapter. I would also like to thank the editors for inviting me to contribute to this collection and acknowledge the editorial work involved.

Notes

1   In Tonga, a constitutional provision keeps the Sabbath day holy (Article 6) and the Constitution opens with the words: "Since it appears to be the will of God that man should be free as He has made all men of one blood therefore shall the people of Tonga and all who sojourn or may sojourn in this Kingdom be free forever" (Article 1). In Samoa, where the constitution incorporates similar phrasing, churches physically dominate villages, and village *fono* (village councils) enforce church attendance, with sanctions in the way of fines and punishments for noncompliance. In both countries, participation in church activities and fund-raising looms large in people's daily routines.

2   Examples of such legislative measures include: in the United Kingdom, the Civil Partnership Act 2004, the Gender Recognition Act 2004, and the Marriage (Same Sex Couples) Bill 2013; in New Zealand, the Civil Union Act 2004, and Marriage (Definition of Marriage) Amendment Act 2013. In Australia, Commonwealth laws include the Civil Partnership Act 2008, the Domestic Relationship Act (1994) effective from 2009, the Discrimination Act (1991) effective from 2011, and the Legislation (Gay, Lesbian, Transgender) Act 2003.

3   The bill of rights provisions in the Tonga Constitution were taken from the 1852 Constitution of Hawai'i, a copy of which Charles St. Julian, who was the Hawaiian consul in Sydney around the mid-1850s, sent to King George

Tupou I when they met on the king's trip to Sydney in 1853. The bill of rights in the much later Samoan Constitution was strongly influenced by the emerging body of universal rights declarations from the United Nations.

4   Section 9, Divorce and Matrimonial Causes Ordinance 1961 No. 20 (Samoa). In Tonga, there is no reference to void or voidable marriages under the Divorce Act Cap 29.

5   The absence of reported cases in the English language electronic data base Paclii.org could be due to the fact that these matters come before village or magistrates courts and are not reported in English, or that they are resolved outside any formal court structure, for example by the *fono* in Samoa.

6   A lesson can be learnt from Fiji, where in 2009 a military decree that decriminalized homosexuality, passed without the use of any democratic process, led to a backlash of violence against homosexuals (George, this volume).

7   Conflicting correspondence between *fa'afāfine* and the expression of other views can be found on the Government of Samoa Law Reform Commission Web page under "Media Coverage": http://www.samoalawreform.gov.ws/News/Media/tabid/6071/language/en-US/Default.aspx (accessed January 2013).

References

Angelo, Anthony H. 1992. Lo Bilong Yumi Yet. In *Essays and Documents on Human Rights in the Pacific*, ed. Victoria University of Wellington Law Review, pp. 33–48. Wellington: Victoria University Press.

Besnier, Niko. 1994. Polynesian Gender Liminality through Time and Space. In *Third Sex, Third Gender: Beyond Sexual Dimorphism in Culture and History*, ed. Gilbert Herdt, pp. 285–328. New York: Zone.

———. 1997. Sluts and Superwomen: The Politics of Gender Liminality in Urban Tonga. *Ethnos* 62: 5–31.

———. 2002. Transgenderism, Locality, and the Miss Galaxy Beauty Pageant in Tonga. *American Ethnologist* 29: 534–566.

———. 2004. The Social Production of Abjection: Desire and Silencing among Transgender Tongans. *Social Anthropology* 1: 301–323.

Civic, Melanie, A. 1995–1996. A Comparative Analysis of International and Chinese Human Rights Law: Universalism versus Cultural Relativism. *Buffalo Journal of International Law* 2: 285–322.

Cobbah, Josiah A. M. 1987. Africa Values and the Human Rights Debate: An African Perspective. *Human Rights Quarterly* 9: 309–331.

Corrin, Jennifer. 1997. Colonial Legacies? A Study of Received and Adopted Legislation in the University of the South Pacific Region. *Journal of Pacific Studies* 21: 33–35.

Currah, Paisley, Richard M. Juang, and Shannon Price Minter, eds. 2006. *Transgender Rights.* Minneapolis: University of Minnesota Press.

Donnolly, Jack. 1984. Cultural Relativism and Universal Human Rights. *Human Rights Quarterly* 6: 400–419.

Edwards, Susan. 1996. *Sex and Gender in the Legal Process.* London: Blackstone Press.

Farran, Sue. 2004. Transsexuals, Fa'afafine, Fakaleiti and Marriage Law in the Pacific: Considerations for the Future. *Journal of the Polynesian Society* 113(2): 119–142.

———. 2009. *Human Rights in the South Pacific: Challenges and Changes.* London: Routledge Cavendish.

———. 2010. Pacific Perspective: Fa'afafine and Fakaleiti in Samoa and Tonga: People between Worlds. *Liverpool Law Review* 31: 13–28.

Farran, Sue, and Alexander Su'a. 2005. Criminal Law and Fa'afafine and Fakaleiti in the South Pacific. *Commonwealth Law Bulletin* 31: 19–31.

George, Nicole. 2008. Contending Masculinities and the Limits of Tolerance: Sexual Minorities in Fiji. *The Contemporary Pacific* 20: 163–189.

Hilsdon, Anne-Marie, Maila Sitivens, Vera Mackie, and Martha McIntyre, eds. 2000. *Human Rights and Gender Politics: Asia-Pacific Perspectives.* London: Routledge.

Hom, Sharon. 1996–1997. Commentary: Re-Positioning Human Rights Discourse on "Asian" Perspective. *Buffalo Journal of International Law* 3: 209–234.

Hunter, Rosemary. 2003. Review of Andrew Sharpe, *Transgender Jurisprudence: Dysphoric Bodies of Law. Griffith Law Review* 12: 387–390.

James, Kerry. 1994. Effeminate Males and Changes to the Construction of Gender in Tonga. *Pacific Studies* 17(2): 39–69.

Jowitt, Anita. 2005. Reconstructing Custom: The Politics of Homophobia in Vanuatu. *Alternative Law Journal* 30: 10–14.

Massad, Joseph. 2002. Re-Orienting Desire: The Gay International and the Arab World. *Public Culture* 14: 361–385.

———. 2007. *Desiring Arabs.* Chicago: University of Chicago Press.

Matangi Tonga. 2010. Tonga Candidates Abhor Abortion, Same-Sex Unions. October 19; http://archives.pireport.org/archive/2010/october/10–19–05.htm (accessed January 31, 2013).

Matzner, Andrew. 2001. Transgender, Queens, Mahu, Whatever: An Oral History from Hawai'i. *Intersections* 6; http://wwwsshe.murdoch.edu.au/intersections/issue6/matzner.html (accessed May 2012).

McIntosh, Tracey. 1999. Words and Worlds of Difference: Homosexualities in the Pacific. Working Papers on Sociology and Social Policy 3/99. Suva, Fiji: University of the South Pacific.

Merry, Sally Engle. 2006. Transnational Human Rights and Local Activism: Mapping the Middle. *American Anthropologist* 108: 38–51.

Meyerowitz, Joanne. 2002. *How Sex Changed: A History of Transsexuality in the United States.* Cambridge, MA: Harvard University Press.

Murphy, Sarah. 2013. Marriage Will Destroy Family Structure Say Tongan Church. *Gay Express,* January 23, 2013; http://www.gayexpress.co.nz/2013/01/marriage -will-destroy-family-structure-say-tongan-church (accessed January 31, 2013).

New Zealand Law Commission. 2006. *Converging Currents: Custom and Human Rights in the Pacific.* Study Paper 17. Wellington: New Zealand Law Commission.

PacificEyeWitness. 2012. Fa'afafine Say No to Same Sex Marriage. August 11, 2012; http://pacificeyewitness.com/2012/08/11/samoa-faafafine-association -sfa-say-no-to-same-sex-marriage (accessed January 2013).

Park, Julie, and Carolyn Morris. 2004. Reproducing Samoans in Auckland "In Different Times": Can *Habitus* Help? *Journal of the Polynesian Society* 113: 227–261.

Philips, Susan. 2004. The Organization of Ideological Diversity in Discourse: Modern and Neotraditional Visions of the Tongan State. *American Ethnologist* 31: 231–250.

Samoa Law Reform Commission. 2010. *Final Report: Crimes Ordinance 1961* 01/10; http://www.samoalawreform.gov.ws/Portals/206/Publications/Final% 20Report_Crimes%20Ordinance%201961%20(final%20%20English% 20version).pdf (accessed January 2013).

Schmidt, Johanna. 2003. Paradise Lost? Social Change and Fa'afafine in Samoa. *Current Sociology* 51: 417–432.

Shore, Bradd. 1982. Sexuality and Gender in Samoa: Conceptions and Missed Conceptions. In *Sexual Meanings: The Cultural Construction of Gender and Sexuality,* ed. Sherry B. Ortner, pp. 192–215. Cambridge: Cambridge University Press.

Thaman, Konai H. 1998. A Pacific Island Perspective of Collective Human Rights. In *Collective Human Rights of Pacific Peoples,* ed. Nin Tomas, pp. 1–9. Auckland: International Research Unit for Maori and Indigenous Education, University of Auckland.

United States Department of State. 2012. *Country Report on Human Rights Practices for 2011;* http://www.state.gov/j/drl/rls/hrrpt/humanrightsreport/ index.htm#wrapper (accessed January 2013).

Valentine, David. 2007. *Imagining Transgender: An Ethnography of a Category.* Durham, NC: Duke University Press.

Notes on Contributors

Kalissa Alexeyeff is a McArthur Research Fellow at the University of Melbourne. Her present project examines globalization and neoliberalism, migration, and gendered affect in the Cook Islands. She is the author of *Dancing from the Heart: Gender, Movement and Cook Islands Globalization* (2009), which explores the significance of dance in the Cook Islands, its colonial history, and its contemporary manifestations.

Niko Besnier is Professor of Cultural Anthropology at the University of Amsterdam. Based on fieldwork in the Pacific Islands and Japan, his current work concerns gender and sexuality at the interface between the local and the global, masculinity and transnational mobility, and the sporting body. His most recent books are *Gossip and the Everyday Production of Politics* (2009) and *On the Edge of the Global: Modern Anxieties in a Pacific Island Nation* (2011).

Reevan Dolgoy conducted fieldwork in Western Samoa and obtained his PhD in 2000 from the Department of Sociology, University of Alberta. He was also a documentary filmmaker, oral historian, and photographer. The chapter included here is a revised version of segments of his dissertation, entitled "The Search for Recognition and Social Movement Emergence: Towards an Understanding of the Transformation of the Fa'afafine in Samoa." He passed away in 2006 at age sixty-four.

Greg Dvorak is an associate professor of cultural studies and history at Hitotsubashi University, and an adjunct lecturer in Asian and Pacific studies at Waseda University in Tokyo. Having grown up on the American military base at Kwajalein Atoll in the Marshall Islands and spent much of his adult life in Japan, his research has largely concerned postcolonial intersections of history, identity, and gender/sexuality between Japan and the United States in Oceania. His recent work explores contemporary Japan–Pacific Islands archipelagic articulations through art and activism, a theme that inspired him to found Project35, a grassroots network of artists and scholars in the region.

Deborah Elliston is a professor in anthropology and women's, gender, and sexuality studies at Binghamton University, State University of New York. Her work in feminist, queer, and Pacific anthropology has been published in the *American Ethnologist, Cultural Anthropology, Pacific Studies,* and *Reviews in Anthropology.* Her current projects include finalizing her ethnography, *Pacific Modern: The Politics of Difference in Polynesian Nationalism*, and continuing fieldwork on questions of sexuality, gender, desire, and labor among sex-worker *raerae*—male-bodied, femininity-performing, men-desiring Polynesians—in the Society Islands.

Sue Farran is Professor of Laws at the University of Northumbria and an adjunct professor at the University of the South Pacific. Her interest is in the interface between legal systems and normative frameworks within and between states and in the relationship among national, regional, and international players in shaping legal responses to contemporary issues. She is the author of *Human Rights in the South Pacific: Challenges and Changes* (2009) and *Law and the Family in the Pacific* (2011), and is currently coediting a collection of essays by Pacific contributors on South Pacific land systems.

Nicole George is a lecturer in Peace and Conflict Studies in the School of Political Science and International Studies at the University of Queensland. Her research focuses on gender, violence, and peace building in the Pacific Islands. She is the author of *Situating Women: Gender Politics and Circumstance in Fiji* (2012). In 2012, she was awarded Australian Research Council funding for a three-year comparative project on women's political resistance to gender violence in New Caledonia, Vanuatu, and Fiji.

Mary K. Good is a Postdoctoral Fellow in the Department of Anthropology at Lawrence University. She defended a PhD dissertation entitled "Modern Moralities, Moral Modernities: Ambivalence and Change among Youth in Tonga" in cultural anthropology at the University of Arizona in 2012. Her research focuses on global modernity, youth, and the development of moral frameworks through language and social action in Tonga.

Linda L. Ikeda received her MSW from UCLA and her PhD in social welfare from the University of Hawai‘i at Mānoa. She has worked with and for immigrant and refugee Asian and Pacific Islander battered women and their children, the suicidal and self-harming, addicted mothers working to regain custody of their children, and *māhūwahine*. From 2005 to 2010, she was connected with Kulia Na Mamo, the only transgender-focused nonprofit organization in Hawai‘i. Since 2006, she has lectured in the Women's Studies Program at the University of Hawai‘i at Mānoa.

Makiko Kuwahara obtained her PhD in anthropology from the Australian National University in 2003. She is an associate professor in the Department of

International Communication at Kinjo Gakuin University in Nagoya. Her recent work concerns gender and sexuality and body modification and decoration in French Polynesia. She is the author of *Tattoo: An Anthropology* (2005).

Sarina Pearson is a Senior Lecturer in the Department of Film, Television and Media Studies at the University of Auckland. She is currently working on a project about Hollywood's representation of the Pacific throughout the twentieth century and the role these images play in producing contemporary Pacific performance and subjectivities.

Geir Henning Presterudstuen was awarded his PhD in anthropology and gender studies from the University of Western Sydney in September 2011 for his thesis, "Masculinity, Manhood and Tradition in Contemporary Fiji." His current research work focuses on processes of gender identification, representation, and sexual practices in postcolonial settings, and on discourses about gender at the interface of notions of tradition and modernity.

Penelope Schoeffel is a Research Fellow at the National University of Samoa. She has taught at universities in Australia, New Zealand, Thailand, and Bangladesh, and has worked as a consultant on gender and development for many international development agencies. Her scholarly interests since the 1970s have focused on the historical transformation of gender relations in Samoa and other Pacific Island cultures. She is currently researching masculinity, representations of tradition, and the exclusion of women from political participation in Samoa.

Christine Stewart graduated with a BA (1st Class Honors) from Sydney University in 1966. She first went to Papua New Guinea in 1968 and earned an LLB from the University of Papua New Guinea in 1976. She has worked in the PNG Law Reform Commission and the Department of the Attorney-General and served as Legislative Counsel in Nauru before embarking on consultancy work in PNG and the Pacific Islands. Her PhD thesis from the Australian National University (2012) examines the effects of criminalizing sex work and sodomy in Papua New Guinea.

Serge Tcherkézoff is Professor of Anthropology and Pacific Studies at the École des hautes études en sciences sociales, a visiting professor at the Australian National University (where he coordinates an EHESS program hosted by ANU), and a part-time professor at the University of Canterbury. His works bring together fieldwork done in Samoa during the 1980s and 1990s with an ethnohistorical critique of European narratives about Polynesia. His most recent coedited work is *Oceanic Encounters: Exchange, Desire, Violence* (2009).

Teresia K. Teaiwa is a senior lecturer and postgraduate coordinator in Pacific studies at Victoria University of Wellington. A Royal Society of New Zealand Marsden
award between 2008 and 2010 enabled her to conduct research on Fijian women
who had served in the Fiji Military Forces and the British Army. She is currently
working on a book based on that research. Her recent activities include editing a
special issue of the *Asia Pacific Viewpoint* journal focusing on militarism and gender
in the Western Pacific (2011).

Index

activism. *See* human rights

adolescence. *See* youth

adoption. *See* kinship: fictive

age, 63, 82

Altman, Dennis, 20–21, 40, 176, 294

authenticity: in French Polynesia, 34, 37, 43

Barth, Fredrik, 7

Beyer, Georgina, 256–257

body, 173–175; modification, 17–18, 94, 99, 106, 109, 129, 137, 350, 261, 350, 361, 364

breast enlargement. *See* body: modification

Chinese, 95, 112n4

Chodorow, Nancy, 124

Christianity, 4, 335; in Fiji, 269, 273, 288n25, 307; in French Polynesia, 98; in Marshall Islands, 187, 189; Methodist Church of Fiji, 278–279, 299, 307, 317n8; Methodist Church of New Zealand, 4; Micronesian Seminar, 189–190, 206n4; New Methodists of Fiji, 312–313; in Papua New Guinea, 329, 337–338; in Samoa, 76, 85, 245–246, 347–348, 354, 360, 361; in Tonga, 225, 227, 347–348, 354, 360, 361

Chuuk, 187

circumcision, 88n1

citizenship, 188–189, 207n12, 222, 232, 268, 269, 274–276, 286n7, 341, 353

class, social, 21; in Fiji, 179–180; in Samoa, 65

clothing: in Fiji, 172–175, 178; in French Polynesia, 35–36, 44–45; in Papua New Guinea, 332, 333; in Samoa, 66; in Tonga, 226

colonialism, 3, 10–11, 23–24; in Fiji, 270, 275, 277, 302; in French Polynesia, 40–42, 48–49, 104–107; in Marshall Islands, 186–187, 190–191; in Papua New Guinea, 335–336, 338–339; in Samoa, 71, 351; in Tonga, 351

"coming out," 47, 141, 196–198

constitution: of Fiji, 298–300, 303, 308

Cook Islands, 5, 8, 164–165

cosmology, 86, 127

coups: political, 298–299, 307

cross-dressing. *See* clothing

development: in Tonga, 221–222, 233–234, 235–236

diaspora. *See* migration

drag shows. *See* shows

Drodrolagi Movement, 273, 314–315

Drozdow-St. Christian, Douglass, 77, 83

empowerment, 216, 222, 235, 236, 238n7

ethnicity, 7

fa'afafine (Samoa), 8–9, 56–72, 73–88, 115–132, 245–246

fa'ateine. *See fa'afafine*

fale aitu. *See* theater: *fale aitu* comedy

family. *See* kinship

Fanaafi Le Tagaloa, Aiono, 117

fashion. *See* clothing